Born-Digital Text
English Language

NEW PERSPECTIVES ON LANGUAGE AND EDUCATION

Founding Editor: Viv Edwards, *University of Reading, UK*

Series Editors: Phan Le Ha, *University of Hawaii at Manoa, USA* and Joel Windle, *Monash University, Australia*

Two decades of research and development in language and literacy education have yielded a broad, multidisciplinary focus. Yet education systems face constant economic and technological change, with attendant issues of identity and power, community and culture. What are the implications for language education of new 'semiotic economies' and communications technologies? Of complex blendings of cultural and linguistic diversity in communities and institutions? Of new cultural, regional and national identities and practices? The New Perspectives on Language and Education series will feature critical and interpretive, disciplinary and multidisciplinary perspectives on teaching and learning, language and literacy in new times. New proposals, particularly for edited volumes, are expected to acknowledge and include perspectives from the Global South. Contributions from scholars from the Global South will be particularly sought out and welcomed, as well as those from marginalized communities within the Global North.

All books in this series are externally peer-reviewed.

Full details of all the books in this series and of all our other publications can be found on http://www.multilingual-matters.com, or by writing to Multilingual Matters, St Nicholas House, 31–34 High Street, Bristol, BS1 2AW, UK.

NEW PERSPECTIVES ON LANGUAGE AND EDUCATION: 119

Born-Digital Texts in the English Language Classroom

Edited by
Saskia Kersten and Christian Ludwig

MULTILINGUAL MATTERS
Bristol • Jackson

DOI https://doi.org/10.21832/KERSTE4808
Library of Congress Cataloging in Publication Data
A catalog record for this book is available from the Library of Congress.
Names: Kersten, Saskia, editor. | Ludwig, Christian, editor.
Title: Born-Digital Texts in the English Language Classroom/Edited by
   Saskia Kersten and Christian Ludwig.
Description: Bristol; Jackson: Multilingual Matters, 2024. | Series: New
   Perspectives on Language and Education: 119 | Includes bibliographical
   references and index. | Summary: "This book is the first to focus
   specifically on born-digital texts in EFL teaching, uniting innovative
   scholarship with practical classroom applications. The book develops a
   theoretically sound framework for curriculum, materials and methods
   design that takes into account the growing ubiquity of born-digital
   texts in the digital age"—Provided by publisher.
Identifiers: LCCN 2023056802 (print) | LCCN 2023056803 (ebook) | ISBN
   9781800414792 (paperback) | ISBN 9781800414808 (hardback) | ISBN
   9781800414815 (pdf) | ISBN 9781800414822 (epub)
Subjects: LCSH: English language—Study and teaching—Foreign speakers. |
   Digital media. | Hypertext literature. | LCGFT: Essays.
Classification: LCC PE1128.A2 B59 2024 (print) | LCC PE1128.A2 (ebook) |
   DDC 428.0071—dc23/eng/20240202
LC record available at https://lccn.loc.gov/2023056802
LC ebook record available at https://lccn.loc.gov/2023056803

British Library Cataloguing in Publication Data
A catalogue entry for this book is available from the British Library.

ISBN-13: 978-1-80041-480-8 (hbk)
ISBN-13: 978-1-80041-479-2 (pbk)

Multilingual Matters
UK: St Nicholas House, 31–34 High Street, Bristol, BS1 2AW, UK.
USA: Ingram, Jackson, TN, USA.

Website: https://www.multilingual-matters.com
Twitter: Multi_Ling_Mat
Facebook: https://www.facebook.com/multilingualmatters
Blog: https://www.channelviewpublications.wordpress.com

Copyright © 2024 Saskia Kersten, Christian Ludwig and the authors of individual chapters.

All rights reserved. No part of this work may be reproduced in any form or by any means without permission in writing from the publisher.

The policy of Multilingual Matters/Channel View Publications is to use papers that are natural, renewable and recyclable products, made from wood grown in sustainable forests. In the manufacturing process of our books, and to further support our policy, preference is given to printers that have FSC and PEFC Chain of Custody certification. The FSC and/or PEFC logos will appear on those books where full certification has been granted to the printer concerned.

Typeset by SAN Publishing Services.

Contents

	Acknowledgements	vii
1	Born-Digital Text in English Language Teaching: The State of Play *Daniel Becker, Saskia Kersten, Christian Ludwig, Peter Schildhauer and Sandra Stadler-Heer*	1
2	The Linguistics of Born-Digital Texts *Saskia Kersten*	30
3	What Counts as Language Learning in a Born-Digital Textual World? *Kathy A. Mills*	42
4	Born-Digital Texts and Digitally Mediated Tasks: A Perfect Match for the Inclusive EFL Classroom? *Celestine Caruso, Judith Hofmann and Kim Schick*	55
5	#hashtagsareforlearning – Hashtags as Digital Texts and their Affordances in the EFL Classroom *Ralf Gießler and Daniel Becker*	71
6	Towards a Critical Digital Literacy Framework: Exploring the Impact of Algorithms in the Creation of Filter Bubbles on Instagram *Peter Schildhauer and Katharina Kemper*	89
7	Exploring the Potential of Live Text for ELT *Valentin Werner*	106
8	From Gaming to Linguistic Action: Let's Play Videos as (More Than) Mediation Tasks *Janina Reinhardt*	122

9	Consuming and Producing Artificial Intelligence (AI)-Generated Text in English Language Classrooms *Sandra Stadler-Heer*	137
10	AI and the Digital Writing Process *Jasmina Najjar and Philip M. McCarthy*	153
11	Learning English as a Second Language through Born-Digital Texts on Social Media in South Africa *Christopher Rwodzi and Lizette J. De Jager*	173
12	'I'm going to teach differently': Changing Perceptions of Writing Instruction through Digital Text Creation *Maya Ashooh, Alecia Marie Magnifico and Bethany Silva*	186
13	Fanfiction Experiences of Japanese Students: Connecting Wild Reading and L2 Learning *Tara McIlroy*	204
14	The Potential of Location-Based Technologies and Mobile-Assisted Language Learning for ELT *Carolin Zehne*	220
15	*Alice for the iPad*: Digital Storybook Apps in the EFL Classroom *Jeanine Steinbock*	233
16	#Literature Goes Digital: Digital Transformations in the ELT Literature Classroom *Christian Ludwig, Michaela Sambanis and Georg Hartisch*	247
	Index	270

Acknowledgements

We would like to thank all the participants of the *Born-Digital Text Symposium*, which took place online in January 2021 during the height of the pandemic and from which this edited volume originates, for their presentations and the lively discussion at this event. To all the contributors, our heartfelt gratitude for their work on the chapters in this book. Thank you also to Paul Scheffler for assisting with the formatting and proofreading of this volume, to the two anonymous reviewers for their helpful comments on a draft version of this book and to Anna Roderick at Multilingual Matters for her encouragement and support throughout the process.

Saskia Kersten and *Christian Ludwig*
München and Berlin, September 2023

1 Born-Digital Text in English Language Teaching: The State of Play

Daniel Becker, Saskia Kersten, Christian Ludwig,
Peter Schildhauer and Sandra Stadler-Heer[1]

1.1 Introduction

Our world is becoming increasingly digital (Hepp, 2021). The impact of information and communication technologies is becoming visible through major transformations in society and culture as we engage in a previously unimaginably broad range of practices (Davidson, 2009: 36), which are anchored in and shaped by the digital (Stalder, 2018: 65). In this digital information age, as Carrington (2001) poignantly puts it, print is increasingly 'downgraded to an auxiliary source of information' (Carrington, 2001: 19 as quoted in Davidson, 2009: 36). While digital artifacts (items produced, accessed and stored in the digital realm), are assuming more and more importance in our daily lives, in English language education print texts and print media practices seem to continue to prevail. As Davidson (2009: 36), drawing on the work of Lankshear and Knobel (2003) and Carrington (2005), already pointed out: 'While young children's literacy practices out of school now encompass a range of digital technologies, school literacy practices remain largely focused on print-based skills'. As digital citizens, however, born-digital teenagers communicate and express themselves through social media and access global knowledge networks to find information, making use of a cornucopia of non-print related skills and competences (Hintz *et al.*, 2018; Ribble & Bailey, 2007; Tewksbury & Rittenberg, 2015). High time, it seems, to finally move away from the idea of digital media being 'add-ons in the core work of teaching about print-based texts' (Davidson, 2009: 36) towards the teaching of texts which are created and live in the digital realm, harnessing the knowledge and experiences with digital technology that learners bring to the classroom every day.

Taking this as a starting point, this edited volume is dedicated to the use of born-digital texts in Foreign Language Education (FLE), arguing that the literacies necessary to consume and produce born-digital texts *should* have the same place in the classroom as traditional print-related literacies, i.e. reading and writing on paper (Knobel & Lankshear, 2007: 2). Obviously, integrating digital artifacts such as social media texts, digital music and photography, videos or digital stories into the classroom requires us to rethink and expand our understanding of how foreign languages should be taught, and open up towards more innovative methods and new ways of learning. Here, autonomous and personalised learning are two of the key concepts that need to be considered (Holmes *et al.*, 2018), especially as today's teenage generation access entertainment and information on their mobile devices anytime and anywhere, with most of the content being tailored to their individual needs (cf. Section 1.4).

Against this background, this introductory chapter first provides a snapshot of life in the digital age, particularly focusing on how digital culture shapes the way we interact with others and make meaning. Following this, the chapter discusses the concept of born-digital texts, a term which so far has received little to no scholarly attention. Third, it looks at the potential of born-digital texts for FLE, arguing that the abilities to understand and 'generate multi-modal texts and to understand principles of making multi-modal meanings' (Lankshear & Knobel, 2003: 77) have become at least as important as the skills necessary to 'handle conventional alphabetical print texts' (Lankshear & Knobel, 2003: 77). In particular, it examines how born-digital texts are closely related to the idea of learner-centered, differentiated and inclusive education in which all learners share their in-the-wild interactions with digital artifacts and fulfil their individual potential. Following this, it briefly discusses why born-digital texts also need to play a more prominent role in teacher education, offering trainee teachers and teachers-to-be the opportunity to experience teaching and learning with multiple born-digital resources. To conclude, the last section provides an overview of the contributions to this volume, all of which illustrate how a diverse range of born-digital texts can be used in contemporary language learning contexts.

1.2 Living in a Digital Culture

No matter whether self-driving cars, smart homes, or virtual entertainment, technology is rapidly developing, offering new innovations and breakthroughs every day. While many of us embrace the opportunities that come with technological advances, it cannot be denied that we are facing unprecedented and profound social, political and cultural changes that come with digital innovation. In his latest book, *Undinge: Umbrüche der Lebenswelt* (2021), the German philosopher Byung-Chul Han argues that information and communication technologies irreversibly alter the relationship between humankind and the world. He states: 'Not objects but information determines our world. We no longer inhabit heaven and earth but Google Earth and Cloud' (Han, 2021: 9). We no longer consume or get attached to objects but information. We are, as Han argues, obsessed with information and data to a degree that we have become information fetishists and datasexuals who record, document and share every aspect of our lives. In a similar vein, the Italian-British philosopher Luciano Floridi (1999) puts forward the idea that we are on the verge of turning into inforgs, informationally embodied organisms, who communicate and exchange information in the metaphysical realm of the global infosphere – the digital counterpart of the analogue biosphere. It is a 'system of services and documents, encoded in any semiotic and physical media, whose contents include any sort of data, information and knowledge, [...] with no limitations either in size, typology or logical structure' (1999: 8). We, as humans, inhabit this realm as informational entities, i.e. inforgs.

Digital technology, this much is clear, fundamentally changes the way we live, communicate and socialize. Floridi (2015b: 1) uses the term 'onlife' to describe this 'new experience of a hyperconnected reality within which it is no longer sensible to ask whether one may be online or offline', but how one lives in a world that is shaped by the digital blur of increasingly overlapping digital and non-digital activities. Society as a whole is moving from information scarcity to information abundance and even information overload (Hintz et al., 2018). A previously unimaginable amount of information is created in the infosphere with everything literally sitting in the palms of our hands. Information and communication technologies are no longer simple tools that make our lives easier but have become 'environmental forces' (Floridi, 2015b: 2) which increasingly alter how we see ourselves, the world and others. They change our self-conception, our mutual interactions, our conception of reality and, last but not least, our interactions with reality (Floridi, 2015b: 2; Otrel-Cass, 2019: 3).

Here, the smartphone may serve as one of many examples. It is no longer just a device but an extension of the human body and mind (Park & Kaye, 2018). It allows us to keep in touch with people anywhere and anytime, tells us where to go in unknown places, fulfills all our entertainment and information needs and tracks our physical activity and location. Unsurprisingly, we seem to find it increasingly difficult to put it down, thus keeping us away from experiences that are not digitally mediated. It changes, for better or worse, how we interact with each other as well as our attitude towards the world. As 'phono sapiens' we are used to the idea that we can easily garner data and zoom in to content that we like, while making anything that we do not consider relevant disappear with a swipe of the finger (Han, 2021: 9). In a way, it makes us more self-preoccupied and self-centered (Pearson & Hussain, 2015), as we are constantly encouraged to present and promote ourselves, and learn that we can make the world what we want it to be. Thus, one may want to conclude that the smartphone, as Han argues, does not only have an emancipatory side, but also brings with it a new form of enslavement:

> Constant availability does not differ fundamentally from slavery. The smartphone turns out to be a mobile labour camp in which we let ourselves be locked in voluntarily. The smartphone is also a pornophone. We expose ourselves voluntarily. (Han, 2021: 33, trans. C.L.)

Information and communication technologies, as Floridi (2015a) points out in the preface to *The Onlife Manifesto – Being Human in a Hyperconnected Era*, bring drastic changes and transformations which urge us to fundamentally rethink and expand our understanding of the previously well-established boundaries between reality and virtuality, as well as between human, machine and nature. They change the way in which we interact with people, create knowledge and share ideas, often across traditional social and cultural boundaries. In other words, the transition from the industrial to the digital age is not merely a technological but also an inherently political and social and, last but not least, cultural one. One illustrative example of this is the ongoing 'gamification' of society. The *homo sapiens* ('man the maker') is gradually replaced by the *homo ludens* ('man the player'). While for the Dutch historian Huizinga (1938) technology and play represented complete opposites, modern digital technologies are now considered to have an inherently playful dimension. As Frissen *et al.* (2015: 10) argue, 'both media explicitly designed for play, such as computer games, as well as digital technologies in general, have an inherent ludic dimension'. The element of play, as Silverstone (1999: 63) states, is 'central […] to media experience'; an element which is 'closely connected with medium-specific qualities like multimediality, virtuality, interactivity, and connectivity' (Frissen *et al.*, 2015: 10). There are many examples of the ludification of almost any cultural domain with computer and online games only being one, albeit the most obvious, example. No matter whether selfies, viral videos, TikTok challenges or even communication itself, one only has to think of blogging and Instagramming; the digital world is our playground, where even identity construction itself has become ludic. As Raessens (2012: 94) points out: 'Play is not only characteristic of leisure, but also turns up in those domains that once were considered the opposite of play', including politics, industry and education.

This digitalisation of communication and culture is incredibly dynamic. As Stalder (2018: 3) puts it: 'What was once just an abstract speculation of media theory, however, now describes the concrete reality of our everyday life'. The 'erosion of old cultural forms, institutions, and certainties' (Stalder, 2018: 3) that McLuhan once predicted is no longer just something we affirm but is now 'easy to identify not only in niche sectors but in the mainstream' (Stalder, 2018: 3). Stalder (2016) refers to this proliferation of cultural opportunities of expression as the digital condition (*Kultur der Digitalität*), a condition which is on the rise and rapidly spreading. Increasingly complex technologies now allow all of us to partake in cultural processes which traditionally were reserved for just a few. He writes:

> More and more people have been participating in cultural processes; larger and larger dimensions of existence have become battlegrounds for cultural disputes; and social activity has been intertwined with increasingly complex technologies, without which it would hardly be possible to conceive of these processes, let alone achieve them. The number of competing cultural projects, works, reference points, and reference systems has been growing rapidly. This, in turn, has caused an escalating crisis for the established forms and institutions of culture, which are poorly equipped to deal with such an inundation of new claims to meaning. (Stalder, 2018: 4)

This digital condition, Stalder suggests, is shaped by three common formal features: referentiality, communality and algorithmicity, each of which will briefly be discussed in the following.

To begin with, the fact that modern media, but also the arts, have become increasingly self-referential is not an entirely new phenomenon in postmodern culture. For quite some time now, literature, the arts and news media no longer simply mediate between the fictional (or real) world and the audience, but report 'increasingly what has been seen, heard or reported before' (Nöth, 2011: 199). In other words, artists, journalists, writers and film directors no longer work with raw material but with 'materials that are already equipped with meaning' (Stalder, 2018: 59). Yet, not only culture and media professionals, but we all have come to use referential techniques as we produce a range of digital media genres and we engage in remixing, remaking, reperforming, recreating, re-enacting and mashing-up. These terms already indicate that we deal with often still recognisable source materials in whatever way we like. For example, we may merge audio with images, photos or even paintings to create a video, usually reverting to already existing materials. According to Stalder, there are three main reasons why self-referentiality has become such a widespread phenomenon in postmodern culture. First, most of the materials that we use were either born in the digital realm, or exist in both analogue and digital format. Thus, they are easily available and economic in that they are affordable or even freely available. Second, reappropriating content is not tabooed or sanctioned in society but rather a common activity in which many people freely and openly engage. Third, it is possible to use the material (cf. Stalder, 2018: 61–62). One may well argue that postmodern referential processes do not differ much from the traditional montage. Yet, as Stalder (2018: 61) argues, cultural objects are no longer simply put side by side but are integrated into one another by 'being altered, adapted, and transformed. [...] it is not the fissures between elements that are foregrounded but rather their synthesis in the present'. For example, in a university course of one of the authors of this introduction, the students were asked to add sound to famous, digitally available paintings, combining their chosen piece of art with modern music, self-written stories, or commentaries. By doing that, the students gave voice to their individual interpretations of the painting through remixing existing cultural material. The example illustrates that many cultural objects that are created today are both new and, at the same time, already exist, often only for a short time as they are (re)used for the creation of new cultural objects. Thus, referentiality is a practice with which individuals can contribute to cultural production. They 'inscribe themselves into cultural processes and constitute themselves as producers' (2018: 58) within an increasingly global community of producers who, often collectively, negotiate meaning.

Probably one of the most prominent examples of postmodern referentiality are memes, which have become an integral part of internet culture since the early 'grumpy cats'. As participatory artifacts which are open, collaborative and adaptable (Aitwani, 2017), memes allow for cosmopolitan practices where young people can productively and creatively engage in multimodal meaning-making within local and global contexts. In very simple terms, memes are 'digital cultural content', e.g. images, GIFs, or videos, often accompanied by short texts, which are copied and shared by many people, often with a slight variation in meaning (Scott, 2022: 110). Thus, an internet meme is not a single item, but rather an interconnected group of artifacts which often can only be understood if users already have an awareness of the underlying meme (Scott, 2022; see also Shifman, 2013). Figure 1.1 shows four iterations of the meme, which all originated in the same source material but have been appropriated by different internet users for their own usage, with the last almost being a metacomment on the meme and its genesis.

The series of instantiations of the meme based on the 'distracted boyfriend' stock photo (for a detailed discussion of this meme, see e.g. Scott, 2022: chap. 6) above illustrates that the synthesis of different elements is often short-lived and of a certain time, since at any time cultural material 'can itself serve as material for yet another rendering' (Stalder, 2018: 61).

The second constituent of the digital condition that Stalder (2018: 81) describes is that of communality. With the pluralisation of society, traditional social institutions such as the church and political parties increasingly disintegrate as the desires and needs of the individual take precedence over those of social communities. Yet, 'nevertheless, or perhaps for this very reason, new forms of communality are being formed in these offshoots – in the small activities of everyday life'; communal formations 'who create the shared meaning that we call culture' (Stalder, 2018: 82). These communal formations, according to Stalder (2018: 84), 'are formed

Figure 1.1 Example of a well-known meme and how it was remixed[2]

in a field of practice, characterized by informal yet structured exchange, focused on the generation of new ways of knowing and acting, and maintained through the reflexive interpretation of their own activity'. Individuals as social beings voluntarily engage in these communal formations or, to use Lave and Wenger's (1991) terminology, Communities of Practice: groups of collective inquiry and reflection in which (informal) reciprocal learning takes place (cf. e.g. Lave & Wenger, 1991; Wenger, 2000). Every day, we continuously text, blog, post, share and like things, engaging in endless threads of communication in the digital realm. In other words, meaning is generated through interaction, and incessant, uninterrupted communication as a 'constitutive element of social existence, the personal desire for self-constitution and orientation [becoming] enmeshed with the outward pressure of having to be present and available to form a new and binding set of requirements' (Stalder, 2018: 84).

TikTok, which has become very common among today's generation of teenagers (see e.g. Statista, 2022, for a breakdown of users by age), is an apt example of this: TikTok as a social media platform fulfills a plethora of functions in people's lives. Users can communicate with other users with similar interests and engage in conversations that are relevant to them as they feel a sense of community through participating in viral challenges, commenting on others' content or uploading content themselves. TikTok and other social media platforms are even beginning to replace 'traditional' search engines, such as Google (Cavender, 2022). Through these forms of communication people can express themselves and be visible as they get attention from others, for example, through likes, comments, or shares. As Stalder (2018: 84) puts it: 'Communication is especially significant to them. Individuals must continuously communicate in order to constitute themselves within the fields and practices, or else they will remain invisible'.

The third mechanism of today's 'decentralized and networked cultural production' that Stalder (2018: 103) describes is that of algorithmicity. Human beings, Stalder contends, would not be able to deal with the massive amounts of data (big data) that are created literally every nanosecond, which is why 'there are algorithmic processes that pre-sort the immeasurably large volumes of data and convert them into a format that can be apprehended by individuals' (Stalder, 2018: 103). In other words, the order that algorithms provide is 'a constitutive element of the digital condition' (Stalder, 2018: 112). One only has to think of a simple Google search to understand the importance of algorithms in today's digitised world: they bring order to chaos as they allow us to find our way through the tsunami of information that the infosphere offers.

The second concept that we would like to present here is Henry Jenkins' participatory culture, which pays tribute to the fact that many of us are not mere consumers of digital services and entertainment, but content producers through the many 'communication and entertainment-focused activities' (Jenkins *et al.*, 2009: 5–6) that we voluntarily engage in every day. According to Jenkins *et al.*, this culture of participation can be defined as one with:

(1) relatively low barriers to artistic expression and civic engagement;
(2) strong support for creating and sharing creations with others;
(3) some type of informal mentorship whereby what is known by the most experienced is passed along to novices;
(4) members who believe that their contributions matter; and
(5) members who feel some degree of social connection with one another (at the least, they care what other people think about what they have created).

Many teenagers today are already (consciously or unconsciously) part of this culture which 'cuts across educational practices, creative processes, community life, and democratic citizenship' (Jenkins *et al.*, 2009: 9). They are members of different (formal or informal) communities such as game clans or chat groups on social media through which they participate in various processes of meaning-making. More specifically, these include:

- affiliations (engaging in formal/informal memberships);
- expressions (producing pop-cultural items such as tutorials, fan videos, or Let's Plays);
- collaborative problem-solving (working together with others, e.g. in online encyclopedias);
- circulations (shaping media flow, e.g. through posting or blogging) (cf. Jenkins *et al.*, 2009: 9).

Both Stalder's theory of the digital condition and Jenkins' model of participatory culture illustrate the fundamental changes (and challenges) that come with digital technologies, increasingly impacting our traditional understanding of the *conditio humana*. What seems to be ahead of us is a data-intensive world, in which technology is no longer a tool, but an infrastructure increasingly determined by independent algorithmic decision-making, based on data and without human mediation. This shows that our society shifts from 'the primacy of standalone things, properties, and binary relations, to the primacy of interactions, processes and networks' (Otrel-Cass, 2019: 3).

The dark side of the digital information society with almost unlimited access to resources is already making itself felt as information can easily be shared by everyone in rapidly expanding networks: information can easily be manipulated, and misinformation be spread. We seem to be entering a new era in which 'a few claims on Twitter can have the same credibility as a library full of research' (Coughlan, 2017). We are moving towards a post-truth society (Han, 2021: 15), a phenomenon that ironically seems to be at least partially rooted in participatory culture and the fact that people can 'find their tribe' online, i.e. often communicate with like-minded people: 'users tend to select and share content related to a specific narrative and to ignore the rest', which, together with 'social homogeneity' (Del Vicario *et al.*, 2016: 558), in turn leads to echo chambers, i.e. the formation of homogeneous groups of friends that have the same or a similar profile and whose beliefs align with the beliefs of others in what the authors refer to as 'homogeneous, polarized clusters'.

Further drawbacks of participating in online communication have become apparent in recent years, be it the revelations of whistleblower Frances Haugen that Facebook (now Meta) was fully aware of the damaging effects of their services (see e.g. Gayle, 2021; Wells *et al.*, 2021), particularly on teenage girls. As Turkle (2021) wrote, '[s]ince many of us grew up with the internet, we thought that the internet was all grown up', but this is not necessarily the case, particularly since the monetisation of clicks and likes in conjunction with the unknown algorithms employed by the providers may well affect the shape and content of social media. Furthermore, more than ever is known about the individuals who post, share and like content and this information is gathered, stored and sold by the platform providers. When communicating online, we inadvertently reveal snippets of our identity, even if we have taken precautions to shield our real identity (see e.g. Kersten & Lotze, 2021, for strategies employed when choosing a username in light of the tension between preserving anonymity and presenting an authentic self), which can be pieced together across services by the breadcrumbs we all invariably leave behind. Awareness of this and other drawbacks is one aspect of digital literacy, discussed in more detail in Section 1.4.

1.3 From Born-Print to Born-Digital

The networked consumption and production of cultural material is only possible because much of the material is available either in analogue and digital format, or digitally alone. In other words, without the availability of resources that can almost effortlessly be shared and remixed, today's networked production would be much more difficult, if not impossible. The wide range of digital material such as videos, songs, blogs, social media posts and archives vividly illustrates that we have departed from the condition of the born-print text of McLuhan's *Gutenberg Galaxy* (1962) and are unstoppably moving towards the condition of exclusively born-digital cultural material. Despite the ubiquity of born-digital texts, 'content that is being created, distributed and used solely in digital form' (Ryan & Sampson, 2018: 2) without an original print-based or analogue version, the concept so far has received little scholarly attention (Erway, 2010: 1).

A better understanding of the nature of born-digital texts requires us to look at both terms: born-digital and text. To start with the latter, we use the word text in the broad sense as any kind of verbal and visual representation of the world, created by a single author or collaboratively. The concept of born-digital texts which we advocate here implies that whatever it is that we find in the digital sphere, is a special type of the notion of 'text'. From this follows the question of what makes a text. As with most concepts that are used widely and intuitively, this question is not easily answered. In fact, text linguistics as a sub-discipline mainly rooted in German-speaking academia in particular spent several decades on the endeavor of finding an appropriate answer (see Adamzik, 2016, for a comprehensive overview of the debate). A key contribution to this debate is Beaugrande and Dressler's (1981) monograph, in which they propose seven criteria of textuality – i.e. criteria an utterance has to fulfill in order to be 'communicative'.

Beaugrande and Dressler consider these criteria as constitutive for texts (see Table 1.1). In other words: if these criteria are not fulfilled, communication would be severely impacted, or could even break down entirely.

Table 1.1 Selected criteria of textuality (based on Beaugrande & Dressler, 1981)

Text-centered criteria	Cohesion
	Coherence
User-centered criteria	Intentionality
	Acceptability
	Informativity
	Situationality
	Intertextuality

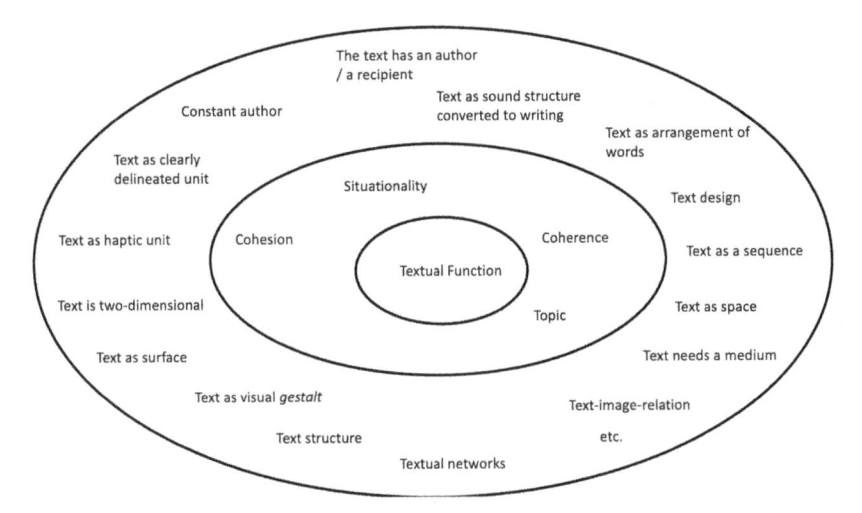

Figure 1.2 shows a diagram with three concentric ellipses. The innermost contains "Textual Function". The middle ellipse contains: Situationality, Cohesion, Coherence, Topic, Text structure, Textual networks. The outermost ellipse contains: The text has an author / a recipient; Constant author; Text as sound structure converted to writing; Text as arrangement of words; Text as clearly delineated unit; Text design; Text as haptic unit; Text as a sequence; Text is two-dimensional; Text as space; Text as surface; Text needs a medium; Text as visual *gestalt*; Text-image-relation; etc.

Figure 1.2 Prototype Model of Textuality Features (Sandig, 2000; trans. P.S.)

With the reception of prototype theory (in particular Sandig, 2000), a consensus was established that still holds today: 'text' is viewed as a category with 'better', even prototypical and peripheral examples. Prototypical members of the category exhibit a number of key features, while peripheral members do so to a lesser extent. Additionally, these features are ranked, i.e. some are more important for an entity to count as a text than others. In the resulting model (Sandig, 2000), several of Beaugrande and Dressler's (1981) criteria reappear as more or less central features of the category 'text' (Figure 1.2).

As Figure 1.2 shows, 'communicative function' is suggested as the number-one criterion for textuality. In other words, any text is an utterance used to achieve a particular purpose in a communicative exchange. Other criteria such as coherence, cohesion, topic, situationality and so on derive from, and are linked to, this core criterion. Further criteria, for example texts being clearly delineated units produced by a single/constant author, are considered less important for an entity to count as text.

This rather flexible approach to criteria for textuality has proven highly useful for describing the specifics of digital texts, such as hypertexts (Rehm, 2006; Żebrowska, 2013) and digital genres such as blogs (Schildhauer, 2016). Coherence is a feature heavily impacted in complex hypertexts (Rehm, 2006), while a key characteristic of blogs, for example, is the fact that they could potentially be infinite as long as their author(s) are motivated enough to add further posts (Schildhauer, 2016). In that regard, texts can be viewed as part of an ongoing negotiation process between producers and recipients (Fritz, 2013) as part of which users can, for example, negotiate the specific function and topic of a blog page (Lomborg, 2014). Most importantly, users declare an entity as text in this negotiation process: whenever YouTubers, bloggers etc. publish a piece online, they declare it as a text (often even of a specific kind) and, thus, as a communicative offer, a meaningful utterance. Whenever recipients accept the offer, establish coherence and create meaning, they declare the entity as text, too (Adamzik, 2016; Schildhauer, 2016). In other words: even entities that, to the eye of an observer, do not fulfil textuality criteria as suggested in Figure 1.2, may be viewed as texts, i.e. perfectly fine communicative utterances, by their producers and (intended) audiences in a particular situation in which they perform a communicative purpose.

Even though the 'purely monomodal text has always been an exception' (Stöckl, 2004: 10; cf. also Kress, 1998), the advent of the so-called 'new' media appears to have worked as a catalyst in a multimodal turn leading to an understanding of texts as entities fusing several sign systems (Luginbühl, 2015). While still considered a peripheral feature in Sandig's (2000) account of textuality, the affordances of digital technologies (Gibson, 1979; Jones & Hafner, 2021) make multimodality a likely candidate for a core feature of born-digital texts.

Based on this prototypical approach to texts, born-digital texts can be described on the basis of two main features: they differ from born-print texts in terms of, first, authorship (i.e. *who* produces a text) and second, the modalities of meaning-making involved (i.e. *how* does a text produce meaning). In the following paragraphs, these two notions will be described in more detail.

First, regarding authorship, born-digital texts depart from the traditional paradigm of 'one text, one author', often to be found in the realm of born-print texts (Nantke, 2018: 1). Rather, they 'challenge the concept of the single author' (Kergel & Heidkamp, 2018: 19) as they shift towards a shared authorship model as the default setting of digital text production. Born-digital texts often rest upon collaborative and interactive efforts, with various individuals being (temporarily or constantly) involved in the production process (Zimmermann, 2015).

This tendency towards collaboration and shared authorship rests upon the fact that public and academic perception of text, as material practice and cultural artefact, has drastically changed over the past two decades. In pre-digital times, once a text was published (e.g. in the form of a paper-based book), its material shape and textual properties were relatively stable. As Hautzinger (1999: 25; trans. D.B.) points out:

> The physical constitution of a book as a haptic object represents authority and stability. Its clear beginning and end give weight to the message of a text since there appears nothing to be added. It forms a unit of its own.

In the context of print culture and analogue production, text was prominently viewed as a closed-off and rather static system, which was 'immutable once written' (Kergel & Heidkamp, 2018: 20). As such, texts evoked a sense of permanence, resulting in a clear hierarchy between author and reader: publishing texts to a larger audience was mostly reserved for professional writers and publishing companies, whereas readers were merely consumers, without the means or opportunities to alter the text in front of them (Eick, 2014: 27).

Yet, with the advent of new digital technologies and outlets for online publication, this absolute view on text as an immutable artefact, and the hierarchical relationship between author and reader, have been increasingly challenged. Beavis (2013: 246), for example, views 'the capacity to copy, mash, change, [and] spoof' as central to digital text production and, in doing so, regards the digital era as a time in which the very notion of textuality is redefined: amidst easy-to-use editing tools and an increasing text distribution via social media platforms, the traditional idea of textual stability is replaced by an understanding of text as an open and dynamic space of semiotic negotiation. As Kuhlen (2004: 221) states, in the digital realm, 'works turn into networks and closed products become public and developing offers to be used and shared'. Be it in the form of social media posts, YouTube videos, or hypertext fiction, many born-digital texts anticipate participation and co-creation as an integral part of their textual design. Thus, readers (in the broadest sense) are invited to alter, add to, and comment on existing texts – or respond with a text of their own. In this context, the traditional line between author and reader becomes increasingly blurred (Pleimfelder, 2018) and text productions resemble a polyphonic amalgam of different authorial voices. Similarly, Tagg (2015: 40) also argues that the line between reader and writer is increasingly blurred in online contexts, since 'readers can take a more active role than traditionally posited for them', for example through below-the-line comments, by bestowing ratings or by publicly responding to a text (e.g. fanfiction) by writing and posting their own. Furthermore, since 'the web is increasingly seen as user-generated, […] it is the users ("the readers") themselves who are also creating and sharing the content that makes up the web' (Tagg, 2015: 41). As such, born-digital texts showcase highly fluid boundaries which are continuously shaped and reshaped by the collaboration and authorship of the many rather than the few.

In addition to the notion of shared authorship, born-digital texts differ from born-print texts in how they textually create meaning. More to the point, it is by now a well-established conviction in research on digital textualities and digital storytelling (e.g. Balaman, 2018; Becker & Blell, 2018; Lütge & Merse, 2021) that born-digital texts are often characterised by their multimodality. Thus, whereas analogue texts most often are presented through only one form of communication (e.g. traditional literary narratives unfold through written language), born-digital texts are defined by 'the existence of multiple (i.e. several [or] many) modes in textual meaning-making' (Towndrow & Pereira, 2018: 3). They rely on the interaction and combination of different semiotic systems, which, according to multiliteracies pedagogy, include oral, written, visual, gestural, tactile and spatial communication (see e.g. Kalantzis *et al.*, 2016). Each of these modes demonstrates its own design (or 'grammar') of representing knowledge, thus making born-digital texts most complex collages of different ways of relating to the world.

On the textual surface, this complex multimodal composition is expressed in the convergence of various media formats – different semiotic modes, in other words, coincide with different 'material channels of dissemination' (Towndrow & Pereira, 2018: 4) and multimodality begets multimediality (and vice versa). In other words, born-digital texts often include 'some mixture of digital graphics, text, recorded audio narration, video and music to present information on a specific topic' (Girmen *et al.*, 2019: 55). In their multimodal composition, therefore, born-digital texts combine both analogue and digital media channels and become contact zones for different forms of media expression. Ultimately, as Owczarek (2018: 12) insinuates, the multimedial character of the genre poses a challenge to readers: in order to understand born-digital texts, readers need to be able to recognise and decipher the diverse media formats as well as the semiotic modes involved, so that 'reading' these digital artifacts (in the broadest sense) becomes a constant interpretative synthesis between modal and medial features of a text.

Preconceived notions of what constitutes a text, therefore, have to be re-examined, as does the notion of what a narrative is, for example. The latter can be illustrated by the 'small stories paradigm' (Georgakopoulou, 2017: 266):

> [Small stories research is a paradigm that] was initially put forth as a counter-move to dominant models of narrative studies that:
>
> (a) defined narrative restrictively and on the basis of textual criteria;
> (b) privileged a specific type of narrative, in particular the long, relatively uninterrupted, teller-led accounts of past events or of one's life story, typically elicited in research interview situations.

As discussed in the contributions in this volume, the existence of born-digital texts impacts not only our theoretical thinking, but also our research into their very nature. Furthermore, their increasing predominance in popular culture should encourage us to explore ways in which we can bring born-digital texts into our classrooms, allowing students to engage with contemporary representatives of our modern communication and information culture.

1.4 Born-Digital Texts in Foreign Language Teaching

Education, it is clear, still largely remains focused on texts that are not born-digital (Kesson, 2021), maintaining 'a strong emphasis on knowledge and skills pertaining to print and print-based texts' (Davidson, 2009: 36). While, at first glance, this may be greeted with incomprehension, there seems to be a number of compelling reasons for the nagging mistrust towards using born-digital material in the classroom. First of all, redrawing the boundaries of the traditional (print-based) text canon may not be an easy undertaking (Schildhauer *et al.*, 2023), as teachers may encounter resistance against born-digital texts because of what Barton and Lee (2013: 11) refer to as moral panics: 'These public discourses, or moral panics, that are largely reinforced by mass media are centered on how the language adopted by young people in their online communication may negatively affect their literacy skills'. Teachers who want to use born-digital texts may be confronted with the very same doubts and reservations that other text types evoked in history. In the 1790 book *Memoirs of the Bloomsgrove Family*, Reverend Enos Hitchcock wrote that:

> [T]he free access which many young people have to romances, novels, and plays has poisoned the mind and corrupted the morals of many a promising youth; and prevented others from improving their minds in useful knowledge. Parents take care to feed their children with wholesome diet; and yet how unconcerned about the provision for the mind, whether they are furnished with salutary food, or with trash, chaff, or poison?

In fact, the current discussion about incorporating born-digital texts into the foreign language classroom is comparable to the discourses on comics, and later graphic novels, around the time of comic censorship in the United States from the mid-1940s until the early 2000s:

> Badly drawn, badly written and badly printed – a strain on young eyes and young nervous systems – the effect of these pulp-paper stimulants is that of a violent nightmare. Their crude blacks and reds spoil the child's natural sense of color; their hypodermic injection of sex and murder make the child impatient with better, though quieter, stories (North, 1940: 56).

In addition to this, the integration of born-digital texts into the classroom may come with a number of other questions, such as the following:

- How can we capture and harness texts for teaching that are by nature ephemeral and subject to change?
- Which born-digital texts do we work with, and which born-digital texts should learners produce?
- How do we link born-digital texts to curricular objects that continue to emphasise print-text-related skills and competences?
- How do we assess born-digital texts that learners produce?

Despite these concerns, there are an overwhelming number of compelling reasons for the integration of born-digital texts in foreign language teaching, which are addressed in more detail in the individual chapters in this volume.

Overall, engaging with born-digital texts in the classroom allows learners to explore texts that have direct relevance to their own communicative practices in which 'written and alphabetical channels for conveying meaning are coupled with, or replaced by, visual, oral, audio, spatial or interactive patterns of meaning-making' (Lütge *et al.*, 2021: 232). Tutorials, YouTube videos and social media posts as examples of born-digital texts offer young people ways to not only express themselves but also find and share information. Thus, incorporating born-digital texts in the classroom means relating language teaching to the learners' lived experiences. Furthermore, born-digital texts often deal with subject matter relevant to learners, in a language that they understand and through the literacy and communicative practices that they use themselves.

With regard to the traditional aims of foreign language teaching, born-digital texts can be used to develop the same skills, competences and literacies as traditional print texts (Table 1.2) while, at the same time, being more accessible to today's generation of learners.

In addition to these traditional curricular goals, born-digital texts can also help to enhance learners' digital competence, i.e.:

> The set of knowledge, skills, attitudes, abilities, strategies, and awareness that are required when using ICT and digital media to perform tasks; solve problems; communicate, manage information; collaborate; create and share content; and build knowledge effectively, appropriately, critically, creatively, autonomously, flexibly, ethically and reflectively for work, participation, learning, socialising, consuming, and empowerment (Ferrari, 2012: 3–4).

In other words, actively engaging with born-digital texts can help learners to acquire the skills they need 'to generate multi-modal texts and to understand principles of making multi-modal meanings' (Lankshear & Knobel, 2003: 77) instead of simply learning to use print texts with digital tools (see e.g. Marx, 2019, for a discussion of what she terms 'pseudo-digitalization' in foreign language textbooks). As learners learn to safely and appropriately access, use and produce born-digital texts, they also come into contact with the critical aspects of today's digital communication and information culture, including aspects such as access (*Are there the same access restrictions as to analogue texts?*), privacy (*Should deleted files be recovered?*) licensing (*When is something in digital form considered published?*) and sourcing (*How can I find out whether a source is legitimate/ trustworthy?*). Thus, the five competence areas in the *The Digital Competence Framework for Citizens* (Vuorikari *et al.*, 2016) can also be applied to born-digital texts (Table 1.3).

Table 1.2 Promoting key foreign language competences through using born-digital texts

Competence	Learners can ...
Functional communicative competence	explore emergent communicative competences which can be observed 'in vivo', paving the way for a wider discussion of language use and change.
Audio-visual competence, reading, writing, listening, mediation	practice their skills with regard to the different modes present in born-digital texts.
Global competence	engage with global and current issues, explore the importance of (cultural) context, and critically discuss aspects of digital cultural ethics, including ethical norms and harm (censorship, digital privacy, the [mis]use of artificial intelligence, online hate speech, or misinformation on social media) (cf. e.g. Aggarwal, 2020; Pegrum *et al.*, 2022).
Text competence	understand that text can be any entity with a purposefully arranged range of signs put together to convey meaning (Lütge *et al.*, 2021: 233) as well as aspects such as genre in the context of digital media.
Language learning competence/learning strategies	train their reflexive use of born-digital texts, drawing on their existing experience with born-digital texts and acquire concrete strategies to deal with born-digital texts.
Language awareness	reflect language use in born-digital texts and use their own language resources to produce born-digital texts.

In addition to the concept of digital competence as summarised in the *The Digital Competence Framework*, the Framework of Digital Literacies 3.0, as outlined by Pegrum *et al.* (2022), provides a further point of departure for exploring the potential of born-digital texts in foreign language teaching. In their framework, print literacy is only one of many, not discrete but overlapping literacies, many of which directly or indirectly point towards born-digital texts. For example, the framework explicitly mentions tagging literacy (+Hashtag literacy), i.e. 'the ability to use metadata in the form of tags to find, make findable and curate digital materials, including through folksonomies or social bookmarking' (Pegrum, n.d.; cf. Becker & Gießler, this volume).

Existing digital literacy and competence frameworks provide a useful starting point to investigate the potential of born-digital texts to prepare students for the demands of the 21st century. However, taking into account the ubiquity of born-digital texts in today's digital media landscape, we propose to understand born-digital text literacy as a separate literacy defined as follows:

> Born-digital text literacy comprises the knowledge of, and skills to, safely and purposefully access, understand, use and create texts which originate in digital format and require the digital to be properly understood.

Table 1.3 The five key competence areas of the *The Digital Competence Framework for Citizens* (Vuorikari et al., 2016)

Competence area	Description
Information and data literacy	To articulate information needs, to locate and retrieve digital data, information and content. To judge the relevance of the source and its content. To store, manage and organise digital data, information and content.
Communication and collaboration	To interact, communicate and collaborate through digital technologies while being aware of cultural and generational diversity. To participate in society through public and private digital services and participatory citizenship. To manage one's digital presence, identity and reputation.
Digital content creation	To create and edit digital content. To improve and integrate information and content into an existing body of knowledge while understanding how copyright and licences are to be applied. To know how to give understandable instructions for a computer system.
Safety	To protect devices, content, personal data and privacy in digital environments. To protect physical and psychological health, and to be aware of digital technologies for social wellbeing and social inclusion. To be aware of the environmental impact of digital technologies and their use.
Problem solving	To identify needs and problems, and to resolve conceptual problems and problem situations in digital environments. To use digital tools to innovate processes and products. To keep up to date with the digital evolution.

The diversity of born-digital materials as well as the knowledge and experiences that learners bring to the classroom call for more learner-centred approaches and teaching methods. Ideally, these incorporate learners' everyday digital practices and experiences with born-digital texts in the digital world in educational environments.

Both the concept of, and the calls for, more learner-centredness – often also termed personalisation, individualisation, or differentiation – are not new. In fact, learner-centeredness has been a key element in foreign language classrooms since the turn towards measuring language competences in the 1960s and 1970s. Since then, teachers have carefully selected context-specific learning materials and tasks to moderate, monitor and guide the foreign language acquisition of their individual learner groups (Moeller & Koubek, 2001). More recently, advances in digital technologies allow for even more personalised learning, since digital tools enable teachers to gather, organise, evaluate and give feedback based on more individual data of each student. Thus, teachers are more equipped to meet the needs of each individual student even beyond the four walls of the classroom, the time constraints of a regular face-to-face lesson, and irrespective of whether the teacher is in the presence of the learner.

When implementing (technology-enhanced) personalised learning, teachers and learners need to consider:

> the personalization of **why** something is to be learned (the learning aims, which are typically the decisions of policymakers);

the personalization of **how** it is to be learned (the learning approach);
the personalization of **what** is to be learned (the learning content and pathways);
the personalization of **when** it is to be learned (the learning pace);
the personalization of **who** is involved in the learning (the learning group); and
the personalization of **where** the learning takes place (the learning context) (Holmes *et al.*, 2018: 10; emphasis in the original).

Intelligent tutoring systems, smart learning management systems, or learning network orchestrators are examples of specific technologies that can meet the complex requirements of personalised learning (Holmes *et al.*, 2018: 11). Presently, studies 'cannot state which technology-enhanced personalized learning tools are the best or, more importantly, which will work best in particular classrooms' (Holmes *et al.*, 2018: 58). Indeed, there might not be a one-size-fits-all tool at all given the complexity of personalisation. Recent research does however show that the use of open teaching methods in digital learning environments is central to personalised learning and has 'a positive effect on both self-reported digital skills and self-perceived ICT-related beliefs in learning' (Schmid & Petko, 2019: abstract). Drawing on teaching methods that are more open (for example, project- or inquiry-based learning, learning stations, or weekly plans), teachers become facilitators of learning pathways that train both individual and collaborative problem-solving skills in the context of pre-selected authentic activities (Holmes *et al.*, 2018). Blending traditional face-to-face lessons and online learning scenarios can be another step in empowering teachers and learners to create authentic learning spaces that mirror students' daily life, which oscillates between digital and analogue spaces. Teachers and learners thus form a Community of Practice (Lave & Wenger, 1991) in which both the teacher's, and the individual learners', roles and competence levels change during the teaching and learning process from newcomer (A1) to explorer (A2), integrator (B1), expert (B2), leader (C1) and then ultimately to pioneer (C2) (Redecker & Punie, 2017).

1.5 Born-Digital Texts in Teacher Education

Education in the digital age is increasingly influenced by the rapidly expanding field of digital humanities, which works at the intersection of digital media studies and the different fields of the humanities. The methodological innovation and changed learner-teacher roles that come with the use of born-digital texts also requires us to prepare teachers for the demands and challenges of teaching in the digital age. Only then can teachers enable their future students to better understand how individuals interact, read and write in the digital age, and the importance of ethical behaviour in an increasingly digital world (cf. also the contribution by Ashooh *et al.* in this volume). Addressing born-digital texts and their use in the classroom in teacher education programmes can provide a critical window into contemporary media practices as well as help future teachers of English:

- reflect on their own media habits;
- develop their own digital and information competences;
- learn how to deal with misinformation;
- demystify born-digital content;
- understand their responsibilities as producers and consumers of born-digital texts; and
- acquire the skills and competences needed to create, curate and consume born-digital texts, including aspects such as archival theory, digital ethics, digital memory (partly based on Brooks, 2019: n.p.; Turner, 2019).

More importantly, a more systematic integration of born-digital texts, such as hashtags (cf. Becker & Gießler, this volume), memes, or chat language into foreign language teacher pre- and in-service education can show teachers how to incorporate existing, as well as evolving, born-digital texts into their classrooms more easily and effectively. More specifically, they can learn how to:

- link born-digital texts to existing curricular guidelines and goals;
- best choose texts that they may want to use in the classroom, especially in the light of the ephemeral nature of born-digital texts;
- complement traditional texts with more innovative, born-digital material;
- evaluate and assess born-digital texts created by their learners; and
- adapt and try out new learner-centred methods to work with born-digital texts.

Only if future teachers receive training in handling born-digital texts and possess born-digital text competences, can they in turn develop these skills in their learners. The ephemerality, complexity and authenticity of many, if not all, born-digital texts makes them a classroom resource that comes with certain challenges, especially as teachers 'swim against the tide of normative and conventional literacy routines of the classroom' (Honan, 2009: 21). Thus, practitioner research plays a vital role in normalising the use of born-digital texts as through classroom-based research teachers to improve their use of born-digital texts and thus support their own professional development (cf. Ludwig, 2018: 16–23; Gabel & Heim, 2019: 7–10). Additionally, (digital) formal and informal teacher networks and professional associations for exchanging experiences, sharing best-practice examples and resources, and discussing methods and activities can help compensate for limited professional experience with born-digital texts in the classroom. Last but not least, teacher action research can contribute to the development of educational policies and curricula explicitly, including not only digital competences, but also competences and skills related to born-digital texts.

1.6 The Contributions to this Volume

The chapters in this volume address key questions around the study of born-digital texts in FLE, and look at how the increasingly broad variety of born-digital texts can be used in language learning contexts, both applying established approaches and methods to dealing with texts and making innovative suggestions for curriculum, syllabus and materials design with regard to born-digital texts. By doing that, the chapters also provide a grounding in the current discussions around digital media tools and platforms in education contexts (cf. e.g. Bündgens-Kosten & Schildhauer, 2021; Ludwig, 2022; Lütge & Merse, 2021).

The volume centres around two broad themes. The first four chapters set the scene and background of the relevance of born-digital texts for Foreign Language Education and thus discuss the contributions, contexts and challenges of born-digital texts in ELT more broadly. The first chapter, 'Born-Digital Text in English Language Teaching: The State of Play' by Daniel Becker, Saskia Kersten, Christian Ludwig, Peter Schildhauer and Sandra Stadler-Heer addresses and counters the cultural pessimism often associated with digital communication as a whole and born-digital texts in particular. Furthermore, it outlines the relevance of born-digital texts for both foreign language learning and teacher education. In the second contribution by Saskia Kersten, 'The Linguistics of Born-Digital Texts', the linguistic dimension of born-digital texts is explored more explicitly, discussing relevant concepts such as affordances and audience design, and more broadly issues that have been debated in the context of digitally-mediated communication. Following this, Kathy A. Mills in 'What Counts as Language Learning in a Born-Digital Textual World?' explores the boundaries and potential limits of language learning in a born-digital textual era and provides a rationale for the inclusion of born-digital texts in the modern language and literacy classroom. Moreover, she raises provocations regarding the born-digital practices of reading and text production that will count in recreational, educational and community spaces, and in the future literacies of Industry 4.0. The chapter concludes with a discussion of the challenges and implications for language and literacy pedagogy and curriculum, including issues of diversity and inclusion, and the scope and sequencing of born-digital practices for curriculum across levels of schooling. Celestine Caruso, Judith Hofmann and Kim Schick discuss in their chapter titled 'Born-Digital Texts and Digitally-Mediated Tasks: A Perfect Match for the Inclusive EFL Classroom?' whether and to what extent digitally-mediated tasks lend themselves for incorporation in an inclusive

EFL classroom. Using the foil of a task as a practical example, they explore in which ways digitally-mediated Task-Based Language Teaching (TBLT) can cater to multilingual learners and learners with Developmental Language Disorder alike, and conclude that teaching language learning strategies and considering home languages may be a fruitful way to navigate the intricate web of digital media, TBLT and inclusion.

The second theme, 'The Practice of Teaching (with) Born-Digital Texts', encompasses the remainder of the chapter, since these focus on the discussion of concrete approaches, methods and tools for the implementation of born-digital texts in classroom contexts. It introduces particular forms of born-digital texts and their relevance for the foreign language classroom in more detail.

The first of these chapters 'Hashtags as Digital Texts and their Affordances in the EFL Classroom' by Ralf Gießler and Daniel Becker, discusses the potential of hashtags as 'born-digital texts' for English language education. More specifically, it argues that a hashtag can be defined as a digital text in its own right, which offers valuable learning opportunities for learners of English as a foreign language. Following this, Peter Schildhauer and Katharina Kemper in 'Towards a Critical Digital Literacy Framework: Exploring the Impact of Algorithms in the Creation of Filter Bubbles on Instagram' focus on the social media feed as a born-digital genre, explore its potential impact on constructing users' worldviews and discuss its implications for foreign language education from a critical digital literacy perspective. Following this, they report on a small-scale experiment in which one Instagram account each was set up to simulate a stereotypical affiliate of the Republican and Democrat Party. The results of the study illustrate the power of algorithms to shape public opinion. They use the results of the study to set up a critical digital literacy framework which aims at empowering learners to critically reflect on and productively engage with texts generated by algorithms.

Traditional broadcasting is declining, while, at the same time, media consumption in general is on the rise. Taking this as a starting point, Valentin Werner in 'Exploring the Potential of Live Text for ELT' argues for the recognition of live texts as a born-digital text type and discusses its relevance for the EFL classroom.

As discussed in Section 1.2 of this introductory chapter, the ludification of society is on the rise. Against this background, 'From Gaming to Linguistic Action: Let's Play Videos as (More Than) Mediation Tasks' by Janina Reinhardt looks at Let's Play videos (LPs) as born-digital linguistic and cultural artifacts in their own right. Using a task-based games-as-text approach, she argues that by watching, analysing, discussing and creating LPs, learners of English as a foreign language can improve their linguistic skills as well as their digital media competence. Following this, the contribution by Sandra Stadler-Heer, 'Consuming and Producing Artificial Intelligence (AI)-Generated Text in English Language Classrooms', pays tribute to the fact that we are entering an age of Artificial Intelligence-Mediated

Communication (AI-MC) as it proposes to expand existing definitions of born-digital text toward text that is produced by artificial intelligence. It proposes content- and context-specific solutions for teaching the (knowledgeable) consumption and production of artificial intelligence-generated text. The chapter concludes with practical implications of consuming and producing artificial intelligence-generated text in English language classrooms and proposes concrete formulations of competence facets for integrating AI-MC in existing 21st-century curricula of foreign language education.

Continuing the discussion of the role of AI in the generation of born-digital texts, 'AI and the Digital Writing Process' by Jasmina Najjar and Philip M. McCarthy explores the role of generative AI in the tertiary education writing process by discussing various tools that could be used by students to assist during their academic writing as well as the implications the use of these tools has on academic writing more generally.

Next, the contribution by Christopher Rwodzi and Lizette J. De Jager, 'Learning English as a Second Language through Born-Digital Texts on Social Media in South Africa', explores the role of born-digital texts in South African education, particularly focusing on resource-constrained township schools in which digital platforms and born-digital texts can help to achieve learner-desired outcomes. Using a qualitative approach and a descriptive case study design, they attempt to better understand the potential of born-digital texts in socialization contexts in townships in South Africa. The chapter concludes by offering selected guidelines regarding how to teach born-digital texts in the South African rural township school context. The contribution by Maya Ashooh, Alecia Marie Magnifico and Bethany Silva, '"I'm going to teach differently": Changing Perceptions of Writing Instruction through Digital Text Creation', equally emphasizes the fact that playful born-digital compositions such as tweets and memes have become increasingly important genres of social and political communication, which are, nevertheless, still largely neglected in US writing classrooms. To help teachers move away from alphabetical, structured genres such as summaries, and envision including born-digital texts in their curricula, the University of New Hampshire hosts an annual National Day on Writing (NDOW), including writing on digital platforms and social media. The contribution examines two years of participation data: the playful texts that writers shared, responsive comments, and a participant exit survey. The results show that introducing participants to creative approaches helped change their perceptions of classroom writing, e.g. participants wrote creatively and discovered born-digital texts to be important factors in building or maintaining students' connections to writing.

The ensuing contribution 'Fanfiction Experiences of Japanese Students: Connecting Wild Reading and L2 Learning' by Tara McIlroy focuses on yet another key skill in the foreign language classroom: reading. It explores potential uses of born-digital fanfiction for second language (L2) learning by better aligning learners' diverse in-the-wild reading experiences which are not yet fully utilized in foreign language learning. More specifically, the chapter reports on a reading experiences survey that reveals Japanese university students' reading preferences. Results suggest that greater awareness of reading preferences and the social nature of reading could assist in integrating born-digital and in-the-wild reading into L2 learning contexts. It concludes with suggestions for the integration of contemporary reading practices and fanfiction into L2 course design. One of the great advantages of using born-digital texts in institutionalized educational contexts is that they can promote out-of-class learning. This fact is also emphasised in the contribution by Carolin Zehne, 'The Potential of Location-Based Technologies and Mobile-Assisted Language Learning for ELT', which explores how location-based technologies can be of benefit in mobile-assisted language learning contexts. In the learning project outlined in the contribution, learners use their smartphones to create their own city tours with born-digital annotated maps. The aim of the project is to enhance learners' digital media skills as well as raise their awareness of concepts such as space, place and location in increasingly digitally mediated environments.

'*Alice for the iPad:* Digital Storybook Apps in the EFL Classroom' by Jeanine Steinbock discusses how the digital revolution is changing the way in which we deal with (canonical) born-print texts, particularly focusing on multimodal digital adaptations of literature. The first part of the contribution discusses digital literature as an emerging literary practice in the digital age. It then moves on to discussing how digital literature as well as digital adaptations of originally born-print texts can enhance learners' digital literacy skills. *Alice for the iPad*, a storybook version of Carroll's *Alice's Adventures in Wonderland*, then serves to illustrate how digital transformation of traditional born-print literature may alter the original text but, at the same time, help to increase learners' engagement with the text and enhance their digital literacies. The chapter by Christian Ludwig, Michaela Sambanis and Georg Hartisch entitled 'Digital Transformations in the ELT Literature Classroom' takes a critical look at state-of-the-art born-digital literature and how it can be integrated into the foreign language classroom, aiming to enhance learners' born-print and born-digital literature skills. Instead of suggesting a mere swap of paper for the screen, they advocate for a more reflective use of both traditional and born-digital literature. By doing that, they attempt to place born-print and born-digital literature in dialogue with each other, arguing that their intricate and complex relationship is worth exploring with regard to multimodal and digital literacy instruction in the contemporary classroom.

We hope that this edited volume helps to shed light on the darkness of born-digital (text) culture (Stapleton & Jaillant, 2022), and encourages teachers, educators and policymakers to shape the digital transformation and create opportunities for learners to critically question existing digital structures and processes and become agents of change.

Münster, München, Berlin, Bielefeld and Eichstätt, September 2023

Notes

(1) Editors and authors are listed in alphabetical order.
(2) See https://www.vox.com/culture/2017/8/25/16200526/distracted-boyfriend-other-woman-stock-photo-meme for information on the original posters and https://knowyourmeme.com/memes/distracted-boyfriend for information on the how the meme developed over time as well as spin offs and variations of the meme.

References

Adamzik, K. (2016) *Textlinguistik: Grundlagen, Kontroversen, Perspektiven*. De Gruyter. https://doi.org/10.1515/9783110339352

Aggarwal, N. (2020) Introduction to the special issue on intercultural digital ethics. *Philosophy & Technology* 33, 547–550.

Aitwani, S. (2017) Taking internet memes seriously: A literature review 2005–2017. See https://www.academia.edu/38491333// (accessed September 2022).

Balaman, S. (2018) Digital storytelling: A multimodal narrative writing genre. *Journal of Language and Linguistic Studies* 14 (3), 202–212.

Beaugrande, R. and Dressler, W.U. (1981) *Introduction to Text Linguistics*. Longman.

Beavis, C. (2013) Literary English and the challenge of multimodality. *Changing English: Studies in Culture and Education* 20 (3), 241–252.

Becker, C. and Blell, G. (2018) Multimedia narratives – Digital storytelling and multiliteracies. *Anglistik: International Journal of English Studies* 29 (1), 129–143.

Brooks, M. (2019) Born-digital archives in the undergraduate classroom. *The Journal of Interactive Technology & Pedagogy* 14. See https://jitp.commons.gc.cuny.edu/born-digital-archives-in-the-undergraduate-classroom/ (accessed September 2022).

Bündgens-Kosten, J. and Schildhauer, P. (eds) (2021) *Englischunterricht in einer Digitalisierten Gesellschaft*. Beltz Juventa.

Carrington, V. (2001) Emergent home literacies: A challenge for educators. *Australian Journal of Language and Literacy* 23 (2), 88–100.

Carrington, V. (2005) The uncanny, digital texts and literacy. *Language and Education* 19 (6), 467–482.

Cavender, E. (2022) For Gen Z, TikTok is more than entertainment. It's a search engine. Young people explain why they're searching social media instead of Google. *Mashable*. See https://mashable.com/article/gen-z-tiktok-search-engine-google (accessed September 2022).

Coughlan, S. (2017) What does post-truth mean for a philosopher? *BBC News*, 12 January. http://www.bbc.com/news/education-38557838 (accessed September 2022).

Davidson, C. (2009) Young children's engagement with digital texts and literacies in the home: Pressing matters for the teaching of English in the early years of schooling. *English Teaching: Practice and Critique* 8 (3), 36–54.

Del Vicario, M., Bessi, A., Zollo, F., Petroni, F., Scala, A., Caldarelli, G., Stanley, H.E. and Quattrociocchi, W. (2016) The spreading of misinformation online. *Proceedings of the National Academy of Sciences of the United States of America* 113 (3), 554–559. https://doi.org/10.1073/pnas.1517441113

Eick, D. (2014) *Digitales Erzählen: Die Dramaturgie der Neuen Medien*. UVK.

Erway, R. (2010) Defining 'born digital'. See www.oclc.org/research/activities/hiddencollections/bornditgital.pdf (accessed January 2021).
Ferrari, A. (2012) *Digital Competence in Practice: An Analysis of Frameworks*. Publications Office of the European Union.
Floridi, L. (1999) *Philosophy and Computing: An Introduction*. Routledge.
Floridi, L. (2015a) (ed.) *The Online Manifesto: Being Human in a Hyperconnected Era*. Springer.
Floridi, L. (2015b) Introduction. In L. Floridi (ed.) *The Online Manifesto: Being Human in a Hyperconnected Era* (pp. 1–3). Springer.
Frissen, V., Lammes, S., de Lange, M., de Mul, J. and Raessens, J. (2015) Homo ludens 2.0: Play, media and identity. In V. Frissen, S. Lammes, M. de Lange, J. de Mul and J. Raessens (eds) *Playful Identities: The Ludification of Digital Media Cultures* (pp. 9–50). Amsterdam University Press.
Fritz, G. (2013) *Dynamische Texttheorie*. Gießener Elektronische Bibliothek.
Gabel, S. and Heim, K. (2019) Action research in pre-service teacher education: A step towards autonomy? *ELT Research: The Newsletter of the IATEFL Research Special Interest Group* 34, 7–10.
Gayle, D. (2021) Facebook aware of Instagram's harmful effect on teenage girls, leak reveals. *The Guardian*, 14 September. See https://www.theguardian.com/technology/2021/sep/14/facebook-aware-instagram-harmful-effect-teenage-girls-leak-reveals (accessed September 2022).
Georgakopoulou, A. (2017) Small stories research: A narrative paradigm for the analysis of social media. In L. Sloan and A. Quan-Haase (eds) *The SAGE Handbook of Social Media Research Methods* (pp. 266–281). SAGE. https://doi.org/10.4135/9781473983847.n17
Gibson, J.J. (2014[1979]) *The Ecological Approach to Visual Perception: Classic Edition*. Psychology Press.
Girmen, P., Özkanal, Ü. and Dayan, G. (2019) Digital storytelling in the language arts classroom. *Universal Journal of Educational Research* 7 (1), 55–65.
Han, B. (2021) *Undinge: Umbrüche der Lebenswelt*. Ullstein Verlag.
Hautzinger, N. (1999) *Vom Buch zum Internet? Eine Analyse der Auswirkungen hypertextueller Strukturen auf Text und Literatur*. Röhrig.
Hepp, A. (2021) *Auf dem Weg zur digitalen Gesellschaft: Über die tiefgreifende Mediatisierung der sozialen Welt*. Halem.
Hintz, A., Dencik, L. and Wahl-Jorgensen, K. (2018) *Digital Citizenship in a Datafied Society*. Polity.
Hitchcock, E. (1790) *Memoirs of the Bloomsgrove Family*. Thomas and Andrews.
Holmes, W., Anastopoulou, S., Schaumburg, H. and Mavrikis, M. (2018) *Personalisiertes Lernen Mit Digitalen Medien. Ein Roter Faden [Technology-enhanced Personalised Learning: Untangling the Evidence]*. Robert Bosch Stiftung. See http://www.studie-personalisiertes-lernen.de/en/tepl.html# (accessed September 2022).
Honan, E. (2009) Fighting the rip: Using digital texts in classrooms. *English Teaching: Practice and Critique* 8 (3), 21–35.
Huizinga, J. (1938) *Homo Ludens: Vom Ursprung der Kultur im Spiel*. Random House.
Jenkins, H., with Purushotma, R., Weigel, M., Clinton, K. and Robison, A.J. (2009) *Confronting the Challenges of Participatory Culture Media Education for the 21st Century*. The MIT Press.
Jones, R.H. and Hafner, C.A. (2021) *Understanding Digital Literacies: A Practical Introduction* (2nd edn). Routledge.
Kalantzis, M., Cope, B., Chan, E. and Dalley-Trim, L. (2016) *Literacies* (2nd edn). Cambridge University Press.

Kergel, D. and Heidkamp, B. (2018) The digital turn in higher education: Towards a remix culture and collaborative authorship. In D. Kergel, B. Heidkamp, P.K. Telléus, T. Rachwal and S. Nowakowski (eds) *The Digital Turn in Higher Education: International Perspectives on Teaching and Learning in a Changing World* (pp. 15–22). Springer.

Kersten, S. and Lotze, N. (2021) Anonymity and authenticity on the web: Towards a new framework in internet onomastics. *Internet Pragmatics* 5 (1), 38–65. https://doi.org/10.1075/ip.00074.ker

Kesson, H. (2021) Examining the influence of teaching reading of born digital texts on student reading and writing of arguments. Dissertation, Temple University. ProQuest Dissertations Publishing.

Knobel, M. and Lankshear, C. (2007) *A New Literacies Sampler*. Lang.

Kress, G.R. (1998) Visual and verbal modes of representation in electronically mediated communication: The potentials of new forms of text. In I. Snyder (ed.) *Page to Screen: Taking Literacy into the Electronic Era* (pp. 53–79). Routledge.

Kuhlen, R. (2004) Kollaboratives Schreiben. In C. Bieber and C. Leggewie (eds) *Interaktivität: Ein Transdisziplinärer Schlüsselbegriff* (pp. 216–239). Campus Verlag.

Lankshear, C. and Knobel, M. (2003) New Technologies in early childhood literacy research: A review of research. *Journal of Early Childhood Literacy* 3 (1), 59–82.

Lave, J. and Wenger, E. (1991) *Situated Learning: Legitimate Peripheral Participation*. Cambridge University Press.

Lomborg, S. (2014) *Social Media, Social Genres: Making Sense of the Ordinary*. Routledge.

Ludwig, C. (2018) Action research and language learner autonomy: An exploration journey. In C. Ludwig, A. Pinter, K. Van de Poel, T. Smits, M.G. Tassinari and E. Ruelens (eds) *Fostering Learner Autonomy: Learners, Teachers and Researchers in Action* (pp. 16–23). Candlin & Mynard.

Ludwig, C. (2022) *Digital Englisch Unterrichten*. Friedrich Verlag.

Luginbühl, M. (2015) Media linguistics. *10plus1*. See http://10plus1journal.com/wp-content/uploads/2015/09/00_OPENER_Luginbuehl.pdf (accessed September 2022).

Lütge, C. and Merse, T. (eds) (2021) *Digital Teaching and Learning: Perspective for English Language Education*. Narr.

Lütge, C., Merse, T. and Stannard, M. (2021) Digital textualities: Innovative practices with social media, digital literatures and virtual realities. In C. Lütge and T. Merse (eds) *Digital Teaching and Learning: Perspectives for English Language Education* (pp. 231–254). Narr.

McLuhan, M. (1962) *The Gutenberg Galaxy: The Making of Typographic Man*. University of Toronto Press.

Marx, N. (2019) Zur Pseudodigitalisierung in Fremdsprachenlehrwerken. In E. Burwitz-Melzer, C. Riemer and L. Schmelter (eds) *Das Lehren und Lernen von Fremd- und Zweitsprachen im Digitalen Wandel* (pp. 162–172). Narr.

Moeller, A.K. and Koubek, E. (2001) Foreign language teaching and learning. In N.J. Smelser and P.B. Baltes (eds) *International Encyclopedia of the Social & Behavioral Sciences* (pp. 5733–5737). Elsevier. https://doi.org/10.1016/B0-08-043076-7/02423-2

Nantke, J. (2018) Multiple Autorschaft als digitales Paradigma und dessen Auswirkungen auf den Werksbegriff. *Textpraxis – Digitales Journal für Philologie* 3 (2), 1–25.

North, S. (1940) A national disgrace and a challenge to american parents. *Childhood Education* 17 (2), 56. https://doi.org/10.1080/00094056.1940.10724519 (accessed October 2022).

Nöth, W. (2011) Self-referential postmodernity. *Semiotica* 183–1/4, 199–217.

Otrel-Cass, K. (2019) Hyperconnectivity and digital reality: An introduction. In K. Otrel-Cass (ed.) *Hyperconnectivity and Digital Reality Towards the Eutopia of Being Human* (pp. 1–8). Springer.

Pearson, C. and Hussain, Z. (2015) Smartphone use, addiction, narcissism and personality. *International Journal of Cyber Behavior, Psychology and Learning* 5 (1), 17–32.
Pegrum, M. (n.d.) Digital literacies. See https://markpegrum.com/overview-of-digital-learning/digital-literacies/ (accessed October 2022).
Pegrum, M., Hockly, N. and Dudeney, G. (2022) *Digital Literacies*. Routledge.
Raessens, J. (2012) The ludification of culture. See https://d-nb.info/1234468034/34 (accessed October 2022).
Redecker, C. and Punie, Y. (2017) *Digital Competence Framework for Educators* (DigCompEdu). European Union. See https://ec.europa.eu/jrc/sites/jrcsh/files/digcompedu_leaflet_de-2018-09-21pdf.pdf (accessed September 2022)
Rehm, G. (2006) Hypertextsorten: Definition, Struktur, Klassifikation. Doctoral thesis, Justus-Liebig Universität. See http://geb.uni-giessen.de/geb/volltexte/2006/2688/ (accessed October 2022).
Ribble, M. and Bailey, G. (2007) *Digital Citizenship in Schools*. International Society for Technology in Education.
Ryan, H. and Sampson, W. (2018) *The No-Nonsense Guide to Born-Digital Content*. Facet Publishing. https://doi.org/10.29085/9781783302567
Sandig, B. (2000) Text als prototypisches Konzept. In M. Mangasser-Wahl (ed.) *Prototypentheorie in der Linguistik: Anwendungsbeispiele – Methodenreflexion – Perspektiven* (pp. 93–112). Stauffenburg Verlag.
Schildhauer, P. (2016) *The Personal Weblog: A Linguistic History*. Lang.
Schildhauer, P., Gerlach, D. and Weiser-Zurmühlen, K. (2023) Considerations on artifacts of digital culture in English language teaching: Conspiracy theories on the instagram newsfeed. In J. Sauer, P. Schildhauer and A. Schröder (eds) *Standards – Margins – New Horizons 2.0: Canons for 21st Century Teaching* [PFLB Special Issue], 242–257.
Schmid, R. and Petko, D. (2019) Does the use of educational technology in personalized learning environments correlate with self-reported digital skills and beliefs of secondary-school students? *Computers and Education* 136, 75–86. https://doi.org/10.1016/j.compedu.2019.03.006
Scott, K. (2022) *Pragmatics Online*. Routledge.
Shifman, L. (2013) *Memes in Digital Culture*. The MIT Press.
Silverstone, R. (1999) *Why Study the Media?* Sage.
Stalder, F. (2016) *Kultur der Digitalität*. Suhrkamp.
Stalder, F. (2018) *The Digital Condition* (trans. V.A. Pakis). Polity Press.
Stapleton, L. and Jaillant, L. (2022) 'Born digital' shedding light into the darkness of digital culture. *AI & Society* 37, 819–822. https://doi.org/10.1007/s00146-021-01358-y
Statista (2022) Distribution of TikTok users worldwide as of April 2022, by age and gender. See https://www.statista.com/statistics/1299771/tiktok-global-user-age-distribution/ (accessed September 2022).
Stöckl, H. (2004) In between modes: Language and image in printed media. In E. Eija Ventola, C. Charles and M. Kaltenbacher (eds) *Perspectives on Multimodality* (pp. 9–30). Benjamins.
Tagg, C. (2015) *Exploring Digital Communication: Language in Action*. Routledge.
Tewksbury, D. and Rittenberg, J. (2015) *News on the Internet: Information and Citizenship in the 21st Century*. Oxford University Press.
Towndrow, P.A. and Pereira, A.J. (2018) Reconsidering literacy in the 21st century: Exploring the role of digital stories in teaching English to speakers of other languages. *RELC Journal* 49 (2), 1–16.
Turkle, S. (2021) How to fix social media. *The Wall Street Journal*, 29 October. See www.wsj.com/articles/how-to-fix-social-media-11635526928 (accessed September 2022).
Turner, K.H. (2019) *The Ethics of Digital Literacy: Developing Knowledge and Skills Across Grade Levels*. Rowman & Littlefield.

Vuorikari, R., Punie, Y., Carretero, S. and Van den Brande, L. (2016) *DigComp 2.0: The Digital Competence Framework for Citizens. Update Phase 1: The Conceptual Reference Model*. Publication Office of the European Union.

Wells, G., Horwitz, J. and Seetharaman, D. (2021) Facebook knows instagram is toxic for teen girls, company documents show. *The Wall Street Journal,* 14 September. See https://www.wsj.com/articles/facebook-knows-instagram-is-toxic-for-teen-girls-company-documents-show-11631620739 (accessed September 2022).

Wenger, E. (2000) Communities of practice and social learning systems. *Organization* 7, 225–246.

Żebrowska, E. (2013) *Text – Bild – Hypertext*. Peter Lang.

Zimmermann, H. (2015) *Autorschaft und digitale Literatur: Geschichte, Medienpraxis und Theoriebildung*. WVT.

2 The Linguistics of Born-Digital Texts

Saskia Kersten

2.1 Introduction

This chapter discusses the current linguistic debates around born-digital texts, in particular the question of whether there is such a thing as a new variety of language used on the internet, i.e. what sometimes has been termed *Netspeak* or *Internet English,* and has been debated by scholars with regards to digitally-mediated interaction (DMI). It will argue that anyone using born-digital texts in the English language classroom should be careful not to be too reductionistic about language features that may or may not be present in a text that originated in the digital domain. Instead, it advocates that the affordances of the platform that may result in particular language being used at all and/or used in novel ways are discussed, thus highlighting overarching concepts with their learners, such as audience design, context design, collaborative co-construction of meaning and emerging local norms.

2.2 The Problem with Netspeak

In his book *Language and the Internet,* Crystal (2006: 274f) stated that because of the 'sheer scale of the present internet', he is convinced that 'we are on the brink of the biggest language revolution ever'. While digital technologies no doubt have an impact on the way we interact, whether this indeed led to a language revolution and a new variety of English as predicted by Crystal will be discussed below.

What is without question is that digitalisation impacts both language and literacies in fundamental ways (Androutsopoulos, 2021: 1). In the following, this chapter will outline the linguistic aspects of born-digital texts, discuss whether digital technology has indeed given rise to what Crystal (2006) terms *Netspeak,* what linguistic conventions and genres have emerged in the wake of born-digital texts and how linguistic skills can be fostered in the English language classroom using these texts.

2.3 Born-Digital Texts: Not as Good as 'Traditional' Texts?

As seems to be the case with the advent of any kind of new technology, digital communication was both enthusiastically embraced and eyed suspiciously from inception. Many decried the (imagined) detrimental effect on language. For example, John Humphrys lamented in his 2007 *Mail Online* article entitled 'I h8 txt msgs: How texting is wrecking our language' that '[o]ur written language may end up as a series of ridiculous emoticons and ever-changing abbreviations'. Texting in particular seems to induce these moments of pearl-clutching, most likely because the use of abbreviations, emoticons and emojis is seen as a typical feature of born-digital texts, not 'serious' communication.

From the advent of digitally-mediated interaction (DMI), that is more specifically the proliferation of email which is generally posited to be the oldest form of what used to be called computer-mediated communication (Dürscheid & Frehner, 2013: 35; Halenko *et al.*, 2021), many linguists (e.g. Baron, Crystal, Herring) raised the question whether there were unifying linguistic features that characterise the new genre.

The question of technological determinism, i.e. whether the medium shapes user behaviour (and thus the language used), was prevalent in the beginning of scholarly interest in digital communication and born-digital texts, as was the view that this type of communication is somehow deficient compared to written and spoken language (Herring *et al.*, 2013). Because electronic contexts were framed as 'impoverished' (Brennan, 1998: 1) based on the assumption that because the communication was mediated, this led to 'an impoverished set of inputs' (Houghton *et al.*, 2018: 112), the texts produced under these conditions were likewise seen as lacking.

Many researchers posited that people compensate for the lack of paralinguistic cues through the use of, for example, emoticons (for a discussion of this view, see Bieswanger, 2013). What is striking, however, is that paralinguistic cues are generally absent from most forms of written communication and yet very few would accuse printed books or business letters of being deficient or 'less than' verbal face-to-face communication.

This compensatory view – or 'deficit model', as Jones and Hafner (2021) call it – is the result of the comparison of DMI with other 'traditional' forms of communication. Tellingly, the view of what is compensated for changes depending on the modes DMI is compared with: when judged against other forms of written communication, DMI 'is found to lack precision, clarity, and "correctness"', and when judged against face-to-face communication, 'it is found to lack richness' (Jones & Hafner, 2021: 95). It is therefore not particularly illuminating to constantly compare born-digital texts with 'traditional', i.e. non-digital, texts. Instead, they should be judged on their own terms and by their own merits, since DMI has 'introduced into social life a whole array of new kinds of interactions which were not possible using traditional writing or voice-based conversations' (Jones & Hafner, 2021: 95).

2.3.1 Netspeak revisited

While there seem to be some shared characteristics and conventions that have emerged or are emerging in born-digital texts, researchers who study digitally-mediated communication generally reject the notion that such a thing as a generalizable *Netspeak* or *Internet English* exists. *Netspeak* (modelled on Orwellian terms ending in *-speak*, e.g. *Newspeak*) in particular was first posited by Crystal (2001: 17ff) based on 'a widely held intuition' (Crystal, 2001: 18) who argued this term to be less cumbersome than, for example, 'computer-mediated communication' (Crystal, 2006: 20). Several researchers have since argued against the notion that there is a set of generalisable features that are present in all born-digital texts (see e.g. Androutsopoulos, 2006; and Herring & Androutsopoulos, 2015; for a succinct overview of this discussion see Bieswanger, 2013: 465–466).

Bieswanger (2013), for example, discusses four micro-linguistic (i.e. below the syntactic level) features that have been argued to be characteristic of digitally-mediated interaction, namely emoticons, non-standard spelling, abbreviation and non-standard punctuation (this aspect will also be discussed in more detail below), and points out that the use of these features varies considerably across platforms, modes and even topics on the same platform (see also Bieswanger & Intemann, 2011) as well as among different users.

2.3.2 The built-in obsolescence of research on born-digital texts

Since platforms evolve and change very rapidly, one issue that researchers face is that their findings are in danger of being obsolete or outmoded almost as soon as they are published. For example, many studies investigating characteristic features of born-digital texts or emerging conventions were based on forum threads or internet relay chat discussions, both forms of DMI which are less common nowadays. Reddit and Quora are two sites which most closely resemble forum threads and regularly make it onto the lists of most used social media sites but they commonly are on the low(er) rungs of the ranking with e.g. Reddit having around 430 million active users compared to top-ranked Facebook with 2.91 billion active users. Furthermore, the affordances (see Section 2.4.1 below) of these platforms have changed significantly, and thus past findings based on internet relay chats may no longer accurately depict current usage.

On the other hand, with around 4.74 billion active social media users worldwide, and with the average time spent on social media of nearly two and a half hours daily which in turn makes up more than a third of the total time spent online (as of October 2022, according the *The Global State of Digital* report 2022), it would be foolish to ignore DMI both in research and in teaching, since it could be an important source of extramural (i.e. out-of-classroom) learning time that could be tapped into to offer opportunities for both language learning and more general digital skills.

The next section outlines concepts and frameworks that can inform the research and teaching of born-digital texts, namely affordances, audience design and interactional linguistics.

2.4 Concepts and Frameworks

2.4.1 Affordances

As outlined above, for a long time researchers were primarily focused on the idea that the 'digitalness' of the media used to create born-digital texts has an impact on their form. In more recent years, however, the discussion has shifted to the view that different media have different affordances that may shape the kind of text that is created, by making use of what a given platform has to offer (see also Gießler & Becker, this volume, for a discussion of the affordances of hashtags).

'Simply put, affordances are enablings and constraints for behavior provided by some object or environment to some agent' (Wikström, 2017: 12). For example, this can be seen in terms of the permissible length of posts or messages, as is the case for Twitter, where longer contributions that exceed the character limit of a single tweet can be presented as a thread, and that other born-digital artifacts can form part of a tweet (through the inclusion of multimodal material such as GIFs or videos) and how users can interact with content, for example through liking, favouriting or disseminating them through retweets and quote tweets.

The term 'affordance' was first coined by Gibson (2015[1986]: chap. 8) who originally conceived of affordances for any form of interaction with the environment which may also be dependent on the user of the environment, since for example bodily differences can impact how an object can be interacted with: 'Knee-high for a child is not the same as knee-high for an adult, so the affordance is relative to the size of the individual'.

In addition to the observation that affordances are relational, Bucher and Helmond (2018: 235) highlight that the environment is perceived through the lens of the affordances; an affordance is not the structural feature itself but rather 'the possibilities for action it may provide'.

> [T]he flatness of a tabletop is not an affordance, but rather a feature that can yield the affordance of putting things on it to an agent for whom 'putting' is a meaningful action. That is, the salient affordance is not the flatness, but the put-on-ableness (Wikström, 2017: 12).

In the context of digitally mediated communication, the user perceives the medium as having a range of possible actions, often linked to a feature. Importantly, the actions are not limited to the features as they were intended to be used by the developers, since 'there is a long history of the mismatch between designers' original expectations and the ways people bend technologies to their own purposes' (Barton & Lee, 2013: 27). An example for this is the star button that used to be available for Twitter users to favorite a tweet (see also Bucher & Helmond, 2018), which was used by many akin to a bookmark for tweets with e.g. information they wanted to revisit later. Starring, i.e. favouriting, was the antecedent of the 'like' heart that can now be activated by double clicking on a tweet, thus emulating the 'like' mechanism of other platforms such as Instagram.

When the change from the 'fav star' (as it was then known) to the 'like' heart was rolled out in November 2015, this led to a wide-ranging discussion among Twitter users about the difference between faving and liking. For example, in a post on LinkedIn, Abihsira (2015) states that the function of the fav star is fundamentally different from the like heart, and that the change from star to heart will change the context that is generated on the site. In a similar vein, Newton (2015) called the fav star 'a versatile little button' and lists a number of functions that it served for him that a like or heart button (which he calls 'a kind of universal currency of the social web') does not.

There may once have been an intended use of the star button by the platform's developers, but it is the social practice of what users actually do with a feature that shapes the affordances (Barton & Lee, 2013). A consequence of this is that a list of properties or features of a given platform is ultimately futile, not only because of the mutability of platforms where features may change from one release or update to the next, but also because affordances are, as outlined above, socially constructed (Barton & Lee 2013). The technological affordances, for example, may affect 'what can be done easily' and 'what can be done conventionally' (Barton & Lee, 2013) but this does not mean that this is how users actually use it.

This is also why Barton and Lee (2013) argue that blog is not a genre, since the blog itself is first and foremost a designed space that can be used in multiple ways, and it is how people make use of the affordances of the predesigned spaces that then in turn gives rise to certain genres, since the constraints and possibilities of a given blogging platform may lend themselves more to writing a particular type of text (Barton and Lee (2013) use the example of a blog with its highly structured chronological layout to illustrate this point).

A change in affordances may impact born-digital texts, in particular if user behaviour is additionally shaped by unknown and unseen algorithms that appear to rely on users' liking behaviour. Born-digital texts are therefore not only shaped by the use users make of the affordances of a given platform, but by the audience (real, perceived or imagined).

2.4.2 Audience design

The notion of audience design based on Bell's (1984) model has been applied to the analysis of born-digital texts, not least to explain how authors of social media posts address several conflicting goals that impact the way texts are shaped: namely the conundrum between the need to provide sufficient information about themselves in order to be recognisable or 'gain social capital' (Tagg, 2015: 153), the fact that they may be communicating with diverse (and ultimately unknowable) audiences (the latter is often referred to as context collapse; see Marwick & boyd, 2011; Wesch, 2009) and how quickly disclosed information in the form of born-digital texts can be disseminated online.

Creators of born-digital texts on social media therefore have to manage what Tagg (2015: 153) refers to as 'social convergence', that is the fact that even though a text may address a particular audience with all the associated stylistic choices (e.g. the appropriate level of formality), it may also be read by audiences other than the intended one since 'a wider, unknown audience may also have access to posts'. For an analysis of what users do when faced with these dilemmas, the framework of audience design (Bell, 1984) posits that the role of the audience is not predetermined but rather allocated, reallocated and, at times, renegotiated (Tagg, 2015).

Furthermore, what Barton and Lee (2013: 56) call the 'situated language ecology of individual users' shapes born-digital texts. They use the choice of which language (or languages) is/are used and in which writing systems as an example: if a text is intended for a general, largely unknown audience (or imagined audience, see Marwick & boyd, 2011), users may prefer to use English rather than a local language, or post in their local language but also an equivalent or complementary translation (see Sebba, 2012, cited in Barton & Lee, 2013: 57).

Audience design is therefore, after affordances, the second most important aspect that shapes born-digital texts and that could be explored with learners (see Section 5 on classroom application below).

Knowledge of who may consume a text online, and who may have produced it with what audience in mind, are important components of critical digital literacy as outlined in, for example, Becker and Gießler (this volume) and Werner (this volume), as well as the *European Framework for the Digital Competence* (DigComp; see Redecker, 2017; Vuorikari *et al.*, 2022).

2.4.3 Context design

Building on the idea of audience design and work on the ethnography of communication, Tagg and Sergeant (2021: 3) developed a theory of context design, which 'accounts for the dynamic, socially co-constructed nature of context, especially as this is a feature of social media, so as to better understand the particular nature of online communication'.

Although context design is not unique to born-digital texts, it is of particular importance since the production of these texts is virtual and not embodied, and is therefore 'often achieved through the exploitation of site affordances, sometimes in ways far removed from their original design purpose' (Tagg & Sergeant, 2021: 7).

They go on to say that social media sites are, by definition, social spaces where posters position themselves in relation to other posters and readers, but also particular discourses, ideologies and social roles which in turn shape the communication that takes place. Finally, they identify a need for a social digital literacies education, which will be examined in the discussion in Section 2.5 later.

2.4.4 Interactional (socio)linguistics

According to Imo (2015), interactional linguistics is an analytic framework well-suited to the analysis of born-digital texts and defines the main tenet of interactional linguistics, quoting Linell (2005: 21) as follows: 'Interactional, spoken language is designed to cope with meaning-making in specific situations, and in real time and space. It has its home base in talk-in-interaction, which is a complex social interplay between actors'. The first principle is reflexivity, which means that context and discourse are related, further that certain patterns of language are expected in particular text types and that it is sequential and jointly constructed (Imo, 2015: 3–4).

It can be argued that this definition does not only apply to spoken interaction but also communication involving born-digital texts, e.g. texting, chatting and commenting on social media posts (if the latter evolves into a dialogic exchange, which of course is not always the case).

Busch (2021a), for example, analysed new forms of punctuation in this paradigm. Instead of explaining form and function of punctuation that does not conform to the norm as trying to emulate orality as was previously done following the Koch and Oesterreicher (1985, 1994, 2012[1]) model, he posits that digital messages (in this case WhatsApp messages) that are part of the informal writing practices of adolescents have a contextualised function and meaning that is constructed collaboratively by the interlocutors. Pappert (2017) investigated emojis and emoticons in a similar fashion. As an example, Imo (2015) describes the fact that when texting most people do not write all they want to say in one message, but often send multiple messages as a locally negotiated norm. Yet another example, namely the use of message-final full stop, will be discussed in more detail by way of illustration below.

2.4.5 The message-final full stop in born-digital interaction

In the following, I will outline one area that lends itself well to being explored in relation to emerging linguistic practices in DMI in classroom contexts, namely that punctuation marks undergo a functional shift in line with the interactional principle (Busch, 2021a, 2021b). Like other features of the language of born-digital texts, punctuation was a focus of analysis of early digitally mediated communication research; it was predominantly the absence or the iteration of punctuation marks that was commented upon, and the main focus tended to be on how punctuation deviated from the perceived norm of what written communication 'should' be and viewed predominantly as a means to emulate oral communication.

What can be observed, however, is that in DMI, punctuation marks do not function as grammatical or phonological markers but rather serve as interactional cues (Busch, 2021c). These practices emerge through the interaction of interlocutors and may then become conventionalised across a wider group as a group-specific practice since they are 'practices of punctuation [...] inseparably connected to the social and mediational setting in which writing and reading take place [...]. Punctuation emerges as a device for organizing written interactions sequentially and establishing shared meanings between participants' (Busch, 2021a: 2).

What learners may be able to observe in their own implicit use of punctuation in texting or other born-digital contexts is the development of 'a new local norm' (Busch, 2021a; see also Imo, 2015): full stops at the end of messages are omitted since they are rendered redundant by an affordance of the medium, namely that messages are already visibly bounded; that is, in Busch's (2021a) words, 'postings already appear visually as bracketed'. Since the function of delineating the end of a message is already encoded in another visual feature afforded by the platform (in this case the bubble the message is delineated by), the message-final full stop becomes available to be imbued with a new function: 'the period has the potential to be meant and to be understood as a contextualization cue' (Busch, 2021a: 4). If a message-final full stop is included, 'readers likely assumed that the period was not included arbitrarily but was included to add meaning to the response' (Houghton *et al.*, 2018: 116).

In his German-language WhatsApp data, Busch (2021a, 2021b) finds that users use a message-final full stop when sending, for example, a negative (and thus dispreferred) response. Furthermore, the data show that this is a deliberate strategy, rather than a functionless idiosyncrasy, thus providing strong evidence that a local norm has indeed been established, and that a message-final full stop has become a context cue that is understood as such by the interlocutors. Busch (2021a) compares the function of the message-final full stop to that of the 'pronounced "period" at the end of a spoken utterance', i.e. when a speaker says for example 'And that's it. Period [or: Full stop, in other varieties of English].' to indicate a firm stance and signal to others that they neither invite nor appreciate further discussion on that topic.

2.5 Classroom Application

As already mentioned above, with around 4.74 billion social media users worldwide whose average time spent consuming and producing born-digital texts is nearly two and a half hours daily (as of October 2022, according to the *The Global State of Digital* report compiled by WeAreSocial and Hootsuite), it would be remiss of English language teaching not to incorporate their learners' extramural practices of 'digital writing, composing, remixing and interacting [...] [that] blur boundaries between institutional and vernacular literacies' (Androutsopoulos, 2021: 1).

Tapping into these non-institutional practices to investigate with the learners what new patterns of communication are adopted by them is the perfect foil to build on literacy practices learners may have already developed (Busch, 2021b), but may not consciously think about, thus raising their language awareness and their digital literacy. The most important point here is not to view the extramural production of born-digital texts as less than other texts, but instead to avoid the deficit framing of born-digital communication and embrace it as a legitimate form of communication that is worthy of classroom discussion. This may also lead to increased motivation in the learners, since it legitimises their practices and lays the groundwork for nuanced discussions around social norms rather than prescriptive rules in the context of language use.

In a second step, and in line with Tagg and Sergeant (2021: 8), these literary practices could then also be situated within a broader societal context (see also the *Digital Competence Framework for Citizens* by Vuorikari *et al.*, 2022).

In order to achieve this, Busch's (2021a, 2021b, 2021c) findings regarding the local norm that developed around the use of message-final full stops could be used to reflect on one's own practices (for example, who in a class thinks that ending a message with a full stop signals rudeness and/or abruptness?). Since this may be a tacit norm that not everybody has come into contact with, this would ideally lead to a discussion about the kind of rules that we appear to follow, but that have not been codified explicitly. Furthermore, learners could reflect on which local norms shape their communicative behaviour when producing or consuming born-digital texts.

This in turn highlights the impact of audience and context design or, in the language of *The Digital Competence Framework for Citizens* (DigComp 2.2, Vuorikari *et al.*, 2022: 99), fosters the competence to:

- be aware of behavioural norms and know-how while using digital technologies and interacting in digital environment;
- adapt communication strategies to the specific audience; and
- be aware of cultural and generational diversity in digital environments.

2.6 Conclusion

Exploring born-digital texts enables learners to develop and reflect on their own digital practices inside and outside the classroom and to critically evaluate how affordances of a medium, as well as audience and context design, may influence the language used. In bringing these aspects into the classroom, the collaborative co-construction of born-digital texts is highlighted.

Incorporating born-digital texts should thus form an important component of the curriculum, not least because of their pervasiveness and ubiquity as part of the lifeworlds of learners of English all over the world. They are an educational resource that can thus be studied as texts in their own right, as exemplified by numerous other chapters in this volume, and can be tapped into and utilised for discussions designed to raise language awareness and foster digital literacies of learners. As Barton and Lee (2013) noted, language choice itself may be one of the arising local norms. It would therefore also be possible to reflect with learners on when they use English as a means of communication with born-digital texts, and what impacts these choices, highlighting the relevance and role of English in relation to other languages in digitally-mediated communication more broadly.

Note

(1) Koch and Oesterreicher (2012) is an English version of their seminal 1985 paper.

References

Abihsira, V. (2015) The difference between a like and a favorite, and what Twitter's update signals for content marketers. *LinkedIn*. https://www.linkedin.com/pulse/difference-between-like-favorite-what-twitters-update-vicky-tobianah, accessed September 2023).

Androutsopoulos, J. (2006) Introduction: Sociolinguistics and computer-mediated communication. *Journal of Sociolinguistics* 10 (4), 419–438. https://doi.org/10.1111/j.1467-9841.2006.00286.x

Androutsopoulos, J. (2021) Investigating digital language/media practices: Awareness, and pedagogy: Introduction. *Linguistics and Education* 62, 100872.

Barton, D. and Lee, C. (2013) *Language Online: Investigating Digital Texts and Practices*. Routledge.

Bieswanger, M. (2013) Micro-linguistic structural features of computer-mediated communication. In S.C. Herring, D. Stein and T. Virtanen (eds) *Pragmatics in Computer-Mediated Communication* (pp. 463–486). De Gruyter Mouton.

Bieswanger, M. and Intemann, F. (2011) Patterns and variation in the language use in English-based discussion forums. In M. Lüginbühl and D. Perrin (eds) *Muster and Variation: Medienlinguistische Perspektiven auf Textproduktion und Text* (pp. 157–187). Peter Lang.

Brennan, S.E. (1998) The grounding problem in conversations with and through computers. In S.R. Fussell and R.F. Kreuz (eds) *Social and Cognitive Psychological Approaches to Interpersonal Communication* (pp. 201–225). Lawrence Erlbaum.

Bucher, T. and Helmond, A. (2018) The affordances of social media platforms. In J. Burgess, A. Marwick and T. Poell (eds) *The SAGE Handbook of Social Media* (pp. 233–251). SAGE.

Busch, F. (2021a) The interactional principle in digital punctuation. *Discourse, Context & Media* 40, 100481.

Busch, F. (2021b) *Digitale Schreibregister: Kontexte, Formen und Metapragmatische Reflexionen*. De Gruyter.

Busch, F. (2021c) Enregistered spellings in interaction: Social indexicality in digital written communication. *Zeitschrift für Sprachwissenschaft* 40 (3), 297–323.

Crystal, D. (2001) *Language and the Internet* (1st edn). Cambridge University Press.

Crystal, D. (2006) *Language and the Internet* (2nd edn). Cambridge University Press.

Dürscheid, C. and Frehner, C. (2013) Email communication. In S.C. Herring, D. Stein and T. Virtanen (eds) *Pragmatics of Computer-Mediated Communication* (pp. 35–54). De Gruyter Mouton.

Gibson, J.J. (2015 [1986]) The ecological approach to visual perception. Psychology Press.

Halenko, N., Savić, M. and Economidou-Kogetsidis, M. (2021) Second language email pragmatics: Introduction. In M. Economidou-Kogetsidis, M. Savić and N. Halenko (eds) *Email Pragmatics and Second Language Learners* (pp. 1–12). John Benjamins.

Herring, S.C. and Androutsopoulos, J. (2015) Computer-mediated discourse 2.0. In D. Tannen and A.M. Trester (eds) *The Handbook of Discourse Analysis* (pp. 127–151).

Herring, S.C., Stein, D. and Virtanen, T. (2013) Introduction to the pragmatics of computer- mediated communication In S.C. Herring, D. Stein and T. Virtanen (eds) *Pragmatics of Computer-Mediated Communication* (pp. 3–32). De Gruyter Mouton.

Houghton, K.J., Upadhyay, S.S.N. and Klin, C.M. (2018) Punctuation in text messages may convey abruptness. Period. *Computers in Human Behavior* 80, 112–121.

Humphrys, J. (2007) I h8 txt msgs: How texting is wrecking our language. *Mail Online*, 24 September. https://www.dailymail.co.uk/news/article-483511/I-h8-txt-msgs-How-texting-wrecking-language.html (accessed September 2023).

Imo, W. (2015) Interaktionale Linguistik und die qualitative Erforschung computervermittelter Kommunikation. *Arbeitspapierreihe 'Sprache und Interaktion' (SpIn)*, Nr. 65. http://arbeitspapiere.sprache-interaktion.de

Jones, R.H. and Hafner, C.A. (2021) *Understanding Digital Literacies: A Practical Introduction* (2nd edn). Routledge.

Koch, P. and Oesterreicher, W. (1985) Sprache der Nähe – Sprache der Distanz: Mündlichkeit und Schriftlichkeit im Spannungsfeld von Sprachtheorie und Sprachgeschichte. *Romanistisches Jahrbuch* 36, 15–43.

Koch, P. and Oesterreicher, W. (1994) Schriftlichkeit und Sprache. In H. Günther and O. Ludwig (eds) *Schrift und Schriftlichkeit: Ein interdisziplinäres Handbuch Internationaler Forschung* (pp. 587–604). De Gruyter.

Koch, P. and Oesterreicher, W. (2012) Language of immediacy – Language of distance: Orality and literacy from the perspective of language theory and linguistic history. In C. Lange, B. Weber and G. Wolf (eds) *Communicative Spaces: Variation, Contact, and Change – Papers in Honour of Ursula Schaefer* (pp. 441–473). Peter Lang

Marwick, A.E. and boyd, d. (2011) I tweet honestly, I tweet passionately: Twitter users, context collapse, and the imagined audience. *New Media & Society* 13 (1), 114–133.

Newton, C. (2015) Twitter officially kills off favorites and replaces them with likes. *The Verge*. See https://www.theverge.com/2015/11/3/9661180/twitter-vine-favorite-fav-likes-hearts (accessed September 2022).

Pappert, S. (2017) Zu kommunikativen Funktionen von Emojis in der WhatsApp-Kommunikation. In M. Beißwenger (ed.) *Empirische Erforschung Internetbasierter Kommunikation* (pp. 175–212). De Gruyter.

Redecker, C. (2017) *European Framework for the Digital Competence of Educators: DigCompEdu*. Publications Office of the European Union.

Tagg, C. (2015) *Exploring Digital Communication: Language in Action* (1st edn). Taylor & Francis.

Tagg, C. and Seargeant, P. (2021) Context design and critical language/media awareness: Implications for a social digital literacies education. *Linguistics and Education* 62, 100776.

Vuorikari, R., Kluzer, S. and Punie, Y. (2022) *Digcomp 2.2: The Digital Competence Framework for Citizens – with New Examples of Knowledge, Skills and Attitudes*. Publications Office of the European Union.

We Are Social and Hootsuite (2022) The global state of digital report. See https://wearesocial.com/us/blog/2022/10/the-global-state-of-digital-in-october-2022/ (accessed September 2023).

Wesch, M. (2009) YouTube and you: Experiences of self-awareness in the context collapse of the recording webcam. *Explorations in Media Ecology* 8 (2), 19–34.

Wikström, P. (2017) I Tweet like I talk: Aspects of speech and writing on Twitter. Doctoral thesis, Karlstads universitet, Karlstad. Retrieved from http://urn.kb.se/resolve?urn=urn:nbn:se:kau:diva-64752 DiVA database.

3 What Counts as Language Learning in a Born-Digital Textual World?

Kathy A. Mills

3.1 Introduction

While born-digital texts might be shifting what counts as language learning, each generation has shown a tendency toward juvenoia – a heightened fear of social change on young people. For example, language educators in a born-digital era now bemoan the inaptitude of students to write substantial, essay-length texts. Students fire off a rapid succession of misspelt, abbreviated posts and messages online. Yet a Sunday Magazine editorial in 1871 had already observed the so-called decline in writing standards:

> The art of letter-writing is fast dying out. When a letter cost nine pence, it seemed but fair to try to make it worth nine pence. Now, however, we think we are too busy for such old-fashioned correspondence. We fire off a multitude of rapid and short notes, instead of sitting down to have a good talk over a real sheet of paper. (XKCD, 2013)

Language educators note the propensity of youth to have short attention spans as they scroll through social media. Yet over a century ago in 1891, Israel Zangwill wrote that 'intellectual laziness and the hurry of the age have produced a craving for literary nips. The torrid brain…has grown too weak for sustained thought' (XKCD, 2013). These words could have been penned yesterday.

This chapter considers the boundaries or limits of language learning in a born-digital textual era. Born-digital texts are defined as texts that originate in a digital form, such as desktop publishing, spreadsheets, email, web pages, digital photographs, digital games, videos, ebooks, sound recordings, digital slideshows, social media posts, digital art, augmented reality texts and much more (see Selfe & Hawisher, 2012; Kersten, Chapter 1 of this volume).

According to some theorists, many of these born-digital texts that live in digital spaces do not rely on alphabetical print or written words as the principal mode of meaning (Selfe & Hawisher, 2012). The implications of born-digital texts, particularly the implications of using texts that have a greater reliance on images and other non-logocentric modes, are currently underexplored in language learning classrooms.

The concept of born-digital texts originates in discourses on digital preservation of collections for governments, libraries and organisations. Born-digital texts differ from analogue materials, or non-digital texts, that are scanned or translated into a digital format for digital preservation and wider accessibility (Beagrie, 2015). For some, the term 'born-digital texts' does not include digital texts that are produced digitally for a print medium, such as a hard copy book. Yet others argue that the distinction is not always clear cut. For example, a book is often 'born' as a digital manuscript and is then produced as both ebooks and printed copies. Given that these differences matter to digital content creation and copyright regulations, some have further categorized born-digital texts as either 'exclusively digital' or 'digital-for-print' (Mahesh & Mittal, 2009).

In the context of the present focus on born-digital texts in language learning and teaching, one might query why digital texts need to be prefaced as 'born' digital, as opposed to other frequently used terms in language and literacy learning, such as digital texts, digital media, multimodal texts, New Literacies, or multiliteracies. Apart from the metaphorical emphasis on living texts since they are 'born', why does the digital origin of texts and their circulation in digital spaces matter to language and literacy scholars? Could distinctions between born-digital texts or not, or between those that are exclusively digital or digital-for-print, be relevant to debates about hierarchies of texts that matter in curricula? For example, the language teaching curriculum often gives priority to an analogue literary canon over popular texts, such as comics and video games (Gutierrez *et al.*, 2023).

Do conceptualizations of born-digital texts have relevance in debates about equity, accessibility and remixing of knowledge? Do these digitally created texts have implications for pedagogical decisions in language classrooms? Do born-digital texts contain more images or sound, or are they more multimodal than other digital-for-print texts, such as books? Are they always less alphabetical and if so, what are the implications for language learning? Do born-digital texts matter in terms of the materiality of the medium, and if so, what are the implications when users interact corporately with diverse born-digital texts (e.g. internet infographic vs. textbook diagram)? Who is 'giving birth to' or remixing these digital texts, and who does not, or cannot, produce them?

This chapter provides a rationale for the inclusion of born-digital texts in the language and literacy classroom, extending theories of multiliteracies, multimodality and the New Literacy Studies. It raises provocations regarding the born-digital practices of reading and text production that will count in recreational, educational and community spaces and in the future literacies of Industry 4.0 (Mills *et al.*, 2022). The chapter raises questions about the role of alphabetical text and other modes in born-digital texts, along with the challenges and implications for language and literacy pedagogy and curriculum. It debates the ideological hierarchies of born-digital and analogue practices and text selection in language learning. Finally, it includes a brief discussion of digital divides, diversity and inclusion, pointing to research that identifies who most often wins, and who misses out in language classrooms, even when born-digital text production is used for 21st-century relevance.

3.2 Defining Language and Literacy in a Born-Digital Textual Era

For several decades now, literacy theorists have argued that conceptions of literacy as spoken and written words are insufficient for capturing the changing nature of communication in digital communication environments. Some of the key traditions that have influenced these ideas have included theorists of multiliteracy by the New London Group (2000), theorists of multimodality (Kress, 2000; Mills *et al.*, 2020) and theorists of the New Literacy Studies (Gee, 2005; Street, 2003). At the same time, teachers in educational sites are often tasked with the requirement to teach an English language curriculum that has been focused on written language skills, such as vocabulary, spelling and grammar, while worldwide, students and teachers groan under the weight of standardized testing regimes that are often focused on decontextualized language skills (Mills, 2008). The notion that definitions of language and texts need to be broadened beyond analogue practices of reading and writing alphabetical print has been long argued and won in research. For example, Scribner and Cole (1981: 236) defined literacies 40 years ago as 'socially organised practices [that] make use of a symbol system and a technology for producing and disseminating it'. Operationally, there has been varying degrees of technology take-up beyond the technology of the book in the reality of language education sites, levels of schooling, geographical sites and assessment practices.

Barton (2001: 95) argued that in opening definitions of literacy to incorporate every kind of digitally mediated communication, that dominant language theories such as the New Literacy Studies have accepted notions of language and literacy that have 'fuzzy borders'. Barton explains that not only do we read novels and academic works, but we 'read timetables, maps, and music', and of course, 'there is a great deal in common in the practices associated with these diverse texts' (Barton, 2001: 95). At the time of Barton's writing, most of those texts would have been analogue, while today most of the texts in that list are born-digital – maps are most commonly digital apps, while novels, academic articles and timetables are either born digital to live in digital spaces, or are produced digitally for print (e.g. ebooks vs. books, online vs. print articles; Mills, 2016).

Theorists of multiliteracy have similarly been critiqued on their concept that language is a system of multimodal meaning-making, a view of which Kress (2000) of the New London Group (NLG) has argued is also 'fuzzy round the edges' (Kress, 2000: 186). Importantly, Kress (2000) distinguishes between written and spoken words, images, gestures and music as particular forms of representation – which are now all used in born-digital texts, but not necessarily so. Language learning must now account for the multiplicity of communications media associated with the convergence and wider accessibility of digital technologies. This is in part because conventional views of reading and writing, along with their narrow repertoires of genres and conventions, is not keeping up with the reality of the multifarious textual practices in society, insufficient for describing the sign systems of digital texts (Mills, 2010a). Today, if we exclude born-digital texts from language learning, particularly if we count 'digital-for-print' texts in our definition, then most texts in society would be excluded from the curriculum. The ease with which students and teachers can produce, consume, remix and transmit texts in society is facilitated by technologies for multimodal, born-digital textual production.

One of the more humorous criticisms of the multiliteracies argument, particularly in relation to opening up literacies to include multiple modes, was made by Cameron (2000: 206) who questioned: 'I sometimes find myself wondering where literacies stop. Why not count, say arable farming as a literacy practice on the grounds that it marks the landscape?'. In a similar vein, when evaluating the work of the New London Group on multimodality, Prain (1997) suggested that by counting images, audio and other multimedia as forms of literacy, that the modes of design in the theory of multiliteracies potentially opens an unwieldy array of text types to be addressed in the reality of a narrow language curriculum in education. Likewise, Prain pointed to the lack of semiotic tools developed for their textual analysis. A related criticism was that the New London Group's conception of multimodal texts was too blurred for the purposes of formulating English curricula, and at the turn of the century, was not nuanced enough for classroom discussion with students (Mills, 2010a, 2016).

In this unwieldy array of born-digital text types in which language teachers now find themselves, ideological questions then arise about which modes should count, or count more, in the language curriculum. Interestingly, in a review of the digital turn in the New Literacy Studies (Mills, 2010a), I observed that across the majority of the original NLS research in formal learning sites, the media, text types and genres selected were still the kinds that prioritize alphabetical print or written words, but with other modes combined, such as song lyrics (Junquiera, 2008), and digital stories with spoken-word poetry (Hull & Nelson, 2005). Few would deny that reading and writing practices using words on paper-based text formats are necessary, but not sufficient, for communicating across the multiple platforms of meaning-making in society (Mills, 2010a), but fewer are willing in classroom language practice to give born-digital text the same status as words.

In earlier funded research of multimodal literacy practices, we tried to balance the prioritizing of print literacy concepts required in the school curriculum with our multimodal innovation, which sometimes resulted in hybrid learning tasks, such as writing lengthy web texts, like blogs, that were never actually permitted by the school system to go live (Mills, 2015). When filming videos in the English curriculum – a text type that gives high priority to moving images – we required students to record their ideas on paper, read websites for ideas and write scripted storyboards with full dialogue, in our efforts to meet national print-based literacy standards (Mills & Exley, 2014). In our selection of text types, alphabetical print or written words carried a significant functional load of the meaning-making due to logocentric language curriculum requirements in schools. In other words, despite theorists emphasizing the importance of multimodality in the language curriculum with all modes being equal (Mills, 2010b), in practice, curriculum requirements for language learning worldwide continue to create hierarchies of modes that place the skillful use of words at the top of curriculum mandates, while other modes continue to be present, but occupy the periphery.

3.3 Are Born-Digital Texts Less Alphabetical?

Following from definitions of language and multimodal theory, an important consideration of born-digital texts for language learning is the extent to which alphabetical texts or words are included in these textual formats. Teachers might consider that if born-digital texts should be used in language learning, is something lost in the teaching about English semantics, syntax and graphophonic elements that typically feature prominently in English curricula?

Increasingly, texts that circulate in society, which are also used in academic and educational environments, have digitally-mediated content – images, video, audio, photos and websites – that are essential, rather than extraneous, to publishing projects (Selfe & Hawisher, 2012). For example, leading digital academic publications, such as Delagrange's (2011) *Technologies of Wonder*, are published electronically for wide accessibility, and such texts are born to live in digital spaces. Theorists such as Selfe and Hawisher (2012: 690) maintain that such digital publishing projects in academic contexts are characterized by 'the same intellectual weight as books, the same specific gravity, reach, and scope, but…do not simply rely on alphabetical text as the primary carrier of meaning'. They argue against those who regard images, audio and video as marginal to meaning making with alphabetical text: 'We call these texts "born-digital" to signal authors' refusal to treat mediated elements – audio, images, text and video – simply as illustrative context' (Selfe & Hawisher, 2012: 690).

Born-digital texts produced for educational purposes, often with image-rich layouts and links, are by no means less academic, less complex, or less serious than analogue texts. Certain genres of born-digital texts are also not less logocentric, such as unrestricted access journal articles, academic ebooks, digital research repositories, reports, online syllabi, online legal documents, digital inventories and digital databases. Conversely, we can look to many examples of analogue texts that are very image-based, such as comic books, anime, graphic novels, picture books for children and adults, wordless picture books, magazines, coffee-table books, recipe books, ancient hieroglyphics, photobooks, scrapbooks, newspapers, pictorial reference books (e.g. atlases), product packaging, textbooks and illustrative fiction. A walk through a bookshop will reveal substantial use of images throughout a wide array of analogue textual genres marketed to all age groups.

Importantly, theorists of multimodality have demonstrated that elements such as images are more than the sum of their parts, working in powerful ways with words to multiply meanings (Lemke, 2002). This is because word meanings are often modified in the context of image meanings. Many textual features of born-digital texts have a complexity of multimodal design that is by no means eclipsed by written text. For example, images can be constructed or deconstructed in ways that attend not only to denoting literal meanings, but to connotative interpretations of values, attitudes and emotional meanings that are implicit through multilayered visual design techniques. For example, images can be narrative or non-narrative representations, and transactional or non-transactional, while semiotic choices as simple as the size or placement of an object in the center or margins of an image influences the encoding of informational value (see for more detailed discussion, Kress & van Leeuwen, 2021).

Some have argued that visual communication has become more central in recent years with the rise of mass media, global advertising, the internet – including Web 2.0 production of texts by everyday users and social media – and changes to the costs and technologies for reproducing images in a digital age (Kress & van Leeuwen, 2021; Mills, 2016). In addition to linguistic grammars, visual, audio and other grammars (e.g. gestural, proxemics, facial expression, body movement, gaze), play a key role in language learning, and these social-semiotic resources include culturally specific meanings that are shared by groups. Thus, in a born-digital textual world, language learning needs to extend beyond linguistic grammars to include meaning-making that embraces powerful confluences of modes. In a born-digital world, the language incompetent is not one who cannot use words, but the one who cannot use words, images and other modes supported by digital technologies.

3.4 Are There Hierarchies of Analogue and Born-Digital Texts in Language Learning?

Debates about the place of born-digital texts in the language learning curriculum extends existing contentions about the selection of suitable analogue texts for inclusion in classrooms (see, for example, Mills, 2005). While most would agree that language learning should involve a variety of texts, both born-digital and analogue, in practice, implicit hierarchies often dictate which texts should be given the greatest priority, and which texts should only occupy the margins of the curriculum. Such hierarchical views of texts in the language classroom leads to the exclusion of certain born-digital texts, such as video games, while excluding whole genres, such as romance and science fiction. More recent born-digital texts, like mixed reality and augmented reality narratives are emerging in classroom use but are likely to be evaluated by some as less legitimate than certain texts from a print-based English canon, particularly if the latter are mandated in the curriculum.

Ideologically, textbooks and European literature have always been privileged in English education. A flow-on effect of this ideology in a born-digital textual era is that analogue and digital textbooks and 'classic' English literature may have higher status than other kinds of popular texts, since these texts are considered the most legitimate forms of knowledge in an officially sanctioned curriculum (Mason & Giovanelli, 2017). Similarly, there will be continued efforts to preserve a Western, analogue canon in language learning, based on a belief in the unchanging merit of historically ratified cultural capital. While theorists of the New Literacy Studies, multimodality and multiliteracies have long argued for digital texts in the English curriculum, in practice, school leaders, teachers, parents, politicians and other educational stakeholders still often espouse a cultural heritage view of text selection that privileges the traditional use of so-called 'higher' forms of analogue culture and English literature in the curriculum (Macken-Horarik, 2014). Given the prevalence of the cultural heritage view of literature selection in schools, even as born-digital texts become more commonplace, one is potentially more likely to find a Kindle edition of Shakespeare in the English language curriculum than digital anime, romance, or science fiction.

Text selection, born-digital or otherwise, in the language and literacy curriculum requires critical judgment regarding the ideologies, cultural assumptions and social formations that seek to reproduce the dominant cultural views and tastes of the most powerful in society, and which marginalize the perspectives of others (Luke, 1994). Text selection along Western lines inequitably reproduces a dominant literary tradition because culturally diverse groups – Indigenous, low socioeconomic and other marginalized social groups – have a stake in language competency in a multicultural society (Mills, 2005).

Conserving historically validated texts may have a place in citizenship and Western education systems, but language learning should not be seen unquestionably as a conduit for cultural transmission. Rather, text selection, whether analogue, digital-for-print, or born-digital to live in digital spaces, should be critiqued as ideological social practices. Educators should interrogate the interests that are served by texts that are selected for use in language classrooms, while seeking to illuminate counter-cultural or alternative positions in multicultural and globally connected, born-digital textual environments. Text selection in the language learning classroom in a born-digital era is a complex cultural, economic and political act. Mainstream or dominant tastes are normalized as the status quo and taught as 'culture' through the exclusion of born-digital texts that live in the digital realm.

The selection of texts in language learning should consider the way in which born-digital media are used for a variety of legitimate social purposes. For example, silencing born-digital popular culture, such as animation, interactive e-literature, fanfiction, video games, 360-degree films and augmented reality also misses valuable opportunities to make the most of learners' interests, reproducing a homogenized, print-based, or at least, digital-for-print, English canon. Born-digital text selection needs to reflect the diverse range of digitally mediated images, popular texts, blogs, videos, infographics, discussion websites (e.g. Reddit), question and answer sites (e.g. Quora), and other social media that language learners experience beyond education sites, and that reflect the range of situated digital media practices that are needed to participate in society.

Born-digital texts on the web are not only multimodal, but they are often characterized by hypermodality – the way in which hypermedia is interconnected with other texts on the internet, creating multiple textual trajectories that contain interrelated sounds, images and written text (Lemke, 2002). For example, a web page is connected to other web pages, content and websites, with clickable links on certain words, paragraphs, videos and images that connect to other related texts beyond the website, or sometimes indexing other parts of the same website. Born-digital texts also have modified genres or text structures that differ to books. For example, instant messaging is more brief, spontaneous and interactive than many other written texts. It is characterized by a responsive, spoken-like form that contains a combination of abbreviations and conventional spelling that are recognizable to those who use the discourse, with differing rules depending on the social context, roles and relationships (Mills, 2010a).

The hypermodality of born-digital texts and other features reshape the nature of reading and interacting with texts, requiring new kinds of reading skills that language learners need to apply in their real-world interactions with others. For example, research of digital reading has demonstrated that analogue reading environments have more predictable reading pathways than born-digital textual environments – where readers activate hyperlinks in non-linear ways with continual interruptions from notifications, hotspots, popups and alerts (Mills *et al.*, 2022). Additionally, digital readers demonstrate tendencies toward browsing, keyword searching, and less in-depth textual processing (Liu, 2012). These born-digital reading environments require self-regulation skills to support reading comprehension to plan, focus, prioritize and filter distractions (Kieffer *et al.*, 2013). Readers of born-digital texts engage in greater use of 'meshing' – communicating content that one is viewing – and 'stacking' – multitasking with several devices (Davidson & Harris, 2019), skills which make more cognitive demands on language learners than reading analogue texts. The exclusion of born-digital texts in language learning will limit the development of these digital reading comprehension skills that are not intuitive or automatic, but which can be successfully taught (Mills *et al.*, 2022).

3.5 Who is Creating Born-Digital Texts and Who is Missing Out?

Language learning in a born-digital textual world is shifting as waves of new media augment and redefine the nature of text production. Since the advent of Web 2.0 – the read-write web – and later, social media, many language users globally have been able to share and read texts that circulate more rapidly to wider audiences (Mills, 2015). Young people can now create, edit and filter born-digital images and video in mere seconds using popular social media platforms, such as Snapchat, Instagram and TikTok. Yet beneath the surface of global media trends and phenomena, the fractured lines of digital inequality continue to create born-digital textual divides, with substantial differences in media use type, frequency and quality based on socioeconomic status, parental education, gender, geographical location and ethnicity (Warschauer & Tate, 2018). While those with the economic resources, cultural capital and technical infrastructure are 'giving birth to' or remixing born-digital texts, there are many who do not, and cannot, produce them.

For example, in my critical ethnographic research, access to born-digital text production using a teacher's enactment of the multiliteracies pedagogy, was influenced by the complex intersection of pedagogy, power relations and discourses in the language classroom (Mills, 2010b). The context was an upper elementary classroom where students from culturally diverse backgrounds were introduced to stop-motion animation production. Born-digital text production extended the prior experiences of students to varying degrees. More pointedly, transformation occurred naturally for socioeconomically dominant, white students in an immersion of student-centered environment in which collaborative design involved minimal teacher direction. Conversely, socioeconomically marginalized students and those who were culturally and linguistically diverse, experienced greater difficulties with born-digital text production because of the mismatch between their experiences and the English language of the classroom. For these marginalized students, the transition from their cultural experiences to born-digital text creation required a multifaceted negotiation between the discourses of the classroom and their own language experiences (Mills, 2008).

Culturally diverse learners were constrained in their use of their home and community discourses in the context of Australian schooling, where English is the dominant language taught and assessed in the curriculum. While the teacher sought to address cultural inclusiveness in classroom practice, the migrant and Indigenous students were least familiar with the implicit expectations for self-directed and collaborative learning. These students only contributed to making born-digital texts when the teacher or other students communicated directions to them personally and overtly. Conversely, the school discourses were familiar to students from the dominant white culture because these ways of being were aligned with the students' previous schooling experiences (Mills, 2008, 2010b).

Interestingly, the use of coercive power in the school had a considerable influence on students' access to born-digital text production. The students' resistance to the school rules functioned as a form of domination, which resulted in prohibiting some of the economically marginalized boys from digital design. Analogue writing tasks, including writing out repetitive sentences in copy books, was the sanction for rule breaking. The way that coercive power was used in the school was to maintain the boys' existing lack of access to born-digital text production at home. This was not a chance event, but was linked to the power and status of the students in the context of the dominant culture (Mills, 2008, 2010b), and similar patterns of exclusion have been reported in other studies.

3.6 Implications for Further Research

Meaningful access to digital technologies for everyday language use involves more than internet connections, hardware and software – though these are all important, as the pandemic has highlighted during times of emergency remote schooling worldwide (Vuorikari *et al.*, 2020). Digital initiatives in education across all areas of the curriculum, language learning and beyond, also require curriculum support, infrastructure, teacher professional development, collaboration, cultural and identity alignment and other social mechanisms to support sustainable change (Warschauer & Tate, 2018). Born-digital textual practices, particularly those of production, are now becoming central to social inclusion, which is also connected to economic resources, literacy skills, health provisions, affordable housing, education and cultural participation for positive long-term life outcomes.

Importantly, born-digital text production needs language educators who are reflexively aware of their own cultural and language bias. This is because educators' classroom decision-making can become part of the structural inequality that requires transformation to better serve the interests of socially marginalized groups. In the 21st century, cultural and linguistic diversity is an ever-present reality, requiring equitable attention to the digital divides that now impact language learning. Born-digital text consumption is common in everyday language practices, while opportunities for innovative, multimodal text production continues to be unevenly distributed, both within schools and in society more broadly. The refusal to regard born-digital text production and multimodal design as central to language learning is no longer a sustainable view, and access to modes beyond alphabetical and analogue texts is now an essential part of full participation in society, and a vital feature of socially-just language learning.

3.7 Conclusion

In a born-digital textual age, debates about what counts as language resurface as each new medium emerges. For example, digital media theorists consider that mobile phone use now occurs 'anywhere, anytime', while in public spaces dozens of people preoccupied with digital devices show indifference to those who share their commute. But similar anti-social behavior with everyday texts has been occurring since the 19th century, as William Smith observed in 1886:

> They have their Mercury or Post laid on their breakfast table in the early morning...too hurried to snatch from it the news during that meal...they carry it off, to be sulkily read as they travel, leaving them with no time to talk with the friend who may share the compartment with them. (XKCD, 2013)

Again, some language educators might lament the use of born-digital texts viewed on tablets and other digital devices in homes that silence family conversations, yet well over a century ago writers of *The Journal of Education* in 1907 observed the non-communicative 'modern family gathering, silent around the fire, where each individual has his head buried in his favorite magazine' (Stevens, 2015). Has a born-digital world really shifted conversational language use since the 20th century when magazines were considered a subversive substitute for real language?

Such debates will continue to occupy the liminal zone between print and born-digital media, pointing to a 'divisive bipolar antagonism between "the book" and new media where none exists, and never did' (Delagrange, 2011: x). However, while the emergence of each new digital form of rhetorical production will be critiqued and contested as a legitimate text in the language classroom, sign-makers globally, aligned to cultural groups and social contexts, will continue to choose the meaning-making resources that suit their interests (Kress & van Leeuwen, 2021). These meaning-making resources will rarely contain words alone but will involve modified digital technologies of production at hand that bring together confluences of modes and media in surprisingly rapid ways.

Language educators will continually evaluate an expanded array of analogue and born-digital texts aligned to their epistemic, cultural and pedagogical values, to determine which texts will count and which ones might not, in the language classrooms of the future.

References

Barton, D. (2001) Directions for literacy research: Analysing language and social practices in a textually mediated world. *Language and Education* 15 (2 & 3), 92–104. https://doi.org/10.1080/09500780108666803

Beagrie, N. (2015) *Digital Preservation Handbook* (2nd edn). Digital Preservation Coalition. https://www.dpconline.org/handbook

Cameron, D. (2000) Book review: *Multiliteracies: Literacy Learning and the Design of Social Futures*, by Bill Cope and Mary Kalantzis (eds). *Changing English* 7 (2), 203–207. https://doi.org/10.1080/13586840050137964

Davidson, C. and Harris, R. (2019) *Reading in the Digital Age: Read NZ, Te Pou Muramura*. Research First. https://www.read-nz.org/advocacy/research/

Delagrange, S.H. (2011) *Technologies of Wonder: Rhetorical Practice in a Digital World*. Utah State University Press/Computers and Composition Digital Press.

Gee, J.P. (2005) The New Literacy Studies: From socially situated to the work of the social. In D. Barton, M. Hamilton and R. Ivanic (eds) *Situated Literacies: Reading and Writing in Context* (pp. 177–14). Taylor and Francis.

Gutierrez, A., Mills, K., Scholes, L., Rowe, L. and Pink, E. (2023) What do secondary teachers think about digital games for learning: Stupid fixation or the future of education? *Teaching and Teacher Education* 133, 104278. https://doi.org/10.1016/j.tate.2023.104278

Hull, G. and Nelson, M. (2005) Locating the semiotic power of multimodality. *Written Communication* 22 (2), 224–261. https://doi.org/10.1177/0741088304274170

Junquiera, E.S. (2008) Challenging the boundaries between standard and popular language situated in historical contexts: The communicative practices of Brazilian students crafting hybrid multi-modal ways with words. *Language and Education* 22 (6), 393–410. https://doi.org/10.1080/09500780802152697

Kieffer, M.J., Vukovic, R.K. and Berry, D. (2013) Direct and indirect roles of executive functioning in reading comprehension for students in urban fourth grade classrooms. *Reading Research Quarterly* 48, 333–348. https://doi.org/10.1002/rrq.54

Kress, G. (2000) Multimodality. In B. Cope and M. Kalantzis (eds) *Multiliteracies: Literacy Learning and the Design of Social Futures* (pp. 182–202). Macmillan.

Kress, G. and Van Leeuwen, T. (2021) *Reading Images: The Grammar of Visual Design* (3rd edn). Routledge.

Lemke, J.L. (2002) Travels in hypermodality. *Visual Communication* 1 (3), 299–325. https://doi.org/10.1177/147035720200100303

Liu, Z. (2012) Digital reading. *Chinese Journal of Library and Information Science (English Edition)* 5 (1), 85–94. https://scholarworks.sjsu.edu/cgi/viewcontent.cgi?article=1067&context=slis_pub

Luke, A. (1994) *The Social Construction of Literacy in the Primary School*. Macmillan Education Australia.

Macken-Horarik, M. (2014) Making productive use of four models of school English: A case study revisited. *English in Australia* 49 (3), 7–19. https://www.aate.org.au/journals/english-in-australia

Mahesh, G. and Mittal, R. (2009) Digital content creation and copyright issues. *The Electronic Library* 27 (4), 676–683. https://doi.org/10.1108/02640470910979615

Mason, J. and Giovanelli, M. (2017) 'What do you think?' Let me tell you: Discourse about texts and the literature classroom. *Changing English* 24 (3), 318–329. https://doi.org/10.1080/1358684x.2016.1276397

Mills, K.A. (2005) Deconstructing binary oppositions in literacy discourse and pedagogy. *Australian Journal of Language and Literacy* 28 (1), 67–82. https://www.alea.edu.au/resources/australian-journal-of-language-and-literacy-ajll-2

Mills, K.A. (2008) Transformed practice in a pedagogy of multiliteracies. *Pedagogies: An International Journal* 3 (2), 109–128. https://doi.org/10.1080/15544800801929419

Mills, K.A. (2010a) A review of the 'digital turn' in the new literacy studies. *Review of Educational Research* 80 (2), 246–271. https://doi.org/10.3102/0034654310364401

Mills, K.A. (2010b) *The Multiliteracies Classroom*. Multilingual Matters.

Mills, K.A. (2015) Doing digital composition on the social web: Knowledge processes in literacy learning. In B. Cope and M. Kalantzis (eds) *A Pedagogy of Multiliteracies: Learning by Design* (pp. 172–185). Palgrave Macmillan.

Mills, K.A. (2016) *Literacy Theories for the Digital Age: Social, Critical, Multimodal, Spatial, Material and Sensory Lenses*. Multilingual Matters.

Mills, K.A. and Exley, B. (2014) Time, space, and text in the elementary school digital writing classroom. *Written Communication* 31 (4), 434–469. https://doi.org/10.1177/0741088314542757

Mills, K.A., Stone, B.G., Unsworth, L. and Friend, L. (2020) Multimodal language of attitude in digital composition. *Written Communication* 37 (2), 135–166. https://doi.org/10.1177/0741088319897978

Mills, K.A., Unsworth, L. and Scholes, L. (2022) *Literacy for Digital Futures: Mind, Body, Text*. Routledge.

New London Group (2000) A pedagogy of multiliteracies: Designing social futures. In B. Cope and M. Kalantzis (eds) *Multiliteracies: Literacy Learning and the Design of Social Futures* (pp. 9–38). Macmillan.

Prain, V. (1997) Multi(national)literacies and globalising discourses. *Discourse: Studies in the Cultural Politics of Education* 18 (3), 453–467. https://doi.org/10.1080/0159630970180309

Scribner, S. and Cole, M. (1981) *The Psychology of Literacy*. Harvard University Press.

Selfe, C. and Hawisher, G. (2012) Methodologies of peer and editorial review: Changing practices. *College Composition and Communication* 63 (4), 672–698. http://www.jstor.org/stable/23264233

Stevens, M.D. (2015) Juvenoia (video), 2.56–3.06. VSauce. See https://www.youtube.com/watch?v=LD0x7ho_IYc (accessed 2021).

Street, B. (2003) What's 'new' in New Literacy Studies? Critical approaches to literacy in theory and practice. *Current Issues in Comparative Education* 5 (2), 77–91. https://doi.org/10.52214/cice.v5i2.11369

Vuorikari, R., Velicu, A., Chaudron, S., Cachia, R. and Di Gioia, R. (2020) *How Families Handled Emergency Remote Schooling during the COVID-19 Lockdown in Spring 2020: Summary of Key Findings from Families with Children in 11 European Countries*. Publications Office of the European Union. https://doi.org/10.2760/31977

Warschauer, M. and Tate, T. (2018) Digital divides and social inclusion. In K.A. Mills, A. Stornaiuolo, A. Smith and J. Zacher Pandya (eds) *Handbook of Writing, Literacies and Education in Digital Cultures* (pp. 63–75). Routledge.

XKCD (2013) The pace of modern life (Cartoon). *XKCD. A Webcomic of Romance, Sarcasm, Math and Language*. see https://xkcd.com/1227/ (accessed 2021). Creative Commons Attribution Non-Commercial 2.5 License.

4 Born-Digital Texts and Digitally Mediated Tasks: A Perfect Match for the Inclusive EFL Classroom?

Celestine Caruso, Judith Hofmann and Kim Schick

4.1 Digital Media, Inclusion and TBLT – a Minefield?

Saying that we are living in a digital world seems tautological these days. It is therefore no wonder that digital media have (some might say finally) found their way into Teaching English as a Foreign Language (TEFL) (cf. e.g. Bündgens-Kosten & Schildhauer, 2021; Burwitz-Melzer *et al.*, 2019; Schmidt & Würffel, 2018). Moving away from the idea that digital media need to have an 'added value' in learning, Krommer (2018) claims that digital media are not needed to achieve old aims better, faster or easier, but that they are constituent elements of teaching which can enhance the goals and aims of education altogether. Consequently, keeping digital media out of the classroom not only deprives learners of potentially very effective learning tools and practices, but actually might be a disadvantage for them, as schools should prepare students for their life and future (cf. Black, 2009: 689). Thus, the question should not be if, but how digital media can be integrated into TEFL and how this can be done in a way that benefits every student with their individual needs and challenges.

Digital media are said to be ideal for inclusive teaching, as they seem to be beneficial for all students and their individual needs (cf. e.g. Schulz, 2021). However, before delving into the discussion, the term 'inclusion' needs to be clarified, a term which has often been defined in terms of students with special needs attending regular schools. This, however, is a very narrow perspective on inclusion. A broader perspective considers every person – every learner – to be different and, thus, diversity and heterogeneity to be the normality in society and in the classroom. From this perspective, barriers are not the result of specific learner characteristics, such as a learner's home or dominant language(s), social background or sexual orientation (Grosche & Vock, 2018: 260). Rather, barriers and categories are socially constructed (Gerlach & Schmidt, 2021: 12).

For the purpose of this chapter, we will take a broad perspective on inclusion. Focusing on different dimensions of heterogeneity, e.g. students with Developmental Language Disorder (DLD) or a multilingual background, and analyzing their specific needs and strengths, however, is not a contradiction as long as it serves the overall and long-term purpose of striving for an inclusive society and school system. One needs to be aware of the issues that come with using labels and categories such as 'special needs' or 'DLD' (Schick & Rohde 2022: 17–19, 22–27) as well as of the need for labels that facilitate the development and discussion of measures that help minimize barriers for everybody in the classroom. It is of utmost importance that teaching concepts are developed for all subjects, including foreign language teaching, that take into account the diverse needs of all students. As far as the inclusive EFL classroom is concerned, we consequently do not assume that the use of digital media is automatically beneficial for all students, but that different dimensions of heterogeneity need to be taken into account in order not to add new barriers to the classroom that might result from the use of digital media, e.g. concerning social inequalities and privileges in the access to digital technologies.

In addition to digital media, there is a framework that is often considered to be beneficial for all students and therefore suitable for inclusive teaching: Task-Based Language Teaching (TBLT; cf. Chilla & Vogt, 2017). Open tasks in particular, which enable learners to find task solutions based on their individual cognitive, linguistic, motivational or imaginative resources, combined with the opportunities the digital world offers, seem to make digitally mediated tasks a promising endeavor for the inclusive classroom (Biebighäuser *et al.*, 2012; Dausend & Nickel, 2017; Reckermann, 2017). However, publications in the field of foreign language teaching often aim at discussing and developing inclusive teaching approaches while still not fully taking into account research about the resources and needs of students with different dimensions of heterogeneity (Gerlach & Schmidt, 2021: 25f.). The needs and resources of students in heterogeneous classrooms should shape the implementation of teaching approaches such as TBLT. The existing literature on children with special needs shows that teachers need to provide more guidance, structure and redundancy for these students (e.g. Gerlach & Schmidt, 2021: 25f.; Grosche & Vock, 2018: 265). This does not clash with modern and learner-oriented EFL teaching if we, as Grimm *et al.* (2015: 55–56) argue, base our teaching on (language) learning theories. Constructivism and instructivism are then not seen as incompatible, but rather as two extreme poles on a continuum, based on which EFL can adapt its methods and procedures, depending on the learners' individual needs.

While both digital media and TBLT undoubtedly offer many positive aspects for the inclusive classroom (especially in terms of differentiation), they also pose specific challenges. In other words, using digital media in the context of TBLT does not automatically mean that every student will truly benefit from digitally mediated tasks. The question arises whether the combination of digital media, inclusion and TBLT may thus create a minefield rather than a perfect match. We would argue that this is not the case if the dimensions of heterogeneity, and the advantages and challenges that come along with them are addressed – and this in turn depends on teachers managing to minimize barriers for students within TBLT.

Consequently, another well-known challenge of TBLT, the role of the teacher as a guide on the side/facilitator becomes even more relevant when working with digital media in inclusive EFL classrooms. Teachers have to (at least to some extent) relinquish control and accept that students increasingly become or even already are experts themselves, e.g. in digital media use, multilingualism and their own (language) learning strategies. On the other hand, teachers have to offer more guidance and structure to students with special needs so that they, too, can become experts in their own learning process. Our analysis and presented task example reveal that these different needs can be balanced within TBLT – especially when exploiting the potential benefits of digital media as well. In the following, we will argue why and how teaching language learning strategies and the consideration of various home languages contribute to a minimization of barriers for students with different dimensions of diversity and heterogeneity, and how this is linked to the affordances of digital media within TBLT. The findings contribute to the aim of adapting TBLT and digital media in the field of inclusive foreign language teaching and learning.

4.2 Digital Media

When listing the general positive aspects of integrating digital media into the (foreign language) classroom, the first item on the list is usually that they can have a motivating effect on students as they are part of their everyday lives (cf. Kerres, 2003: 32). However, it has to be kept in mind that digital media alone neither teach the students anything nor motivate them in any way, unless they are embedded in the principles of modern TEFL. Only then can learner-centered approaches be positively influenced by the use of digital media. Individualized and self-regulated learning can thus be initiated and the teacher can take over the role as a facilitator of learning.

On a content and outcome level, digital media can also influence English language teaching. The internet is a place of multiple languages and literacies, with English being the lingua franca of the digital realm (Grimm et al., 2015: 5). Learners are already engaged in many activities in the digital world that can be easily integrated into the EFL classroom. They can be regarded as cultural agents that are actively involved in circulating and producing meaning – and so can their teachers (cf. Hallet,

2004: 207). A cultural framework for this understanding of TEFL is that of participatory culture. Since participatory culture has relatively low barriers for being a consumer and producer (cf. Jenkins *et al.*, 2009: 6) – a prosumer – learners often interact with born-digital texts by producing and consuming them. This may mean engaging with fanfiction in all its forms ('expressions'), being a member of online communities (e.g. in social networks or gaming clans – 'affiliations'), using and contributing to shared spaces of knowledge distribution (e.g. free encyclopedias like Wikipedia), but also participating in alternate reality gaming ('collaborative problem-solving'), or producing and consuming blogs or podcasts ('circulations') (Jenkins *et al.*, 2009: 8). This out-of-school exposure to English should be taken seriously by teachers and integrated into EFL, as it acknowledges the learners' autonomy and expertise (cf. Grau, 2009), which is in line with learner orientation as a principle of EFL teaching. Also, many of the activities in participatory culture encourage learners to use language creatively (by writing their own texts, acting out role plays, etc.) – which is also a central goal of EFL.

When we look at the inclusive EFL classroom, digital media offer some undeniably positive aspects. They can make learning processes and outcomes visible and documentable, as they can be used by the learners to reflect on their own language production easily, in particular with regard to communicative competencies, e.g. by the built-in recording function that tablets and mobile phones, amongst other devices, offer (cf. Windmüller-Jesse & Talarico, 2018: 91). Furthermore, intercultural (communicative) competencies can be fostered through digital media (cf. Windmüller-Jesse & Talarico, 2018: 91) and the aforementioned activities rooted in participatory culture. The focus of these activities is on the creative process underlying them as it not only allows learners to express themselves but also involves a change of perspective, empathy and immersion (cf. Hofmann, 2019: 43). These assets of digital media for the EFL classroom (such as the authenticity of born-digital texts as well as the acknowledgement of the learners' autonomy and expertise in participatory culture) perfectly fit the communicative and learner-centered language learning principles of TBLT.

4.3 Digital Media and TBLT: Digitally Mediated Tasks

Both digital media and TBLT have the potential 'to engage students in active learning and holistic tasks' (González-Lloret & Ortega, 2014: 3). This implies that combining the two offers the possibility to learn a foreign language while fostering digital literacy at the same time (cf. Schmidt & Strasser, 2016: 5; also see Bär, 2019; Biebighäuser *et al.*, 2012; Dausend & Nickel, 2017). The framework of digitally mediated tasks (Caruso, 2020; Caruso *et al.*, 2021; Hofmann, 2019) does not necessarily mean that every aspect of the task is digital, but that digital media are an integral part of the task setting, e.g. as a medium for gathering information, for using or producing (born-digital) texts (in a wider sense), or for scaffolding language input and output. It is, however, perfectly acceptable, for instance, to have a task instruction in form of a 'traditional' worksheet, while the outcome of the task is a born-digital text. Additionally, the scaffolding provided by the teacher may be both analogue and digital (e.g. chunks on a worksheet combined with instructional videos). Ideally, every medium is involved in a way that it is best suited to solve the problem at hand, similar to real-life situations (cf. Caruso et al., 2021: 164). This means that digitally-mediated tasks need to be carefully prepared according to the principles of TBLT. For our context, we rely on the definition proposed by Nunan (2004) who states that a (pedagogical) task:

> [Is] a piece of classroom work that involves learners in comprehending, manipulating, producing or interacting in the target language while their attention is focused on mobilizing their grammatical knowledge in order to express meaning, and in which the intention is to convey meaning rather than to manipulate form. (Nunan, 2004: 4)

A task should further present authentic problems to the learners, who need to negotiate meaning with each other and experiment with language in order to find solutions – a focus on meaning rather than on form (cf. Nunan, 2004: 4).

In the context of an inclusive EFL classroom, digital media can be a scaffold for individualized learning by offering support for all aspects of communicative competence (cf. Windmüller-Jesse & Talarico, 2018: 91). Scaffolding can be understood as temporary support structures that help connect the task demands with the task requirements (for a detailed definition of scaffolding see Gibbons, 2015). Digital tools offer a diverse range of input and output scaffolding (cf. Gibbons, 2015) that facilitate individual task-solutions, for example, with the help of digital dictionaries, explanatory videos, text-to-speech options, recorded voice, animations and drawings. Nevertheless, teachers should prepare additional scaffolds to align the linguistic and cognitive demands of a task to the learners' individual needs and prerequisites. The use of digital media, therefore, may be a double-edged sword since digital media can be used as scaffolds while at other times their use may result in the need for additional scaffolding.

With regard to authenticity, which means that topics and materials need to connect to the pupils' lives and interests (cf. e.g. Ellis, 2003), especially the internet, as a place where born-digital texts are created and live, is an environment in which learners can become agents and actively engage in using, remixing and circulating digital artefacts. The question is how teachers can use authentic digital materials for language learning in the EFL classroom. In order to construct a learner-centered task, it is not sufficient to merely use materials or topics that are presumed to be part of the learners' lives (such as TikTok videos or Instagram stories); rather, learners should already be part of the whole task-planning process. This, however, in addition to the unpredictability of the collaborative processes that take place while learners are working on the task and task outcome changes the role of teachers (as facilitators or guide on the side, cf. Blume *et al.*, 2018: 40) and learners (as creators of classroom discourse) alike.

TBLT in general and the use of digitally mediated tasks in particular challenge the traditional assumption of teachers being in charge: giving up control might seem to feed teachers' insecurities (Müller-Hartmann & Schocker, 2018: 103). The increased agency of learners, however, is one of the major advantages of TBLT – particularly in an inclusive setting, as we will argue in the next section. Incorporating born-digital texts, a reversal of the novice/expert roles may occur, since learners may be more experienced in these cultural discourses than some teachers. This, however, only applies to the artefacts, such as born-digital texts, and the digital world itself – when embedding any media pedagogically into the EFL classroom (i.e. creating digitally mediated tasks), the teacher still remains the expert. Therefore, teacher-learner cooperation is an important task criterion, not only with regard to learner-learner interaction but also on the teacher-learner level, i.e. between learners as experts on the digital world, and teachers as experts on how to create a meaningful learning environment and address specific dimensions of heterogeneity, as we will show in the next section.

4.4 TBLT and Digital Media in Practice: 'Animal Safari'

Our task example 'Animal Safari' has been described in more detail in Caruso (2020) and Caruso *et al.* (2021). In Figure 4.1 (see following page), we will give a general impression of the digitally mediated task. Also, we will introduce two dimensions of heterogeneity: multilingualism and DLD. Afterwards, we will outline how the animal safari task can be adapted to consider the needs and strengths of these two groups of students.

4.4.1 Multilingual students

Multilingualism is normal both in society and the classroom. Different languages and cultures are not stored as separate entities with clear boundaries in a multilingual and multicultural person's mind (see the research on Translanguaging, e.g. Fürstenau *et al.*, 2020: 147–148; García & Li, 2014: 21; Otheguy *et al.*, 2015: 281). The linguistic knowledge and skills, as well as the language learning experience of all languages of a person are closely intertwined, and interact and contribute to the overall

TASK "ANIMAL SAFARI"

Step 1: the names of the animals

- vocabulary-focused subtask
- app BitsBoard: learners create their own vocabulary cards and then practice the vocabulary with a set of games
- learners choose how many words they want to practice and how they want to design the vocabulary cards (drawings, pictures)
- pronunciation can be recorded

➡ schema building activity, in which some key terms are introduced that pupils need in order to complete the task (cf. Nunan 2004)

Step 2: (simplified) lexicon entries

- genre-focused subtask
- app Book Creator: learners create a simplified, yet authentic-looking, multimodal lexicon entry on an animal of their choice
- learners choose how detailed their born-digital lexicon entry will be
- Book Creator allows for the integration of text, images, sounds, hyperlinks, and videos
- scaffolding: e.g. chunks for the facts that can be used or model lexicon entries as generic prototypes

Step 3: animated role play

- task focused on the conversation pattern of introducing oneself (basic communicative principles in primary school, introduced as early as first grade (KMK, 2008, p. 78))
- app Puppet Pals: learners produce a short, animated film which is a born-digital and creative version of the above-mentioned pattern
- transformation of a simplified lexicon entry into a conversation as a way to playfully focus on grammatical issues such as simple questions and answers (Do you like..? — No, I don't like.../Yes, I like...)
- learners can practice and record their dialogue several times and do not have to expose themselves in front of the whole class when presenting it
- easily documented, born-digital learning outcome

- real-life problem orientation: the context of the outcome is a (fictional) meeting, the use is the communication pattern of introducing oneself, and the function is knowing and applying the pattern
- goals: learning about animals, fostering digital literacy, learning to introduce oneself
- scaffolding: needs to be provided in digital and analogue from in every step and can be modified to the individual needs of the learning group
  ➡ learners also create their own scaffolds in every step for the respective next step

Figure 4.1 Task 'Animal Safari' according to Caruso, 2020; Caruso *et al.*, 2021.

communicative competence of a learner (Goethe Institut, n.d.). Multilingual speakers thus utilize their entire linguistic repertoire when constructing meaning in communication.

Following the broad perspective of inclusion, differences between languages and speakers of different languages are a social construct that shape our actions in everyday life and in the classroom. Reexamining such social constructs means questioning the monolingual bias which sees the native speaker and nativeness as the norm and standard for language practice and competence (e.g. May, 2014: 7–10; Ortega, 2014: 32–35).

Even though this change in perspective is reflected in current research and literature, differences based on language are still constructed in educational systems (e.g. Panagiotopoulou & Rosen, 2015; Panagiotopoulou *et al.*, 2018: 129), partially because many stakeholders in the field of education grew up in a system shaped by the monolingual bias. Working towards a more inclusive perspective is, thus, an ongoing process that requires time and effort, e.g. by critically reflecting on our own language learning biographies (e.g. Macedo, 2019: 27–28).

The special potential of the foreign language classroom lies in its contribution to enhancing learners' multilingual and intercultural awareness, with the latter being closely linked to the overall aim of inclusion (Eßer *et al.*, 2018: 11). Teaching multilingualism means considering, reflecting on and actively discussing languages, language learning processes, language practice and language learning experiences that students bring to the classroom (Ballweg *et al.*, 2013: 189).

Teachers cannot be experts on many different languages, cultures and writing systems. In order to be able to embrace other languages and cultures in their classrooms, they should aim at building learners' intercultural competence and language awareness. This means that the true challenge for teachers in inclusive classrooms is to let go of the idea of the teacher as the expert in the classroom, and to accept that multilingual students may know more about (dealing with and acquiring) other languages and cultures than the teacher. Learners will contribute ideas that ideas that the teacher might not be prepared for. This is compatible with TBLT, where teachers are facilitators and guides on the side. Here, teachers can step back and reflect on different languages and cultures together with students and on a metalevel. As an example, our 'Animal Safari' task takes other languages into account as especially multilingual students are encouraged to employ their other languages in all steps of the task (cf. section 4.4.3 and Figure 4.2).

4.4.2 Students with developmental language disorder (DLD)

Typically developing children form hypotheses about language systems and the language acquisition process based on the input they get when engaging in interactions with other speakers of the language and when producing utterances in the target language (Gass & Mackey, 2021).

Most children with DLD have difficulties in language comprehension and in acquiring vocabulary. They are often used to the fact that there are many words and utterances they do not understand and that they often do not notice new or unknown words, or fail to reflect on other causes for their lack of understanding (e.g. background noise, difficult sentence structure, lexical or structural ambiguity). These issues in monitoring their comprehension and failing to react appropriately when comprehension issues arise are commonly reported for children

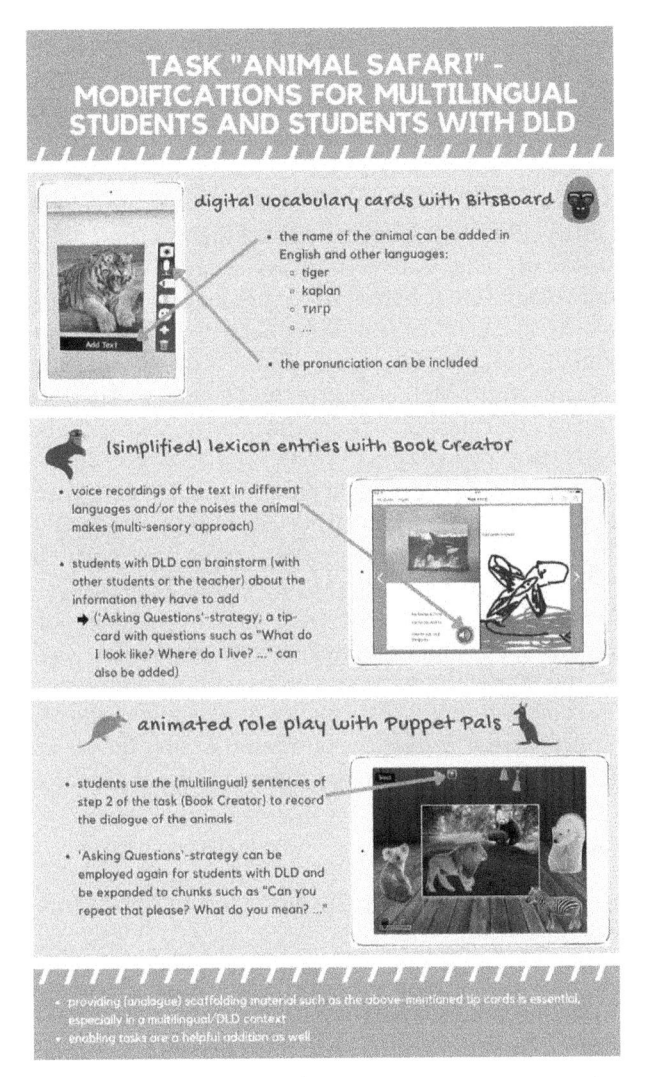

Figure 4.2 Modifications for the task 'Animal Safari' for multilingual students and students with DLD

with lexical and comprehension difficulties in the context of DLD, but also for children with attention deficits (ADHD) and children on the autism spectrum (Klumpp & Schönauer-Schneider, 2020: 47; Schönauer-Schneider & Eberhardt, 2018: 175, 177f, 179; Schick, 2018: 64). Looking out and asking for e.g. the meaning of unknown words is a powerful lexical learning strategy that typically developing children use. Checking comprehension and asking for clarification as part of negotiation of meaning are efficient comprehension, communication and language learning strategies in both L1 and L2 acquisition (Ahmadian & Long,

2022: 62; Gass & Mackey, 2021: 198–203; Klumpp & Schönauer-Schneider, 2020: 47; Marks, 2017: 50–51, 113) and an inherent part of solving tasks (Blume *et al.*, 2018: 38). Reflecting on the listening comprehension and the vocabulary learning process on a metalevel can be a helpful resource for children with lexical and language comprehension difficulties (Marks, 2017; Schick, 2018; Schönauer-Schneider & Eberhardt, 2017: 107–108). Explicitly teaching and practicing comprehension monitoring (e.g. active listening, engaging in negotiation of meaning) and vocabulary learning strategies (e.g. looking for and asking for unknown words, establishing links between words of one or more different languages, saying target words out loud in order to remember them) is thus important. Metacognition and metacognitive strategies are also discussed as one variable that determines the success in L2 listening for typically developing learners (Vandergrift & Baker, 2015: 411–412). Such listening and vocabulary learning strategies can potentially be transferred to all languages of a learner, and foster self-regulated learning as well as learner autonomy. Explicitly teaching and reflecting on language learning strategies may thus be one way of bridging the gap between the needs of students with DLD and the openness of TBLT, as well as the challenges of digital media. Our 'Animal Safari' task example takes lexical and comprehension strategies into account as students are encouraged to test and practice strategies in all steps of the task (cf. section 4.4.3 and Figure 4.2). The task example also shows how digital media can help to make these language learning strategies more efficient and accessible.

4.4.3 Multilingual students and students with DLD within the animal safari task

In order to take into account the dimensions of heterogeneity addressed earlier (multilingualism and DLD), we will analyze how different learner languages can be integrated into our task example, and how language learning strategies can be introduced to, tested and practiced by students while completing the task at hand.

For step 1, this for example means that in terms of vocabulary learning strategies, students can be encouraged to brainstorm and find words they can relate to the animal and to each other, and to sort them according to criteria they ideally come up with on their own (the goal here is to create different kinds of links within their mental lexicon – the teacher can give prompts; cf. Motsch *et al.*, 2018; Schick, 2018):

Example '*monkey*':

- spelled like *money* only with a k; *monkey* and *mouse* both start with [m], *monkey* and *donkey* sound similar and are spelled in a similar way (second syllable);

- *ape* and *monkey* denote similar entities; *tail* (meronymy); *climb* (verb that is semantically linked with *monkey*);
- can be used as a part of a phrasal verb *to monkey around*.

This can be done 'analogue' or digitally, depending on the individual prerequisites of the learning group, with (digital) whiteboards, word clouds and (online) dictionaries (cf. Grimm *et al.*, 2015: 110–111). As an enabling task, students could also collaboratively work on an interactive whiteboard and share their associations, strategies etc., about specific words with their partner(s). Furthermore, students choose:

- *how many* words they want to practice;
- *which words* they want to practice depending on which words they find difficult to remember (and this choice will be individual);
- *their own way* of practicing – e.g. for some students it might be a useful strategy to say a target word out loud several times, while for others it will be more helpful to ask another learner to say the target word again several times so that they have more opportunities to hear the target word.

Students can be encouraged to include words from other languages on the digital vocabulary cards (cf. Figure 4.2) that they can relate to the target word in order to account for multilingualism. Within their group, they can discuss why/how these words from other languages are associated with the target word. Strategy use and multilingualism can be combined in a 'false friends' subtask: in their BitsBoard vocab cards (cf. Figure 4.1), students could also include words that are similar in other languages in terms of phonology or orthography but may not be directly connected semantically (the goal would also be to create different links with their mental lexicon, while at the same time drawing on plurilinguistic competences).

In step 2, the vocabulary learning strategy of 'Asking Questions' about the animal can be tested and employed in order to create the born-digital lexicon entry, e.g. what does the animal look like? Where does the animal live? Where do we find the animal? What does the animal eat? What does the animal like to do? Also, the digital lexicon entries can be created in several languages – when researching where the animal lives, learners are encouraged to also use e.g. texts, hyperlinks and videos from other languages (cf. Figure 4.2).

In step 3, the learners are asked to transform the lexicon entries into an animated role play, in which 'their' animals meet up to talk to each other. For this step, the learners have to modify the third person form of the digital lexicon entry into a dialogue in which they impersonate their own animals. The lexical strategy of 'Asking Questions' about the animal can be employed again, now however with the changed point of view (cf. Figure 4.1): What do you look like? Where do you live? Where can I find you? What do you eat? What do you like to do? Also, other questions and comments can enhance the negotiation for meaning process and can be provided as useful chunks for the interaction: can you repeat that please? What do you mean? I don't understand. Can you give an example? Asking these questions supports students with DLD in monitoring their comprehension and at the same time, these questions serve as powerful vocabulary learning strategies. However, learners with DLD do not automatically use these strategies, but need to be explicitly encouraged to do so by the teacher or other students.

4.5 Implications for Further Research

The example discussed illustrates how multilingual students and students with DLD can be included in TBLT, and with the help of digital media, in inclusive EFL settings. However, our example in particular, and the consideration of different dimensions of heterogeneity within the combination of TBLT and digital media in general still need to be tested in 'real' lessons, in order to provide some empirical evidence about their application. In addition to this, our example only takes into account these two dimensions of heterogeneity – other dimensions need to be considered in further tasks and research.

4.6 Conclusion

In this chapter, we argued that teaching language learning strategies can bridge the gap between the need for stronger guidance for students with DLD and the openness of TBLT – especially in a digitally mediated task. We also argued that including learners' home languages is necessary and possible, especially due to endless possibilities of the digital world combined with TBLT.

Our analysis allows some general conclusions about how to include digitally mediated TBLT in inclusive settings. The digital aspects that are part of the task need to be taken advantage of in ways that barriers for learners are reduced for example by providing additional scaffolding and digital, multimodal options to initiate self-regulated learning. Learners are not only agents in the digital discourse, where they come into contact with multiple languages and literacies, but should also be given the opportunity to become experts in their individual needs and strategies associated with their (language) learning process. This also implies that the role of the teacher has to change, which may lead to a 'split teacher personality': teachers should be active guides on the side, while at the same time providing guidance that is needed to explicitly introduce and support the use of language learning strategies. As a consequence, teachers need to accept a change in the power dynamics in the classroom when their students are in charge of shaping the task components, topics, materials, scaffolds and learning strategies. Thus, when we reconsider the initial question of whether born-digital texts and digitally-mediated tasks are a perfect match for the inclusive EFL classroom, we can say that teaching language learning strategies and considering home languages can be ways through the minefield of digital media, TBLT and inclusion, and that both teachers and students need to be the matchmakers. With our example 'Animal Safari', we presented one possibility of how this can work.

References

Ahmadian, M.J. and Long, M.H. (2022) *The Cambridge Handbook of Task-Based Language Teaching*. Cambridge University Press.

Ballweg, S., Drumm, S., Hufeisen, B., Klippel, J. and Pilypaitytė, L. (2013) *Wie Lernt Man die Fremdsprache Deutsch?* Klett.

Bär, M. (2019) Fremdsprachenlehren und -lernen in Zeiten des digitalen Wandels. Chancen und Herausforderungen aus fremdsprachendidaktischer Sicht. In E. Burwitz-Melzer, C. Riemer and L. Schmelter (eds) *Das Lehren und Lernen von Fremd- und Zweitsprachen im digitalen Wandel* (pp. 12–23). Narr/Francke/Attempto.

Biebighäuser, K., Zibelius, M. and Schmidt, T. (2012) Aufgaben 2.0 – Aufgabenorientierung beim Fremdsprachenlernen mit digitalen Medien. In K. Biebighäuser, M. Zibelius and T. Schmidt (eds) *Aufgaben 2.0 – Konzepte, Materialien und Methoden für das Fremdsprachenlehren und -lernen mit digitalen Medien* (pp. 11–56). Narr.

Black, R.W. (2009) English-language learners, fan communities, and 21st century skills. *Journal of Adolescent and Adult Literacy* 52 (8), 688–697.

Blume, C., Kielwein, C. and Schmidt, T. (2018) Potenziale und Grenzen von Task-Based Language Teaching als methodischer Zugang im (zieldifferent-) inklusiven Unterricht für Schülerinnen und Schüler mit Lernbesonderheiten. In B. Roters, D. Gerlach and S. Eßer (eds) *Inklusiver Englischunterricht–Impulse zur Unterrichtsentwicklung aus fachdidaktischer und sonderpädagogischer Perspektive. QUA-LiS NRW Band, Reihe Beiträge zur Schulentwicklung* (pp. 27–48). Waxmann.

Bündgens-Kosten, J. and Schildhauer, P. (eds) (2021) *Englischunterricht in einer digitalisierten Gesellschaft*. Belz Juventa.

Burwitz-Melzer, E., Riemer, C. and Schmelter, L. (eds) (2019) *Das Lehren und Lernen von Fremd- und Zweitsprachen im digitalen Wandel. Arbeitspapiere der 39. Frühjahrskonferenz zur Erforschung des Fremdsprachenunterrichts*. Narr/Francke/Attempto.

Caruso, C. (2020) Animals, apps and language learning. Digitale Lernaufgaben für die Grundschule. *Grundschulmagazin Englisch* 2, 32–35.

Caruso, C., Hofmann, J. and Rohde, A. (2021) Get 'em while they're young: Complex digitally-mediated tasks for EFL learners in primary schools. *Canadian Journal of Applied Linguistics* Special Issue 24 (2), 187–207. See https://doi.org/10.37213/cjal.2021.31340 (accessed January 2022).

Chilla, S. and Vogt, K. (eds) (2017) *Heterogenität und Diversität im Englischunterricht. Fachdidaktische Perspektiven*. Peter Lang

Dausend, H. and Nickel, S. (2017) *Tap'n' Talk*. Differenzierte Förderung von Sprachproduktionen durch tabletgestützte Lernaufgaben. In S. Chilla and K. Vogt (eds) *Heterogenität und Diversität im Englischunterricht Fachdidaktische Perspektiven* (pp. 179–203). Peter Lang.

Ellis, R. (2003) *Task-Based Language Learning and Teaching*. Oxford University Press.

Eßer, S., Gerlach, D. and Roters, B. (2018) Unterrichtsentwicklung im inklusiven Englischunterricht. In B. Roters, D. Gerlach and S. Eßer (eds) *Inklusiver Englischunterricht – Impulse zur Unterrichtsentwicklung aus fachdidaktischer und sonderpädagogischer Perspektive* (pp. 9–31). Waxmann.

Fürstenau, S., Celik, Y. and Plöger, S. (2020) Language comparison as an inclusive translanguaging strategy: Analysis of a multilingual teaching situation in a german primary school classroom. In J.A. Panagiotopoulou, L. Rosen and J. Strzykala (eds) *Inclusion, Education and Translanguaging: How to Promote Social Justice in (Teacher) Education?* (pp. 145–162). Springer VS.

García, O. and Li, W. (2014) *Translanguaging: Language, Bilingualism and Education.* Palgrave Pivot.

Gass, S.M. and Mackey, A. (2021) Input, interaction and output in L2 Acquisition. In B. VanPatten and J. Williams (eds) *Theories in Second Language Acquisition. An Introduction* (3rd edn, pp. 192–222). Routledge.

Gerlach, D. and Schmidt, T. (2021) Heterogenität, Diversität und Inklusion: Ein systematisches Review zum aktuellen Stand der Fremdsprachenforschung in Deutschland. *Zeitschrift für Fremdsprachenforschung* 32 (1), 11–32.

Gibbons, P. (2015) *Scaffolding Language, Scaffolding Learning. Teaching Second Language Learners in the Mainstream Classroom* (2nd edn). Heinemann.

Goethe Institut. Gemeinsamer europäischer Referenzrahmen für Sprachen: Lernen, lehren, beurteilen. See http://www.goethe.de/z/50/commeuro/103.htm (accessed January 2022).

González-Lloret, M. and Ortega, L. (2014) Towards technology-mediated TBLT. An introduction. In M. González-Lloret and L. Ortega (eds) *Technology-Mediated TBLT. Researching Technology and Tasks* (pp. 1–22). John Benjamins.

Grau, M. (2009) Worlds apart? English in German youth cultures and in educational settings. *World Englishes* 28 (2), 160–174.

Grimm, N., Meyer, M. and Volkmann, L. (2015) *Teaching English.* Narr Francke Attempto.

Grosche, M. and Vock, M. (2018) Inklusion. In D.H. Rost, J.R. Sparfeldt and S.R. Buch (eds) *Handbuch Pädagogische Psychologie* (5th rev. and ext. edn, pp. 260–268). Beltz.

Hallet, W. (2004) (How) Can we close the gap? Zum Verhältnis von Literatur-, Kulturwissenschaften und Didaktik am Beispiel der Intertextualität und Nick Hornby's Roman *High Fidelity*. In L. Bredella, W. Delanoy and C. Surkamp (eds) *Literaturdidaktik im Dialog* (pp. 207–238). Narr.

Hofmann, J. (2019) Romeo and Juliet and my iPad. Partizipative Kultur und digitale Medien im Englischunterricht am Beispiel eines Schulklassikers. In M. Basseler and A. Nünning (eds) *Fachdidaktik als Kulturwissenschaft: Konzepte – Perspektiven – Projekte* (pp. 39–63). WVT.

Jenkins, H., Purushotma, R., Weigel, M., Clinton, K. and Robison, A.J. (2009) *Confronting the Challenges of Participatory Culture. Media Education for the 21st Century.* MIT Press.

Kerres, M. (2003) Wirkungen und Wirksamkeit neuer Medien in der Bildung. In R. Keill-Slawik and M. Kerres (eds) *Education Quality Forum. Wirkungen und Wirksamkeit neuer Medien* (pp. 31–44). Waxmann.

Klumpp, T. and Schönauer-Schneider, W. (2020) Monitoring des Sprachverstehens bei ein- und mehrsprachigen Kindern mit Spezifischen Sprachentwicklungsstörungen (SSES). *Forschung Sprache* 8 (1), 45–65.

Krommer, A. (2018) Wider den Mehrwert! Oder: Argumente gegen einen überflüssigen Begriff. See https://axelkrommer.com/2018/09/05/wider-den-mehrwertoder-argumente-gegen-einen-ueberfluessigen-begriff (accessed January 2022).

Macedo, D. (2019) Rupturing the yoke of colonialism in foreign language education: An introduction. In D. Macedo (ed.) *Decolonizing Foreign Language Education. The Misteaching of English and Other Colonial Languages* (pp. 1–49). Routledge.

Marks, D.-K. (2017) *Effektivität lexikalischer Strategietherapie im Grundschulalter unter besonderer Berücksichtigung mehrsprachig aufwachsender Kinder. Adaption des 'Wortschatzsammler'-Konzepts und Evaluation im Rahmen einer randomisierten und kontrollierten Interventionsstudie*. Shaker.

May, S. (ed.) (2014) *The Multilingual Turn: Implications for SLA, TESOL and Bilingual Education*. Routledge

Motsch, H.-J., Marks, D.-K. and Ulrich, T. (2018) *Der Wortschatzsammler. Evidenzbasierte Strategietherapie lexikalischer Störungen im Kindesalter* (3rd edn). Ernst Reinhardt Verlag.

Müller-Hartmann, A. and Schocker, M. (2018) The challenges of integrating focus on form within tasks. Findings from a classroom research project in secondary EFL classrooms. In V. Samuda, K. Van den Branden and M. Bygate (eds) *TBLT as a Tesearched Pedagogy* (pp. 98–129). John Benjamins Publishing Company. See https://doi.org/10.1075/tblt.12 (accessed January 2022).

Nunan, D. (2004) *Task-Based Language Teaching*. Cambridge University Press.

Ortega, L. (2014) Ways forward for a bi/multilingual turn in SLA. In S. May (ed.) *The Multilingual Turn: Implications for SLA, TESOL and Bilingual Education*. Routledge.

Otheguy, R., García, O. and Reid, W. (2015) Clarifying translanguaging and deconstructing named languages: A perspective from linguistics. *Applied Linguistics Review* 6 (3), 281–307.

Panagiotopoulou, A. and Rosen, L. (2015) Migration und Inklusion. In K. Reich, D. Asselhoven and S. Kargl (eds) *Eine inklusive Schule für alle: Das Modell der Inklusiven Universitätsschule Köln* (pp. 158–166). Beltz.

Panagiotopoulou, A., Rosen, L. and Karduck, S. (2018) Exklusion durch institutionalisierte Barrieren. In R. Ceylan, M. Ottersbach and P. Wiedemann (eds) *Neue Mobilitäts- und Migrationsprozesse und sozialräumliche Segregation* (pp. 115–131). Springer VS.

Reckermann, J. (2017) Eine Aufgabe – 25 richtige Lösungen: Das Potenzial offener Lernaufgaben für den inklusiven Englischunterricht in der Grundschule. In S. Chilla and K. Vogt (eds) *Heterogenität und Diversität im Englischunterricht Fachdidaktische Perspektiven* (pp. 205–233). Peter Lang.

Schick, K. (2018) *Wortschatzförderung im frühen Englischunterricht für Kinder mit lexikalischen Störungen – Eine empirische Studie zum Einsatz von Wortlernstrategien sowie Speicher- und Abrufelementen im Englischunterricht eines ersten Schuljahres einer Förderschule Sprache*. Shaker.

Schick, K. and Rohde, A. (2022) Von integrativem zu inklusivem Englischunterricht. Weiterentwicklung sprachdidaktischer Prinzipien vor dem Hintergrund sonderpädagogischer Förderung. In K. Schick and A. Rohde (eds) *Von integrativem zu inklusivem Englischunterricht. Weiterentwicklung sprachdidaktischer Prinzipien vor dem Hintergrund sonderpädagogischer Förderung. Inquiries in Language Learning* (pp. 15–41). Peter Lang.

Schmidt, T. and Strasser, T. (2016) Digital classroom. *Der fremdsprachliche Unterricht Englisch* 144, 2–7.

Schmidt, T. and Würffel, N. (eds) (2018) Zur Einführung in den Themenschwerpunkt. *FLUL Fremdsprachen Lehren und Lernen: Themenschwerpunkt Digitalisierung und Differenzierung* 47 (2), 3–7.

Schönauer-Schneider, W. and Eberhardt, M. (2017) Work in progress: 'Hä?' Monitoring des Sprachverstehens bei Kindern mit Sprachentwicklungsstörung und Kindern mit Autismus. *Forschung Sprache* 2/2017, 107–113.

Schönauer-Schneider, W. and Eberhardt, M. (2018) 'Hab ich nicht verstanden!' Monitoring des Sprachverstehens bei Kindern mit Sprachentwicklungsstörungen und Kindern mit Autismus. In T. Jungmann, B. Gierschner, M. Meindl and S. Sallat (eds) *Sprach- und Bildungshorizonte. Wahrnehmen – Beschreiben – Erweitern* (pp. 174–179). Schulz-Kirchner.

Schulz, L. (2021) Diklusive Schulentwicklung. *Medienpädagogik* 41, 32–54. https://doi.org/10.21240/mpaed/41/2021.02.03.X

Vandergrift, L. and Baker, S. (2015) Learner variables in second language listening comprehension: An exploratory path analysis. *Language Learning* 65 (2), 390–416.

Windmüller-Jesse, V. and Talarico, M. (2018) Go digital! Chancen und Möglichkeiten digitaler Mediennutzung im inklusiven Englischunterricht. In B. Roters, D. Gerlach and S. Eßer (eds) *Inklusiver Englischunterricht. Beiträge zur Schulentwicklung* (pp. 83–100). Waxmann.

5 #hashtagsareforlearning – Hashtags as Digital Texts and their Affordances in the EFL Classroom

Ralf Gießler and Daniel Becker

5.1 Introduction

In recent years, research in English as a Foreign Language (EFL) education has significantly broadened its spectrum of texts and materials to be explored in the classroom. Thus, next to continued research on analogue texts such as picture books, novels or poems, there has been a surge of studies focusing on new digital texts – including tweets, video games or YouTube videos (cf. Jones, 2018; Kirchhoff, 2019; Watkins & Wilkins, 2011) – and their relevance for EFL learners. As such, English language education has lately taken a digital turn by more prominently addressing how the contemporary EFL classroom can prepare learners to actively participate in a digitised world and the 'salient digital practices of any community' (Sykes, 2019: 130).

In the spirit of these studies and their endeavour to bring current digital communicative practices into the EFL classroom, the present chapter will address one digital text in particular: the hashtag. Recently, hashtags have become an omnipresent phenomenon. Whether they appear in the context of elections (#notmypresident), the entertainment industry (#letthemusiclive) or everyday life (#ootd:outfit of the day), they currently permeate numerous sectors of the political, social and cultural landscape and, in doing so, fulfil various essential functions in today's digital age. Hashtags, for instance, play a pivotal role in generating social and economic capital in the field of marketing, and are vitally involved in creating digital communities, fostering solidarity and empathy. They serve as important structuring devices for digitally mediated discourses, themes and ideas. Hashtags, in other words, have become 'multitasking tools' (La Rocca, 2020: 2) which are deeply embedded in the very fabric of digital culture(s) and which, as such, prominently help to shape a meaningful relationship to the world in the internet era.

Despite their important position in digital language use and communication, hashtags have hardly received any attention in EFL research so far. The present chapter will address this gap by asking to what extent hashtags as omnipresent phenomena in the digital world can be integrated into contemporary EFL teaching and learning practices. It will be argued that a hashtag can be defined as a digital text in its own right, which can be used in the EFL classroom in two ways: they can either be seen from a narrow perspective, in which the hashtag itself (i.e. #-symbol + word/phrase) becomes the learning object, or they can be seen from a broad perspective, in which the hashtag is used in combination with its related tweets and posts. Viewed from each of these perspectives, hashtags as texts offer EFL learners valuable learning opportunities in terms of skills development and language awareness. We will use the concept of affordances in order to show that hashtags provide learners with both linguistic and communicative (narrow perspective) as well as discursive (broad perspective) learning opportunities, which makes this phenomenon a valuable addition to contemporary English language teaching.

The chapter consists of four sections: the first two sections will provide the theoretical foundation: section 5.2 will explore the textuality of hashtags, and section 5.3 offers a short introduction to affordance theory. Based on these considerations, section 5.4 will then examine which specific affordances hashtags as texts can provide in the EFL classroom. Finally, the chapter ends with some more practical implications of using hashtags in English language teaching by discussing some example hashtags used on Twitter in the context of the US presidential elections.

5.2 Defining Hashtags as Texts

When considering what a text is, most people would probably identify novels or newspaper articles as typical representatives of this concept. Perhaps they would also perceive blogs or emails as current digital add-ons to the textual canon. But would they also include hashtags? At first sight, hashtags are highly unlikely candidates to represent texts in a conventional sense: as phenomena which only consist of short individual phrases (or even single words), and which always start with a symbol they seem so utterly different from the prototypical forms of texts mentioned before. And yet, despite their idiosyncrasies, we will show in the following section that they can be defined as a specific form of digital text which shares the structural features of more conventional examples, while also displaying some unique textual features.

In order to explore what kind of texts hashtags are, one first needs to define the term 'text' in general. In contemporary academic debates, text can be seen as a traveling concept (cf. Bal, 2002), which means that it is currently being used in a broad variety of disciplines, including literary and cultural studies, media studies, linguistics or sociology. Each of these disciplines conceptualises the term in a different manner, making the notion of text a highly context-sensitive and fuzzy concept for which no universally accepted definition exists (cf. Brinker *et al.*, 2018: 13). In the present paper we will outline the textuality of hashtags by drawing on definitions provided by text linguistics. On a general level, Martens (1982), for instance, classically defines a text as a 'coherent and self-contained linguistic pattern' (1982: 3; trans. D.B.) that usually appears in a written or spoken form. In a similar manner, Göpferich (1995: 56–57; trans. D.B.) describes text as a 'thematically and/or functionally oriented linguistic construct'. She adds that this construct is usually shaped and situated in a communicative setting, which involves the exchange of information between senders and addressees: texts are 'created with a specific communicative purpose' and they 'fulfill a recognisable communicative function' in social interaction (Martens, 1982: 3). This idea is also indicated by Brinker *et al.* (2018), who define text as follows: 'the term "text" refers to a limited sequence of linguistic signs [...] which is coherent and which, as a whole, signals a recognisable communicative function' (2018: 17; trans. D.B.). On the most basic level then, a text is seen as both a product of communication which displays specific structural properties (i.e. a coherent sequence of signs) as well as an integral part of the process of communication, as it is functionally embedded in social meaning-making practices.

In the light of this minimal definition, hashtags can be seen as texts too. They also fulfil the basic criteria of textuality by displaying a limited and coherent sequence of linguistic signs (i.e. the signs following the #-symbol) and, as already indicated in the introduction, by carrying out essential communicative functions in today's digital world. Yet, compared to more conventional texts, hashtags primarily differ in the size and form of the linguistic pattern they usually exhibit: while most texts studied in text linguistics consist of at least several coherent sentences, as the 'most important structural unit of a text' (Brinker *et al.*, 2018: 14; trans. D.B.), hashtags mostly consist of single sentences or phrases. Predominantly, they are made up of single-word constructions (e.g. #beauty; #selfie), short (imperative) phrases (e.g. #takethemic) or elliptic statements (e.g. #notmypresident) and thus become an example of minimal text composition.

As such, hashtags can be more precisely defined as what Hausendorf (2009) labels 'small texts' (*kleine Texte*). Small texts are 'inconspicuous linguistic forms' (Hausendorf, 2009: 7; trans. D.B.) that are ubiquitous in everyday life – e.g. public signs, aphorisms on calendar pages or slogans on (shopping) bags – but are often overlooked as texts in their own right. Due to their very limited nature, they are relegated to the margins of textuality, where they 'challenge our everyday expectations of what a text is and can be' (Hausendorf, 2009: 5; trans. D.B.). These texts are characterized through a particular set of textual features, which can also be used to describe hashtags as texts in more detail.

Table 5.1 Hashtags as small texts (adapted from Hausendorf, 2009: 6)

Features of Small Text	Implication for Hashtags
Limited size	Limited to words, phrases and/or short sentences
Limited complexity	Single word or phrase constructions/slogans and catchphrases
Formulaic structure	# + signifier
Easily distinguished from surrounding context	#-symbol and hyperlink status mark hashtags as coherent entities
Function	Communicative contouring (see below)

First, small texts are defined by their limited size. They are usually highly restricted in length/word count, as well as the (physical) space they occupy. This can, for example, be observed in the form of short descriptions on the limited space of a warning sign (e.g. *exam in progress, please do not disturb*). The same can be said about hashtags: much like other small texts in public life (e.g. *no mask, no entry*), they often consist of a very limited amount of words (e.g. #metoo; #followme). Furthermore, they abbreviate words to the point of, at times, only using acronyms (e.g. #ootd; #rofl) and even omit spacing between individual lexical items (e.g. #stayathome; #picoftheday), which makes hashtags highly condensed textual spaces in a digital environment.

Second, small texts are also 'small' in relation to their linguistic complexity: as Hausendorf (2009: 7–8; trans. D.B.) points out, texts such as slogans on bags (e.g. *I'm not using plastic bags*) are often 'simple in regard to the syntactical means being used'. Again, this description applies to hashtags, which, in most cases, feature single-word structures (e.g. #fashion; #beautiful), simple descriptive phrases (e.g. #thisisnotjournalism; #iamplasticfree) or imperatives (e.g. #letthemusiclive). Additionally, much like slogans, they predominantly make use of easy-to-understand everyday vocabulary (e.g. #iamwithher; #getoutanddrive).

Third, since small texts are so short, compact and simple, they tend to offer a particularly formulaic and, thus, predictable textual design. As can be seen in the example of calendar aphorisms, specific small texts often share a recurring layout and structure – e.g. aphorisms are usually embedded in an image, are limited to a few lines and most often state the name of the author right after the quote – which means that they can be recognised by their appearance alone. In this context, Hausendorf adds as a fourth feature: just by looking at them and their compact textual shape, one can easily distinguish small texts from the surroundings in which they occur. Both features can be used to describe hashtags, which also display a highly predictable design (there is always a #-symbol followed by a signifier of limited length). Next to being immediately recognisable by their #-symbol, they frequently exist as hyperlinks which, on a mere visual level, makes them easily distinguishable from their digital surroundings (e.g. on social media).

Last but not least, like 'bigger' texts, small texts fulfil specific communicative functions in social interaction. According to Hausendorf, these functions are mostly practical in nature: small texts provide information (e.g. labels in clothing items) or guide (communicative) behaviour (e.g. a set of rules printed on a sign in a park; Hausendorf, 2009: 6). Hashtags fulfil these functions, too, since they guide and shape communication in digital contexts in the sense that they provide a form of *communicative contouring* in digital interactions. In contrast to longer texts, hashtags do not unfold and describe a topic in detail (e.g. in the form of a plot in a novel). Rather, based on a low number of signifiers, they set up a communicative frame which minimally contours the topic to be discussed.

Hashtags establish a communicative frame in two ways: first, they simply label a topic by stating *what* is to be discussed in posts and tweets (e.g. posts about the topic of #photography or #blacklivesmatter). Second, they set the scene for *how* a topic is to be discussed. This scene is established through processes of narrative and/or affective contouring. Thus, by frequently using the imperative, hashtags can construct minimal storylines that narratively frame individual posts. By using the imperative #freebritney, for instance, sketches a minimal narrative arc of moving from a current state of oppression to a future state of liberation. Every post sharing the hashtag is thus positioned in the continuation of the overall 'story' of emancipating former pop star Britney Spears from the (alleged) tyranny of her father. Furthermore, hashtags provide an outline by coloring the topic at hand in certain emotional tones, thus guiding the reader to perceive a topic from a specific affective stance (cf. Boyd, 2010). This can be seen in the context of #notmypresident, where the wording of the hashtag (i.e. *not* in initial position) already guides users to focus on the negative characteristics of a certain president, while ignoring potentially positive aspects.

With this function of communicative contouring in mind, hashtags offer a basic communicative frame, yet this frame requires the individual reader, and their interaction with the hashtag, to be expanded and completed. Therefore, hashtags can ultimately be defined as inherently unfinished (small) texts. As such, hashtags structurally stimulate reader participation as an inherent feature of their unique textuality. That is what makes them highly dynamic on a semantic level: since hashtags stir different associations in different individuals, their overall meaning becomes fluid and is open to a constant process of 'definition, re-definition and re-appropriation' (La Rocca, 2020: 2). In the end, therefore, hashtags are polyphonic: as highly interactive texts, they do not represent the voice of a single author but create textual spaces of 'polysemic orientation' (La Rocca, 2020: 2) which invite the communicative participation of the many rather than the few.

As small and interactive texts with specific textual features and functions, hashtags deserve attention in foreign language education, as they offer various potentials and learning opportunities for EFL learners. These potentials can best be described when considering hashtags from the perspective of affordances.

5.3 The Concept of Affordances

According to the American psychologist John Gibson, affordances can be defined as 'properties of the environment that activate or offer potential action by an agent' (La Rocca, 2020: 5). The basic assumption is that 'environmental features are experienced as having a functional meaning' (Pedersen & Bang, 2016: 734, cited in Kordt, 2018: 148). Buttons for pushing, knobs for turning, handles for pulling or levers for sliding are cues, perceived in the environment by an individual that indicate possibilities for action. Whether visual stimuli become clues that trigger human action depends on the goals and needs of the individual. After several hours of walking, a hiker may feel the need to rest and will therefore accept the 'invitation' of a fallen tree to take a seat on it: 'Needs control the perception of affordances (selective attention) and also initiate acts' (Gibson, 1982: 411).

Our argument is that the concept of affordances can serve as a heuristic tool for describing the didactic potential of hashtags for language education. The symbol # is a visible cue that can be conceptualised as an affordance that invites communicative and discursive action. This is highly relevant for understanding hashtags: once the symbol # is perceived in a Twitter post, the user or reader can decide to respond to it. Twitter, for example, features affordances with regard to hashtags in the following three ways: first, the platform allows users to create hashtags; second, once perceived by users hashtags invite different types of action such as retweeting, writing one's own posts (La Rocca, 2020: 5); and third, 'the possibility of hashtags to change their original meaning thanks to retweets and quotings' (La Rocca, 2020: 5). The meaning of hashtags in a broader sense can change throughout the course of interaction in social media: the original, intended meaning of a hashtag such as #notmypresident can widen and lead to other intentional, metaphorical or figurative usages of the original hashtag, 'independently from [...] the initial creator of the hashtag itself' (La Rocca, 2020: 5).

5.4 The Affordances of Hashtags in the EFL Classroom

As pointed out in the previous section, affordances are opportunities for action which individuals perceive in interaction with objects in their respective environment. Based on this understanding, the following section will explore the specific opportunities for action that EFL learners might find in hashtags, when engaging with them in the environment of the EFL classroom. More precisely, by assuming that individuals predominantly perceive those affordances in an object that will help them achieve specific goals in a specific situation (see above), the next section will focus on the specific opportunities for learning that hashtags offer to EFL learners, which can support them in their overarching endeavour of becoming proficient in communicating and participating in the English language and its various contexts. It will be argued that hashtags can provide linguistic, communicative and discursive affordances, depending on the perspective from which they are perceived in the EFL classroom.

5.4.1 Narrow perspective: Linguistic and communicative affordances

Seeing hashtags from a narrow perspective means to only focus on the hashtag itself as learning material in the EFL classroom. Thus, EFL learners merely engage with the minimal textual unit of the #-symbol and its ensuing signifiers in the form of single words or short phrases. In this interaction, hashtags afford various opportunities for learners to develop their foreign language competences on a linguistic and communicative level.

5.4.1.1 Linguistic affordances

First, hashtags provide EFL learners with the opportunity to explore the English language and its linguistic patterns. More precisely, as highly condensed small texts, hashtags display specific lexical and grammatical structures for learners to engage with. Since hashtags for instance usually fulfil the general function of labelling and contouring topics for online communication (see Section 5.2), they often consist of hypernyms that represent specific lexical and semantic fields. These hypernyms range from concrete (e.g. #photography, #music) to abstract (e.g. #selflove), which makes single-word hashtags an ideal textual foundation for EFL learners to examine a broad array of hyponymous relationships in the English language. For that purpose, learners might for example be asked to create a list of all the words they associate with a specific hashtag and/or they would expect in posts following this hashtag. In that way, learners become aware of individual words in their lexical and semantic context, which can facilitate the acquisition of new lexical items, since 'lexical items which are semantically related seem to be stored together' in the mental lexicon (Hutz, 2012: 106).

Furthermore, hashtags also afford opportunities to learn more about collocations. As small texts with a limited size, hashtags often feature short phrases with a high density of collocates. These become most apparent in the classroom when juxtaposing lexically similar multi-word hashtags with each other: by simultaneously engaging with hashtags such as #stayathome, #stayawake, #staypositive or #stayhealthy, for example, learners can get to know the lexical 'neighborhood' (Thornbury, 2002: 7) of *stay*.

In this context, hashtags provide the frame for a 'miniature corpus analysis', as they offer a limited textual space in which learners can analyse how specific words are combined accurately in phrases and sentences.

On the grammatical level, hashtags afford opportunities to deal with phenomena such as the imperative or elliptic constructions. Hence, on the one hand, hashtags as small texts often fulfil an appellative function in digital interaction (cf. Brinker *et al.*, 2018: 109), as they encourage individual users to actively participate in communication. Frequently, this communicative appeal of hashtags is linguistically reflected in the use of the imperative form (e.g. #letthemusiclive; #getoutside; #beyourownboss). As such, hashtags become a worthwhile foundation for EFL learners to expand their grammatical repertoire: according to Goh and Burns (2012: 59), the ability to accurately perform speech acts such as requests, instructions or commands belongs to the 'core speaking skills' of any proficient language user, which makes the imperative an important linguistic phenomenon for learners to be aware of and understand. By often being limited to only short imperative phrases, hashtags allow learners to achieve this task, since they offer the opportunity to examine the imperative in isolation and, thus, to focus on its formal composition out of 'the base form without a noun or pronoun' (Scrivener, 2010: 112). Hashtags may thus serve as an authentic starting point for gaining a basic understanding of the imperative, before then considering this phenomenon in more communicative contexts by, for example, having learners create their own imperative hashtags for either their own social media posts or posts provided by the teacher.

On the other hand, as pointed out above, hashtags as small texts tend towards linguistic abbreviation, which includes the frequent use of ellipses (e.g. #notmypresident; #notjustsad). Elliptic expressions are a common occurrence in digital communication (Kersten & Lotze, 2013) so that learners who want to participate in contemporary discourse need to be able to comprehend this abbreviated form of language use. Once more, hashtags afford an ideal opportunity for EFL learners to engage with this exact phenomenon: given their status as unfinished and incomplete texts, hashtags often also feature unfinished and incomplete language that can be completed by individual learners (e.g. #notjustsad might become 'I am not just sad', or even 'I am not just sad but…'). In that way, learners have the chance to become aware of how short phrases are related to larger syntactic structures, thus making hashtags potential texts for further considering the function of ellipses in broader linguistic contexts.

5.4.1.2 Communicative affordances

Lexical and grammatical competences, however, are not sufficient on their own. Rather, in contemporary English language education '[l]anguage use […] comprises the actions performed by persons who as individuals and as social agents develop a range of competences, both general and in particular communicative language competences' (Council of Europe, 2001: 9). Next to knowing how the English language works, most importantly EFL learners are meant to be 'empower[ed]' (Council of Europe, 2001: 9) to appropriately use this language in different communicative settings in an increasingly globalised world. In order for learners to develop these communicative competences successfully, the EFL classroom needs to offer incentives for communication in English that 'learners consider meaningful, relevant and interesting in their own everyday lives' (Diehr & Frisch, 2008: 45; trans. D.B.). In other words: communicative competences can be developed best when there are opportunities for communication that make learners want to express themselves in the foreign language.

Hashtags can provide such motivating opportunities. They are omnipresent in social media and contemporary youth cultures (cf. Sykes, 2019) and thus present an instance of communication most relevant for many learners' everyday existence. Furthermore, as small texts that structurally anticipate an individual's communicative participation, hashtags become an ideal textual foundation for engaging learners in meaningful communicative action. They invite learners to share their own experiences on a specific topic. In that way, learners can become social agents who participate in broader communicative settings in which other users can likewise contribute their opinions under the same hashtag. This communicative affordance is additionally underlined by the wide range of topics that hashtags communicatively contour. When learners engage with popular hashtags such as #myfamily, #whatigotforchristmas or #globalgoals, they have the chance to communicate about both personal (e.g. family) as well as social (e.g. challenges of a global age) concerns and, depending on their age and level of proficiency, they can find appropriate and meaningful incentives for practising their communicative competences. More specifically, they might work with hashtags by both writing and speaking about them, when, for example, they write their own post based on a specific hashtag or when learners are asked to orally exchange ideas with a partner based on a hashtag's communicative framework.

5.4.2 Broad perspective: Discursive affordances

Next to these linguistic and communicative affordances, hashtags also provide discursive affordances. In combination with their respective tweets and posts, hashtags can be understood as a discursive move and as a critical component of expert social media practices (Sykes, 2019: 129). Hashtags extend the social context of the information being shared and place it within a larger social landscape. #whatigotforchristmas may turn a casual conversation about Christmas presents into an extended discourse about sustainability, the joy of giving and the consumer lifestyle. Such digitally mediated discourse in social media like Twitter is dynamic, co-constructed and may give rise to societal debates with relevant or even high stakes and impactful topics.

There are good reasons why EFL learners should engage with such discourse and study the patterns of digital discourse: they can engage with communities and their discourses beyond the classroom, e.g. in academic domains or the public sector. The scope of topics that can enter language education is broad since hashtags are used for a number of functions. Each function affords an opportunity for multilingual, multicultural engagement:

(1) Marketing and public relation function,
(2) Interpersonal interaction,
(3) Organizing text around a topic or phenomenon. (Sykes, 2019: 130)

Due to the ubiquity of hashtags and their nature to invite participation in digital discourses, hashtags and the tweets and posts accompanying them must be considered as a relevant text type for foreign language education. Learners can examine cultural, economic and interpersonal phenomena by studying and responding to the communicative affordances of hashtags. By examining hashtags in a broader sense they can explore subtle, yet critical cultural and political practices in a globalised society. The 'rich dynamicity of hashtags' (Sykes, 2019: 130) becomes apparent, for example, when different groups of people create different hashtags for the same event. Selecting hashtags that are of critical importance to a current political or cultural event or pop cultural movement becomes a learning opportunity: learners can trace the # throughout its use, exploring the ways it is used and the implications for its insertion in certain types of posts. Used in that way, hashtags can facilitate close reading and deep analysis of cultural patterns, ideologies and identities (Sykes, 2019: 134).

How do these considerations relate to current key objectives in language education? Hallet (2009) points out that the foremost goal of foreign language education is to develop learners' discourse competences. According to Matz (2020: 57), discourse competences entail social participation and empowerment of the individual. In this vein, discourse competence goes beyond the use of language for communicative purposes in the sense of basic interpersonal skills. Discourse competence is about understanding how meaning is and can be represented (Kalantzis & Cope, 2012: 4). The underlying assumption is that any knowledge has a linguistic-discursive orientation. For example, knowledge about culture-specific customs for giving tips manifests in specific speech acts and communicative actions in the given situation (cf. German 'stimmt so' with the Italian custom to leave a tip on the silver tray the bill arrived on after payment). Discourse competence can be subdivided into five different abilities (Hallet, 2009: 85, cited in Matz, 2020: 57):

(1) the ability to recognize and use the linguistic and generic patterns offered;
(2) the ability to strengthen and diversify foreign-language concepts;
(3) the ability to recognize and critically use the models of foreign language communication;
(4) the ability to identify individual discourse components and collective discourse objects in the communication at hand;
(5) the ability to recognize the represented and modelled discourses (and their object, relate them to lifeworld discourses and participate in these discourses with their own perspectives and views).

Hashtags as small texts have a particular potential to foster the ability to identify discourse components and discourse markers and how they relate to lifeworld discourses. When learners engage with hashtags in the narrow and the broader sense, when they open up to the linguistic, communicative and discursive affordances of hashtags, they are likely to enter a metareflection upon language use and the way meanings of words and phrases change in particular discourses over time. Such reflection is beneficial for developing discourse competence as defined by Hallet (2009) and is in agreement with key objectives in current language education.

5.5 Using Hashtags in the EFL Classroom – An Example

Now that we have defined hashtags as small texts and outlined their linguistic, communicative and discursive potential by referring to affordance theory, we would like to illustrate with the help of a commonly used hashtag how things can be carried into practice when teaching a particular topic. The topic we chose for the sake of illustration is the US presidency. One very popular hashtag for discussing this topic was and still is #notmypresident (#nmp). A keyword search on the website hashtagify.com proves that it is widely used on Twitter. On a scale of 1–100 (with 100 indicating highest popularity) #nmp ranges at 67 (January 2021).

The hashtag #nmp provides discourse affordances for EFL learning. With the help of this hashtag learners could explore how US citizens talk about the presidency and the election. We selected four tweets on the topic and will discuss communicative and affective contouring, instances of retweeting and meaning changes.

This tweet by the user @edgiesversion illustrates nicely how communicative contouring in digital interactions works. Based on a low number of signifiers, a communicative framework which minimally contours the topic to be discussed is set up. The author expresses disagreement with the former Californian governor's optimism that Biden will unite America again by simply saying 'Sorry Arnold'. A minimal storyline is created when the author uses 'Not possible' to express his doubts about the governor's hope to 'bring the country back together' again. By using the

> **edgiesversion** @edgiesversion · Jan 4, 2021
> Sorry Arnold. Not possible. #RESIST @JoeBiden is #NotMyPresident.

Arnold ✓ @Schwarzenegger · Jan 4, 2021
It was fantastic to talk to President Elect @JoeBiden today about bringing the country back together. I#M here to help in any way I can.

Figure 5.1 Tweet example #notmypresident (https://twitter.com/edgiesversion, 12.1. 2021)

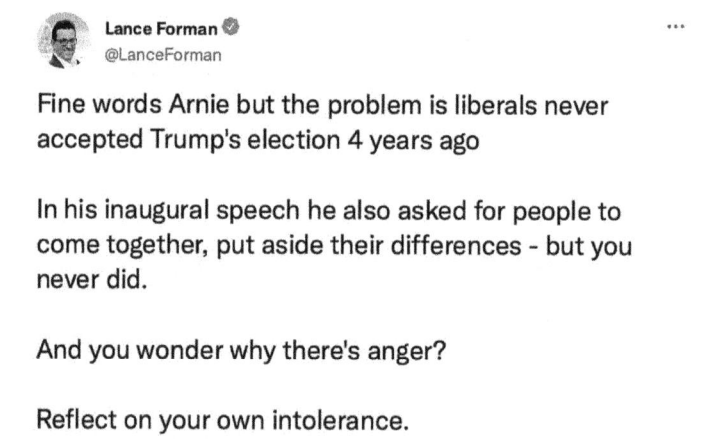

Lance Forman ✓
@LanceForman

Fine words Arnie but the problem is liberals never accepted Trump's election 4 years ago

In his inaugural speech he also asked for people to come together, put aside their differences - but you never did.

And you wonder why there's anger?

Reflect on your own intolerance.

12:00 PM · Jan 10, 2021

4.7K Retweets   **930** Quote Tweets   **7.2K** Likes

Figure 5.2 Tweet example #notmypresident (https://twitter.com/LanceForman, 10.1.2021)

hashtag #notmypresident the author explains why he thinks that this will not be possible. The tweet by @edgiesversion (Figure 5.1) with a retweet by @Schwarzenegger and demonstrates how hashtags in the narrow sense can construct micro-storylines that narratively frame individual posts.

The tweet by @LanceForman explains the problem that Trump's election was not accepted by liberals which gave birth to the hashtag #notmypresident, as Shaz explains (see Figure 5.2). Both tweets show first the origins of the hashtags, and second, how the meaning of the hashtag has undergone change. After the election in 2020 it is now used by Trump supporters to declare their rejection of the Democrat Joe Biden. @Sharona911

Sassy Sunny
@Sassy_Sunny

@Lanceforman @Schwarzenegger @NoraMulready
Exactly, we've been hearing #NotMyPresident for the past 4 years. Now they're wanting us to just shut up and accept Biden? No thanks.

12:00 PM · Jan 10, 2021

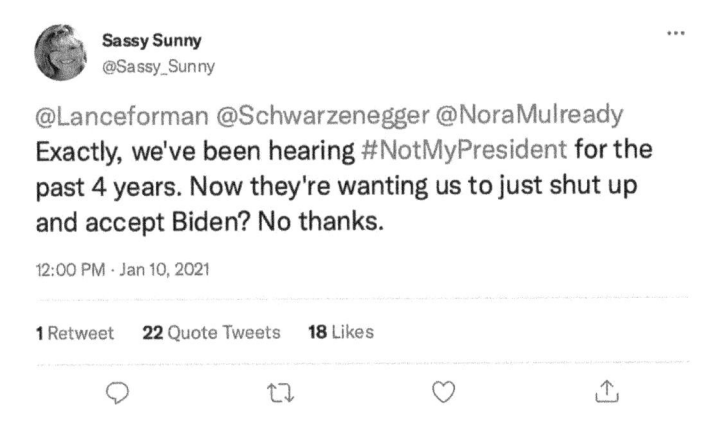

1 Retweet   22 Quote Tweets   18 Likes

Figure 5.3 Tweet example #notmypresident (https://twitter.com/LanceForman, 10.1.2021)

concedes that the creation of the hashtag #notmypresident was not very wise, yet she maintains that liberals did not ever want to question or even do harm to the democratic system.

Finally, the tweet by @Sassy_Sunny (Figure 5.3) reveals to what extent the hashtag #notmypresident led to the great divide in American society in pre- and even post-election times. Trump supporters appear to be deeply hurt after having to endure dozens of tweets containing that particular hashtag. The author's resistance is to accept the result of the election is pivotal as it sheds light on a deeply rooted distrust of the democratic system as such.

These examples demonstrate how different groups of people use the same hashtag for similar events with differing outcomes (elections in 2016 and 2020). Reading and interpreting hashtags as small texts in the broader sense can deepen insights into the interpretation of that event at a given point in time and in contemporary history. It is evident that hashtags create a learning opportunity as learners can trace the # throughout its use, exploring the ways it is used and the reasons and implications for its insertion in certain types of posts. In that sense hashtags afford starting points for participating in discourse that is relevant for understanding current Anglophone cultures and social movements.

How could tasks look like that exploit these potentials of the hashtag and the given tweets for language education? We would like to suggest a three step approach:

(1) Identify Trump supporters in the following tweets.
(2) Outline a short history of the hashtag #notmypresident. Who used the hashtag for which purpose?
(3) Create a new #hashtag and respond to Sassy Sunny's tweet.

The first task prompts learners to deal with the hashtag in a narrow sense. As they strive to understand the phrase and relate the word *president* to a concrete person (either Trump or Biden), learners exploit the

84 Born-Digital Texts in the English Language Classroom

> **Shaz** 🔥🔥🔥
> @sharona911
>
> @Lanceforman @Schwarzenegger @NoraMulready
> Liberals made a hashtag of #NotmyPresident (yes, very stupid. I agree). Yet we never saw the basic tenants of democracy or the election as fraudulent.
> And my friend is a big difference.
>
> 12:00 PM · Jan 10, 2021
>
> **35** Retweets   **6** Quote Tweets   **214** Likes

Figure 5.4 Tweet example #notmypresident

linguistic affordance of the #nmp. By inference learners can work out that for example @edgiesversion is a Trump supporter. Task 2 requires learners to compare the tweets and work out that the hashtag #notmypresident is still in use – by Democrats in the past (Figure 5.4) and more recently again by Trump supporters. Learners exploit the communicative affordance of the hashtag as they engage in meaningful receptive communicative action which results in reading comprehension and contributes to the development of reading skills. Task 3 exploits the discursive affordance of the hashtag and summons learners to join the debate and express their own views on the vulnerability of the election system and the stability of the democratic system as such, when people like @Sassy_Sunny frankly oppose the idea of accepting the president-elect.

5.6 Methodological Considerations for Teaching Hashtags

By referring to a minimal definition of text, we suggest that hashtags serve to be treated as texts in language education. Still, the nature of hashtags as small texts requires a high amount of didactic effort to make them accessible to learners and work towards developing learners' foreign language discourse skills. Even though foreign language learners may look at hashtags as a more accessible kind of text due to their mere length, the overall comprehension of the hashtag in its given social context still poses challenges. The elliptic structure requires more intense inference; situating the hashtag in its wider social context may require elaboration of key concepts and direct instruction about societal or political trends. Reducing the processing load, while attempting to achieve overall and detailed understanding of hashtags, is therefore a key didactic goal. On these grounds we argue that a well-structured methodological procedure, commonly suggested for dealing with reading comprehension texts (e.g.

Oakhill *et al.*, 2015: 11ff.), should also be employed when hashtags are used in the language classroom. In what follows we will outline what a pre-while-post procedure for reading hashtags can look like. For the sake of illustration we will refer back to the examples tweets with #nmp mentioned in the section above.

In a pre-reading task, the key concepts and schemata which are needed for comprehension should be activated. Introducing key concepts such as presidential elections, political groups and the function of an inaugural speech will prepare the ground for brainstorming and intelligent guessing, e.g. when learners are encouraged to make predictions about #notmypresident: Guess who uses and used this hashtag in the US? Why did US citizens make up this hashtag?

A while-reading task should prompt EFL learners to explore the language and linguistic patterns used in the hashtag in its broader sense. The goal is that learners engage with the specific lexical items (e.g. intolerance) and some of the grammatical structures they encounter in the hashtag (e.g. see sth. as). Furthermore, hashtags also afford opportunities to learn more about collocations as they often feature short phrases with a high density of colocates (e.g. put aside one's differences; bringing sth. back together). Learners could explore how the communicative appeal of hashtags is linguistically realized in the use of the imperative form (e.g. reflect on your own intolerance) or structures like *to want s.o. to do sth.* as in Sassy Sunny's tweet: 'Now they're wanting us to just shut up and accept Biden'. Another goal of the while-reading phase is for learners to reconstruct social discourse and the different roles of discourse participants, which is realized by the second prompt: 'Outline a short history of the hashtag #notmypresident. Who used the # for which purpose?'. It is through close reading and a comparative analysis of tweets that the place of hashtags in the larger social (and political) landscape can be reconstructed. The ability 'to identify individual discourse components and collective discourse objects in the communication at hand' (Hallet, 2009: 85) is therefore crucial for the development of learners' discourse skills. When exploiting the potential of Hashtags as small texts in language education, learners need to be set tasks that direct them to identify discourse components and discourse markers in specific tweets. It is only after this identification of key components that the reconstruction of hashtags and how they relate to lifeworld discourses is realised in a didactic sense.

In a post-reading task, learners can be prompted to take action and 'join the conversation' by both writing and speaking about hashtags. Learners can respond to a given tweet (here: Sassy Sunny's tweet) by using the hashtag at stake. More advanced learners may also create new hashtags when responding to a tweet. A prerequisite for responding to hashtags is that learners recognize distinct discourse markers and specific linguistic means (lexical items; phrases; collocations). On the basis of their understanding of the linguistic affordances of hashtags, 'they relate them to lifeworld discourses and participate in these discourses with their own perspectives and views' (Hallet, 2009: 85). Such productive tasks realise a product- and author-based approach and strengthen learners' agency as language users and discourse participants in a communicative classroom.

5.7 Conclusion

In the context of English language education, hashtags offer a range of affordances and, thus, can be viewed as a valuable addition to the current canon of digital texts which the *Companion Volume* to the *CEFR* addresses in the scales for online conversation and discussion. The example presented in this chapter also illustrates that the reception and production of hashtags cannot be captured 'in traditional competence scales focusing on the individual's behavior in speech or writing' (Council of Europe, 2018: 96).

They do not only allow learners to gain insights into lexical and grammatical patterns of the English language, but also provide opportunities for meaningful communication and the development of communicative competences in the classroom. In addition, they can raise learners' awareness of digital discourse patterns and the representation of cultural and societal trends in social media. The contribution of hashtags to higher level discourse skills is reflected in the level descriptions of B1. At this level learners should be able to 'engage in real-time online exchanges with more than one participant, recognizing the communicative intentions of each contributor' (Council of Europe, 2018: 97). At B2+ learners can link their contributions to previous posts in the thread and can thus understand cultural implications (Council of Europe, 2018: 97).

Once learners 'join the debate', hashtags serve as a stimulus for developing EFL learners' discourse abilities, as they become an invitation for participation in discourse communities. As such, in both a narrow and a broader sense, hashtags are dynamic small texts that 'can be tapped for deep, reflective engagement at all levels of language learning' (Sykes, 2019: 130).

And yet, the present chapter is only a first glimpse into the potential hashtags might unfold as digital texts in the EFL classroom. Aspects such as the selection and use of hashtags are in need of further exploration. While this chapter provides insights into some theoretical foundations, it only briefly touches upon the more practical issues of task design and the different types of methods and activities that might foster the development of discourse competence (cf. Hallet, 2009). The paper's theoretical insights may become a foundation for further empirical research on the design process of materials with hashtags. Furthermore, future studies may also examine how learning materials based on hashtags are used by learners in the classroom. In summary, the following questions may give direction to future research about hashtags:

- Identifying hashtags and their discursive affordances: Can learners identify hashtags and related tweets on their own in social media platforms? What kind of instruction and guidance do learners need? What does a more structured approach for intermediate learners look like that will enable them to exploit hashtags in all their richness?
- Materials design: A guided exploration of hashtags requires well-structured materials and prompts. Which principles of materials design guide the production of materials that contain hashtags as small texts? How can experienced teachers and material writers be trained to produce these kinds of materials?
- Reading skills for hashtags: How does reading hashtags in online communication differ from reading ordinary texts? Which strategies do learners need to fully explore the cultural implications and re-interpretations of hashtags?

References

Bal, M. (2002) *Travelling Concepts in the Humanities: A Rough Guide*. University of Toronto Press.

Brinker, K., Cölfen H. and Pappert S. (2018) *Linguistische Textanalyse: Eine Einführung in Grundbegriffe und Methoden* (9th edn). Erich Schmidt Verlag.

Council of Europe (2018) *Common European Framework of Reference for Languages: Learning, Teaching, Assessment. Companion Volume with new Descriptors*. Council of Europe.

Diehr, B. and Frisch, S. (2008) *Mark Their Words: Sprechleistungen im Englischuntericht der Grundschule fördern und beurteilen*. Westermann.

Goh, C.C.M. and Burns, A. (2012) *Teaching Speaking: A Holistic Approach*. Cambridge University Press.

Göpferich, S. (1995) *Textsorten in Naturwissenschaften und Technik. Pragmatische Typologie – Kontrastierung – Translation*. Narr.

Hausendorf, H. (2009) Kleine Texte: Über Randerscheinungen von Textualität. *Germanistik in der Schweiz: Online-Zeitschrift der SAGG* 6, 5–19.

Hallet, W. (2009) Romanlektüren und Kompetenzentwicklung: Vom narrativen Diskurs zur Diskursfähigkeit. In W. Hallet and A. Nünning (eds) *Romandidaktik. Theoretische Grundlagen, Methoden, Lektüreanregungen* (pp. 73–88). Wissenschaftlicher Verlag Trier

Hutz, M. (2012) Storing words in the mind: The mental lexicon and vocabulary learning. In M. Eisenmann and T. Summer (eds) *Basic Issues in EFL Teaching and Learning* (pp. 105–117). Winter.

Jones, R.D. (2018) *Developing Video Game Literacy in the EFL Classroom: A Qualitative Analysis of 10th Grade Classroom Game Discourse*. Narr.

Kersten, S. and Lotze, N. (2013) Microblogs global: Englisch. In T. Siever and P. Schlobinski (eds) *Microblogs Global: Eine Internationale Studie zu Twitter & Co. aus der Perspektive von zehn Sprachen und elf Ländern* (pp. 75–112). Peter Lang Edition.

Kirchhoff, P. (2019) Your story in 280 characters max. Twitter Fiction für das kreative Schreiben nutzen. *Der fremdsprachliche Unterricht Englisch* 53 (160), 40–45.

Kordt, B. (2018) Herausforderungen und Chancen eines affordanztheoretischen Ansatzes in der Fremdsprachenforschung mit Beispielen aus einer Studie zur Umsetzung von EuroComGerm in der Schule. *Zeitschrift für Fremdsprachenforschung* 29 (2), 147–168.

La Rocca, G. (2020) Possible selves of a hashtag: Moving from the theory of speech acts to cultural objects to interpret hashtags. *International Journal of Sociology and Anthropology* 12 (1), 1–9.

Martens, G. (1982) Was ist ein Text? Ansätze zur Bestimmung eines Leitbegriffs der Textphilologie. *Poetica - Zeitschrift für Sprach- und Literaturwissenschaft* 21, 1–25.

Matz, F. (2020) Taking a stance: The role of critical literacies in learning with literature in a world at risk. In D. Gerlach (ed.) *Kritische Fremdsprachendidaktik* (pp. 53–67). Narr.

Oakhill, J., Cain, K. and Elbro, C. (2015) *Understanding and Teaching Reading Comprehension*. Routledge.

Scrivener, J. (2010) *Teaching English Grammar: What to Teach and How to Teach It*. MacMillan.

Sykes, J.M. (2019) Emergent digital discourses: What can we learn from hashtags and digital games to expand learners' second language repertoire? *Annual Review of Applied Linguistics* 39, 128–145.

Thornbury, S. (2002) *How to Teach Vocabulary*. Pearson.

Watkins, J. and Wilkins, M. (2011) Using YouTube in the EFL classroom. *Language Education in Asia* 2 (1), 113–119.

6 Towards a Critical Digital Literacy Framework: Exploring the Impact of Algorithms in the Creation of Filter Bubbles on Instagram

Peter Schildhauer and Katharina Kemper

6.1 Introduction

At the time of writing this chapter, Instagram is one of the most popular social networking sites on a global scale, and especially attracts adolescents and young adults (Statista, 2021a). In secondary school classrooms in Germany, for example, teachers can expect that between 54% and 83% of their students use Instagram at least several times a week (mpfs, 2020: 41). Consequently, the centerpiece of Instagram, the *feed*, has become an integral part of the digital landscape. Social media feeds in general display a continuous stream of posts and comments and are born-digital texts in line with the overall topic of this collected volume (Becker *et al.*, this volume). In particular, social media feeds are based on the three key aspects that Stalder (2017) identifies as characteristics of digital culture:

- Referentiality: In a digital culture, cross-references are built between cultural artifacts by curating, mixing and remixing existing content. That is essentially what we can observe on social media feeds when users like, share and modify content.
- Community: Digital culture is marked by the emergence of participant networks around certain interests such as topics, professions or political action (see e.g. Del Vicario *et al.*, 2016). A user's network is decisive for which content appears on a user's feed as it is compiled from their recent contributions.

- Algorithmicity: In creating a user's social media feed, platforms employ algorithms that are supposed to personalize a user's experience. These algorithms draw on a user's previous interactional behavior (liking, sharing, following, time spent on a certain post etc.; Instagram, 2020; Mahapatra, 2020) and have two points of attack: first, they are employed to suggest potential new accounts a user could follow, and second, they rank the content to be displayed on the feed according to its (assessed) relevance to a user. Therefore, algorithms influence what the social media feed looks like for each individual user in two ways: directly, via the display of posts, and indirectly, via suggestions of accounts to follow, whose content will be primarily displayed on the feed.

It is particularly the feature of algorithmicity that led some scholars to alert us to potential dangers of social media feeds (amongst others): Pariser (2011, 2012, 2015) argues that algorithms may lead to the emergence of so-called filter bubbles in which users encounter items that are in line with their world views and therefore confirm rather than challenge views already held. The ultimate result might be polarization rather than exchange across diverse groups (Beam et al., 2018a).

Considering these potential dangers, we argue that any language classroom should foster critical digital literacy: students should be made aware of the potential impact of algorithms on their social media feeds and, hence, their world views. What is more, students should be enabled to assume agency and burst the (potential) bubble. In what follows, we therefore first review the connected concepts *filter bubble* and *echo chamber* with a particular focus on the potential impact recommendation algorithms on social media may have in their emergence (6.2.2). On this basis, we argue that learners need to be equipped with critical digital literacy and suggest an initial corresponding framework (6.3.1). In order to foster this competence, we propose an experimental approach that allows students to experience how Instagram's recommendation algorithm may lead users into a filter bubble. We exemplify this approach with a focus on the US presidential election 2020 (6.3.2) and use first insights from classroom practice to fine-tune our critical digital literacy framework (6.3.3) before transferring our insights into an exemplary teaching concept (6.3.4). Finally, we provide an outlook on future research (6.4).

6.2 Filter Bubbles

6.2.1 Towards a working definition

The terms *filter bubble* and *echo chamber* have developed into buzzwords, with the effect that they are sometimes used without being properly defined (Bruns, 2019). For that reason, we disentangle the various different uses of the terms first in order to develop a working definition for the present chapter. The conceptualizations we identified roughly relate to two conceptual dimensions:

- Perspective: individual user vs. networked community;
- Agency: technology vs. human.

An account of the filter bubble that strongly relates to the perspective of the individual user is Pariser's. He defines the filter bubble as 'the unique universe of information' (Pariser, 2011: 9) which personalized algorithms create for us. These algorithms work invisibly in the background and can lead to the fact that users mainly encounter information that 'supports what they already believe' (Pariser, 2015). This, in turn, can foster 'self-segregation into groups of like-minded people' (Sunstein, 2017: 9), making constructive dialogue more difficult. On the agency dimension, Pariser stresses the impact of technology (e.g. algorithms on social network sites) in creating filter bubbles. In an attempt to re-equip users with agency, Pariser (2011, 2015) suggests ways of using personalizing algorithms productively.

While Pariser's view has found support (e.g. Bozdag, 2013; Bozdag & van den Hoven, 2015; Mehlhose *et al.*, 2021), it has also been criticized. Bruns (2019: 121) argues that in 'a hyperconnected yet deeply polarized world, the most important filter remains in our heads, not in our networks'. Besides questioning the existence of filter bubbles and allocating agency to humans (instead of algorithms), Bruns also represents the networked community perspective. This is most visible in his attempt to define the concepts filter bubble and echo chamber: 'An echo chamber comes into being when a group of participants choose to preferentially *connect* with each other, to the exclusion of outsiders [...]. A filter bubble emerges when a group of participants, independent of the underlying connections with others, choose to preferentially *communicate* with each other, to the exclusion of outsiders' (Bruns, 2019: 29). Thus, echo chambers are concerned with network structures on social network sites, while the term *filter bubble* denotes a specific kind of information flow within groups. Bruns argues that neither concept exists in its pure form and that both are, thus, scalar phenomena.

Even though Bruns's and Pariser's accounts focus on different aspects of the dimensions mentioned above, they can be linked theoretically: if algorithms aiming at personalization suggest whom to follow on a social network site on the basis of a similarity principle (Masrour *et al.*, 2020), following these recommendations can lead to a network of like-minded users (see also Bruns, 2019, suggesting the same mechanism). As users prefer content that is in line with their own belief system (e.g. Del Vicario *et al.*, 2016; Iyengar & Hahn, 2009), this may increase the likelihood of encountering confirmatory content on the social media feed.

It is this view of the concept *filter bubble* which we would like to adopt in the present chapter. It highlights the perspective and agency of the individual user while at the same time acknowledging the *potential* impact algorithms may have indirectly via suggestions on whom to follow. From an individual user's perspective, it is the content encountered on a social media feed that matters, rather than the underlying network responsible for circulating it. Therefore, we discard the concept *echo chamber* for the purposes of this chapter. We choose this focus on the individual user, their view on the social media feed and their agency in interacting with the algorithm because this perspective is most relevant to the educational approach we suggest below.

6.2.2 Filter bubbles on social network sites – What research tells us

Over the last decade, researchers have debated whether filter bubbles actually exist. The evidence is mixed and also depends on which of the perspectives outlined in 6.2.1 are highlighted by a specific study. Research focusing on the networked community similar to Bruns (2019) is often based on big data network analyses of a certain sphere on a social networking site. These studies detect clusters that look like echo chambers, but that are often also interlinked, i.e. no sealed enclaves (e.g. Bruns *et al.*, 2017; Boy & Uitermark, 2020). The perspective of individual users is often captured by survey studies which make respondents self-report on the diversity of their information diet (e.g. Beam *et al.*, 2018a, 2018b; Brundidge, 2010; Dubois & Blank, 2018; Parmelee & Roman, 2020). These studies:

- acknowledge the possibility of selective exposure to content that confirms a user's beliefs (e.g. Brundidge, 2010);
- caution us not to overestimate the impact of filter bubbles. However, all of these studies are based on the 'ignorability assumption' (Hill *et al.*, 2007) that people who do not take (or opt out of) the surveys behave the same way as those who do participate. Consequently, actual filter bubble effects may be higher than reported by the particular respondents;
- find filter bubble effects for subsets of their population, especially Republicans in the US (Parmelee & Roman, 2020) or users with a low interest in politics and news diversity (Dubois & Blank, 2018).

Research related to the individual perspective also employs experiments that test the outcomes of self-programmed algorithms (for Instagram: Mehlhose *et al.*, 2021) or to overcome filter bubble effects (Masrour *et al.*, 2020). This research reveals that recommendation algorithms have the potential to support the formation of filter bubbles.

To sum up: first, the filter bubble is not only a theoretical concept but has empirical support. Second, filter bubbles do not appear to be a phenomenon as absolute and inescapable as Pariser initially portrayed them. The studies show that users find ways to engage with a healthy, diverse information diet – exploiting the affordances of social media sites in a productive way (e.g. Beam *et al.*, 2018b). Social networking sites provide a set of tools that influence, but do not *determine* how we use them. Third, the highest risk for being trapped in a filter bubble exists for users with little interest in information diversity in the first place (Dubois & Blank, 2018). These users are particularly relevant for an educational approach: they, too, are or have once been students in language classes, whose educational task it is to prepare students for 'democratic citizenship' (Council of Europe, 2001: 3), which includes a critical understanding of digital media mechanisms (Council of Europe, 2013: 56). The importance of this awareness is even acknowledged by opponents of the filter bubble concept (Dubois & Blank, 2018; Bruns, 2019).

6.3 An Experimental Approach to Filter Bubbles for the English Language Classroom

6.3.1 Towards a critical digital literacy framework

Algorithms never start with a clean, unbiased sheet of information (Carrington, 2018: 69–70). They are 'designed to function according to particular powerful ways of perceiving the world, political assumptions and the codes of conduct to which their designers and promoters have subscribed' (Williamson, 2017: 59), which may, essentially, result in biased output (Sandvig *et al.*, 2016). For example, Instagram's recommendation algorithm is designed according to the economic interest of keeping users on the platform as long as possible in order for them to view (and click on) an abundance of ads. This goal is pursued by creating a social media feed that caters to their interests (Mahapatra, 2020): the algorithm aims at a balance between similarity to content previously liked and shared by a user, as well as slight difference to previous content in order to avoid boredom by arousing curiosity (Meta, 2022).

In line with actor-network theory (Leander & Burriss, 2020; Markham, 2013; Tufekci, 2015), we can therefore view algorithms as (co-)authors of the social media feed, as 'computational agents that are not alive, but that act with agency in the world' (Tufekci, 2015: 207). This underlines the need to make visible the ways in which they contribute to the social media feed and, ultimately, to shaping our world views (Williamson, 2017: 61).

Such a critical approach to texts as non-neutral products which need to be deconstructed is close to what critical literacy postulates, which is often defined as the 'use of the technologies of print and other media of communication to analyze, critique, and transform the norms, rule systems, and practices governing the social fields of institutions and everyday life' (Luke, 2014: 21). Following this train of thought, Leander and Burriss (2020) suggest extending the traditional toolbox of critical literacy to a critical *digital* literacy which explicitly takes into account the fact that digital texts are co-created by non-human agents. Specifically, they propose moving from 'traditional' critical literacy questions such as 'Who wrote the text and what was their motivation? How do power and privilege operate in the text?' to questions such as: 'Where can you identify the influence of computational agents in the composition and/or distribution of the text? Who built the computational agent(s) and how do they operate?' (Leander & Burriss, 2020: 1273). With a focus on our specific topic at hand, we suggest the following questions as a starting point, which we will fine-tune in the following sections:

(1) In what way may algorithms play a role in generating the Instagram feed and where/how can we identify this influence?
(2) What impact may this potentially have on the users' perception of specific topics and issues?
(3) How could we take action to reduce the impact of algorithms on the users' views of a specific topic/issue?

(1) and (2) move from text analysis to reflecting the potential impact on others', and personal, worldviews. (3) does justice to the transformative stance taken by critical literacy (see also Gerlach, 2020). In sum, these questions constitute a framework for approaching the algorithmicity of social media feeds, which promises to promote critical digital literacy as the 'ability to understand how this system works and how to formulate creative (and often collective) strategies to change it' (Jones & Hafner, 2021: 154).

With Jones (2021), we assume that opening the black box and viewing the algorithm as code is not likely to lead learners to the deeper insights targeted by the framework. The most promising way of uncovering the workings of the algorithm is by devoting attention to and deconstructing the product it creates, the social media feed (Jones & Hafner, 2021), as a born-digital text. We therefore propose that learners need to be given the opportunity of experiencing and reflecting on the effects of the algorithm on us – and our agency in interaction with the algorithm.

6.3.2 An experiment: Instagram and the 2020 US presidential election

In order to make the potential influence of algorithms on Instagram's feed transparent, the experimental setup exploits the first point of attack outlined above, i.e. the recommendation of potential accounts to follow, which then shapes the content a user will encounter on the news feed. We developed the following procedure:

(1) At least one 'fresh' Instagram account is created. In doing so, it is essential that every attempt of the software to access existing accounts, contacts and location information is denied. This creates a 'cold start

problem' (Mahapatra, 2020), in which the input of previous interactional data is missing that recommendation algorithms need.
(2) A prominent Instagram account is located and followed; ideally this account expresses a strong political and/or ideological position and exhibits an extended network of further accounts.
(3) This sets the recommendation algorithm in motion: it generates suggestions for further accounts to follow by exploring all accounts which the chosen account follows, and the accounts which these in turn follow in a snowball system (Mahapatra, 2020). All suggested accounts are followed.
(4) The Instagram feed is now generated from this experimental network. Instagram claims that users see everything posted by the accounts they follow, but not in chronological order. The algorithm that displays posts on the Instagram feed uses a complex ranking system based on recency, previous likes and interaction history (Instagram, 2020).
(5) The resulting feed can be explored.

Ideally, the steps (1) to (5) are completed twice, to create *two* experimental accounts which take politically/ideologically contrasting accounts as their individual starting points. This would allow the influence of the recommendation algorithm to be highlighted by comparing the resulting Instagram feeds.

We tested this setup in the context of the 2020 US presidential election. We chose this context because during major elections, processes of opinion formation become particularly salient. This is especially true for the US context with its two-party system, which makes encounters with partisan content more likely. This additional amplification effect is desirable in the light of the goal of making students experience what impact recommendation algorithms could potentially have.

We set up two Instagram accounts with the aim of simulating what the Instagram feed would look like if supporters of either presidential candidate allowed the Instagram algorithm to take the lead when building their network. In step (2), therefore, we actively searched for and followed the account of the respective presidential candidate (i.e. Donald Trump vs. Joe Biden). In step (3), Instagram presented a list of suggestions of accounts to follow. Among these were members of the Trump family, Mike Pence, Students4Trump, FoxNews etc., vs. Jill Biden, Kamala Harris, Barack Obama, CNN and so on. As a result, we created two networks of 75 accounts each.

In (4) we explored the accounts by drawing on the instruments provided by Multimodal Critical Discourse Analysis (Mayr, 2016). Both feeds were remarkably homogeneous regarding the political views expressed by the accounts. The experimental Trump supporter was confronted with many posts related to the election, and in particular (from 4 November onwards) regarding election fraud. Many posts praised Trump's virtues, while Biden was often portrayed as senile and corrupt. The feed of the experimental Biden supporter displayed similar topics and strategies, e.g. pointing out Trump's flaws and displaying the support Biden gained all over the country.

We also detected striking differences. The topic of Covid-19, for instance, hardly played a role on the Trump feed (and was downgraded in its significance), while it featured prominently on the Biden feed, mainly in relation to its dangers, rising case numbers and the resulting need to wear masks. The Biden feed also addressed aspects related broadly to the topics of diversity/social justice, such as anti-semitism, the first black US cardinal and police violence against black Americans. In relation to this topical field, one video stood out as it appeared on both feeds. The framing, however, was different in each case: the material shows a shooting scene in which several (white) police officers shoot a black man who apparently waves a knife. On the Biden feed, the footage was provided by the CNN account and part of the caption read as follows:

Example 1: CNN, 27 October 2020
Police in Philadelphia shot and killed a Black man waving a knife on the street plunging the city into protests that resulted in injuries to 30 officers as the police commissioner quickly acknowledged the encounter 'raises many questions' [...]

The written part of the post focuses on the proportionality of shooting a man 'waving' a knife and the resulting protests. By use of the active voice, the police officers are portrayed as agents of the shooting. The corresponding post on the Trump feed downplays the officers' agency by using the passive voice, justifies fatal violence against what is framed as an attack and anticipates unjustified protests:

Example 2: anonymized account, 27 October 2020
Walter Wallace jr was shot dead by the police in Philadelphia. This was very obviously deserved considering he was charging the police with a knife. But of course people hear 'black man killed by police' then they flock to the streets to protests ☺

In the different framings that become apparent, we can observe different ideologies at work, namely one (on the Biden feed) sympathizing with the Black Lives Matter movement, and another (on the Trump feed) which is skeptical or even opposed to this movement. Similar observations hold true for the Covid-19 examples and others.

This means that the experiment offers a glimpse at two different discourse spheres in which real world social practices are recontextualized in different ways or are deemed differently relevant (while climate change does not appear in the Republican sphere, gun laws do not appear on the Democratic feed). From the perspective of our experimental users, we created two filter bubbles: two very consistent spheres in which confirmatory content circulated, similar to Pariser's predictions.

At the same time, the posts related to political topics were not the only ones presented on the two Instagram feeds. For instance, the Trump feed displayed a considerable number of sports-related posts (e.g. by @sportscenter and @bleacherreport); around Christmas 2020 we encountered many seasonal contributions on both feeds – often without political references. Despite the partisan approach taken when setting up the two accounts, both feeds also displayed non-partisan posts and some degree of variation. This observation aligns with the research reviewed in Section 6.2 that characterizes filter bubbles as *scalar* phenomena. In other words: though experimental in its setup, our approach produces results predictable from current research and, therefore, can serve as a basis to make students experience the emergence of filter bubbles first hand.

6.3.3 First experiences from the classroom: The third-person effect

For a first trial, the two Instagram feeds created during the experiment were embedded within one EFL lesson of a year 12 class. In order to give the students a first-hand experience of the algorithms at work, they were given a 15-minute time frame to explore the accounts. In the beginning, the students were informed about the two accounts originating from a research project. The students were then asked to describe the differences between the two accounts. This task was meant to elicit the students' reactions to the accounts. The students were further asked to make guesses on the aim of the research project and to give ideas about how the accounts could have been created. These tasks were aimed at starting the conversation about algorithms and possible filter bubble effects as well as to collect the students' existing knowledge.

The most prominent insight from that initial trial is a potential discrepancy between what students know about algorithms and how they experience them. The students were aware of the fact that the Trump feed was a result of recommendation algorithms. Their emotional reactions resulted from a strong discrepancy between their own world views and the ones constructed by the experimental feed. Generally, the students appeared to be aware of the existence of algorithms that curate social media feeds. However, when it comes to their assessment of the influence of algorithms, a bias occurred. They seemed to rate the influence of algorithms on their own social media feeds lower than on those of persons with contradicting world views.

This observation coincides with the third-person effect, people's tendency 'to overestimate the influence that mass communications have on the attitudes and behavior of others' and vice versa, underestimate this influence on themselves (Davison, 1983: 3). It was found in various contexts, e.g. news coverage, advertisements, the influence of violent media and the perceived effects of political campaigns (Conners, 2005: 5). Later studies detected third-person effects in the perception of fake news on social media (Chung & Kim, 2021; Lee, 2021).

Consequently, the students' responses to algorithm-supported filter bubbles may also emerge from third-person effects. As these perception phenomena (by their nature) go unnoticed, they could possibly stand in the way of acquiring critical digital literacy as defined above. It may therefore be useful to approach the reflection in two steps. In our framework, we already stated that students should reflect on: 'what impact may algorithms potentially have on my own perception of a certain topic?'. This question can lead to increased knowledge about the general potential impact of algorithms. In order to encourage students to overcome the third-person effect by reflecting on their own estimation of the algorithms' impact on themselves, we suggest asking 'how do I assess the actual

Table 6.1 Phases, goals and critical digital literacy foundation of the teaching unit

Phase	Teaching Goals	Questions from CDL Framework
Phase 1: Understand	The students participate in discourses by **conducting** an experiment on the workings of algorithms on social media platforms (Instagram) and **analyzing** and **comparing** the resulting 'Republican' and 'Democratic' Instagram feeds.	In what way may algorithms play a role in generating the Instagram feed and where/how can we identify this influence?
Phase 2: Reflect	The students **demonstrate awareness** of biases in their perception by pointing them out, using specific examples. They **discuss** their perception of the effects of algorithms on themselves, persons close to them (family, friends) and third persons.	What impact may this potentially have on other users', but also my own perception of specific topics and issues? How do I assess the actual impact of algorithms on my perception of a certain topic? In what way does my perception of the effects of the algorithms lead me to behave in a certain way – which is possibly less careful than I should be?
Phase 3: Connect	The students **collect** ways of taking action to reduce the impact of algorithms on the individual. They do so by drawing on their insights from the phases 1 and 2 as well as by consulting adequate sources (e.g. Eli Pariser's suggestions on how to use personalization algorithms productively). The students take action and participate in discourses by **creating** products of their choice (flyers, websites, desktop backgrounds) which inform a specific audience (e.g. peers, younger students).	How could I/we take action to reduce the impact of algorithms on user's/our/my own views of a specific topic/issue such as the presidential election?

impact of algorithms on my perception of a certain topic?' as well as 'in what way does my perception of the effects of algorithms lead me to behave in a certain way – which is possibly less careful than I should be?'. This elaborate reflection process may highlight the individual's agency in the interaction with algorithms as underlined in 6.2.1 above. It needs to be scaffolded well by the instructor, who in turn is supported by suitable material. The next section presents some suggestions.

6.3.4 Fostering critical digital literacy – An exemplary teaching concept

In what follows, we suggest a tentative teaching concept aimed at advanced learners of English. In keeping with the experiment (6.3.2) and the initial trial, the material has been designed surrounding the topic of US politics. Following our critical digital literacy (CDL) framework (6.3.1) and its enhancement due to insights from practice (6.3.3), the teaching concept is structured in three phases as summarized in Table 6.1.

During the first phase, *understand*, the students get acquainted with discourses surrounding algorithms on social media and engage with social media feeds in classroom discussions. Students are active participants from the beginning (Hallet, 2007: 32) and conduct a version of the experiment outlined in section 6.3.2 themselves. They set up and carry out a downscaled version during which they are asked to follow roughly 10 accounts (as compared to the 75 accounts we followed during the experiment). We recommend this focused version because it keeps the main principles of the experiment intact but should result in more concise social media feeds that lend themselves best for further discussion in class. By engaging with and experiencing the workings of algorithms on social media in the conduct of the experiment, the students receive agency and engage in real-life discourses (see Figure 6.1 for an example).

The second phase, *reflect*, provides insights into the third-person effect. In the light of our discussion above (6.3.3), we suggest using questions that move gradually from awareness of filter bubbles to the students' families and friends and lastly towards their own judgments:

(1) How easily do you think people believe fake news on social media? To what degree can algorithms push political polarization?
(2) How easily do you think your family and friends are influenced by filter bubbles?
(3) What about you? How easily are you influenced by algorithms?

In order to include the perspective of families and friends, students could conduct interviews with them on their respective views regarding the influence of algorithms on their own/others' world views. Potentially, the reflection phase could be framed by using a scale on which the learners rate how influenced they perceived themselves to be. This scale could be

conducting the experiment

Algorithms have an influence on what our social media feeds look like. But how big exactly is this influence of algorithms? How much do they shift our social media feeds into specific directions and influence us? To find out, we will focus on the effects of algorithms. You will conduct a black box experiment:

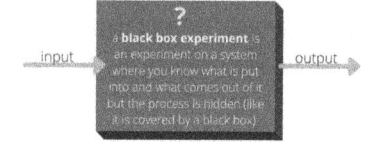

input → a black box experiment is an experiment on a system where you know what is put into and what comes out of it but the process is hidden (like it is covered by a black box) → output

How to set up the experiment:
For the following steps, use school devices only and make sure you don't disclose any personal information and don't use personal e-mail addresses.

1. Create a new Instagram account. As your first input, start following, for example, Alexandria Ocasio-Cortez @aoc. Now, follow all accounts that Instagram suggests.
2. Create another new Instagram account. As your first input for this account, start following an account that opposes your input in 1., for example, Ted Cruz @sentedcruz. Now, follow all accounts that Instagram suggests.
3. For both accounts, keep refreshing and monitoring the Instagram feed for a week or so. Pay special attention to posts that deal with the same issues and bookmark them.

analysing the experiment

Think- Phase:
On your own, begin to analyse the results of your experiment. Keep in mind to fact-check regularly. This ensures that you can identify polarising messages and fake news and are able to engage with the content you encounter in a critical manner.

1. Jot down some general observations - what do you find striking when looking at the two Insta-feeds?
2. Select one post from each feed. Ideally, try to find posts that deal with a similar topic.
   a. Describe the image: What is depicted? Which layout is used?
   b. Describe the caption: What message is conveyed? How do message and image link?
   c. Describe further details: What hashtags are used?

Pair-Phase:
With a partner, compare your observations from the think-phase and answer the following questions.

1. To what extent do the Instagram feeds of your two fictional people differ?
2. To what extent do they deal with similar topics?
3. What messages are transmitted?
4. What are the characteristics of a typical Instagram post?

Share-Phase:
Collect your results and prepare to present them to the rest of the class.

Figure 6.1 Instruction sheet for students – Setting up the experiment

used once before conducting the experiment and a second time to conclude the reflection phase (Figure 6.2).

Using this scale can also trigger reflection on the questions 'how do I assess the actual impact of algorithms on my perception of a certain topic (here: the US presidential election)?' and 'in what way does my perception of the effects of the algorithms lead me to behave in a certain (maybe less careful) way – which is possibly less careful than I should be?'.

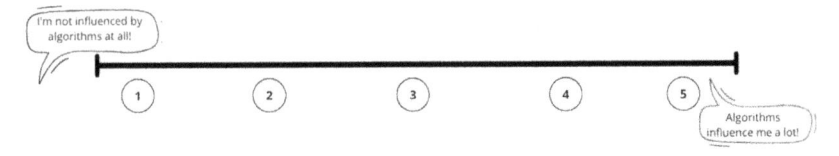

Figure 6.2 Reflection scale

connect

Now it is time for the last phase of our topic where you get to pass on what you have learned! At our school, we want to create more digital awareness and knowing how algorithms on social media work as well as how they affect us is part of that. You can now create material to inform other students from our school. You get to decide how you want to inform the other students:

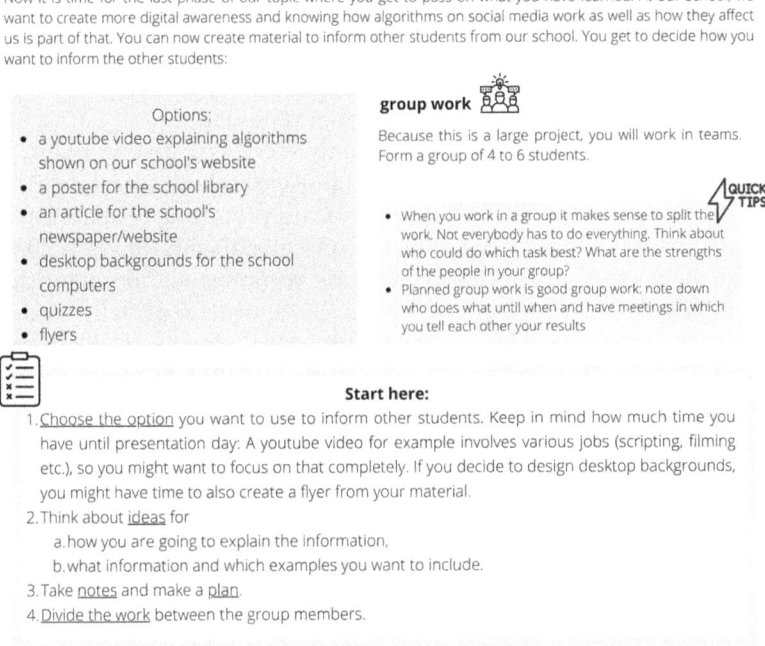

Options:
- a youtube video explaining algorithms shown on our school's website
- a poster for the school library
- an article for the school's newspaper/website
- desktop backgrounds for the school computers
- quizzes
- flyers

group work

Because this is a large project, you will work in teams. Form a group of 4 to 6 students.

QUICK TIPS
- When you work in a group it makes sense to split the work. Not everybody has to do everything. Think about who could do which task best? What are the strengths of the people in your group?
- Planned group work is good group work: note down who does what untill when and have meetings in which you tell each other your results

Start here:
1. Choose the option you want to use to inform other students. Keep in mind how much time you have until presentation day: A youtube video for example involves various jobs (scripting, filming etc.), so you might want to focus on that completely. If you decide to design desktop backgrounds, you might have time to also create a flyer from your material.
2. Think about ideas for
   a. how you are going to explain the information,
   b. what information and which examples you want to include.
3. Take notes and make a plan.
4. Divide the work between the group members.

Figure 6.3 Connecting insights – Re-engaging with discourses

During the third phase, the students *connect* their acquired content knowledge, the insights from the discussions and reflections. First, they consider ways to reduce the impact of (recommendation) algorithms on individual users. Second, they create a product that builds a bridge from discourses inside the classroom to real-life discourses (Figure 6.3).

We suggest (multimodal) texts that can be used to educate, for example, younger students of the school about the workings of algorithms on social media platforms. It is a real-life goal that can be easily implemented at any school because there are spaces where these informational products could be hung or presented (e.g. the library, in some schools a computer room, on tablets or other devices). In creating these products, students integrate their insights about the topic, and train their media skills as well as their language skills by presenting it appropriately. At the same time, it allows students to operate at a language level they consider appropriate as they can, for example, decide to include visuals wherever they deem necessary.

6.4 Questions for Further Research

The present chapter opens numerous avenues for further research. First, we exemplified our experimental approach by using the setting of the US presidential election. It may be worthwhile exploring to what extent the approach also works for other discourses and which pedagogical potentials and challenges arise. Our own work on the climate change discourse (Kemper & Schildhauer, 2022) indicates that this transfer is possible and that more conceptual research is needed.

Second, while Instagram can certainly serve as a case in point, the dynamics of the wider social media landscape should be taken into account. In particular, TikTok appears to be a promising field for further research: it is rapidly gaining popularity on a global scale (Statista, 2021b) and its mechanism also draws heavily on recommendation algorithms (e.g. Bandy & Diakpoulos, 2020). TikTok appeals especially to users younger than the typical Instagram audience: in Germany, the platform is most popular with users aged 12–13 (mpfs, 2020). Consequently, it is imperative to develop concepts for fostering critical digital literacy targeted at younger learners than the fairly advanced students we had in mind in this chapter.

Third, our contribution is based on first classroom trials, from which we developed refined suggestions for the critical digital literacy framework. Future research should take this concept back to the classroom to investigate its implementation and refine it further on this basis. In the light of the challenges we outlined above regarding the third-person effect, we can assume that a particularly sensitive form of teacher-student interaction may be needed to achieve these aims and that microanalysis of interaction sequences may establish what good practice may look like in that regard (Schildhauer *et al.*, in press).

6.5 Conclusions

In this chapter, we argue that algorithmicity is a key feature of the social media feed that makes it a truly born-digital text. We showed that this feature may lead to the emergence of filter bubbles with potential consequences on how users encounter content and form their world views. In order to address this educational issue, we took three interconnected steps:

(1) We suggested an experimental approach to exploring the role of algorithms in the creation of filter bubbles, using the example of the 2020 US presidential election. We argued that this allows students to experience the workings of recommendation algorithms rather than envision them from a description (or even from algorithm code) in an abstract way.
(2) We developed a critical digital literacy framework that takes the role of algorithms as co-authors of social media feeds into account.
(3) Based on first insights from classroom practice, this framework was developed further in order to account for the challenge of dealing with third-person effects and illustrated with specific task suggestions.

We consider this a first step towards critical digital literacy with a focus on the algorithmicity of (many) born-digital texts, a key feature of digital culture that opens exciting avenues for future conceptual work.

References

Bandy, J. and Diakopoulos, N. (2020) #TulsaFlop: A case study of algorithmically-influenced collective action on TikTok. See https://arxiv.org/pdf/2012.07716 (accessed December 2021).
Beam, M.A., Hutchens, M.J. and Hmielowski, J.D. (2018a) Facebook news and (de)polarization: Reinforcing spirals in the 2016 US election. *Information, Communication & Society* 21 (7), 940–958.
Beam, M.A., Child, J.T., Hutchens, M.J. and Hmielowski, J.D. (2018b) Context collapse and privacy management: Diversity in Facebook friends increases online news reading and sharing. *New Media & Society* 20 (7), 2296–2314.
Boy, J.D. and Uitermark, J. (2020) Lifestyle enclaves in the Instagram city? *Social Media + Society* 6 (3), 1–10.
Bozdag, E. (2013) Bias in algorithmic filtering and personalization. *Ethics Inf Technol* 15 (3), 209–227.
Bozdag, E. and Van den Hoven, J. (2015) Breaking the filter bubble: Democracy and design. *Ethics Inf Technol* 17 (4), 249–265.
Brundidge, J. (2010) Encountering 'difference' in the contemporary public sphere. The contribution of the internet to the heterogeneity of political discussion networks. *Journal of Communication* 60 (4), 680–700.
Bruns, A. (2019) *Are Filter Bubbles Real?* Polity.
Bruns, A., Moon, B., Münch, F. and Sadkowsky, T. (2017) The Australian twittersphere in 2016: Mapping the follower/followee network. *Social Media + Society* 3 (4), 1–15.
Carrington, V. (2018) The changing landscape of literacies. Big data and algorithms. *Digital Culture & Education* 10 (1), 67–76.
Chung, M. and Kim, N. (2021) When I learn the news is false: How fact-checking information stems the spread of fake news via third-person perception. *Human Communication Research* 47 (1), 1–24.
Conners, J.L. (2005) Understanding the third-person effect. *Communication Research Trends* 24 (2), 2–22.
Council of Europe (2001) *Common European Framework of Reference for Languages: Learning, Teaching, Assessment*. Council of Europe. See http://www.coe.int/t/dg4/linguistic/source/framework_en.pdf (accessed December 2021).
Council of Europe (2013) Reference framework of competences for democratic culture. See https://rm.coe.int/prems-008318-gbr-2508-reference-framework-of-competences-vol-1-8573-co/16807bc66c (accessed December 2021).

Davison, W. (1983) The third-person effect in communication. *The Public Opinion Quarterly* 47 (1), 1–15.
Del Vicario, M., Bessi, A., Zollo, F., Petroni, F., Scala, A., Caldarelli, G., Stanley, H.E. and Quattrociocchi, W. (2016) The spreading of misinformation online. *Proceedings of the National Academy of Sciences of the United States of America* 113 (3), 554–559.
Dubois, E. and Blank, G. (2018) The echo chamber is overstated: The moderating effect of political interest and diverse media. *Information, Communication & Society* 21 (5), 729–745.
Gerlach, D. (2020) Einführung in eine kritische Fremdsprachendidaktik. In D. Gerlach (ed.) *Kritische Fremdsprachendidaktik. Grundlagen, Ziele, Beispiele* (pp. 7–31). Narr.
Hallet, W. (2007) Literatur und Kultur im Unterricht: ein kulturwissenschaftlicher didaktischer Ansatz. In W. Hallet and A. Nünning (eds) *Neue Ansätze und Konzepte der Literatur- und Kulturdidaktik* (pp. 31–49). Wissenschaftlicher Verlag Trier.
Hill, S.J., Lo, J., Vavreck, L. and Zaller, J. (2007) The opt-in internet panel: Survey mode, sampling methodology and the implications for political research. See https://www.researchgate.net/publication/228893430_The_Opt-In_Internet_Panel_Survey_Mode_Sampling_Methodology_and_the_Implications_for_Political_Research (accessed December 2021).
Instagram (2020) Using Instagram. Feed. See https://help.instagram.com/1986234648360433/?helpref=hc_fnav&bc[0]=Instagram%20Help&bc[1]=Using%20Instagram (accessed December 2021).
Iyengar, S. and Hahn, K.S. (2009) Read media, blue media. Evidence of ideological selectivity in media use. *Journal of Communication* 59 (1), 19–39.
Jones, R.H. (2021) The text is reading you. Teaching language in the age of the algorithm. *Linguistics and Education* 62 (2). https://dx.doi.org/10.1016/j.linged.2019.100750.
Jones, R.H. and Hafner, C.A. (2021) *Understanding Digital Literacies. A Practical Introduction*. Routledge.
Kemper, K. and Schildhauer, P. (2022) *Beware of filter bubbles!* Am Beispiel climate change Algorithmen auf Instagram und deren Einfluss auf die Meinungsbildung erforschen. *Der fremdsprachliche Unterricht Englisch* – Issue *Global Digital Players*, 36–39.
Leander, K.M. and Burriss, S.K. (2020) Critical literacy for a posthuman world: When people read, and become, with machines. *British Journal of Educational Technology* 51 (4), 1262–1276.
Lee, T. (2021) How people perceive influence of fake news and why it matters. *Communication Quarterly* 69 (4), 431–453.
Luke, A. (2014) Defining critical literacy. In J.Z. Pandya and J. Ávila (eds) *Moving Critical Literacies Forward: A New Look at Praxis Across Contexts* (pp. 20–31). Routledge.
Mahapatra, A. (2020) On the value of diversified recommendations. See https://about.instagram.com/blog/engineering/on-the-value-of-diversified-recommendations (accessed December 2021).
Markham, A. (2013) The algorithmic self: Layered accounts of life and identity in the 21st century. *AoIR Selected Papers of Internet Research* 14 (0), 1–5.
Masrour, F., Wilson, T., Yan, H., Tan, P.-N. and Esfahanian, A. (2020) Bursting the filter bubble: Fairness-aware network link prediction. *AAAI* 34 (01), 841–848.
Mayr, A. (2016) Multimodal critical discourse analysis (MCDA). In H. Stöckl and N.-M. Klug (eds) *Handbuch Sprache im multimodalen Kontex*t (pp. 261–276). De Gruyter.
Mehlhose, F.M., Petrifke, M. and Lindemann, C. (2021) Evaluation of graph-based algorithms for guessing user recommendations of the social network Instagram. Paper presented at the 15th International Conference on Semantic Computing (ICSC), 27–29 January, Laguna Hills.

Meta (2022) Instagram features. How Instagram feed works. See https://help.instagram.com/1986234648360433/?helpref=hc_fnav&cms_id=1986234648360433 (accessed August 2023).

mpfs (2020) Jugend, Information, Medien. Basisuntersuchung zum Medienumgang 12- bis 19-Jähriger. See https://www.mpfs.de/fileadmin/files/Studien/JIM/2020/JIM-Studie-2020_Web_final.pdf (accessed December 2021).

Pariser, E. (2011) Beware online 'filter bubbles'. Paper presented at March 2011 TED Conference.

Pariser, E. (2012) *The Filter Bubble. What the Internet is Hiding from You*. Penguin Books.

Pariser, E. (2015) Did Facebook's study kill my filter bubble thesis? See https://www.wired.com/2015/05/did-facebooks-big-study-kill-my-filter-bubble-thesis/ (accessed December 2021).

Parmelee, J.H. and Roman, N. (2020) Insta-echoes: Selective exposure and selective avoidance on Instagram. *Telematics and Informatics* 52. https://doi.org/10.1016/j.tele.2020.101432.

Sandvig, C., Hamilton, K., Karahalios, K. and Langbort, C. (2016) Automation, algorithms, and politics. When the algorithm itself is a racist: Diagnosing ethical harm in the basic components of software. *International Journal of Communication* 10 (0), 4972–4990.

Schildhauer, P., Gerlach, D. and Weiser-Zurmühlen, K. (in press) (Mental) Challenges of a post-truth society. Tackling conspiracy theories in the English Language classroom. In D. Becker, M. Eisenmann, C. Ludwig and T. Summer (eds) *Mental Health in English Language Education* (pp. 181–195). Narr.

Stalder, F. (2017) *Kultur der Digitalität* (3rd edn). Suhrkamp.

Statista (2021a) Most popular networks of teenagers in the United States from fall 2012 to fall 2020. See www.statista.com/statistics/250172/social-network-usage-of-us-teens-and-young-adults/ (accessed December 2021).

Statista (2021b) Distribution of TikTok users in the United States as of March 2021, by age group. See https://www.statista.com/statistics/1095186/tiktok-us-users-age/ (accessed December 2021).

Sunstein, C.R. (2017) *#Republic. Divided Democracy in the Age of Social Media*. Princeton University Press.

Tufekci, Z. (2015) Algorithmic harms beyond Facebook and Google: Emergent challenges of computational agency. *Colorado Technology Law Journal* 13 (1), 203–218.

Williamson, B. (2017) *Big Data in Education. The Digital Future of Learning, Policy and Practice*. Sage.

7 Exploring the Potential of Live Text for ELT

Valentin Werner

7.1 Introduction

Several recent surveys have indicated that audience numbers and viewing times of traditional broadcast media, such as TV and radio are decreasing, especially when it comes to live reporting (Ofcom, 2022; Statista, 2021a, 2021b). By contrast, media consumption at large is growing, mainly due to the rise of digital media and web-based alternatives to traditional live broadcasting. One media artifact that squarely falls into this category is live text, which has emerged in the late 1990s. Live text (LT)[1] qualifies as a genuine born-digital text (BDT) type (see Becker *et al.*, this volume) as it exploits the affordances of digital media. More specifically, it epitomizes major trends both as regards changes in the technical and communicative infrastructure in general (see e.g. Kergel & Heidekamp-Kergel, 2020) as well as in digital journalism in particular. LT has been defined as a 'single blog post on a specific topic to which time-stamped content is progressively added for a finite period' (Thurman & Walters, 2013: 83). In general, it has been described as an immediate form of journalism well-suited for the coverage of (pre-scheduled) events with limited duration, such as sports matches, political events (elections, presidential debates, inauguration ceremonies, etc.), natural disasters or terrorist attacks (Thurman & Walters, 2013; see also Michael & Werner, 2021, in press).

Previous descriptions have labeled LT as a hybrid in multiple respects: first, stylistically, as it mashes different journalistic styles, for instance fact-based reporting, evaluative commenting and glossing (Werner, 2016); second, structurally, as it combines textual and visual elements (see Section 7.2), and third, textually and linguistically, as the content is regularly updated and the discourse emerges as the events reported upon unfold. Thus, LT has been called a dynamic 'text-in-motion' (Hauser, 2008: 5), 'text-in-process' (Chovanec, 2018: 511) or 'open news discourse' (Thorsen & Jackson, 2018), delineating LT from static textual practices available in traditional reporting. LT is further characterized by interactivity, as audience contributions may be embedded into the discourse, as well as by its ability to connect digital and physical spaces (Ng, 2013). LT therefore provides a dynamic, interactive and multimodal environment that has been claimed to also be functionally hybrid as it instantiates infotainment (Baym, 2008; McEnnis, 2016).

While scholarly engagement with LT has been wide in media and communication studies (see e.g. Thurman & Walters, 2013; also, Matheson & Wahl-Jorgensen, 2020), there are also a few studies that have tackled linguistic and multimodal aspects, for instance of sports-related (e.g. Chovanec, 2018; Werner, 2016, 2019) and political LT (e.g. Michael & Werner, 2021, in press; Tereszkiewicz, 2014). Such studies have considered the language of the main commentary, have analyzed the usage of formulaic language and stance expressions, and have dealt with the issue of spoken-written hybridity of LT as a BDT.

Within the context of ELT, however, LT has been ignored to date.[2] A prospective point of departure are several contributions on the use of blogging in ELT in general (e.g. Chen, 2019; Elola & Oskoz, 2009; Ishihara & Takamya, 2019; Raith, 2010). However, these are restricted to the issue of the development of sociocultural competence through telecollaboration with blogs. Another type of blogging, that of educational 'microblogging' with the help of tweets, features in other publications (e.g. Lomicka & Lord, 2011; Reinhardt, 2019).[3] As the focus is restricted to social media usage, unfortunately, LT is not considered.

In view of the arguably understudied and to date underused nature of LT as a genuine BDT for purposes of ELT, the present contribution aims to develop multiple perspectives on LT. These comprise a media/communication studies perspective that considers LT as a multimodal artifact and an applied media linguistics perspective that explicitly takes into account discourse properties and thus serves to illustrate structural features of LT as a BDT. The aforementioned perspectives will serve as a base to inform the vantage point of ELT that explores LT as a BDT with potential classroom relevance.

More specifically, the following questions will be addressed:

- How does LT relate to more traditional forms of reporting?
- What characterizes LT as a BDT due to recent technological advances and increasing media 'prosumption' (Beer & Burrows, 2013)?
- What are the potential affordances of LT for ELT?

The remainder of the present chapter is structured as follows: Sections 7.2 to 7.4 contextualize LT as a BDT and provide information on its communicative situation, core linguistic aspects as well as on selected multimodal properties. Section 7.5 addresses the core concern of implications for ELT, highlighting opportunities and challenges when it comes to classroom usage of LT, and offers a lesson outline. Section 7.6 is dedicated to implications for further research before a concluding overall summary is presented in Section 7.7.

7.2 The Communicative Situation

To provide some background information on the genesis of LT as a BDT and to facilitate the ensuing analysis, it is helpful to offer a basic overview of the production and consumption circumstances of LT, followed by the presentation of one example of a concrete LT instantiation.

As a rule, LT appears on the websites of news outlets (such as https://www.theguardian.com/tone/minutebyminute or https://www.mirror.co.uk/live/) and is produced with commercial content management platforms by freelance journalists or (increasingly) regular editors. The editors usually are in front of a TV screen rather than present at the events on which they report and the discourse may be single- or, more likely, multiple-authored, with editors sometimes taking on specific roles, for example one editor being responsible for play-by-play commentary, another one for color commentary in sports LT (Werner, 2016, 2019) or editors from different departments commenting on their areas of specialization (domestic politics, economy, etc.) in political LT. The consumption of LT typically is quick and cursory, often happens individually on mobile devices, and sometimes as a second-screen by-medium besides the primary televisual mediation of an event (Bitkom, 2018). Note that LT may not only be followed while an event actually is in progress but can also be accessed at a later point in time when it is made available on a website.

Figure 7.1 shows an example of LT from the British news outlet *The Guardian*, illustrating LT reporting on a major political TV event (the first 2020 US presidential debate).

Figure 7.1 exemplifies what could be considered a traditional layout based on a squared ordered page with black on white/grey print. At the same time, it illustrates the modularity of LT. For instance, zone 1 contains the heading of the LT and several clickable links that lead to the respective 'key moment' posts in the main commentary. Zone 2 lists the names of the commentators, provides an X/Twitter ID, social media links and a vertical timeline with key moments in reverse chronological order (again linked to the relevant sections in the main commentary). Zone 3 contains the main commentary in reverse order. The individual posts in this zone are time-stamped and may feature links, photorealistic and abstract imagery, as well as multimodal elements (in the example shown an embedded video clip).[4] Note that the main commentary contains material from different producers, including other media sources, official channels (e.g. from political parties and organizations) as well as from private people, with X/Twitter being the channel of choice for such input.

While the textual commentary represents the core part of any LT, it is evident that LT consists of a range of additional structural features permitted by the digital medium and is characterized by multimodality and modularity, uniting different carriers of information within one large semiotic unit. Overall, LT can therefore be described as a spatiotemporal

Figure 7.1 Screenshot of LT from *The Guardian* (Belam *et al.*, 2020) with different navigational and content zones highlighted

interactive medium involving linear and nonlinear data (Bateman *et al.*, 2017; Werner, 2019): LT is *spatial* as it is represented on a two-dimensional space on a webpage but also *temporal/dynamic* as its content is updated regularly. It is *unscripted*, as the unfolding of events cannot be fully planned, and also *interactive*, as the digital format facilitates exchange between commentators and audience. While the posts appear in a *linear* (reverse chronological) fashion, *nonlinearity* refers to the fact that posts may link to other sources, articles, videos, Tweets, etc.

7.3 Linguistic Aspects

As the main commentary is the core part of LT, and as it contains textual material that will in all likelihood be the focus of any language-educational engagement, selected linguistic aspects of LT commentary as a particular instantiation of BDTs (see also Kersten, this volume) are described subsequently.

It has been observed that the lexicon of LT is largely determined by the respective LT type: not surprisingly, football LT features football discourse, for instance, where formulaic language, specialized vocabulary and expressions relating to spatial and temporal location for the creation of a mental image of the football pitch are pervasive (Werner, 2016, 2019). Likewise, political LT represents political discourse and is characterized by specialized vocabulary (e.g. *rally*, *nominee*, *campaign*, etc.) and a high incidence of reporting verbs (*say*, *claim*, *state*, etc.) (Michael & Werner, 2021).

A further aspect discussed from a linguistic perspective is whether LT can be viewed as an example of stylistic lag and emulated speech. This means that it relies on communicative and linguistic conventions of established live media formats that rely on the spoken mode (TV and radio reporting), adapted to the (written) digital medium (Hauser, 2008). Corpus data of sports LT (Werner, 2016) are suggestive of a restricted use of pertinent features, such as expressive punctuation and capitalization and indication of vowel lengthening (see examples 1 and 2), interjections (example 3) or the presence of informalisms (examples 4 and 5) and even fewer of the elements of emulated speech have been found to occur in political LT (example 6; Michael & Werner, 2021, 2023).

(1) **WEST BROM HAVE A SHOT!!!!!!!!!!!**
(2) **Ooooh!** Ireland, in the centre circle, passes to the right and starts running
(3) **Wowee.** The celebrations behind Mignolet's goal are inevitably wild.
(4) Bournemouth payers are hugging **and stuff**
(5) More like **snowin'** Hargreaves, **amirite?**
(6) **Hi from Miami, team!** I will be on the lookout for anything that could give Biden or Trump an edge in all-important Florida

It has also been noted that LT embodies discourse with a significant commentator presence. This implies that the main commentary features strongly personalized commentator voices using exophoric reference and expressions of stance (examples 7 to 9).

(7) I'd like to see **that** again.
(8) Alonso is booked for fouling the keeper Adrian. **That**'s a bit harsh **I think**.
(9) **I think** Trump's championing a heroic view of American history resonates with a lot of conservatives.

Finally, as already indicated above, LT discourse can be categorized as a stylistic hybrid that mixes commentary, evaluation and – particularly in sports LT – statistical background information (see examples 10 to 12).

(10) Moving on to Coronavirus, Biden says Trump has no plan – and 200,000 people have died. He says, correctly, that in the early days of the virus, Trump had praised China and President Xi's response to the virus.
(11) Kenny's long ball downfield is hit and hope and Klavan soon snuffs that out. That's all Everton have mustered in truth and that's not good enough really. It's been totally one-way traffic.
(12) A gentle reminder that this fixture has seen a record 21 red cards issued across the 50 Premier League meetings, with 14 for Everton and seven for Liverpool.

7.4 Beyond Text: Live Text as a Multimodal Artifact

It was already mentioned above that LT as a BDT exploits the affordances of the digital medium and represents a truly multimodal artifact. Therefore, it is sensible to briefly inspect the role of paratextual material (i.e. items used in addition to the text of the main commentary) that may determine the style and content of LT. Such a perspective is motivated by observations on general patterns in the current mediascape, which include a central role of images in present-day digital representations (Caple, 2017), the increased availability of statistics (Clarke, 2017), as well as audience participation as a growing mass media trend (Chovanec, 2018; McEnnis, 2016).

Figure 7.2 shows that images indeed play an important part as, especially, photorealistic images commonly occur in LT. Tweets, which can be seen as indicative of the interactive properties of LT and the opportunity for direct audience involvement, and audiovisual material appear to be less pervasive, while abstract imagery (e.g. figures and tables with statistical information) also occurs occasionally. Thus, LT obviously seems to follow parts of the broader media trends described and relies on various textual and additional elements to convey an overall message.

Previous research (see, e.g. Werner, 2019) has also found that LT implements certain strategies to foster audience participation and community building only possible in the digital medium, establishing 'light communities' (that is, temporary communities converging around a shared interest or event; see Blommaert & Varis, 2015: 127) through 'mediated quasi-interaction' (Chovanec, 2010: 234). For LT, this includes invitations for mail-ins and Tweets and selectively[5] including and addressing them in the main commentary (see examples 13 to 16) as well as relation to insider/collective knowledge (examples 15 and 16).

(13) Thoughts? Predictions? Hopes? Fears? Send them my way.
(14) 'Thoughts? I think United need to make a statement tonight. It's all for City to lose,' says Ahmed Aly. 'Predictions? 3–2 to United. Hopes? I hope it's not a drab nil-nil draw after all those column inches about "the game of the season." Fears? Spiders.'

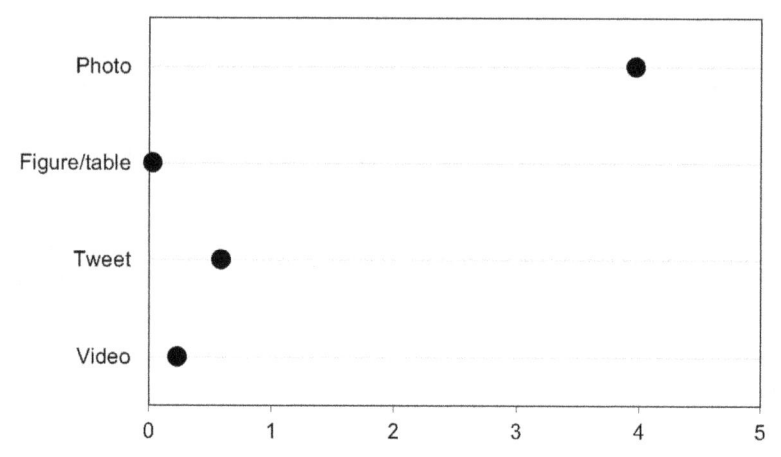

Figure 7.2 Occurrences of paratextual material in sports LT from *The Guardian*, normalized per 1000 words of commentary (adapted from Werner, 2019)

(15) 'Allardyce fiddling with his earpiece is the new Wenger struggling with his coat zip,' emails Marie. I like it, I like it.
(16) This, as Tom Jordan points out, is the kind of dirty, tough game Diego Costa would have loved. Chelsea have lacked a bit of mongrel.

Arguably, these strategies foster 'prosumption' on part of the audience, who are not restricted to mere passive consumers of media content. The humor created through these apparently informal exchanges furthermore can be viewed within the context of what Siehr (2016) has termed 'comedy journalism', where information and entertainment are mashed up.

7.5 Implications for ELT

In the following, the focus will shift from description to how LT can inform ELT. From the foregoing sections, it should have become clear that LT can be viewed as an artifact integrating online and offline practices, that it represents a complex artifact necessitating the analysis of linear and non-linear data and that it constitutes a multimodal ensemble relying on text, images and other communicative means. It is characterized by some instances of stylistic lag and its producers exploit multimodal affordances (e.g. the opportunity to integrate content from various sources and other producers),[6] so that it has clearly developed into a BDT format of its own. LT fulfills several functions, as it informs, entertains and serves to build a community. It further breaks the unidirectionality of communication found in traditional broadcast media and thus loosens the hierarchy (producer vs. consumer) in journalism through exploiting the affordances of the digital sphere, creating multi-layered and multi-authored ('polyvocal') discourse. LT therefore is a prime example of the current trend of media convergence; that is, it illustrates how formerly separate communicative practices are consciously combined to make their points (Bateman *et al.*, 2017).

All of these aspects make LT a potentially relevant and interesting concern in ELT, as it epitomizes many qualities of BDTs. Subsequently, opportunities and challenges when working with LT in the classroom are presented from a broader perspective and ideas for practical application are offered.

7.5.1 Opportunities

Above all, LT embodies authentic news discourse in a digital format. In this regard, LT may serve as authentic and complex input for reading comprehension activities, and therefore appears to be squarely in line with central demands of current ELT practice. Using such authentic texts, BDTs included, is a core demand in many curricula, especially at higher proficiency levels (CEFR B1 and beyond). Relevant activities, fostering what has been termed 'online reading comprehension' (Coiro, 2012: 412), involve the analysis of linguistic structures used in such texts, and further include the interpretation of statistics and figures as well as comparisons with similar texts in other media types. Following the scheme for typical educational functions of digital media developed in Lütge and Merse (2021), it is suggested that LT can at least be used for the functions of *information* and *reflection*.

A first specific focus could be raising awareness about the properties of LT as a genuine BDT type. This involves drawing attention (i) to the dynamicity of LT production and its potential open-endedness as a 'text-in-motion', (ii) to the fact that LT establishes multi-layered and multi-authored discourse (how are different voices and parts of the LT combined to achieve an overall effect?), and (iii) to the hybridity of LT in multiple respects, for instance as regards its:

- Style (spoken vs. written/informal vs. formal): when do the commentators use more formal or informal ways of expression?
- Function (information vs. entertainment): when and how do the commentators inform, when and how do they evaluate?
- Extent of audience engagement (consumption vs. production): who can contribute to LT?

All of the aforementioned characteristics clearly delineate LT from traditional journalistic text types and can moreover be viewed as starting points for discussions that problematize the consumer/prosumer role of the audience in present-day media societies. Such activities are squarely in line with the educational function of reflection; that is, digital media as subject of reflection, critically reconsidering the roles and effects of media on learners and society (Lütge & Merse, 2021).

Another potential focus could be the development of multimodal/digital literacy (see e.g. Bulfin & McGraw, 2015; Jones & Hafner, 2021). This will involve explicit contrastive work in which LT is compared with other, traditional news text types. Relevant activities could aim at comparing dynamic LT reporting with non-dynamic *post-hoc* reporting of an event in a newspaper article or also with dynamic reporting on traditional channels such as TV or radio. Again, linguistic structures in terms of formal/informal language use and stylistic nuances could be a core concern, as could be analyses of what distinguishes LT as a genuinely multimodal artifact from related monomodal texts. Such activities recognize the growing significance of multimodal literacy, which is especially fostered through the increased circulation of digital texts (Mills & Unsworth, 2017), and may eventually be conducive to the development of multiliteracies (Cope & Kalantzis, 2016) as a general competence.

On a different note, addressing the content of individual LTs opens avenues for engagement with current target-culture events. LT as a BDT thus also fulfills the educational function of information, that is, using digital sources to research, collect and evaluate new information and knowledge, or to discover topical issues (Lütge & Merse, 2021). As LT offers linked information, for instance to publications by other media organizations, political parties, sports clubs, etc., and generally represents multi-authored and multi-layered discourse on a topic, there is ample opportunity on part of the learners for individual further research and the reflection of positions, for instance in a political debate. Depending on the topic treated in a specific LT, core areas that commonly feature in language curricula, such as society, politics, economy, environment, or values and norms can be addressed with a view to developing multiple perspectives within the broader framework of intercultural learning.

7.5.2 Challenges

In spite of the aforementioned affordances, it will be recognized that there are several potential obstacles for integrating LT into the ELT classroom, and that authentic LT is in all likelihood best suited for advanced learner populations.

As sketched above, LT constitutes an – in several respects – hybrid artifact and a highly complex meaning-making activity. Among other things, to be able to grasp the full meaning of LT, learners need to already have a broad range of vocabulary, potentially including specialized vocabulary. In addition, they need advanced skills when it comes to textual comprehension and interpretation, which also involves the comprehension and interpretation of additional multimodal material, and a certain degree of (inter)cultural knowledge.

There are also a few practical limitations: One is the restricted topic range of LT. Even though it was stated above that LT in principle is used to cover all kinds of current events, due to audience interest most LTs focus on politics and sports. This curbs the range of topics that can be dealt with in the classroom when LT is used as a starting point for intercultural learning (see Section 5.1) and may also impact on learner interest. A second issue is the restricted opportunity to consume LT 'as it happens', that is, when the event reported upon is *actually* in progress. This may have to do with time differences (e.g. the US presidential debates will not coincide with hours of instruction in Europe, or a football match will not take place during schooling hours, for instance) and the fact that LT reporting may well extend beyond the time boundaries of one class. The question that arises is whether a post-hoc approach to LT – that is, looking at the completed LT – is considered attractive as the dynamic nature of its textual genesis is discounted. Another potential weakness is that LT at first sight only allows more interpretative rather than productive tasks, even though learner submissions to a LT in progress, for instance in the form of a social media post, would be conceivable in principle.

7.5.3 Practical example

While several potential broader avenues for learner engagement with LT were sketched in Section 7.5.1, a specific practical example for how LT can be integrated into ELT classroom practice is offered successively. Given the potential challenges examined in Section 7.5.2, the activities are geared to learners at an upper-intermediate to advanced level. The lesson outline adapts the classical pre-while-post-activity structure and is intended to cover a 90-minute class. Materials used are (i) the complete version of the LT shown in Figure 7.1 (political LT reporting by *The Guardian* on the televised first 2020 US presidential debate between incumbent Donald Trump and contender Joe Biden) and (ii) a traditional monomodal print (or online) news report on the same event. It is assumed that the lesson is embedded into a longer sequence that deals with the issue of parliamentary and presidential democracies in target-language cultures.

Lead-in/pre-reading: Before the learners are presented with the actual LT and the news article, to tune into the topic, to raise their expectations and to activate their knowledge, they will be shown a still image that shows the two candidates and the moderator in the TV studio where the debate is recorded (e.g. https://static.dw.com/image/55099142_403.jpg). Learners are then asked to describe what and who they see on the picture and are asked to speculate on the context, while the instructor takes notes on the learners' observations (on a whiteboard or screen). It was noted above that specialized vocabulary, particularly items relating to (US) political discourse, is needed to understand the discourse of LT. Therefore, in a second step, such vocabulary is previewed with the help of an activity where passages from the LT and the news article that contain relevant items (*campaign, incumbent, Democratic candidate, GOP*, etc.) are given to individual learners. They are asked to read the passage, identify any unknown words and to use context clues to determine their meaning. As a fallback option, they may be allowed to use a dictionary. Next, they should post their findings to a Padlet or add (sticky) notes to a (magnetic) whiteboard, which can then be used as a resource for all learners. Finally, the class is divided into two equally sized groups, one focusing on LT, the other one on the traditional news report. The LT group receives a brief informational text that fills them in on LT as a BDT type for journalistic coverage and the special role of the online audience in this media format, while the news report group receives an informational text on the gatekeeper/filter role of traditional journalism.

While-reading: The LT group is now presented with the LT (or parts thereof), ideally in its original format on an electronic device. Optionally, learners may view a short video of the live debate as screened on TV along with the associated LT posts to raise awareness that LT is a digital remediation of a mediated (televised) political event. The news report group is given a traditional news report, ideally also in its original (monomodal) format. Learners are asked to go through the texts individually and are provided with a worksheet with several guiding questions pertaining to structural and linguistic aspects of the LT and the news report, respectively. This is intended to make them aware of the specifics of LT (time-stamped posts in reverse order, presence of multimodal elements, potentially active role of the audience, etc.; presence of partly informal tone, evaluative language, etc.) and of traditional news discourse (linear pyramid structure, formality of media language, presence of reporting verbs, typically passive audience, etc.). They are also instructed to complete a list of the debate topics addressed.

Post-reading: Subsequently, learners are asked to pair up with someone from the other group and share and compare their findings. This comparison is structured by the guiding questions used during the while-reading phase, with a view to fleshing out the properties and affordances of LT as a recent addition to BDT news media formats. As a follow-up activity (with the whole class or in smaller groups), it is conceivable to assess several larger issues pertaining to the development of multimodal/digital literacy, taking into account current practices of (digital) media production and consumption. Topics could include discussion of (i) whether the gatekeeping function of traditional news media is justified or should be overcome given the present-day realities and affordances of online news practices, (ii) whether audience participation and prosumption (potentially possible in LT, usually not possible in traditional reporting) should be viewed as a welcome development in the mediascape and (iii), on a related note, who the audience is that is actually represented in the LT.

What lies outside of the scope of the lesson outline presented so far, but is conceivable in terms of a productive activity, is to subsequently switch the learners' role to LT producers and provide them with a short televisual excerpt (of a political debate or of a sports match), asking them to write several posts themselves. Such a real-time text production activity places high demands on the learners, of course, but could lead to further reflection on linguistic means necessary to fulfill the different LT functions. A follow-up activity could consist of learners evaluating the LT produced by other learners.

Homework: Several options are conceivable for broader engagement with the content of the lesson. Learners could be asked to conduct some further research, for instance on the issue of why the US presidential debates usually only feature two candidates (unlike in many European democracies, for instance), leading them to explorations of differing political cultures and voting systems, or on specific topics featuring in the debate (e.g. healthcare, climate change, racism, immigration policies in the US, etc.). Based on opinions expressed in the debate and by the LT commentators and on the further research conducted, learners can also be asked to produce a text (e.g. an argumentative essay) on a disputed issue.

7.6 Implications for Further Research

While LT, as shown in Section 7.5.3, indeed can be exploited for ELT purposes and offers several additional opportunities that could only briefly be described in Section 7.5.1, it is evident that due to the scarcity of language-educational research on this particular BDT type the present contribution has to leave some gaps.

Given the fact the LT is geared toward adults – and in the case of sports LT even an adult specialist audience – it was indicated at several points that LT places high lexical demands on learners. To be in a position to determine the appropriate level of vocabulary knowledge and the required amount of scaffolding, for instance during a pre-reading phase (see Section 7.5.3), it would be helpful to establish specific lexical profiles (cf. Nation, 2013) for LT and LT subtypes.

A second desideratum is an extension of the description and application of LT beyond the examples used in the present contribution, which all stemmed from one (UK-based) media organization, *The Guardian*. Including contrastive views involving media outlets from other target-culture contexts and with other editorial stances and intended audiences will substantially broaden the perspective but may also further complicate the picture for an already complex research object. On a related note, all the examples presented relied on sports and political LT and it may be worthwhile to explore differences between these and other LT subtypes in more detail.

7.7 Conclusion

The present contribution aimed to explore the affordances of LT in the context of ELT and identified LT as a genuine BDT text type that is a popular option for online journalistic coverage of live events. It was shown that LT to date has not explicitly been considered in ELT.

An outline of the communicative situation and linguistic and multimodal aspects of LT illustrated that LT possesses its inherent complexities. It could also be demonstrated that LT offers several opportunities for classroom-based engagement if potential challenges are considered and a basic example lesson outline, which certainly is subject to modifications depending on the LT subtype and individual LT manifestation used, was introduced. The present contribution indicated where engagement with LT is squarely in line with demands of current curricula and how relevant activities possibly connect to the larger issues of digital and multimodal literacy as well as intercultural learning. As LT is a BDT that is in all likelihood here to stay, future engagement on the part of applied linguists and ELT practitioners will be vital to realize its full language-educational potential.

Acknowledgements

I acknowledge support by the Open Access Publication Fund of the University of Bamberg.

Notes

(1) In the context of media and communication studies, LTs are often alternatively labelled live blogs, which relates them to their sister genre the (we)blog, which originally emerged as informational or discussion-based websites that present dated diary-style text entries (known as posts), regularly in reverse chronological order.
(2) For an example that discusses the use of sports LT in the German literacy classroom, see Siehr (2016).
(3) Note that Reinhardt (2019) in his review states that traditional blogging may become a niche practice in the near future and may lose some of its relevance for language education.
(4) To contrast the LT with a sports LT from the same outlet, you may refer to https://www.theguardian.com/football/live/2022/jan/02/chelsea-v-liverpool-premier-league-live, for instance. Sports LT will often additionally present extensive statistical information in zone 2.
(5) For some examples of Tweets embedded into the main commentary, see the linked LT examples. They simultaneously illustrate the practice of gatekeeping through the LT producers when it comes to audience contributions.
(6) See the linked LT examples for further examples of sourcing practices in LT.

References

Bateman, J., Wildfeuer, J. and Hiippala, T. (2017) *Multimodality: Foundations, Research and Analysis*. Mouton de Gruyter. https://doi.org/10.1515/9783110479898

Baym, G. (2008) Infotainment. In W. Donsbach (ed.) *The International Encyclopedia of Communication*. Wiley-Blackwell. https://doi.org/10.1002/9781405186407.wbieci031

Beer, D. and Burrows, R. (2013) Popular culture, digital archives and the new social life of data. *Theory, Culture & Society* 30 (4), 47–71. https://doi.org/10.1177/0263276413476542

Belam, M., Greeve, J.E., Singh, M. and Sullivan, H. (2020) First 2020 presidential debate as it happened: Trump tries to steamroll Biden in chaotic clash. See https://www.theguardian.com/us-news/live/2020/sep/29/presidential-debate-latest-news-tonight-watch-trump-biden-taxes-coronavirus-updates (accessed December 2020).

Bitkom (2018) Jeder Dritte verfolgt Sportevents live im Netz. See https://www.bitkom.org/Presse/Presseinformation/Jeder-Dritte-verfolgt-Sportevents-live-im-Netz.html (accessed November 2021).

Blommaert, J. and Varis, P. (2015) *Enoughness, Accent and Light Communities*. Tilburg University. https://research.tilburguniversity.edu/files/30482406/TPCS_139_Blommaert_Varis.pdf (accessed January 2022).

Bulfin, S. and McGraw, K. (2015) Digital literacy in theory, policy and practice: Old concerns, new opportunities. In M. Henderson and G. Romeo (eds) *Teaching and Digital Technologies: Big Issues and Critical Questions* (pp. 266–281). Cambridge University Press. https://doi.org/10.1017/CBO9781316091968.026

Caple, H. (2017) Results, resolve, reaction: Words, images and the functional structure of online match reports. In D. Caldwell, J. Walsh, E.W. Vine and J. Jureidini (eds) *The Discourse of Sport* (pp. 209–227). Routledge.

Chen, J. (2019) 'To blog, not to block': Examining EFL learners' language development and intercultural competence in the blogosphere through the sociocultural lens. In T. Dobinson and K. Dunworth (eds) *Literacy Unbound: Multiliterate, Multilingual, Multimodal* (pp. 225–245). Springer. https://doi.org/10.1007/978-3-030-01255-7_12

Chovanec, J. (2010) Online discussion and interaction: The case of live text commentary. In L. Shedletsky and J.E. Aitken (eds) *Cases on Online Discussion and Interaction* (pp. 234–251). IGI. https://doi.org/10.4018/978-1-61520-863-0.ch012

Chovanec, J. (2018) *The Discourse of Online Sportscasting: Constructing Meaning and Interaction in Live Text Commentary*. Benjamins. https://doi.org/10.1075/pbns.297

Clarke, B. (2017) Representations of experience in the language of televised and radio football commentaries. In D. Caldwell, J. Walsh, E.W. Vine and J. Jureidini (eds) *The Discourse of Sport* (pp. 34–55). Routledge.

Coiro, J. (2012) The new literacies of online reading comprehension: Future directions. *The Educational Forum* 76 (4), 412–417. https://doi.org/10.1080/00131725.2012.708620

Cope, B. and Kalantzis, M. (2016) *A Pedagogy of Multiliteracies: Learning by Design*. Palgrave Macmillan. https://doi.org/10.1057/9781137539724

Elola, I. and Oskoz, A. (2009) Blogging: Fostering intercultural competence development in foreign language and study abroad contexts. *Foreign Language Annals* 41 (3), 454–477. https://doi.org/10.1111/j.1944-9720.2008.tb03307.x

Hauser, S. (2008) Live-Ticker: Ein neues Medienangebot zwischen medienspezifischen Innovationen und stilistischem Trägheitsprinzip. *kommunikation@gesellschaft* 9 (1), 1–10. https://nbn-resolving.org/urn:nbn:de:0228-200809090

Ishihara, N. and Takamiya, Y. (2019) Pragmatic development through blogs: A longitudinal study of telecollaboration and language socialization. In M. Khosrow-Pour (ed.) *Computer-Assisted Language Learning: Concepts, Methodologies, Tools, and Applications* (pp. 829–854). IGI. https://doi.org/10.4018/978-1-4666-6174-5.ch007

Jones, R.H. and Hafner, C.A. (2021) *Understanding Digital Literacies*. Routledge. https://doi.org/10.4324/9781003177647

Kergel, D. and Heidkamp-Kergel, B. (2020) Digital transformation of communication and learning: A heuristic overview. In D. Kergel, B. Heidkamp-Kergel, R.C. Arnett and S. Mancino (eds) *Communication and Learning in an Age of Digital Transformation* (pp. 39–54). Routledge. https://doi.org/10.4324/9780429430114-5

Lomicka, L. and Lord, G. (2011) A tale of tweets: Analyzing microblogging among language learners. *System* 40, 48–63. https://doi.org/10.1016/j.system.2011.11.001

Lütge, C. and Merse, T. (2021) *Digital Teaching and Learning: Perspectives for English Language Education*. Narr.

Matheson, D. and Wahl-Jorgensen, K. (2020) The epistemology of live blogging. *New Media & Society* 22 (2), 300–316. https://doi.org/10.1177/1461444819856926

McEnnis, S. (2016) Following the action: How live bloggers are reimagining the professional ideology of sports journalism. *Journalism Practice* 10 (8), 967–982. https://doi.org/10.1080/17512786.2015.1068130

Michael, H. and Werner, V. (2021) Live text coverage of political events: Combining content and corpus-based discourse analysis. In I. Hendrickx, L. Verheijen and L. van de Wijngaert (eds) *Proceedings of the 8th Conference on CMC and Social Media Corpora for the Humanities* (pp. 66–70). Radbound University. https://doi.org/10.20378/irb-51860

Michael, H. and Werner, V. (2023) Hybrid news (in the) making: A content and corpus-based discourse analysis of political live blogs on the 2020 US presidential debates. *Journalism Practice*. https://doi.org/10.1080/17512786.2023.2215254

Mills, K.A. and Unsworth, L. (2017) Multimodal literacy. In G. Nobilt (ed.) *Oxford Research Encyclopedia of Education*. Oxford University Press. https://doi.org/10.1093/acrefore/9780190264093.013.232

Nation, P. (2013) *Learning Vocabulary in another Language*. Cambridge University Press. https://doi.org/10.1017/CBO9781139524759

Ng, J. (2013) Genuinely new: The strategy of remix in live blogs. *Authorship* 1 (4). https://doi.org/10.21825/aj.v2i2.793

Raith, T. (2010) The use of weblogs in language education. In A. Tatnall (ed.) *Web Technologies: Concepts, Methodologies, Tools, and Applications* (pp. 1596–1613). IGI. https://doi.org/10.4018/978-1-60566-190-2.ch015

Reinhardt, J. (2019) Social media in second and foreign language teaching and learning: Blogs, wikis, and social networking. *Language Teaching* 52 (1), 1–39. https://doi.org/10.1017/S0261444818000356

Ofcom (2022) Media Nations 2021: Interactive report. See https://www.ofcom.org.uk/research-and-data/tv-radio-and-on-demand/media-nations-reports/media-nations-2021/interactive-report (accessed December 2021).

Siehr, K.-H. (2016) Der Live-Ticker als Gegenstand von Sprach- und Medientextreflexion. In F. Kern and K.-H. Siehr (eds) *Sport als Thema im Deutschunterricht: Fachliche Grundlagen – Unterrichtsanregungen – Unterrichtsmaterialien* (pp. 101–128). Universitätsverlag Potsdam.

Statista (2021a) Mediennutzung weltweit 2021. See https://de.statista.com/statistik/studie/id/57701/dokument/mediennutzung-weltweit/ (accessed December 2021).

Statista (2021b) Mediennutzung in Europa 2021. See https://de.statista.com/statistik/studie/id/24564/dokument/mediennutzung-in-europa-statista-dossier/ (accessed December 2021).

Tereszkiewicz, A. (2014) 'I'm not sure what that means yet, but we'll soon find out': The discourse of newspaper live blogs. *Studia Linguistica Universitatis Iagellonicae Cracoviensis* 131, 299–319. https://doi.org/10.4467/20834624SL.14.018.2326

Thorsen, E. and Jackson, D. (2018) Seven characteristics defining online news formats: Towards a typology of online news and live blogs. *Digital Journalism* 6 (7), 847–868. https://doi.org/10.1080/21670811.2018.1468722

Thurman, N. and Walters, A. (2013) Live blogging – Digital journalism's pivotal platform? *Digital Journalism* 1 (1), 82–101. https://doi.org/10.1080/21670811.2012.714935

Werner, V. (2016) Real-time online text commentaries: A cross-cultural perspective. In C. Schubert and C. Sanchez-Stockhammer (eds) *Variational Text Linguistics: Revisiting Register in English* (pp. 271–305). Mouton de Gruyter. https://doi.org/10.1515/9783110443554-013

Werner, V. (2019) A multimodal analysis of football live text commentary. In M. Callies and M. Levin (eds) *Corpus Approaches to the Language of Sports: Texts, Media, Modalities* (pp. 201–240). Bloomsbury. https://doi.org/10.5040/9781350088238.ch-009

8 From Gaming to Linguistic Action: Let's Play Videos as (More Than) Mediation Tasks

Janina Reinhardt

8.1 Introduction

Let's Plays (LPs), also described as 'gameplay videos' (Piittinen, 2018: title) are a category of online videos consisting of commented and published screen recordings of the playing of video games (Burwell, 2017: 41; Donick, 2020: v; Fromme & Hartig, 2020; Schmidt & Marx, 2020: 132; Venus, 2017: 24). In many cases, the recording is produced during a streaming session, edited, and uploaded in several episodes to video platforms (Leisten, 2020: 11), where some of them are watched and commented on millions of times (Ackermann, 2017: 1).

Among 12 to 19-year-olds, 30% watch such videos on YouTube at least several times a week (MPFS, 2020: 46, 73f.). LPs have not only become very popular among young people, they have also garnered interest in scientific research (see Ackermann, 2017; Hale, 2016a, 2016b; Nguyen, 2016; Piittinen, 2018; Schmidt & Marx, 2020) as well as pedagogical theory and application (see Burwell, 2017; Buser, n.d.; Hennekes, n. d.; Leisten, 2020; Zielinski, *et al.*, 2017).

Against this background, this article explores the potential of LPs for foreign language classrooms. To show their relevance for the teaching of language, literature and culture, it first examines why LPs are an interesting phenomenon from a media studies perspective and how they relate to today's participatory culture and contemporary ways of meaning-making. In a second step, it analyses the use of LPs as a pedagogical topic and tool. For this purpose, I present their general value in school contexts and their competence-oriented use in foreign language education.

8.2 Let's Plays as 'Cultural Artefacts', 'Texts' and 'Readers' Responses'

As Ackermann (2017: 1) notes, the term *Let's Play* seems to be a misnomer because it contains a paradox: while its literal meaning is a linguistic invitation to play together, the actual concept refers to media products intended for consumption. The interactivity usually attributed to computer games is thus eschewed in favour of a shared reception experience. However, this apparent contradiction can be at least partially resolved: when the term was coined in May 2006, *Vanilla Ice*, the (presumably) first Let's Player, called for active participation in the text-based strategy game *The Oregon Trail*, by not only meticulously documenting his gameplay through screenshots and written comments, but also leaving game decisions to the users of the forum (Ackermann, 2017: 2f.). The meaning of the word *Let's Play* has since shifted (from gameplay documentations in a forum to audio-visual recordings), but even today viewers of LPs usually have the opportunity to influence the course of the game (e.g. by participating in a vote), to initiate explanations (e.g. by asking questions) or at least to share their own opinions (e.g. by writing comments). While it is true that watching someone play a game is less active than playing the game yourself, it is not true that the audience of LPs is relegated to a purely passive role (Tilgner, 2017). Consumers of LPs do actively participate in game decisions, may give instructions and express their opinions. Furthermore, adolescents show their favorite videos to, and discuss them with, their peers and may also try out the games or even create their own LPs. In this sense, LPs have turned into a means of social and communicative participation in the world of young people.

LPs can thus be considered to be an (inter)active and participatory consumption and production practice of contemporary popular culture (see also Introduction; Fromme & Hartig, 2020; Jenkins *et al.*, 2006: 3; Kremser, 2015). As Grünberger (2017: 195) points out, they are important (youth) cultural artefacts, since this contemporary media phenomenon does not only capture gaming habits and media-related language use, but also reflects current events and trains of thought. At the same time, LPs represent a means of self-expression that allows for the satisfaction of the basic anthropological need of communicating the self as a narrative to another (Grünberger, 2017: 196). Furthermore, Let's Plays are a contemporary form of text interpretation, opening up new dimensions of computer games by exploring virtual spaces of possibility and allowing players to express their thoughts and feelings (Fischer, 2021: 44). From a reception theory perspective (see Michler, 2015: 136f. for such a perspective on literature teaching), LPs are a form of sharing individual players' experience of playing a game. They show the effect of the game on the player, the player's individual perception of what is happening, and their subjective understanding of anything implicitly or explicitly mentioned in the gameplay.

LPs can thus be understood as mediatised interpretations of games, a modern form of 'readers' responses'. Since 'video games are indeed outside the [text game] spectrum, as something that is an experience of the player rather than an object to be played' (Kuhn, 2016: 21), the interpretation of a game may be directly linked to its gameplay. More precisely, the interpretation will not be a purely analytical reading of a self-contained text, but an interpretation through commentary of a player's interaction. Using a broad definition of text, LPs can therefore be seen as interpretive audio-visual texts (i.e. commented screencasts) about a player's experience with imaginative audio-visual texts (i.e. video games). What is special about this kind of interpretation is that the games are not simply interpreted, but simultaneously staged as literary or artistic works (Çakir, 2022: 140ff.).

In LPs, the communication situation is much more complex than in traditional texts or games: there is not only an author, a text and a recipient, but also interaction between player, audience, video recording/ transmission and game that leads out of the actual game, overlays it and thus represents a media form that goes beyond a conventional paratext (Othold, 2017: 51). As Burwell (2017: 41f.) observes, LPs are a 'remixed digital text' and a 'unique hybrid of gameplay and video'. Since games and LPs are both born-digital texts (see Introduction), LPs can be seen as (complex interpretative) born-digital texts about (immersive imaginative) born-digital texts. Thus, LPs are a highly relevant text type for study in schools.

8.3 Let's Plays as a Pedagogical Topic and Tool

As shown above, LPs are very interesting from a media studies perspective. Since media education and an introduction to our digital world are part of many school curricula (see e.g. KMK, 2017 for Germany), LPs are also relevant for teaching. However, this assumption should not be taken for granted; rather it should be carefully considered why the integration of LPs in school contexts really makes sense. This section will therefore show that LPs do have their place in the classroom.

As digital media play a considerable role in young people's everyday lives, they should also be included in school teaching practices (Bär, 2019: 12). Two media habits that are particularly common among teenagers are the playing of digital games and the streaming of videos. More than two thirds of 12 to 19-year-olds play digital games at least several times a week (see MPFS, 2020, 2021) and video streams are watched equally frequently by even more teenagers (87% in 2020, 83% in 2021). Since LPs unite these two media practices, one can assume that LPs are part of many youngsters' everyday lives. Hence, it is no surprise that LPs were found to be the third most popular YouTube genre (MPFS, 2020), and that 12% of the young people indicated they use Twitch at least several times a week: a platform that is mainly used in gaming for live streaming Let's Plays (MPFS, 2021). However, this media practice is inherently gendered: most YouTube genres are consumed more frequently by boys than by girls, and this difference is most pronounced in LPs (boys: 43%, girls: 16%, MPFS, 2020). If LPs are included in school education for the sake of integrating pupils' media habits, this may thus lead to boys seeing their lives reflected in class, which in turn may increase their motivation to participate in these sessions.

However, LPs are not only interesting from a learner-centred and motivational perspective, but also from a competence-oriented point of view. From an interdisciplinary perspective, *21st-century skills* (Battelle for Kids, 2019) and *digital literacies* (Jones & Hafner, 2021) can be useful frameworks of reference. Both try to determine the abilities students need to acquire if they want to become active participants in our world. In the first case, it is assumed that there are four major skills – also called *the four Cs* – that students need in order to be 'prepared for [the] increasingly complex life and work environments in today's world [...]. These skills include:

- Creativity and Innovation;
- Critical Thinking and Problem Solving;
- Communication;
- Collaboration'. (Battelle for Kids, 2019: 2)

These skills can easily be fostered by integrating LPs in lessons: as LPs are a mediated form of communication, in which gameplay is shown and commented on, communicative awareness will be raised if LPs are not only watched but also analysed and discussed with regard to the use of their communicative means. If they are also produced and collaboratively revised and edited, this leads to creative and collaborative use of media. Critical thinking can be promoted through all these activities, but it can be taken further by using LPs as a starting point for reflection on gaming culture, media habits and gaming addiction.

The second framework looks at the impact of digital media on society and the literary skills they require – also called *digital literacies* – that students need to acquire to navigate our increasingly mediatised world.

> 'Digital literacies' are ways in which people use the mediational means available to them to take actions and make meaning in particular social, cultural, and economic contexts. [...] They involve not just being able to 'operate' tools like computers and smartphones, but *also* the ability to adapt the affordances and constraints of these tools to *particular* circumstances. At times this will involve mixing and matching the tools at hand in creative new ways that help us do what we want to do and be who we want to be. (Jones & Hafner, 2021: 18)

Since LPs are a complex form of media communication, their reception, production and discussion can help foster a reflective and possibly innovative use of these media tools. Furthermore, the definition above can be read as a justification for modifying text types in specific learning tasks. If pupils are to learn to mix and match digital texts, it may also be legitimate to adapt the LP genre to an educational content (e.g. a particular educational game) or a particular communication situation (e.g. classmates or exchange students as addressees). Additionally, the passing on of media experiences and their integration in social interaction can be considered a communicative goal (see e.g. KMK, 2017: 17 for Germany). For the acquisition of this competence, LPs seem to be a predestined means, as they represent a mediatised form of communicating gaming experiences.

Finally, it should also be mentioned that LPs can be used as a means of reflection not only on media and gaming in general, but also on the content and logic of a specific game. As games offer an immersive experience (see also Donnick, 2020: 64f.), gameplay can be a means to make historical events or foreign places tangible. Since personal experience and emotional involvement lead to increased motivation and deeper engagement, making, sharing and discussing such gaming experiences can thus lead to more affective and effective learning. In this way, historical events, social practices and ethical choices can be addressed in a different – potentially more memorable – way. Through this, cognitive processes such as decision-making in situations that pose an ethical dilemma could, for example, be embedded in Citizenship or Religious Education lessons (see also Leisten, 2020). Furthermore, alternate worlds can be explored, leading to new perspectives on the reality we live in. Since video games are set in universes that usually have a clear connection to our lifeworld, LPs can be seen as an attempt to interpret not only fictional worlds, but also the world in which the Let's Player lives. Whatever that interpretation turns out to be, LPs will thus encourage deeper reflection on the content and design tools of the game, the alternate world in which it is set, and the real world(s) in which we live.

In summary, there are good reasons for using LPs in the classroom. From a learning and teaching perspective, LPs are useful to foster 21st-century skills as well as digital literacy, and from a methodological point of view, they prove to be a timely means of enabling young people to discuss subject matter and personal experiences. In the next section, these basic considerations will be followed up by specifications for foreign language teaching.

8.4 Let's Plays as a Resource for Foreign Language Teaching

So far, only arguments of general didactics and methodology have been presented. However, if LPs are to be implemented in foreign language teaching, subject-specific considerations should also be undertaken. To this purpose, the competence model from the German *Bildungsstandards für die Allgemeine Hochschulreife* (a national framework for language teaching, KMK, 2012) and the *Common European Framework of Reference* (CEFR, an international framework for language teaching, Council of Europe, 2020) shall be considered. As will be shown, LPs can promote text and media literacy – or *multiliteracies* (The New London Group, 1996) – in the form of an authentic, medially complex mediation task.

If LPs are to be used in foreign language teaching, learning objectives must be targeted accordingly. This means that subject-specific competences must be integrated in such a way that the target language and culture are at the centre of LP reception and production. For the use of LPs in the foreign language classroom, this means that:

(1) The use of LPs should not only promote 21st-century skills and digital literacies, but also knowledge and skills related to target language(s) and culture(s);
(2) LPs should be used as a contemporary means of enabling young people not only to learn about foreign languages and cultures in an authentic context, but also to reflect on and discuss these encounters in the target language.

As the *lingua franca* of the global gaming community is English (Hallet, 2018: 5; Jones & Schmidt, 2020), the use of LPs in foreign language classes may be most straightforward for English. Video games and LPs are valuable resources for language teaching because they offer (linguistically) immersive experiences (see also Kuhn, 2016) and a virtual *Sprachbad* ('language bath', meaning an immersive exposition to linguistic input). They are thus a great means to encourage students to use the target language in an authentic context by talking about their personal experiences.

Since actions and impressions are usually verbalised in LPs, they offer new ways of working on language skills. More precisely, verbalisation is put into a visually accessible context. As Schmidt and Marx (2020: 131) put it, 'a player's own game actions are explicated verbally which makes the game play more transparent as an action and thus more attractive for viewers'. If LPs are integrated in foreign language teaching, linguistic actions become meaningful because students use language in an authentic language task (i.e. the production of LPs) instead of simply practising picture/action descriptions, as is often the case in textbook exercises. Furthermore, these linguistic actions are recorded so that language and content can be shared and discussed afterwards. As a guiding question, it could be discussed how comments generate added value that makes LPs worth watching for their viewers (for a scientific study on this topic, see Schmidt & Marx, 2020).

Table 8.1 The creation and discussion of LPs as a complex mediation task (Based on Council of Europe 2020: 33, North & Piccardo 2016: 25–27)

	Mediation	LPs as a complex mediation task
Creative, interpersonal language use	→ Mediating communication social interaction	Explaining one's own gaming experience in a way a target group understands and finds interesting
Transactional language use	→ Mediating a text extraction and processing of information	Using existing LPs as text models (e.g. by copying linguistic means or structures) and making sense of the game as a text
Evaluative, problem-solving language use	→ Mediating concepts using languages as a tool for reflection	Forming opinions on a game/LP (e.g. by contrasting cultural viewpoints) and discussing the reception and production of LPs

Such a guiding question leads to the concepts of 'addressee orientation' and 'situational appropriateness', two concepts inherent to the field of mediation. Students should learn to transmit content in a way that is appropriate to the addressee and the situation, ideally by adding explanations necessary for comprehension and dealing creatively with languages (and further code systems). Against this background, LPs seem particularly suited for an authentic mediation task. This idea can be further supported when looking into the current version of the *CEFR*, which describes communication by classifying language activities into four modes of communication (i.e. reception, production, interaction, mediation) and three basic functions (i.e. creative and/or interpersonal, transactional, evaluative and/or problem-solving). Consequently, the creation and discussion of LPs can be seen as a mediation task covering all three language uses (see Table 8.1).

In the German *Bildungsstandards*, mediation is one of the five sub-areas of *functional communicative competence* (KMK, 2012: 14). If LPs are treated as a specific type of (born-digital) text, there will, however, rather be a focus on *text and media* literacy (see KMK, 2012: 20), since the understanding, interpretation and use of LPs in their communicative context(s) is at the core of interest. The creation and discussion of LPs can thus be seen as a complex mediation task aimed at promoting text and media literacy. Consequently, the underlying learning goals are not only language skills, but also the recognition of conventionalised, culturally shaped features of LPs, the use – or reflected non-use – of these features in the production of one's own LPs, as well as reflection on the individual reception and production process.

When focusing on text and media literacy, the concept of *multiliteracies* should also be considered. It refers to a pedagogy 'in which language and other modes of meaning are dynamic representational resources, constantly being remade by their users as they work to achieve their various cultural purposes' (The New London Group, 1996: 64). This is to say that new media forms and application contexts constantly reshape communication. Language use is thus being modified by digital media, and the modes of meaning making are becoming increasingly diversified. For teaching foreign languages, this means that students must encounter more multimodal texts in order to learn to understand the interplay of different sign systems; on the other hand, it means that authentic, and also digital, communication must be integrated into language classes (Schildhauer & Bündgens-Kosten, 2021: 15). A first step in this direction can be the integration of LPs, as these are medially complex born-digital texts (see above) and authentic forms of youth communication. If students create and discuss LPs, they will not only work on language skills, but also deepen their understanding of how language(s) and other sign systems work by engaging in an authentic mediation task.

8.5 Let's Plays in Practical English Language Teaching

LPs have already been discussed in the context of English language teaching by Becker (2021), Burwell (2017) and Hennekes (n.d.). Among other things, they both mention the possibility of having students create LPs themselves. This idea is taken up below and transformed into a complex learning task – a mediation task to promote students' 21st-century skills and multiliteracies. The task, which should be feasible for students aged 14–16 with a level of A2+ or B1 in English, could be as follows:

> Create your own Let's Play of about three to five minutes in which you show, explain, and comment on one (or more) particularly interesting game scene(s) or activity(ies).

The focus of the unit is therefore on the production of LPs, but the reception and discussion of LPs should of course be included, and the task is framed by several activities facilitating and structuring the learning process (for a similar approach for games instead of LPs, see Stannard & Blanckenburg, 2018). Before students produce LPs themselves, they need to know what constitutes this text type; they must encounter and analye its specific characteristics, communicative goals and contexts of use. They should also have the opportunity to revise their productions cooperatively and to present and discuss the final results. Such a learning task could thus have the following five phases (see Figure 8.1 on the next page).

8.5.1 Introduction

At the beginning, teachers should investigate what experiences and media habits their students have with games and LPs. This could be done through an online survey or through partner interviews. Afterwards,

130 Born-Digital Texts in the English Language Classroom

```
┌─────────────────────────────────────────────────────┐
│                  1. Introduction                    │
│         Talk about gaming and LP experience         │
└─────────────────────────────────────────────────────┘
                          ⇩
┌─────────────────────────────────────────────────────┐
│                    2. Reception                     │
│ Collect, watch, and analyse examples of LPs (from meaning to form) │
└─────────────────────────────────────────────────────┘
                          ⇩
┌─────────────────────────────────────────────────────┐
│                    3. Production                    │
│  Create their own LPs (with linguistic & technical scaffolding) │
└─────────────────────────────────────────────────────┘
                          ⇩
┌─────────────────────────────────────────────────────┐
│                     4. Revision                     │
│       Give feedback on other LPs & rework own LPs   │
└─────────────────────────────────────────────────────┘
                          ⇩
┌─────────────────────────────────────────────────────┐
│         5. Exposition, discussion & conclusion      │
│              Present and value results              │
└─────────────────────────────────────────────────────┘
```

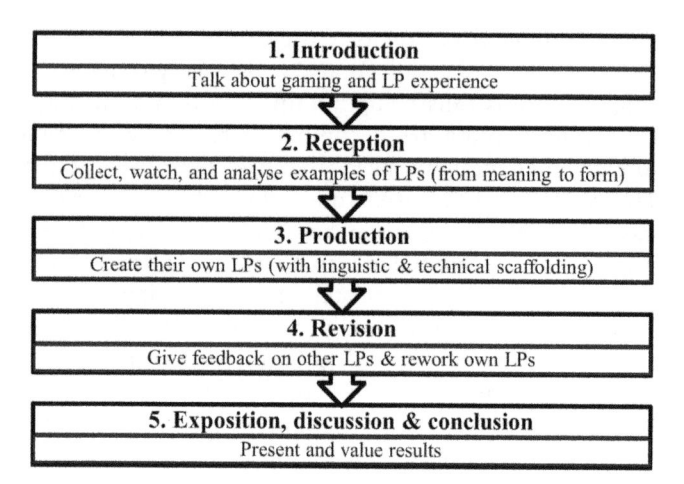

Figure 8.1 Five-phase model of LP-production in a text-based learning task

students need to be informed what the teaching unit is about and that they will produce their own LPs. Finally, one or more working definition(s) of an LP should be provided as a basis for the next phase and as a point of reference for the conclusion.

8.5.2 Reception

During the reception phase, LPs should be explored, analysed and made usable for students' own productions. For this purpose, instances demonstrating not only appropriate models, but also the diversity of this text type should be deliberately selected. Possible criteria for the selection of examples could be the use of the target language, the significance/popularity of Let's Players (e.g. measured by views/likes), and characteristics of the learning group (e.g. preferences for certain genres, or choice of Let's Player of the same age and gender). Besides, certain topics/games could be deliberately presented by the teacher (e.g. a narrative sequence with direct relevance for students' lifeworld) or avoided (e.g. ego shooters). The following three examples introduce popular English-speaking Let's Players with various backgrounds, speech styles and varieties of English, show very different games and provide strategies for making gameplay watchable (see Table 8.2; for more examples, see Becker, 2021: 97f.).

Before watching the videos, research on the Let's Players should be conducted. Then, while viewing the first two or three minutes of each LP, students should focus on what is being presented and how this is made interesting. After that, a collection of further examples can be compiled collaboratively (e.g. with a database tool). Since creativity needs input, it is important to address a variety of topics.

Table 8.2 Selected examples for Let's Plays (last access: 25 August 2022)

Link to a **Let's Play** *Title of game* (Genre)	**Let's Player** (followers) real name nationality gender	Short **comment**
https://vu.fr/aTRE *Minecraft hardcore* (Sandbox & survival game)	PewDiePie (111 M) Felix A. U. Kjellberg Swedish Male	The Let's Player with currently the most followers plays a classic game and gives (also culture-specific) comments.
https://bit.ly/3qClbf1 *Akinator* (AI guessing game)	Jacksepticeye (28.7 M) Seán W. McLoughlin Irish Male	The Let's Player demonstrates a freely available web-based game by making the artificial intelligence guess himself.
https://rb.gy/t3dmwp *Among us* (Social deduction game)	Pokimane (6.69 M) Imane Anys Moroccan Canadian, female	In this LP, Pokimane speaks in French with several francophones to find "the impostor" although she has not been practising her (attrited L1) French in a long time.

Game openings or key scenes are of course suitable, but so are many other points such as representations of race and gender, culture-specific content, such as a certain school system, special media design elements such as camera perspectives, or hidden messages (e.g. so-called *Easter eggs*). It is possible to also include LPs in non-target languages, provided they are briefly described in English. In this way, many different inspirations can be collected and multilingualism (both of students and of this text type) can be made visible.

After collecting examples, students can (e.g. in groups or as a think-pair-share activity) again discuss which games and topics are chosen. Once the LPs have been analysed regarding their content, the focus should be shifted to their linguistic and medial form(s). On the linguistic level, it is important to know how to start and end LPs, and which technical words (e.g. *glitch*, *space bar*, *noob*, …) or phrases (e.g. *Today, we are playing… / Let's click on …*) may be helpful. Also, mediational means such as sounds, animations or subtitles could be focused. In doing so, students develop their own scaffolding for the production task. At the end, they know possible content, useful phrases and strategies to make LPs watchable.

Table 8.3 Five freely available games (last access: 25 August 2022)

Akinator (https://en.akinator.com/)	5–10 min.	A web-based guessing game, in which an artificial intelligence tries to figure out who or what you are thinking of by asking you yes/no-questions
Can I have a glass of water? (https://monty-monster-studios.itch.io/can-i-have-a-glass-of-water)	10–20 min.	A mini horror game, in which you must fetch a glass of water for your daughter in the middle of the night
Mission us (https://www.mission-us.org/play/)	1–3h each	Five interactive narrative games about important events in US history, designed for learning purposes
Life is Strange **Episode 1** (https://store.steampowered.com/agecheck/app/319630/)	At least 2h each	The first part of a decision-based adventure game, in which an 18-year-old photography student discovers that she can rewind time
Life is Strange 2 **Episode 1** (https://store.steampowered.com/app/532210/)		The first part of a decision-based adventure game about a 16-year-old Mexican American and his nine-year-old brother, who has telekinetic powers

8.5.3 Production

The first step in the production of an LP is to select a game. For this purpose, selection criteria (e.g. age restriction, free availability of at least demo versions and some focus on English language and culture) should be established – possibly in conjunction with the pupils. In addition, examples of games should be given to those who lack ideas or do not want to spend money on a computer game. In the following table, two shorter games and two longer game series that are freely available have been compiled (see Table 8.3; for approaches on how to use the longer games in class, see Becker & Matz, 2020 and Blume & Hübner, 2021).

As this task is very complex and requires many different skills, students should be introduced to this form of media production gradually. As far as technical implementation is concerned, at least one possible tool should be presented in class and alternative solutions should be allowed. Since web-based tools may lack data security, pre-installed programmes like *Xbox Game Bar* or installable freeware, for example *OBS Studio*, may be preferable over web-based tools like *Screencast-o-matic* or video conference applications (e.g. *Zoom*).

As a very first pre-task exercise, the historical form of LPs could be explained and used to create their first media products. For example, pupils could try out one of the shorter games, record their gameplay in screenshots and then comment on these images in writing. Then, short extracts from LPs without sound or from non-target language LPs could be mediated into English by recording voiceovers or adding subtitles. Another possible pre-task exercise would be to have students play and record the beginning of the same free game, watch at least one other recording and give feedback to classmates on how to improve their recording and presentation techniques. For the final task, one could suggest recording only the gameplay first and subsequently creating a voice-over for the screencast. An alternative would be to write a storyboard that can be worked through and recorded in several steps. As for post-production, students should be encouraged to help one another, as individual media skills may be at different levels. Again, support for at least one tool (e.g. OpenShot) should be provided by the teacher.

8.5.4 Revision

Once the videos have been recorded and edited, pupils should have a chance to receive feedback from peers and teachers, to rework their products and to finally present them. An interesting method for this could be an adaption of the Writers' Conference (see Giesau, 2019).

8.5.5 Exposition, discussion and conclusion

Finally, the products of the task should be published (e.g. on a secured learning platform), valued and discussed. The students could vote for the three best LPs, and these could – if their authors agree – be shown during a school event, for example a parents' evening or an end-of-year party. Other issues related to games and LPs, such as gaming addiction or marketing strategies, could also be discussed at this stage. At the end, the original working definition(s) from the introductory phase should be reviewed and adapted if necessary.

8.6 Conclusion

As has been shown, LPs are born-digital texts (i.e. commented screencasts) about born-digital texts (i.e. video games), represent a mediatised form of interpretation, and can be considered youth-cultural artefacts. They are recorded individual responses to games from one (or more) player(s). As such, they are easily accessible for analysis, discussion and imitation, thus forming a participatory culture. In teaching, they can be used to foster 21st-century skills as well as multiliteracies. For teaching English as a foreign language, they have great potential not only from a textual and analytical point of view, but also regarding their use as an authentic mediation task.

As there is currently a lack of empirical studies on the use of LPs in foreign language classrooms, a major desideratum for future studies is to carry out action research in this area. For this purpose, learning outcomes could be evaluated, and different stakeholders (students, teachers, parents, experts) could be interviewed to elicit their views on the subject. Furthermore, linguistic studies could be conducted to find out typical expressions and structures in this type of text, which could be used for the development of language support.

Incorporating LPs in the foreign language classroom is an endeavour worth exploring, as it offers opportunities for authentic communication as well as the option to lead to individualised media production. It is thus a means to prepare our students for the future by making them engage in a participatory culture. Let's not just play with language: let's enable our students to share and discuss their individual experiences – medially, verbally and in a reflected way.

References

Ackermann, J. (2017) Einleitung Phänomen Let's Play – Entstehung und wissenschaftliche Relevanz eines Remediatisierungsphänomens. In J. Ackermann (ed.) *Phänomen Let's Play-Video: Entstehung, Ästhetik, Aneignung und Faszination aufgezeichneten Computerspielhandelns.* Springer VS.

Bär, M. (2019) Fremdsprachenlehren und -lernen in Zeiten des digitalen Wandels. Chancen und Herausforderungen aus fremdsprachendidaktischer Sicht. In E. Burwitz-Melzer, C. Riemer and L. Schmelter (eds) *Das Lehren und Lernen von Fremd- und Zweitsprachen im digitalen Wandel. Arbeitspapiere der 39. Frühjahrskonferenz zur Erforschung des Fremdsprachenunterrichts* (pp. 12–24). Narr Francke Attempto.

Battelle for Kids (2019) *Framework for 21st Century Learning: A Unified Vision for Learning to Ensure Student Success in a World where Change is Constant and Learning Never Stops.* BFK. See http://static.battelleforkids.org/documents/p21/P21_Framework_Brief.pdf (accessed January 2022).

Becker, D. (2021) *Videospiele im Fremdsprachenunterricht.* Narr Francke Attempto.

Becker, D. and Matz, F. (2020) Your life is still yours to live. *Der fremdsprachliche Unterricht Englisch* 165, 32–38.

Blume, C. and Hübner, A. (2021) Von Rebellen und Patrioten: Ein digitales Lernspiel für den fremdsprachlichen Englischunterricht. In J. Bündgens-Kosten and P. Schildhauer (eds) *Englischunterricht in einer digitalisierten Gesellschaft* (pp. 154–188). Beltz.

Burwell, C. (2017) Game changers: Making new meanings and new media with video games. *The English Journal* 106 (6), 41–47.

Buser, M. (no date) Let's play – Gamekultur in der Schule. See https://www.gamekultur-inderschule.ch/lets-play.html (accessed January 2022).

Çakir, D.C. (2022) Social gaming: Let's Plays und virtuelle Bühnen Inszenierung einer medialen Form der Literatur in Computerspielphänomenen der Gegenwart. In E. Kreuzmair, M. Pflock and E. Schumacher (eds) *Feeds, Tweets & Timelines – Schreibweisen der Gegenwart in Sozialen Medien.* See https://www.transcript-verlag.de/media/pdf/25/4a/3e/oa9783839463857.pdf (accessed September 2022).

Council of Europe (2020) *Common European Framework of Reference for Languages: Learning, Teaching, Assessment.* Council of Europe Publishing, Strasbourg. https://rm.coe.int/common-european-framework-of-reference-for-languages-learning-teaching/16809ea0d4 (accessed January 2022).

Donick, M. (2020) *Let's Play ! Was wir aus Computerspielen über das Leben lernen können.* Springer Fachmedien.

Fischer, S. (2021) *Moralische Spiele auf YouTube: Die Darstellung ethischer Computerspiele im Let's Play und ihre Diskussion in den Userkommentaren.* Springer Fachmedien.

Fromme, J. and Hartig, T. (2020) Let's Plays als Szene informeller Bildung? Möglichkeiten und Grenzen partizipativer Medienkulturen im digitalen Zeitalter. In V. Dander, P. Bettinger, E. Ferraro, C. Leineweber and K. Rummler (eds) *Digitalisierung – Subjekt – Bildung: Kritische Betrachtungen der digitalen Transformation* (pp. 159–182). Verlag Barbara Budrich. See https://doi.org/10.2307/j.ctvvb7n3h.12 (accessed January 2022).

Giesau, M. (2019) Schreibkonferenz [handout from the Mercator-Institue's *Methodenpool für sprachsensiblen Fachunterricht*]. See https://methodenpoolapp.de/pdfs/Schreibkonferenz.pdf (accessed February 2022).

Grünberger, N. (2017) Narrative Konstruktion von Selbst und Sozialität. Auf der Suche nach Produktions- und Rezeptionsmotiven von Let's Play-Videos. In J. Ackermann (ed.) *Phänomen Let´s Play-Video* (pp. 195–207). Springer SV.

Hale, T. (2016a) Archives, identity and apparatus: Let's play and videogame fandom. In B. Kuhn and A. Bhéreur-Lagounaris (eds) *Levelling Up: The Cultural Impact of Videogames* (pp. 137–150). Inter-Disciplinary Press.

Hale, T. (2016b) Formen von Let's Plays und vergleichbare Formate. In J. Ackermann (ed.) *Phänomen Let´s Play-Video* (pp. 257–263). Springer SV.

Hallet, W. (2018) What's (in) a digital classroom? Levels of digitalization in FL Learning and teaching. See https://languagelearninglog.de/wp-content/uploads/2018/02/180202_Hallet_Whats_a_digital_classroom-1.pdf (accessed January 2022).

Hennekes, M.A. (no date) Let's Plays im Unterricht. See https://www.mandree.de/letsplays-im-unterricht/ (accessed January 2022).

Jenkins, H., Clinton, K., Purushotma, R., Robinson, A.J. and Weigel, M. (eds) (2006) *Confronting the Challenges of Participatory Culture: Media Education for the 21st Century*. MacArthur Foundation. See https://www.macfound.org/media/article_pdfs/jenkins_white_paper.pdf (accessed January 2022).

Jones, R.D. and Schmidt, T. (2020) Wanna play? Using games, gaming, and gamification in the EFL classroom. *Der fremdsprachliche Unterricht Englisch* 165, 2–6.

Jones, R.H. and Hafner, C.A. (2021) *Understanding Digital Literacies: A Practical Introduction* (2nd edn). Routledge.

KMK (=Kultusministerkonferenz) (2012) Bildungsstandards für die fortgeführte Fremdsprache (Englisch/Französisch) für die Allgemeine Hochschulreife. See https://www.kmk.org/fileadmin/Dateien/veroeffentlichungen_beschluesse/2012/2012_10_18-Bildungsstandards-Fortgef-FS-Abi.pdf (accessed January 2022).

KMK (=Kultusministerkonferenz) (2017) Bildung in der digitalen Welt Strategie der Kultusministerkonferenz. See https://www.kmk.org/fileadmin/Dateien/pdf/PresseUndAktuelles/2018/Digitalstrategie_2017_mit_Weiterbildung.pdf (accessed September 2022).

Kremser, N. (2015) Let's Play! Eine theoretische Annäherung im Rahmen von Participatory Culture und die Frage nach der verlorenen Interaktivität. *Paidia – Zeitschrift für Computerspielforschung*, 24 June. See https://www.paidia.de/lets-play-eine-theoretische-annaeherung-im-rahmen-von-participatory-culture-und-die-frage-nach-der-verlorenen-interaktivitat/ (accessed January 2022).

Kuhn, B. (2016) Theories of gaming: Are video games text, game, or somewhere in between? In B. Kuhn and A. Bhéreur-Lagounaris (eds) *Levelling Up: The Cultural Impact of Videogames* (pp. 21–28). Inter-Disciplinary Press.

Leisten, S. (2020) *Wer will ich sein? Ethisches Lernen an TV- und Videospielserien sowie Let's Plays*. Schüren.

Michler, C. (2015) *Einführung in die Didaktik der romanischen Sprachen und Literaturen*. University of Bamberg Press. See https://fis.uni-bamberg.de/bitstream/uniba/39373/1/SGuK22MichlerDidaktikopusse_A3a.pdf (accessed January 2022).

mpfs (=Medienpädagogischer Forschungsverbund Südwest) (2020) JIM-Study: Jugend, Information, Medien. Basisuntersuchung zum Medienumgang 12- bis 19-Jähriger. See https://www.mpfs.de/fileadmin/files/Studien/JIM/2020/JIM-Studie-2020_Web_final.pdf (accessed January 2022).

mpfs (=Medienpädagogischer Forschungsverbund Südwest) (2021) JIM-Study: Jugend, Information, Medien. Basisuntersuchung zum Medienumgang 12- bis 19-Jähriger. See https://www.mpfs.de/fileadmin/files/Studien/JIM/2021/JIM-Studie_2021_barrierefrei.pdf (accessed August 2022).

Nguyen, J. (2016) Performing as video game players in Let's Plays. *Transformative Works and Cultures* 22. See http://dx.doi.org/10.3983/twc.2016.0698 (accessed January 2022).

North, B. and Piccardo, E. (2016) *Developing Illustrative Descriptors of Aspects of Mediation for the CEFR*. Council of Europe. See https://rm.coe.int/common-european-framework-of-reference-for-languages-learning-teaching/168073ff31 (accessed February 2022).

Othold, T. (2017) Let's not play – Kooperatives nicht-spielen. In J. Ackermann (ed.) *Phänomen Let's Play-Video. Entstehung, Ästhetik, Aneignung und Faszination aufgezeichneten Computerspielhandelns* (pp. 43–53). Springer Fachmedien.

Piittinen, S. (2018) Morality in let's play narrations: Moral evaluations of gothic monsters in gameplay videos of Fallout 3. *New Media & Society* 20 (12), 4671–4688. See https://doi.org/10.1177/1461444818779754 (accessed January 2022).

Schildhauer, P. and Bündgens-Kosten, J. (2021) Englischunterricht in einer digitalisierten Gesellschaft: The times they are a-changin' oder there is nothing new under the sun? In J. Bündgens-Kosten and P. Schildhauer (eds) *Englischunterricht in einer digitalisierten Gesellschaft* (pp. 9–23). Beltz.

Schmidt, A. and Marx, K. (2020) Making Let's Plays watchable: An interactional approach to gaming visualizations. In C. Thurlow, C. Dürscheid and F. Diémoz (eds) *Visualizing Digital Discourse: Interactional, Institutional and Ideological Perspectives* (pp. 131–150). De Gruyter Mouton.

Stannard, M. and von Blanckenburg, M. (2018) Digitale Spiele im Fremdsprachenunterricht. *Praxis Fremdsprachenunterricht* 2018 (4), 9–12.

The New London Group (1996) A pedagogy of multiliteracies: Designing social futures. *Harvard educational review* 66 (1), 60–93. See www.doi.org/10.17763/haer.66.1.17370n67v22j160u (accessed January 2022).

Tilgner, A. (2017) Gaming 2.0: Von der Fanproduktion zum Kulturgut – Let's Play-Videos als Schnittstelle zwischen passiver Rezeption und aktiver Partizipation. In J. Ackermann (ed.) *Phänomen Let's Play-Video. Entstehung, Ästhetik, Aneignung und Faszination aufgezeichneten Computerspielhandelns* (pp. 209–222). Springer Fachmedien.

Venus, J. (2017) Stilisierte Rezeption. Überlegungen zum epistemischen Status von Let's-Play-Videos. In J. Ackermann (ed.) *Phänomen Let's Play-Video. Entstehung, Ästhetik, Aneignung und Faszination aufgezeichneten Computerspielhandelns* (pp. 19–29). Springer Fachmedien.

Zielinski, W., Aßmann, S., Kaspar, K. and Moormann, P. (eds) (2017) Spielend lernen! Computerspiele(n) in Schule und Unterricht. See https://www.grimme-forschung.de/fileadmin/Grimme_Nutzer_Dateien/Medienbildung/Dokumente/SR-DG-NRW_05-Spielend_lernen.pdf (accessed January 2022).

9 Consuming and Producing Artificial Intelligence (AI)-Generated Text in English Language Classrooms

Sandra Stadler-Heer

9.1 Introduction

This chapter discusses how the intricacies of information science and programming languages have already, and will continue to transform the way we use natural languages and interact across cultures in different languages in yet unthinkable ways. The origin of this transformation lies with artificial intelligence (AI), which Kaplan and Haenlein (2019: 17) define as 'a system's ability to interpret external data correctly, to learn from such data, and to use those learnings to achieve specific goals and tasks through flexible adaptation'. At least for now, AI's ability to interpret external data, however, remains limited as it cannot solve every given task. In relation to mathematics, for instance, du Sautoy (as cited in Samuel, 2019) points out that AI cannot 'come up with new ideas' and even when 'trained on mathematical ways of thinking', it cannot pass a school-level paper. Apparently, AI, ultimately reliant on binary code, is not capable of solving a complex (mathematical) problem verbalized with the help of humans' natural language, i.e. described with context-specific words in an analogous test. While this momentary inability to train AI to communicate effectively with 'us' is frustrating, recent research nevertheless claims that 'digital technology is considered one of the most important drivers of linguistic change in a modern period' (Abbasova & Mammadova, 2019: 364). Such developments are a call to investigate these changes, especially in the field of English language teaching (ELT).

Concerning the English language classroom, it transpires that the latest technological developments turn have major implications for how languages are learned in institutional settings. The fact that we are entering an age of Artificial Intelligence-Mediated Communication (AI-MC) (Hancock *et al.*, 2020), and that more and more text is produced online by artificial intelligence calls for a reconsideration of our current notion of text authorship. I will therefore expand on existing definitions of 'born-digital text' (e.g. Ye & Doermann, 2015) in order to address how AI-MC is already shaping the way we interact through language. Indeed, the latest theoretical re-conceptualizations and findings on AI-MC highlight the inherent need to discuss its implications for (human) agency in digitized environments (Hancock *et al.*, 2020).

This chapter debates selected implications of the advent of AI-MC for the digital competence development of (language) learners (Amiri, 2000; Redecker & Punie, 2017; Vista, 2020); a topic which has not yet been integrated into the development of intercultural communicative competence, one of the major learning objectives of foreign language teaching. To begin with, the following outlines suggestions for content- and context-specific solutions for teaching the (mindful) consumption and production of AI-generated texts. The chapter proposes concrete steps for integrating AI-generated text in existing 21st-century curricula of L2 language education and concludes with implications for research into AI-generated text in English language classrooms.

9.2 Born-Digital Text – Terminological Discrepancies

This chapter was devised, researched and written by a human. It took countless attempts to formulate sentences, to divide the chapter into sections and to develop the overall line of argumentation. The final version of this chapter was only approved for publication after drawing on multiple resources, after repeated consultation with the editors of this collection, and after informal debates with people surrounding me in my private and professional life. The amount of time and human-to-human interaction that went into this text initially typed into a Word document is certainly higher than pressing a 'generate text' button on a website like the Talk to Transformer website (InferKitDemo, 2022). The Generative Pretrained Transformer 3 (GPT3), which can be accessed via the Talk to Transformer website, is a highly sophisticated chatbot based on a large language model, which is a neural network trained on more than 200 billion words (Hutson, 2021). GPT3 can generate streams of text by request. This chapter as well as the text generated by GPT3 are both born-digital texts (Table 9.1), a term presently used inconsistently across different academic disciplines, namely in reference to people, to human-made digital materials and, most recently, in reference to text produced by artificial intelligence (see also the Introduction).

Initially, Palfrey and Glaser (2008) established the term born-digital as a reference to people who have grown up in an environment shaped by smartphones, social media and permanent access to online content via WiFi networks, the so-called digital natives. The National Archives (n.d.) uses the term born-digital in relation to things other than people and

Table 9.1 Defining born-digital texts

Born-digital records	Metadata
1. Email	1. Identifier, for example a file path
2. Text-based documents (for example Word documents, Google documents)	2. File title
3. Presentations (for example PowerPoint)	3. File format
4. Spreadsheets (for example Excel)	4. Dates, for example the date of creation, the date last modified, the date last accessed
5. PDFs	5. Checksum
6. Images and videos	6. Closure information, if applicable, e.g. the retention period or the exemption applied
7. CAD drawings	7. Description
8. 3D models	8. Copyright information
9. Data sets and data bases	9. Protective marking

Source: The National Archives (n.d).

differentiates between born-digital records and metadata (Table 9.1). On their website, they define '[b]orn-digital records [as] records that have been natively created in digital format (rather than digitized from paper records)'.

The list displayed in Table 9.1 focuses exclusively on text authored by humans. Surprisingly, neither the list of born-digital records nor the metadata mention 'software code' as a separate category. Also, scholarly papers, such as Faustina Joan and Valli (2019: Figure 1), do not include the textual infrastructure, i.e. the programming language needed to generate digital text, in their definition and subsequent analysis of born-digital text. Even the Wikipedia entry for 'born-digital' (2022) only considers human-made front-end text to be born-digital. Indeed, most current definitions of born-digital text predominantly describe the front-end text of the digital space but do not consider the programming language operating in the back-end to make text visible and readable online in linguistic or graphic patterns.

However, the idea that software code is digital text and a programming language is needed to make, for instance, digital archiving possible, is not new. During a debate available on YouTube under the title *Born Digital*, Lowood (2014), an expert in computer games, and his colleague mention software code as a distinctive form of born-digital text. To make software code accessible and indeed run for an extended period, even after computer updates, code authors must consider sustainability as a design factor, as it is crucial for transparency and for implementing quality standards in the field of computer science.

Since the mid-2010s, another category of born-digital text has emerged, namely text produced by artificial intelligence. Drawing on natural language processing technology, different AI systems, for example InferKit (2022), produce millions of lines of text every second. GPT3 can write songs, stories, press releases, guitar tabs, interviews, essays or technical manuals (Hutson, 2021). It is also trained to 'summarize legal documents, suggest answers to customer-service enquiries, propose computer code, run text-based role-playing games or even identify at-risk individuals in a peer-support community by labelling posts as cries for help' (Hutson, 2021). Although computer linguists might call this an oversimplification, it could be argued that AI-produced text comes into existence without prior review or consultation. InferKit (2022), for instance, 'was modeled on a great variety of different web pages, some of which contained [offensive or sexual] content'. As a result, the 'generator may produce offensive or sexual content' and humans are warned 'Use at your own risk!' (InferKit, 2022). The Frequently Asked Questions section states that newly generated text is not stored. The question of who owns the generated text is termed a 'complicated issue' and worth citing in full, considering the discussion of how to integrate AI-MC in classroom practices later in this chapter.

> We can't give legal advice, so if you rely on a solid answer you'll need to consult a legal professional. We do however waive any rights we may have in the text you generate and grant you license to use it for any purpose (to the extent that we have that right), royalty-free and without warranty. You don't have to credit us anywhere.
>
> To hint at the complexity of this issue, consider that the neural networks were originally: (1) designed and trained by large tech companies who licensed their code under the MIT license, (2) learned from millions of web pages containing content in which many people hold copyright, (3) are hosted by us (we waive all rights to the content) and (4) are conditioned on the prompt you give it (your own content). (InferKit, 2022)

As text generated by InferKit can be used without citation, identifying text generated by artificial intelligence becomes a complex issue, if not impossible. Indeed, research shows that individuals are 'largely incapable of distinguishing between AI- and human-generated text' (Kreps *et al.*, 2022). While ignorance can be bliss, AI-generated text is found to have 'the potential to shift language norms and expectations even when communicators are not using these tools, and produce long-term language change over time' (Hancock *et al.*, 2020: 4). A study on Gmail's smart reply suggestions in text messaging shows that these AI-generated messages are overly positive ('sounds great!') (Hohenstein & Jung, 2018) to facilitate trust between human communicators (Hohenstein & Jung, 2020). As a result, AI is used to 'optimize communications and achieve interpersonal goals' by 'augmenting our natural ability to communicate with one another and improving the affordances of such interactions' (Hancock *et al.*, 2020: 9). Moreover, human users of AI-mediated communication feel less responsible when communication fails, this being the only instance when they actually ascribe agency to AI (Hohenstein & Jung, 2020).

With more and more research pointing to the influence of AI-generated text on interpersonal dynamics (Hohenstein & Jung, 2020), it is time to develop (L2) language learners and teachers' competences in AI-MC. The following section on current developments in (language) curriculum design, digital competence development and research in professional development can help teachers to evaluate their own professional development of digital competences and AI-generated text before they engage in classroom activities with their learners.

9.3 Curricular Developments: AI-Generated Text in English Language Teaching

Over two decades ago, Amiri (2000) asked whether language teachers should be able to code. Amiri (2000) argued for making language teachers IT-literate as they would then move from being 'mere consumers of computer-based materials' to becoming 'consumers and producers of computer-based materials'. Teachers could actively produce high-quality learning materials themselves and be in the position to critically evaluate existing materials. Being more competent in this field, they would consequently be more likely to enable their learners to become consumers and producers of born-digital texts. This line of argumentation is also found in the Charta of Digital Education (2020): For humans to be able to shape the digital and analogue world, they must assess new digital tools from a technical perspective (How does it work?), an application-oriented perspective (How do I use it?) and a sociocultural perspective (What impact does it have?) (Nagel, n.d.).

The importance for citizens being digitally competent is also emphasized in the Digital Competence Framework for Educators (DigCompEdu; Redecker & Punie, 2017). While digital competences are to be acquired by learners, only 25.9% of teachers learned how to use digital media during teacher training (Eickelmann et al., 2019). In the German context, for instance, no numbers are available for how many teachers can create digital content; neither are numbers available to what degree teachers are digitally literate in the first place. However, national standards of education in a digital world exist to ensure that teachers prepare learners for learning and assessment in digital learning spaces, and that learners develop subject-specific digital competences to participate actively and in a self-determined manner in a digital world (KMK, 2017: 6f.). This also includes being able to recognize and formulate algorithms (KMK, 2017: 12). Learners should:

- know and understand the functioning and basic principles of the digital world,

Table 9.2 Competences related to AI-generated text and AI-MC

L2 language teachers learn how to	L2 language learners learn how to
1. acquire knowledge about AI-generated text(subject specific competence and digital, Punie & Redecker, 2018).	1. become information and data literate.
2. consume AI-generated text knowledgeably in their professional environment, as a digital resource and in their teaching (Punie & Redecker, 2018: Figure 4).	2. communicate digitally and collaboratively.
3. produce learning designs on AI-generated text and AI-MC as a result of professional development.	3. create digital content with the help of AI and use AI-MC responsibly.
4. empower learners and facilitate learners' competences in relation to AI-MC.	4. solve problems related to AI-MC.

Source: Adapted from Redecker (2017).

- recognise and formulate algorithmic structures in digital tools,
- use structured, algorithmic sequence to solve a problem (2017: 12).

According to the DigCompEdu, to be digitally competent means to be information and data literate, to be able to communicate, to create content, to produce and use digital content responsively and to solve digital problems (Redecker & Punie, 2017). Drawing on these domains of the DigCompEdu, the above progression in facilitating competence development is suggested (Table 9.2).

Table 9.2 reflects the prevalent assumption that teachers need to be competent users of a tool or form of communication themselves, here AI-generated text, before they can teach their learners. On the content level, AI that can be used to generate text is one such tool, and another form of communication that language teachers will need to understand from a conceptual, contextual and linguistic perspective. In the scope of this chapter, I will focus predominantly on the 'How do I use it?' and the 'What impact does it have?' questions of the Charta of Digital Education (2020) and attempt to answer what AI-MC means for English language teaching. Hence, understanding the very last technical details of AI-MC is not the goal of this chapter. Instead, I will focus on the 'complicated issues' the authors of InferKit (2022) address, and how tools drawing on AI-MC might affect language production of both language teachers and learners.

9.4 Developments in Learning Design

To date, online (learning) spaces remain crucially underdeveloped (learning) environments and both (language) teachers and (language) learners lack experience in engaging with digital tools for learning purposes. Consequently, there is a need for (learning) designs that integrate the specificities of online spaces (Carrillo & Flores, 2020). Wathall's

Consuming and Producing AI-Generated Text in English Language Classrooms 143

Stages of eLearning

Survive
What digitals tools do we use?
What LMS do we use?

Arrive
An entire unit for a **blended learning** approach which involves the best **pedagogical** practices!

Strive
How do the digital tools work?

Thrive
How to use digital tools in a meaningful way to enhance learning?

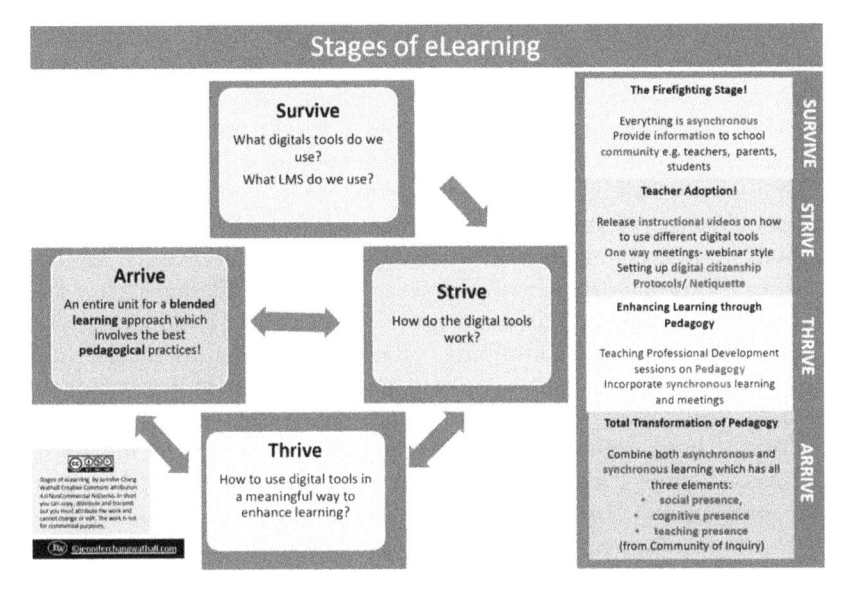

SURVIVE — The Firefighting Stage!
Everything is asynchronous
Provide information to school community e.g. teachers, parents, students

STRIVE — Teacher Adoption!
Release instructional videos on how to use different digital tools
One way meetings- webinar style
Setting up digital citizenship Protocols/ Netiquette

THRIVE — Enhancing Learning through Pedagogy
Teaching Professional Development sessions on Pedagogy
Incorporate synchronous learning and meetings

ARRIVE — Total Transformation of Pedagogy
Combine both asynchronous and synchronous learning which has all three elements:
* social presence,
* cognitive presence
* teaching presence
(from Community of Inquiry)

Stages of eLearning by Jennifer Chang Wathall Creative Commons attribution—NonCommercial NoDerivs. In short you can copy, distribute and transmit but you must attribute the work and cannot change or edit. The work is not for commercial purposes.
@jenniferchangwathall.com

Figure 9.1 The Stages of eLearning (Source: Wathall, 2020)

infographic on the stages of eLearning (2020) provides a research-based, and yet easy to access, toolkit for both teachers and learners to develop strategies for engaging with unknown digital tools. I will use Wathall's approach to propose a learning design for integrating AI-generated texts as a tool for learning about how AI impacts human communication.

Teachers can approach teaching with a new tool by making an informed decision about which tool to use (Figure 9.1) and draw on the positive effects of the Community of Inquiry approach (Carrillo & Flores, 2020). When they decide to include AI tools, for instance GPT3 or Gmail's smart replies, in their language lessons and use AI-generated text, they must take on both a user and consumer perspective. Slipping into the role of the user, teachers – and later also their learners – need to figure out what AI does (STRIVE). Teachers then need to ask whether AI-generated text can be used meaningfully for language learning (THRIVE). Learners would ask in this stage how using AI-generated texts shapes their understanding of the foreign language. Finally, teachers plan an entire blended learning unit on AI-generated text and involve the best pedagogical practices including social, cognitive and teaching presence (Garrison *et al.*, 2000) (ARRIVE).

9.5 Possible Uses of AI in English Language Teaching

The following teaching sequences aim to systematically develop language learners' critical awareness towards using and consuming

AI-mediated text. The tasks foster L2 language learners' competences according to the steps proposed by Wathall (2020) and the DigCompEdu (Redecker & Punie, 2017) as adapted in Table 9.2. All examples are intended as teaching guidelines for pre- and in-service teachers who are not coding experts, but (becoming) experts in developing (digital) intercultural communication. All activities have been tried out in grades 8 and 10 (13- to 16-year-olds) of a German secondary school. Results from classroom discussions in the teaching interventions show the potential of such subject-specific task formats on born-digital text types for reclaiming agency and for developing AI-related communicative competences (Table 9.2).

The learning designs on consuming and producing born-digital text start at a basic level and conclude with classroom debates on AI-generated text or AI-MC. All tasks consider both the consumer's and the producer's perspective of born-digital text to initiate a discussion on the impact of AI-MC on language use. Tools that have been preselected include or produce some form of born-digital text. All tasks can be completed within a 10–15 minute sequence depending on prior experience, learner group and individual L2 language competences. Alternatively, individual activities or tasks can be completed as standalone lessons.

9.5.1 Consuming born-digital text

The first activities in the task sequence require learners to engage with types of AI-generated text (Table 9.3 and Table 9.4); becoming literate in a topic is the first necessary step in becoming competent (Table 9.5). This first task sequence fosters learners' receptive skills through engaging with born-digital text. All immersive tasks are, however, matched with interactive and cooperative learning activities initiating communication about their experiences as consumers of these types of texts.

9.5.2 Producing born-digital texts

Having established what born-digital and AI-generated texts are, the second task sequence addresses the interplay of software code and human written text on websites to illustrate how teachers and learners are consuming computer-generated text implicitly on a day-to-day basis (Table 9.6). The following tasks aim to demystify beliefs that one needs to be able to code to produce born-digital texts, and starts with an activity presenting examples of front-end and back-end text of a website. Students should be given room to explore their experience of seeing different languages on one website and how this shifts their focus (Hirvela, 1996). This is followed by an activity in Scratch that can help L2 language learners to code stories. The learning design helps both learners and teachers to develop concepts and attitudes towards born-digital text and how it is already shaping our world. After completing these productive tasks in which students and

Table 9.3 Selected teaching material 1: Example of an AI-generated text

Description	In the following text, the first three sentences (in bold) were written by a human. They were entered in a model that automatically generates further text (from The Washington Post onwards). The AI-generated text is produced based on AI calculating from the texts it was trained on which words would follow.
Human	**President Trump is buying Greenland in a surprise deal. The state of California is traded in return. The deal was well received by Republicans.**
Non-Human (AI-generated)	The *Washington Post* reports: 'Trump said the country's unique geography and natural mineral resources would be 'an asset' to the state over its lifespan. He is expected to move swiftly to make good the investment in the $10.8 billion purchase of a national park that he and the president of Denmark, Jens Stoltenberg, announced last year. 'The sale of the state could help the US in its fight against global warming, which is already heating up the planet. The government of Denmark says the purchase will pay for a 10-year expansion of a national park in the north of the island, which is one of the world's most biodiverse areas.' This move doesn't come as a surprise to political analysts. A recent study by the World Wildlife Fund and the Smithsonian's National Center for Atmospheric Research revealed several Arctic nations have substantial oil reserves and natural gas reserves and they are in talks to trade them in for the Arctic. 'Canada and Russia are the two most active, buying all but 2 percent of the Arctic's undiscovered oil and gas reserves, based on an analysis of data from 2008 to 2016,' explains the Wall Street Journal. 'As many as 11 countries also have interests in the Arctic. The U.S. and Britain, which both lost an ocean fleet to Islamic State militants in the last year, are both among them, as are China, Germany and India.'

Source: Thompson (2019).

teachers could experience their active engagement, the effects that AI-MC can have on interaction are debated, intending to promote conscious consumption and critical engagement as well as informing about the differences in human-to-human and computer-mediated language.

9.6 Implications for Future Research

This chapter provided some first conceptual glimpses into learning designs on born-digital text and AI-MC. More design-based, as well as practitioner research, on how L2 language teachers and learners can consume and produce AI-generated text is necessary. It is imperative to establish qualitative research practices conducted in online or face-to-face L2 language classrooms by in-service teachers or researchers, to actively monitor and discuss the 'potentially critical impact' (Hancock *et al.*, 2020: 9) of AI-MC on maintaining intact interpersonal relationships through communication. This could be in the form of interviews, or by drawing on the categories of design-based research to optimize digital learning materials. These efforts must be undertaken alongside studies in

Table 9.4 Exemplary tasks to promote digital competences related to consuming AI-MC in the L2 language classroom.

Level of Competence	Task
Beginners: Consuming AI-generated text	**Topic A: Debating text authorship** Introductory Text (**Table 9.3**) 1. Read the text and say what it is about. 2. Please guess: by whom/when was this written? 3. What questions arise for you when I tell you that the author is a computer program?
Intermediate Learners: Consuming AI-generated text	Raising awareness for AI-generated text: Maybe you ask yourself now 'How can I find out whether something was written by a human or an artificial intelligence?' Go to this website (https://www.bot-or-not.de/gedichte.html) and decide whether these poems written by humans or an artificial intelligence. **For fast finishers:** How can you find out if who you talk to online is a bot or not? Read through Table 9.5, pick the feature you find most interesting and be prepared to explain it in class. You may use a dictionary and do further research online. Engage in a classroom discussion and debate the following statements by Marcus du Sautoy: 1. 'AI is quite successful in poetry because it's able to create something that leaves enough ambiguity so the reader can use a lot of their creativity to bring the poems to life.' 2. 'What you do as a novelist is very interesting to me because I think we actually come much more hardwired for language than we realize. The evidence suggests that a child learns language with exposure to very little data, which chimes in with Chomsky's idea that we do come preprogrammed. And that preprogramming is millions of years of evolution. Whereas we haven't been through such an evolutionary process in creating our mathematical language. So math is something that AI could perhaps fast-track, much quicker than being able to tell the stories that you tell.' Source: https://www.vox.com/2019/5/10/18529009/ai-art-marcus-du-sautoy-math-music-painting-literature **Transfer:** Should AI-generated text only be used to produce art and not factual text, like news reports? Alternative texts: e.g. samples of automated journalism.
Advanced learners: Consuming AI-generated text	**Topic B: Talking to an AI** **Gaining information and data literacy:** Let's try out to talk to an artificial intelligence online. Website: https://www.kuki.ai/ Think carefully about what you want to ask the Kuki, "the world's most popular English language social chatbot" (2022). Find out more about Kuki on the following website: https://www.kuki.ai/research. Prepare a one-minute talk on social bots and your experiences of chatting online with a bot. **For fast finishers:** How can you find out if who you talk to online is a bot or not? Read through **Table 9.4**, which explains which features bots have. Pick the feature you find most interesting and be prepared to explain it in class. You may use a dictionary and are allowed to do further research online. **Think-Pair-Share:** Think about when you would choose to (rather) talk to an AI than a human. Come up with a list of topics and reasons. Present it to your partner. Be prepared to present one topic in class. **Transfer I:** Some people consult social bots when they are feeling sad (Exemplary news report: https://edition.cnn.com/2020/08/19/world/chatbot-social-anxiety-spc-intl/index.html). Can you imagine why? **Transfer II:** Mental health, AI and the ethics of medical data. What do you do when you are feeling sad? Do you tell somebody when you feel sad? How do you feel when talking about problems? Who do you want to know about your problems?

Table 9.5 Features that help recognize and separate bot-like from human-like behavior

Class	Number of features	Description (*Note: This task introduces tech-specific vocabulary. You may not understand every word at once. See which terminology is used in this scientific field. You may use a dictionary and are allowed to do further research on terms online.*)
Network	112	*Network features* capture various dimensions of information diffusion patterns. We build networks based on retweets, mentions and hashtag co-occurrences, and extract their statistical features. Examples include degree distribution, clustering coefficient and centrality measures.
User	56	*User features* are based on Twitter meta-data related to an account, including language, geographic locations and account creation time.
Friends	208	*Friend features* include descriptive statistics relative to an account's social contacts (followees), such as the median, moments and entropy of the distributions of their number of followers, followees, posts and so on.
Timing	24	*Timing features* capture temporal patterns of content generation (tweets) and consumption (retweets); examples include the signal similarity to a Poisson process (Ghosh *et al.*, 2011), the average time between two consecutive posts, and such.
Content	411	*Content features* are based on linguistic cues computed through natural language processing, especially part-of-speech tagging; examples include the frequency of verbs, nouns and adverbs in the phrases produced by the account.
Sentiment	339	*Sentiment features* are built using general-purpose and Twitter-specific sentiment analysis algorithms, including happiness, arousal-dominance-valence and emotion scores (Golder & Macy 2011; Bollen *et al.*, 2011).

Source: Extended from Ferrara *et al.*, 2014: XX,4.

subject-specific development of digital competences related to AI-MC. Researchers in teacher training and professional development should accompany the former efforts and feed the results into their own studies on the development of technological pedagogical content knowledge of (future) L2 language teachers. Ideally, researchers should engage in longitudinal studies of competence development.

While research on the nature of AI-MC text is growing, more subject-specific research considering ethical implications of AI-MC between humans and non-humans is necessary. Here, studies in the field of L2 language learning could investigate beliefs and perceptions of learners and teachers of AI-MC and investigate their trust in born-digital texts read in an L2 classroom. This would make already existing findings (Gillespie *et al.*, 2021) more concrete and applicable for individual learning contexts.

Finally, cross-disciplinary research on new forms of teaching with and about AI-MC, on material design and development of high-quality learning materials, is as relevant as strengthening teachers' competences to use, produce and evaluate digital learning designs. Here, interactive and gamified language learning tasks (Költzsch & Stadler-Heer, 2021) may also present an alternative for engaging with AI-MC. Cross-disciplinary research teams may do well to invest in the time-consuming development of open-access high-quality language learning tasks as these have the potential to promote creativity, social competences and communicative skills needed by L2 language learners.

Table 9.6 Exemplary tasks to promote digital competences related to producing AI-generated text in the L2 language classroom

Level of competence	Task
Beginners: Producing born-digital text	**Topic: Writing/Programming websites.** Activity: Highlight all hypertext markup language of the back-end version of this website (**Figure 9.2**). Compare it to the front-end version (**Figure 9.3**). How does seeing the hypertext markup language affect your reading of the text? Possible answers: Leads my attention away from the text. Shifts my focus on text structure rather than content. Transfer: Which elements of a website can you influence while writing it? Name at least 10 different features.
From intermediate learner status: Producing born-digital text	**Topic: Telling our own stories with the help of code.** We have just learned that there are programming languages needed to make natural languages visible as texts online. Classroom discussion: Generally speaking, how do you feel when you see/read such a new programming language? (Pupils might feel different kinds of emotions, all are valid). Teacher: 'When I feel overwhelmed by new things, I always like to look for advice from experts. In the field of AI, I found this recommendation by experts (the first sentence might be enough!):' '[…] **Even if you have no machine learning experience, you can start with some of the simpler tools and expand from there**. [Here are some examples:] Use AI photo editing tools like Deep Art, an AI art generator like Deep Dream Generator, an AI image generator like Artbreeder (a.k.a. GANBreeder), an AI painting generator like AI Painter, a[n] AI cartoon maker like Cartoonify, or draw with a neural network using Quick Draw. As tools to make AI art **become more mainstream, AI artworks will increasingly embed themselves in our culture**.' 2019 AIArtists.org. Founded by Marnie Benney and Pete Kistler. https://aiartists.org/ai-generated-art-tools **Task: Let's write our own stories with the help of** *Scratch*. Your task is to 'code' your own story in Scratch. Scratch's graphical user interface will help you to visualize how programming language and natural language mix. What text is written in the 'back-end' and what text becomes visible in the front-end? Switch the language settings to English. Your story needs to be related to a topic in our curriculum. Be prepared to present your project in class. You will have 5 lessons to complete the project. Tipp: You can find an example story by LordSalad (2015) here: https://scratch.mit.edu/projects/86173393/

(*Continued*)

Table 9.6 (Continued)

Level of competence	Task
Advanced learners: Producing born-digital text	**Topic: AI-generated text and the effects of AI-MC.** Example from *Hancock et al. (2020: Figure 1), Gmail's AI-generated suggested responses often trend positive.* Have a great time! Glad to hear it! Nice! ← Reply → Forward Introductory question: Do you use the automated responses suggested as text when talking to other humans via your smartphone? Why do you use them? Do they convey the message that you want to send? Question: What happens when AI-MC plays a role in suggesting or generating messages by one of the communicators (Hancock *et al.*, 2020: 5)? For an answer to this question see the conclusion of this paper. Open classroom project: In groups, plan an exhibition on the topic 'Interaction through Language'. How do you want to interact with other people and/or with AI? Which role does language play in face-to-face or online interaction? Include an artistic product that visualizes your vision. Intended learning goal: Conscious consumption/interaction of/with AI.

Upcoming Events

```
<p style="text-align: justify;">The following list provides an overview of events
organised or attended by members of the research network. Please feel free to contact
us about/at these events.</p>
<p style="text-align: center;"><strong>Call for Abstracts</strong></p>
<p style="text-align: center;"><strong>LiLLT ReN Symposium at the AILA World Congress 2023 in
Lyon</strong></p>
<p>We are pleased to announce that can now call for individual submissions for our hybrid
LiLLT ReN Symposium - Researching Literature in Language Learning and Beyond at the 2023 AILA
World Congress in Lyon in July 2023.</p>
<p>The abstracts of the symposia are now accessible on the platform (<a
href="https://aila2023.sciencesconf.org/" target="_blank" rel="noopener
noreferrer">https://aila2023.sciencesconf.org/</a>) by going to the "Symposia" tab. You will
find several ways to search within them (authors, formats, etc.).</p>
<p>We would also like to inform you of the procedure for the call for individual
submissions:</p>
<p>1)     The call is available on the main website of the congress: <a
href="https://aila2023.fr/call-for-papers/" target="_blank" rel="noopener
```

Figure 9.2 Example of backend text (Source: LiLLT, 2022)

9.7 Conclusion

Given that the engagement with born-digital text is a young research field this chapter can only serve as a starting point to build L2 language learners' competences in engaging critically with selected types of AI-MC text. At present, '[m]any open questions remain about how AI tools will be used to optimize communications and achieve interpersonal goals' (Hancock *et al.*, 2020: 9). This is to be understood as a call for action. The proposed teaching example brings AI-generated texts into language

Upcoming Events

> The following list provides an overview of events organised or attended by members of the research network. Please feel free to contact us about/at these events.
>
> Call for Abstracts
>
> LiLLT ReN Symposium at the AILA World Congress 2023 in Lyon
>
> We are pleased to announce that can now call for individual submissions for our hybrid LiLLT ReN Symposium - Researching Literature in Language Learning and Beyond at the 2023 AILA World Congress in Lyon in July 2023.
>
> The abstracts of the symposia are now accessible on the platform (https://aila2023.sciencesconf.org/) by going to the "Symposia" tab. You will find several ways to search within them (authors, formats, etc.).
>
> We would also like to inform you of the procedure for the call for individual submissions:
>
> 1) The call is available on the main website of the congress: https://aila2023.fr/call-for-papers/

Figure 9.3 Example of frontend text (Source: LiLLT, 2022)

classrooms and makes them the topic of human communication. By engaging with latest research findings and developments in digital technologies and the use of AI-mediated text teachers and learners of languages train their AI-related competences. Only then can they play an active role in shaping how languages are consumed and produced in both online and offline settings.

Figures

LiLLT (Literature in Language Learning and Research Network) (2022) Upcoming Events. Accessed 7 June 2022. <https://lilltresearch.net/>.

Wathall, J.C. (2020) Stages of eLearning. Accessed 7 June 2022 <https://www.jennifer-changwathall.com/single-post/how-blended-learning-has-evolved>.

References

Abbasova, M. and Mammadova, N. (2019) The role of digital technology in english language teaching in Azerbaijan. *International Journal of English Linguistic*s 9 (2), 364–372.

Amiri, F. (2000) It-literacy for language teachers: Should it include computer programming? *System* 28 (1), 77–84.

Born Digital (2014) Youtube. See https://www.youtube.com/watch?v=ZQY8xBEl1vI (accessed January 2022).

Carrillo, C. and Flores, M.A. (2020) COVID-19 and teacher education: A literature review of online teaching and learning practices. *European Journal of Teacher Education* 43 (4), 466–487.

Eickelmann, B., Bos, W., Gerick, J., Goldhammer, F., Schaumburg, H., Schwippert, K., Senkbeil, M. and Vahrenhold, J. (eds) (2019) *ICILS 2018 #Deutschland –Computer- und informationsbezogene Kompetenzen von Schülerinnen und Schülern im zweiten internationalen Vergleich und Kompetenzen im Bereich Computational Thinking*. Waxmann.

Faustina Joan, S.P. and Valli, S. (2019) A survey on text information extraction from born-digital and scene text images. *Proceedings of the National Academy of Sciences, India Section A: Physical Sciences* 89, 77–101. https://doi.org/10.1007/s40010-017-0478-y

Ferrara, E., Varol, O., Davis, C., Menczer, F. and Flammini, A. (2014) The Rise of social bots. *Communications of the ACM* XX, 1–9. https://doi.org/10.1145/2818717

Garrison, R., Anderson, T. and Archer, W. (2000) Critical inquiry in a text-based environment: Computer conferencing higher education. *The Internet and Higher Education* 2 (2–3), 87–105. https://doi.org/10.1080/02607476.2020.1755205.

Gillespie, N., Lockey, S. and Curtis, C. (2021) *Trust in Artificial Intelligence: A Five Country Study.* The University of Queensland and KPMG Australia. https://doi.org/10.14264/e34bfa3

Hancock, J.T., Naaman, M. and Levy, K. (2020) AI-Mediated communication: Definition, research agenda, and ethical consideration. *Journal of Computer-Mediated Communication*, 1–12.

Hirvela, A. (1996) Reader-response theory and ELT. *English Language Teaching Journal* 50 (2), 127–134. https://doi.org/10.1093/elt/50.2.127

Hohenstein, J. and Jung, M. (2018) AI-supported messaging: An investigation of human-human text conversation with AI support. *CHI EA '18: Extended abstracts of the 2018 CHI conference on human factors in computing systems* (pp. LBW089:1–LBW089:6). ACM.

Hohenstein, J. and Jung, M. (2020) AI as a moral crumple zone: The effects of AI-mediated communication on attribution of responsibility and perception of trust. *Computers in Human Behavior*. https://doi.org/10.1016/j.chb.2019.106190.

Hutson, M. (2021) Robo-writers: The rise and risks of language-generating AI. *Nature*. Accessed 04 May 2022 https://www.nature.com/articles/d41586-021-00530-0.

InferKitDemo (2022) Text generation. Accessed 19 January 2022, https://inferkit.com/docs/generation.

Kaplan, A. and Haenlein, M. (2019) Siri, Siri, in my hand: Who's the fairest in the land? On the interpretations, illustrations, and implications of artificial intelligence. *Business Horizons* 62, 15—25.

KMK (2017) German standards of education in a digital world. See https://www.kmk.org/fileadmin/Dateien/pdf/PresseUndAktuelles/2017/Strategie_neu_2017_datum_1.pdf (accessed January 2022).

Költzsch, D. and Stadler-Heer, S. (2021) Gamifying language learning: How Gamification can support learning in the language classroom. *11th International Conference the Future of Education,* 449–454. Pixel e Filodiritto Editore. https://doi.org/10.26352/F701_2384-9509

Kreps, S., McCain, R.M. and Brundage, M. (2022) All the news that's fit to fabricate: AI-generated text as a tool of media misinformation. *Journal of Experimental Political Science* 9 (1), 104 – 117. DOI: https://doi.org/10.1017/XPS.2020.37

LordSalad (2015) Great fire of london history homework, November 2. Accessed 7 June 2022 <https://scratch.mit.edu/projects/86173393/>.

Nagel, F. (n.d.) Charta digital education. See https://charter-digital-education.org (accessed June 2022).

Palfrey, J. and Gasser, U. (2008) *Born Digital: Understanding the First Generation of Digital Natives.* Basic Books.

Redecker, C. (2017) Synthesis of the DigCompEdu framework. See https://publications.jrc.ec.europa.eu/repository/handle/JRC107466 (accessed September 2023).

Redecker, C. and Punie, Y. (2017) Europäischer Rahmen für die Digitale Kompetenz von Lehrenden (DigCompEdu). *European Union.* Accessed 7 June 2022 <https://ec.europa.eu/jrc/sites/jrcsh/files/digcompedu_leaflet_de-2018-09-21pdf.pdf>.

Samuel, S. (2019) Artificial intelligence can now make art. Artists, don't panic. *Vox*, 17 May. Accessed 05 January 2022 <https://www.vox.com/2019/5/10/18529009/ai-art-marcus-du-sautoy-math-music-painting-literature>.

Thompson, C. (2019) StoryAI, a bot that autocompletes a story for you. *Boingboing*, 27 August. See https://boingboing.net/2019/08/27/storyai-a-bot-that-autocomple.html (accessed June 2022).

The National Archives (n.d.) Born-digital records and metadata. See https://www.nationalarchives.gov.uk/information-management/manage-information/digital-records-transfer/what-are-born-digital-records/ (accessed August 2022).

Vista, A. (2020) Teaching coding as a literacy: Issues, challenges, and limitations. *Academia Letters*, Article 5. https://doi.org/10.20935/AL5

Ye, Q. and Doermann, D. (2015) Text detection and recognition in imagery: A survey. *IEEE Transactions on Pattern Analysis and Machine Intelligence* 37 (7), 1480–1500.

10 AI and the Digital Writing Process

Jasmina Najjar and Philip M. McCarthy

10.1 Introduction

This chapter focuses on the role of AI (Artificial Intelligence) in the tertiary-level writing process. More specifically, we consider the role of AI as it pertains to the challenges faced by non-native English speakers in college-level writing courses. These challenges have been extensively documented, and stem from both linguistic and cultural differences that are likely to impact students at any stage of the writing process. The writing process itself refers to the recursive practice involved in creating papers, essays, reports, stories and other similar documents (Beaufort, 2007; Flower & Hayes, 1981). This process may involve several interconnected stages, including generating ideas researching, drafting, revising, integrating feedback, editing, peer reviewing and submitting. In modern-day writing process textbooks (e.g. McCarthy & Ahmed, 2021), authors assume that technology is available and will be applied. For example, instructors present materials with PowerPoints, and introduce readings using online collaborative learning platforms; meanwhile, students find resources using electronic databases and submit papers through learning management systems. Therefore, it is not surprising that the papers instructors expect from students are also fundamentally underpinned by technology; indeed, the final paper itself is seldom likely to have featured many (or any) analogue components. As such, a modern-day composition course itself can be considered a technology-driven born-digital writing process.

In recent years, researchers such as McCarthy *et al.* (2021b) have extensively documented the role of technology in writing. However, as the authors note '[…] by this time tomorrow, new technology will have been made available, and yet another group of authors will have been tasked with trying to catalogue and convey the ever-expanding galaxy of gadgetry' (McCarthy *et al.*, 2021b: 338). *Tomorrow* has now arrived, and its name is AI. Correspondingly, it is the purpose of this chapter to discuss some of the galaxy of AI gadgetry that can be applied to facilitate the writing process for college level non-native English speakers. This said, we understand that the individual names that best represent today's AI will change frequently, and some of the names we currently include will, no doubt, soon be listed alongside that of Yahoo!, MySpace and America Online that once seemed destined to have a long and prosperous future. As such, the following sections will mention the names of currently available AI tools, but rather than describing in detail any of the tools, we reflect on the writing process and the kinds of AI technology that are likely to impact each of its stages.

In order for such a discussion to take place, we must first establish what exactly we mean by AI: to us, AI refers to technology that mimics or replicates human behavior (Russel & Norvig, 2016). However, it is important to note that the field of AI is very broad. The interests that primarily concern a chapter on digital text are the AI subfields of Natural Language Processing (NLP) and generative AI (see for example, McNamara *et al.*, 2014; Olga *et al.* 2023). These two subfields maintain a considerable overlap and numerous shared interests, even though they remain distinct in terms of their focus. That is, NLP focuses on computational approaches to understanding, classifying, interpreting, processing and/or generating human language. Meanwhile, the focus of generative AI is on creating new content, whether that content be human-like language, pictures, music, or numerous other applications. When speaking in terms of the technology-driven writing process, it is this distinction in focus that needs to be kept in mind. This said, given the relatively recent emergence of generative AI (and the corresponding numerous concerns it has spawned), it is this subfield (and this term) that is the primary focus of the current chapter.

10.2 Generative AI and Academic Integrity

For most instructors, it took less than a few minutes of interaction with a system like ChatGPT for there to be sincere concerns as to how the technology could impact academic integrity. Academic integrity, as defined by the International Center for Academic Integrity, is 'a commitment, even in the face of adversity, to six fundamental values: honesty, trust, fairness, respect, responsibility, and courage. From these values flow principles of behaviour that enable academic communities to translate ideals into action' (ICAI, n.d.). Following the public release of generative AI, headlines soon provided ample evidence: 'Artificial intelligence is getting better at writing ... universities should worry about plagiarism' (Kelley, 2023) and 'Ways to prevent students from using AI tools in their classes' (Mindzak & Eaton, 2021). The rapid rise of AI had long been predicted; however, the extent of the impact on the writing classroom still came as a shock to many. To counter generative AI, measures were quickly devised and included established and updated systems like Turnitin and SafeAssign. There were also newer tools such as AI Text Classifier,

Originality.AI, GPTZero as well as a plethora of others. Unfortunately, as people soon realised, all such available tools were far from accurate and were easily fooled (Williams, 2023): Instagram accounts such as @aitherevolution featured numerous posts about how to use undetectable.ai and related tools to ensure AI-generated text could not be detected. Today, the race to catch up continues. Defensive technology will get better; however, the development of generative AI itself is hardly likely to slow down either. As such, it is already high time for us as instructors to play our part. Ultimately, it is we who are best positioned to make a friend of this seeming foe.

Fortunately, not everybody views the arrival of AI as a threat. For example, during an interactive session on academic integrity at the American International Consortium of Academic Libraries (AMICAL) 2023 Conference, attendees (faculty members, librarians, IT experts and administrators) from 30 American-modeled educational institutions based in 20 different countries, all agreed that attempting to ban AI outright was both unrealistic and unreasonable. This said, attendees acknowledged that many students lack the confidence necessary to prioritise assignments, generate original content and develop an independent voice. Attendees also accepted that many non-native English-speaking students may rely extensively on AI technology such as Google Translate and related paraphrasing AI tools, for example Quillbot. Issues such as these drive some students to intentionally cut corners and many others to (un)intentionally stray from the designated pathway. That is, the line where integrating sources ends and plagiarism begins can be very gray, whether because of a lack of understanding, a difference in culture or perceived inconsistencies in instruction. Therefore, it is also important to understand that non-American institutions following the American liberal arts model of higher education typically adhere to the American/Western definition of academic integrity. This adherence may increase the likelihood of non-American/Western students' non-intentional violation of expectations, thus highlighting the need to define academic integrity in different cultural contexts so that culture-specific challenges can be addressed, especially since writing is a social act as Heap (1989) and others assert. This issue impacts how students may perceive AI as a 'generator' that creates a complete product rather than as an 'assistant' that guides them throughout the process. Therefore, there is a need for classroom and university-wide policies that first fit each university's unique cultural context, second, address the rapid developments in AI and third, support career preparedness (Najjar & Akpan, 2023).

Collecting and coalescing strategies and policies is vital; however, few instructors have the time to wait for administrators to recognise challenges and articulate solutions. As such, given the concerns regarding academic integrity, many instructors have been quick to experiment with different types of writing assignments. Some assignments have been devised to make it difficult for students to use generative AI or to completely remove AI from the equation and others to ethically integrate AI. Based on observations by Najjar (2023), 'pen and paper' in-class timed writing assignments promote academic integrity and provide a snapshot of students' skills and levels, but they are far from ideal since in the real world (be it in learning environments or in the workplace) the bulk of writing is digital and involves the use of technology. This said, it is possible to create alternative assignments that are useful, relevant and technologically ethical. Observations show the importance of shifting the emphasis from product to process to encourage academic integrity, while promoting authentic learning that better mirrors real-life situations. Observations also suggest that the type of assignment can be helpful. For instance, multimodal assignments (e.g. videos and podcasts) that involve the analysis of multimedia and include personal reflection and opinion seem to reduce the likelihood of the unproductive or unethical incorporation of generative AI (Najjar, 2023).

Developing productive assignments that reduce or eliminate generative AI should certainly be encouraged. However, it is equally beneficial (and probably *more* beneficial) to rethink assignments in a way that allows the ethical integration of AI systems. Such assignments better reflect the current and future landscape while also enhancing the prospect of student learning across the writing process (Najjar, 2023). In order to do so, several generative AI issues first need to be considered. These issues include linguistic justice, authorship and reliability. Once students have discussed and understood these issues, instructors are free to re-envision the digital writing process as one that is inclusive of the newest tools that technology has provided. Accordingly, the remainder of this chapter addresses these challenges and opportunities.

10.2.1 Linguistic justice and creativity

When AI is tasked with improving writing, this practice raises questions of *linguistic justice*. Linguistic justice is the principle and/or pursuit of everyone having equal access and opportunity to use their own language or dialect, without discrimination or oppression since, as Baker-Bell (cited in Bankhead III, 2021) states, there is no 'homogenous, standard, one-size-fits-all language'. However, AI can often favour certain varieties of English over others, which may influence people's language choices, preferences or expressions and even impose certain norms or standards that may not be appropriate or respectful for everyone. According to Nee *et al.* (2022: para 1), this influence can create inequalities and impact language, power and social identity. As the authors put it, we need to examine 'natural language processing tools (along with the datasets that are used to train and evaluate them) [...] not only from the perspective of a privileged, majority language user, but also from the perspectives of minoritized language users'. Whether AI 'improvements' are suggested changes to grammar, spelling, punctuation, wording or style, they all highlight the need to consider linguistic justice as has been pointed out. Also, on a content level, creativity may be limited because of standardised or generic feedback and suggestions. This could discourage different opinions or perspectives or pressure writers to conform (Chubb et al., 2021).

Since many of our students are non-native English speakers, it is worth having class discussions as to the issues of linguistic justice and creativity. By doing so, students can better understand how their choice of using AI and AI tool impacts their style, identity and originality, which is to say, their developing individual voice. In turn, such discussions can encourage students to think critically about each change the AI recommends, thus also developing their own writing abilities. Some questions that can be addressed include: what is your home or dominant language and how does your language impact how you write in English? How many types of English are there, and are any of these varieties superior or inferior? How do AI tools affect your linguistic identity and expression? Do AI tools enhance or diminish your linguistic diversity and creativity? How do you balance following AI's suggestions and maintaining your own voice? How can we promote linguistic justice and respect for linguistic diversity in our society when using AI to help us write? What are some of the actions that you can take as a language learner and user to address linguistic justice when using AI when writing? Note that a critical analysis assignment (described later in this chapter) can be adapted to focus on these issues and raise awareness.

10.2.2 Authorship and ownership

As with the issue of linguistic justice, AI has also sparked considerable debate about authorship. Such has been the debate that both journals and style guides have been swift to update their advice. One prominent example of the stance taken by journals comes from *Frontiers* (www.frontiersin.org), an extensive research publisher that features the inclusion of AI in its mission statement. In its guidance section for submissions, Frontiers (2023: para 1) explains that generative AI systems (e.g. ChatGPT) may not be included as an author (or co-author), since 'Generative AI technologies cannot be held accountable for all aspects of a manuscript and consequently do not meet the criteria required for authorship'. However, Frontiers does not have issues with the use of generative AI per se, they merely warn that authors are '… responsible for checking the factual accuracy of any content created by the generative AI technology' (2023: para 2) and require that the specific generative AI used is detailed in the acknowledgements section. Meanwhile, style guides such as APA offer their own extensive reasoning for the exclusion of ChatGPT: 'Unfortunately, the results of a ChatGPT 'chat' are not retrievable by other readers, and although non retrievable data or quotations in APA style papers are usually cited as personal communications, with ChatGPT-generated text there is no person communicating.' APA adds that 'Quoting ChatGPT's text from a chat session is therefore more like sharing an algorithm's output; thus, credit the author of the algorithm with a reference list entry and the corresponding in-text citation' (McAdoo, 2023: para. 4). The fact that APA appears to indicate a clear way to cite ChatGPT, and by extension similar AI, suggests that there is, at least, a recognition as an 'author' for the creators of the generative AI products. More importantly, such recognition means that there is also an ethical way for students to use AI as an assistant. In sum, the current picture is not entirely clear as, seemingly, ChatGPT can be a reference within a paper, but cannot be an author *of* a paper.

Questions also abound as to ownership, intellectual property and copyright. Appel *et al.* (2023: para 1) highlight that 'the legal implications of using generative AI are still unclear, particularly in relation to copyright infringement, ownership of AI-generated works, and unlicensed content in training data'. This issue is linked to how generative AI works. They argue that the AI does not create something out of nothing or from scratch, rather it is going through massive archives of texts and images to respond to a prompt (i.e. it provides a response from content already in existence). While this reasoning has intuitive merit, it could also be argued that human cognition operates in much the same way; after all, our own creative intelligence is largely the result of accessing and processing the numerous experiences we have collected and evaluated (Gardner, 1983). Thus, if AI cannot be credited as creating something out of nothing then neither can humans.

Given the debate outlined above, we need to consider what exactly happens each time we give generative AI a prompt or share content that we have created, especially since some experts argue that there is a risk that the confidentiality of the texts and the writer might be breached. This breach may occur since some information might inadvertently be revealed because of how generative AI uses large datasets to generate responses (Lauer *et al.*, 2023). That is, much like humans, AI uses all input to learn, improve answers, enhance results and sound more plausible. AI tools typically claim that they delete this input once processing is complete, so as to safeguard privacy and prevent the data from being used for different purposes (Microsoft Corporation, 2023; Google LLC, 2023). In the words of the generative AI integrated into Bing, 'the data processed does not ultimately become part of the data I use in responses … [but] it helps me learn and improve in a general and aggregated way' (Microsoft Corporation, 2023). Although reassuring, such statements do not mean that we should forget about privacy and data protection. Indeed, it is important to check the privacy policy of each AI tool before using it, to think carefully about the content being shared and to go through the appropriate settings (Nield, 2023).

To raise students' awareness, it is worth having a class discussion about these issues. Specifically, students can discuss whether or not AI can be an author (or co-author); whether the use of AI simply needs to be 'acknowledged' rather than 'credited'; what the purpose of citing others' work actually is; whether the purpose of citations apply in the case of AI; what it means to 'build on previous work' and whether the creative work of AI is substantially different from the creative work of people (see Hendricks, 2023). One further previously raised topic is that user input is deleted once it has served its purpose. As such, one question for students is whether such deleting differentiates AI creativity from human creativity; after all, our own creativity is often dependent upon access to our memories, and much as we might often like to erase some of those memories, we are not gifted with quite the same kind of 'delete' options.

10.2.3 Hallucinations, misinformation, inconsistencies and biases

Just as with much information provided on the Internet, AI such as Google's Bard acknowledge that we should not and cannot take things at face value: 'It is important to note that Bard outputs are not peer-reviewed, so you should use them with caution' (Google LLC, 2023). While this acknowledgement is an important disclosure, it is more specific issues such as *hallucinations* that cause greater concern (see Edwards, 2023). In generative AI, hallucinations refer to highly plausible responses that are not factually correct and often seem to be inconsistent with the data upon which the system has been trained. While some hallucinations are easy to identify, such as when DALL-E generates images based on a given text description that are unrealistic, illogical, or simply nonsensical (Given, 2023), other instances of hallucination seem perfectly plausible, such as when generative AI concocts statistics or invents a study supposedly conducted by MIT. Researchers at OpenAI acknowledge this issue: 'Even state-of-the-art models are prone to producing falsehoods – they exhibit a tendency to invent facts in moments of uncertainty' (Field, 2023: para 5). Field highlights that the human minds behind generative AI are looking at measures to eliminate hallucination but also states that experts are not convinced that the issue will completely disappear. Time will tell as to whether (or the degree to which) hallucinations will be nothing more than a generative AI teething problem. In the meantime, instructors need to be aware that students can easily be confused or misled about what is fact and what is false.

Also problematic are the inconsistencies and contradictions that can also emerge with AI. For example, while tools like ChatGPT can generate plausible and accurate text based on a given context or conversation, they can also generate text that is contradictory, incorrect, irrelevant, or incoherent (Given, 2023). Similarly problematically, various studies suggest that AI can reflect or amplify biases (e.g. based on discipline, gender, methodology, race etc.) when it generates content or data, impacting quality (Chubb *et al.*, 2021) since the output is influenced by the biases already present in the system's learning data or the generative AI models (Pohl, 2023). AI is only as neutral as the data it was trained on, so if a significant amount of the learning material suggests X, then generative AI is prone to assuming that X must have significant validity. Needless to say, this issue can have a major impact on the principles and values of fairness, equality and justice; infringe the rights and dignity of individuals or groups; and perpetuate or exacerbate existing social or economic inequalities or injustice. Note that whether the biases are positive or negative, they still equate to the majority becoming associated with that which is true. To address this issue, generative AI systems have been quick to build in safeguards, at least for some prominent issues (see Oxborrow, 2022).

In summary, generative AI tools like ChatGPT can produce realistic but false text based on a given prompt or context (Given, 2023). Regardless of whether this misinformation is unintentionally spread or presented as true, it is obviously problematic. As Villasenor (2020) argues, it can erode trust in information and institutions, polarise opinions and emotions, incite violence or hatred, interfere with elections or policies, or harm reputations or privacy. It is also important to mention is that generative AI tools can impersonate or misrepresent real people or events, by manipulating or fabricating images, audio or video. Clearly, such actions undermine the credibility of evidence or sources. This issue extends to multimodal composition assignments as these circumstances reduce the quality and reliability of the generated content or data, affect user experience and satisfaction and even impair the performance and functionality of the generative AI tools.

The aforementioned issues are certainly a concern, but they are concerns we have long been familiar with. We are already surrounded by misinformation and disinformation because of the internet and social media, although as Kidd (Pohl, 2023: para 25) explains, AI may be especially alarming: 'The fact that you are interacting with these systems as though they're agents is something different that we haven't seen before. The fabrications are also very different from what we've seen with search. There is nothing in these models that has the ability to discern fact from fiction'. Ultimately, however, the challenges of generative AI are not unlike those of the digital world itself, or for that matter, of books, newspapers, TV and even family and friends. That is, humans too can be wrong, and sometimes, we go out of our way to be wrong. As such, we should not expect ChatGPT to be an oracle or agent, we simply have to treat it like any other source of information, and rigorously check it.

This said, just as humans can be held accountable for inaccurate information, so too must generative AI seek to improve itself if it is to avoid legal ramifications (see for example, Vincent 2023). Addressing this challenge has already begun in earnest, with some examples including verification techniques to authenticate content or sources, fact-checking or debunking services to verify information or claims, media literacy education or awareness campaigns to inform and empower people and ethical guidelines or regulations to govern the use and development of generative AI tools (Given, 2023; Villasenor, 2020). From a technological perspective, we can also employ *debiasing* techniques and algorithms to mitigate potential prejudices, preferences, assumptions, stereotypes and favouritisms that may be present in the foundational data or algorithmic models of the generative AI (Friedler *et al.*, 2016).

Of course, instructors themselves cannot be expected to develop the necessary additional technology nor can instructors assure the inclusion of better data and greater diversity to train generative AI models. This said, what we can do is include these issues in discussions and assignments for our students. For example, we can have discussions that clarify and explain the limitations and uncertainties of the generative AI tools, and we can have assignments where students review and correct the generated content or data. We can also pose the question of who gets to be the gatekeeper of fairness because 'safeguards' have to be selected by someone, which raises questions as to who, and how we get to decide what is (and is not) acceptable.

10.2.4 Keeping up

With news stories such as the Texas A&M University professor who failed students because he 'incorrectly used AI software to detect cheating' (Klee, 2023), it is clear that not all educators are well informed about the capabilities and limitations of various AI tools. Indeed, even those in the know have to remain up-to-date since today's news quickly becomes tomorrow's history. For example, when ChatGPT was released for public use on 30 November 2022, its data only reached as far as 2021, but by the end of May 2023, it could access real-time information from Bing search (Hamilton, 2023). These developments mean that some instructor advice, such as assigning current topics to deter students from using the tool, is already obsolete. More importantly, the evolution of the technology is so rapid that the spotlight is now firmly focused on the challenge instructors face to keep up. Given that Microsoft 365 Copilot is promising 'a whole new way to work' (Microsoft News, 2023) and Google is integrating Bard into Google apps and services (Hsiao, 2023), digital culture has been transformed into a brave new world of AI culture, and the learning curve for educators is significant.

Keeping up is hard work and few of us are likely to be subscribing to Generative AI Weekly. The collective departmental knowledge is likely to be considerable, but regular faculty meetings where technology developments are discussed are hardly likely to spark enthusiasm from instructors already burdened with overcrowded classrooms and challenging grading deadlines. One productive way to keep up is simply to discuss with students the capability, availability and also the limitations of current AI developments. For example, instructors can share a list that demonstrates what AI can and cannot do and/or the degree to which it can do it. Students can then share their knowledge or views on each item. Given that many classes are large enough for there to be students who are well tuned into technological developments, instructors would be advised to listen carefully to student contributions and, accordingly, regularly update the list they are sharing. Just as instructors have to keep up, so too must students.

10.3 Generative AI and the Digital Writing Process

10.3.1 The starting point: Critical analysis

A good way to encourage students thinking critically about generative AI before they start the writing process is through analytical assignments such as the born-digital multimodal assignment in Najjar (2023). In this assignment, students were asked to critically analyse one of four essays. Each essay was on a different topic, all of which were generated by ChatGPT: influencer marketing, films and emotional intelligence (EQ), Gen Z and fast fashion. To construct the essays, the instructor prompted ChatGPT to take on the persona of a university student and write a paper that included all sides of the argument, showing research, and references where appropriate.

The students' goal for the assignment was to submit a video essay, complete with a script and slides. The students were advised to familiarise themselves with the research and technology underlying ChatGPT, including its potential benefits and limitations. Students were also encouraged to experiment with ChatGPT so as to better understand the necessary input and subsequent output. To guide student responses a set of questions was distributed. These questions included the following: what are the strengths of the essay? What are the weaknesses of the essay (including the accuracy and validity of the information and evidence provided)? What improvements can be made in terms of content, research and writing style? The video essay assignment concluded with a student reflection on the experience, including their own thoughts on whether they would use ChatGPT and how exactly they would use it.

The findings of the assignment suggested analysing ChatGPT content helped students understand both the benefits and limitations of AI. More specifically, the findings suggested that such an assignment encourages fact checking (and source checking), and informs students as to how AI can be used as a tool to promote learning and enhance performance

(Najjar, 2023). The assignment also appears to have increased students' confidence in their own research and writing abilities as can be evidenced from comments taken from the reflection part of the video essay. For instance, these:

> It is undoubtedly impressive what this AI can do and interesting to see what it comes up with; however, it has proved itself as an unreliable tool for professional writing since it may produce incorrect information, lacks the nuances and depth of human communication, and a certain quality that comes from human-written work. Nevertheless, I would surely use ChatGPT again as I enjoy playing with it; it is fun, interactive, a great start-up for those who experience writing block and a wonderful tool to keep you thinking, but I would unfortunately be unable to rely heavily on it for my academic work.

> While ChatGPT has shown its potential in assisting with writing and research tasks, it should not be a substitute for human input and critical thinking.

Overall, the findings indicate that the assignment had a very positive impact. Indeed, the study indicates that the assignment may have been the most influential work of the semester as it increased student knowledge and understanding of generative AI, caused students to look at AI in a different light and perhaps most importantly, changed how, if, and when students would choose to use AI (Najjar, 2023).

10.3.2 Invention and brainstorming

Whether the final product is an academic essay, video essay, blog post, web page, or podcast assignment, the first stage of the writing process is always coming up with topics, narrowing down those topics and generating content ideas for the selected topics (see for example, McCarthy & Ahmed, 2021). While there are many traditional ways to go about this stage which should still be encouraged, incorporating generative AI is now also an option. For instance, at the time this chapter was written, students could make use of systems such as ChatGPT, Microsoft's ChatGPT4-powered Bing, or Google's Bard. These systems can facilitate invention and brainstorming by generating multiple questions about a certain topic or providing counterarguments, problems, issues, or challenges with the topic under consideration. While there are legitimate concerns about how these tools can be potentially limiting by inhibiting student creativity, reinforcing biases, etc., they can also provide diverse viewpoints by addressing topics from the perspective of a certain persona, or through the lens of various disciplines, theories, or frameworks. As Nerantzi (2023: 21) states, we can explore different perspectives and push the boundaries of Socratic questioning with ChatGPT and similar AI by using them as a 'conversation buddy'. This said, to generate good results, there must be some awareness and understanding of prompt engineering. Also, teachers can use generative AI for invention and brainstorming when creating writing prompts for assignments and/or as a means of glimpsing into the sort of content AI might generate about assigned topics (Najjar, 2023).

As generated by Bing (Microsoft Corporation, 2023), here are some tips and tricks when prompting any text-based AI:

- **Be specific and clear about your research question and hypothesis.** The more details you provide, the easier it will be for me to generate relevant and helpful sources and arguments for you. For example, instead of asking me to help you write a paper about climate change, you could ask me to help you write a paper about the effects of climate change on coral reefs in the Pacific Ocean.
- **Use keywords and phrases that relate to your research question and hypothesis.** This will help me search the web for scholarly articles and books that match your needs. For example, if you want to write a paper about the effects of climate change on coral reefs in the Pacific Ocean, you could use words like coral bleaching, ocean acidification, biodiversity loss, or ecosystem services.
- **Ask open-ended questions that invite critical thinking and analysis.** This will help me generate more diverse and original sources and arguments for you. For example, instead of asking me to give you a thesis statement for your paper, you could ask me to suggest some possible research gaps or controversies for your paper.
- **Be open-minded and curious about the sources and arguments I generate.** Don't dismiss or judge them too quickly, but try to see how they might fit into your paper. You can always ask me to explain or elaborate on any source or argument that interests you. For example, if I suggest that you use a source that argues that coral reefs provide economic benefits to humans, you could ask me how that relates to your research question or hypothesis.
- **Have fun and experiment with different prompts and tools.** You can use any of my predefined tools to help you with your academic writing project, such as search_web, graphic_art, or request_ads. You can also combine them or use them in different ways to get different results. For example, you could use search_web to find some scholarly articles or books about your topic, then use graphic_art to create a diagram or chart based on those articles or books, then use request_ads to find some products or services related to your topic or diagram.

Bard gave a very similar responses (Google LLC, 2023), adding:

- Provide examples of the kind of writing you want me to generate.
- Be patient, and don't expect me to be perfect. I'm still under development, but I'm always learning.

Here are some examples of prompts we created with Bing's help. These prompts follow best practices by including context and assigning roles:

- **Topic selection**: You are a university student studying journalism. Come up with five original topics for an analytical piece based on news that is trending this week.
- **Literature review**: I am a graduate student who is writing a literature review on the topic of artificial intelligence and ethics. You are my research assistant who will help me find and summarise relevant sources for my literature review. Please search the web for five scholarly articles that discuss the ethical issues and challenges of artificial intelligence, and provide me with a brief summary of each article, including the main arguments, findings and implications.
- **Research proposal**: I am a researcher who is writing a research proposal on the topic of social media and mental health. You are my colleague who will help me design and justify my research methodology. Please suggest a suitable research design, data collection method and data analysis method for my research project, and explain why they are appropriate and feasible.
- **Argumentative essay**: I am a university student who is writing an argumentative essay on the topic of whether video games cause violence. You are my tutor who will help me develop and support my thesis statement. Please suggest a possible thesis statement for my essay, and provide me with three main points and evidence that support or challenge my thesis statement.

While this is all very useful, it is easy to see how some students might feel tempted to overly rely on AI. Such over-reliance highlights the importance of emphasising the ethical use of AI.

10.3.3 Research

A core part of the writing process is focused research (see McCarthy & Ahmed, 2021) and, again, generative AI may be of assistance at this stage. As noted above, generative AI systems do not always identify the most credible sources, nor do they guarantee 100% accurate content, but this does not mean that AI is not useful for the type of academic research expected in college level courses. Below, we provide four possible avenues of interest, along with the names of technology that currently facilitates such pursuits. However, it is worth noting that some students are likely to need a degree of guidance on how to most effectively use these AI tools (Najjar, 2023).

First, for a literature review, an assignment could be created requiring students to use an AI research assistant, for example Elicit.org. Such tools can respond to questions by providing a list of relevant academic papers, suggesting related research questions and even summarising key information. Second, to better understand the current discourse community, tools such as ResearchRabbit.ai can be used. For any given topic, such systems allow students to discover authors, explore what researchers have been publishing, see visualisations of how the research is connected, curate research collections, and even get recommendations based on their research interest. Such an assignment causes the discourse community to come to life, thus making it a highly positive experience for many students. Third, to reinforce information literacy skills and raise awareness about the importance of credibility and quality of evidence, we can ask students to use a search engine like Consensus. Such tools use AI to generate evidence-based answers from research papers. Students may then be asked to compare and contrast the results with other systems such as Bing and Bard. Finally, to better understand academic journal articles, we can ask students to engage with AI tools such as ExplainPaper. Abstracts and full articles in complex peer reviewed journals can be especially challenging for non-native English speakers. As such, it is useful to understand and employ tools that can provide explanations for difficult parts of papers as well as break down jargon into easy-to-understand language (Najjar, 2023).

10.3.4 Drafting multimodal assignments

As mentioned previously, multimodal assignments can be highly beneficial not only for students' literacy development but also for productively and ethically integrating generative AI. Below, we consider the drafting stage of the writing process from a multimodal perspective. Fortunately, for such purposes, a wealth of AI has already been made available, and many more will likely follow. For instance, instructors can design an academic writing assignment that requires students to include illustrative and immersive content. Such an assignment allows students to explain complex concepts with visual and auditory aids or present findings with interactive and dynamic media. One currently available AI tool for such an assignment is CoDi. The tool can generate any-to-any content across text, images, video and audio. For example, CoDi can take a text description and produce a video with synchronised audio or take an image and generate a caption and a sound effect (Tang et al., 2023).

If an instructor chooses to assign a video essay, web page, or podcast, AI can empower students to unleash their imagination and realise their full potential, regardless of their technical skills. By using tools such as Synthesia or AI Video Generator, students have the ability to create videos from text prompts and AI avatars. With tools such as Podcastle and Descript (which greatly facilitate recording, editing and publishing of podcasts), students can remove unwanted background noise and record text to speech with realistic voice skins. Meanwhile, based on students' input, tools such as Durable, Wix and Framer help in creating website layout, content and images.

Another possible assignment is PowerPoint Karaoke. In this assignment, students get a taste of improvisation while enhancing their oral presentation skills. The goal for students is to spontaneously weave a coherent narrative of a slide deck that they have not previously seen. One way of conducting the presentation is to divide students into small teams. Each team creates a slide deck for another team, selecting a topic and 10 slides of various random images (Bali *et al.*, 2021). When working on slide decks, students can use AI presentation tools like Tome, Slidesgo, Presentations.AI or Plus AI. These tools, providing a variety of templates and themes, allow students to create slides based on their input. Additionally, there are tools such as Midjourney, DALL.E 2, AI Image Generator and Fotor, all of which use AI to generate realistic or fantastical images from student generated text prompts.

10.3.5 Peer review

Student peer reviews are a vital component of the writing process. Peer reviews enhance student understanding of audience, purpose and organisation, all while facilitating in generating student engagement with the writing process itself (McCarthy *et al.*, 2021a). However, peer reviewing is not without its challenges: that is, feedback can often be disappointing, and peer availability is seldom guaranteed (McCarthy *et al.*, 2021a). To address these issues, generative AI can once again be an option worthy of consideration. While technically not a peer in the strictest definition of the word, AI can assume the role of a peer reviewer, albeit using algorithms and machine learning techniques to analyse a text and provide recommendations. For example, Bing claims it can offer corrections and tips for language and formatting errors; evaluate content for clarity, coherence, logic and relevance; point out weaknesses or gaps in arguments and evidence; suggest ways to improve structure, organisation, transitions and flow; help create effective introductions and conclusions; assist in refining thesis statements, topic sentences and main points; ensure consistency; and provide additional sources and references.

While the above is undoubtedly a rich list of potentially beneficial assessments, we must again stress that caution is the watchword. For example, in our own attempts to use Bing as a 'peer review buddy', it cited a peer-reviewed journal article that does not exist and one other that was substantially off-topic. As Nerantzi (2023: 87) points out, 'Critical engagement with the feedback will be required as with any peer review'; indeed, for the time being at least, perhaps even more vigilance is required.

Keeping such caveats in mind, one useful technique for students to experiment with is *role reversal*. This technique can help students gain insight, develop new perspectives and improve writing skills. The following is an example of a role reversal prompt for a persuasive essay:

You are a teacher who is grading a persuasive essay written by me, a student, on the topic of whether homework should be banned. I have written an essay that argues that homework should be banned because it is stressful, ineffective and harmful. You will read my essay and provide me with constructive feedback on how I can improve my essay, such as pointing out any logical fallacies, weak evidence, or counterarguments that I have overlooked or ignored.

Role reversal can also be conducted as a group activity: using the same example, students can task generative AI with peer reviewing a paper; however, instead of evaluating the feedback individually, groups of students (or even the entire class) can discuss the comments and evaluate those that are most helpful. Such an activity can help students understand the shortcomings of both using AI as a peer reviewing alternative specifically, and the peer reviewing process itself. This said, note that such an assignment requires students to submit their own work into a generative AI system. As mentioned previously, such actions come with concerns as to confidentiality and bias, as well as the potential of stifling student creativity and voice development.

10.3.6 Feedback

Instructor feedback is highly beneficial for student-writer development (Boud & Molloy, 2013). However, research (see e.g. Yu *et al.*, 2021) also suggests that instructors can view the feedback stage of the writing process to be time consuming, frustrating and riddled with challenges. To address this issue, technology such as Auto-Peer is available. Auto-Peer analyses virtually any kind of digital text. The analysis includes a wide variety of writing issues (e.g. paragraph structure, complex sentences, cohesion, topic sentences, word choice and various issues of in-text referencing). However, unlike systems such as Grammarly and Trinka, it is important to recognise that Auto-Peer is a *feedback* tool, not a *corrective* tool. That is, Auto-Peer does not look for relatively simple surface level issues and does not simply replace perceived 'bad writing' with perceived 'good writing'. As such, Auto-Peer does not face the same issues of linguistic justice described earlier in the chapter. Instead, as a feedback system, Auto-Peer simply flags textual elements that are *potentially* problematic. Auto-Peer then explains the issue by providing explanations and examples. Through this feedback, the task of the student is either to modify the text, or, equally importantly from a pedagogical perspective, justify why the flagged text needs no modification. In either case, Auto-Peer facilitates the development of the student's own voice as it is students themselves who get to decide. Auto-Peer also compiles the students' own feedback, which can then be shared with the instructor. The instructor is thus informed of ongoing issues and misunderstandings and can use this data to more effectively and efficiently plan future classes.

AI such as ChatGPT can also offer feedback. However, ChatGPT cannot be aware of the right kind of questions to ask, much less can anyone be sure that appropriate responses are being provided. Moreover, ChatGPT is very eager to provide recommended wording, but in doing so can both prevent learning and lead to potential plagiarism. This said, AI can still serve a facilitative function as a partner to a feedback tool. Indeed, Auto-Peer is gradually introducing ChatGPT 'enhanced' features. That is, for certain writing issues, Auto-Peer can generate suggested *prompts*, that students and instructors can opt to use in conjunction with AI tools. These custom designed prompts can generate explanations and analysis, but not text itself. The prompts can also include 'model examples' so that ChatGPT is better able to provide facilitative feedback. By incorporating prompts in this way, systems like Auto-Peer remain structurally independent of any generative AI system, allowing students, instructors and academic institutes the freedom to use AI productively and ethically, or, indeed, not use AI at all.

While Auto-Peer offers an effective solution to the issue of feedback, other approaches are also available. For example, instructors can record their most frequently made comments using software such as Microsoft Bookmarks. For those willing to invest more time, Microsoft Word has 'Macros', which allow an instructor to use 'Short-Cut' keys to automatically paste comments into a text. Macros are extremely useful; however, coding them is not for the faint-hearted. As such, we can yet again ask AI to help out. That is, we can simply ask ChatGPT to provide the code for us: a task ChatGPT is only too happy to perform. In our own trials, successful ChatGPT coding required lengthy conversations, as initial efforts could often result in misplaced comments (or even no comments at all). However, ChatGPT learns, and eventually we were able not only to insert comments, but to colour code them for aspects such as 'local/global issues', 'recommendations' and 'importance'.

10.4 Conclusion

As Heick (2015: para 16) puts it, 'technology doesn't make teaching better or worse, simpler or more complex – it changes it all entirely'. Generative AI is most certainly going to change digital writing processes. Many of us will soon better understand the feelings of our students, for we are all going to have to learn a lot, learn it quickly, learn it well, and then learn it all over again. This said, if adopted with sincerity and adapted with care, AI can be a willing and constructive asset to the writing classroom: an asset that can play a vital part in any and all of the stages of the digital writing process. Studies such as Thomas and McCarthy (2023) have already demonstrated that if instructors, students and technology can all act together as a team, then excellent outcomes can certainly result. As such, the purpose of our chapter was not to show that living with technology's latest gift was merely possible; instead, it was to show that generative AI offers all of us (students, instructors, administrators and software developers themselves) an exciting opportunity to transform learning. Thus, if goals are clearly defined, discussions openly encouraged and tasks thoughtfully created, then generative AI will only better serve the aspirations of our students, meaning that we might not have to be quite so brave in this brave new world.

Acknowledgements

This research was funded in part by the American University of Sharjah (FRG23-C-S66). The authors acknowledge that some creative ideas were inspired by generative AI systems, including ChatGPT and Bing.

References

Appel, G., Neelbauer, J. and Schweider, D.A. (2023) Generative AI has an intellectual property problem. *Harvard Business Review*, 7 April. See https://hbr.org/2023/04/generative-ai-has-an-intellectual-property-problem (accessed September 2023).

Bali, M., Najjar, J. and Mostafa, H. (2021) PowerPoint Karaoke. *OneHE*. See https://onehe.org/eu-activity/powerpoint-karaoke/ (accessed September 2023).

Bankhead III, M. (2021) Baker-Bell warns of linguistic racism. *UB Now – University of Buffalo*, 22 November. See https://www.buffalo.edu/ubnow/stories/2021/11/baker-bell-linguistic-racism.html (accessed September 2023).

Beaufort, A. (2007) *College Writing and Beyond: A New Framework for University Writing Instruction*. Utah State University Press.

Boud, D. and Molloy, E. (2013) What is the problem with feedback? In D. Boud and E. Molloy (eds) *Feedback in Higher and Professional Education* (pp. 1–10). Routledge.

Chubb, J., Cowling, P. and Reed, D. (2021) Speeding up to keep up: Exploring the use of AI in the research process. *AI & Society* 37 (4), 1439–1457. https://doi.org/10.1007/s00146-021-01259-0

Edwards, B.J. (2023) Why ChatGPT and Bing Chat are so good at making things up: A look inside the hallucinating artificial minds of the famous text prediction bots. See https://arstechnica.com/information-technology/2023/04/why-ai-chatbots-are-the-ultimate-bs-machines-and-how-people-hope-to-fix-them/ (accessed September 2023).

Field, H. (2023) OpenAI is pursuing a new way to fight A.I. 'hallucinations'. *CNBC*, 31 May. https://www.cnbc.com/2023/05/31/openai-is-pursuing-a-new-way-to-fight-ai-hallucinations.html (accessed September 2023).

Flower, L. and Hayes, J.R. (1981) A Cognitive Process Theory of Writing. *College Composition and Communication* 32 (4), 365–387.

Friedler, S.A., Scheidegger, C. and Venkatasubramanian, S. (2016) Fairness and abstraction in sociotechnical systems. *ACM Transactions on Interactive Intelligent Systems* 6 (3), 20.

Frontiers (2023) AI use by authors. See www.frontiersin.org/guidelines/author-guidelines (accessed September 2023).

Gardner, H. (1983) *Frames of Mind: The Theory of Multiple Intelligences*. Basic Books.

Given, L.M. (2023) AI tools are generating convincing misinformation. Engaging with them means being on high alert. *The Conversation*, 27 March. See https://theconversation.com/ai-tools-are-generating-convincing-misinformation-engaging-with-them-means-being-on-high-alert-202062 (accessed September 2023).

Google LLC (2023) *Bard* (July 13 version) [AI chatbot]. See https://bard.google.com (accessed September 2023).

Hamilton, K. (2023) CHATGPT will now have access to real-time info from Bing Search. *Forbes*, 23 March. See https://www.forbes.com/sites/katherinehamilton/2023/05/23/chatgpt-will-now-have-access-to-real-time-info-from-bing-search-report-says/ (accessed September 2023).

Heap, J.L. (1989) Writing as social action. *Theory Into Practice* 28 (2), 148–153.

Heick, T. (2015) Why some teachers are against technology in education [blog post]. *TeachThought*. See https://www.teachthought.com/pedagogy/why-some-teachers-are-against-technology-in-education/ (accessed September 2023).

Hendricks, J. (2023) 7 cool AI tools you've never used before. See https://www.findmycrm.com/blog/cool-ai-tools-youve-never-used-before (accessed September 2023).

Hsiao, S. (2023) What's ahead for Bard: More global, more visual, more integrated. *Official Google Blog*, 10 May. See https://blog.google/technology/ai/google-bard-updates-io-2023/ (accessed September 2023).

ICAI (n.d.) Landing page. See https://academicintegrity.org/ (accessed September 2023).

Kelley, K.J. (2023) Ways to prevent students from using AI tools in their classes. *Inside Higher Ed*, 18 January. See https://www.insidehighered.com/advice/2023/01/19/ways-prevent-students-using-ai-tools-their-classes-opinion (accessed September 2023).

Klee, M. (2023) Professor flunks all his students after CHATGPT falsely claims it wrote their papers. *Rolling Stone*, 17 May. See https://www.rollingstone.com/culture/culture-features/texas-am-chatgpt-ai-professor-flunks-students-false-claims-1234736601/ (accessed September 2023).

Lauer, M., Constant, S. and Wernimont, A. (20233) CSR review matters: Using AI in peer review is a breach of confidentiality. *Center for Scientific Review*. See https://www.csr.nih.gov/reviewmatters/2023/06/23/using-ai-in-peer-review-is-a-breach-of-confidentiality/ (accessed September 2023).

McAdoo, T. (2023) How to cite ChatGPT. *American Psychological Association*. See https://apastyle.apa.org/blog/how-to-cite-chatgpt (accessed September 2023).

McCarthy, P.M. and Ahmed, K. (2021) *Writing the Research Paper: Multicultural Perspectives for Writing in English as a Second Language*. Bloomsbury.

McCarthy, P.M., Al-Harthy, A., Buck, R.H., Ahmed, K., Duran, N.D., Thomas, A.M., Kaddoura, N.W. and Graesser, A.C. (2021a) Introducing Auto-Peer: A computational tool designed to provide automated feedback. *Asian ESP Journal* 17, 9–43.

McCarthy, P.M., Highland, K. and Ahmed, K. (2021b) Integrating technology for reading and writing in the ESL classroom. In Z.S. Genc and I.G. Kaçar (eds) *TESOL in the 21st Century: Challenges and Opportunities* (pp. 323–348). Peter Lang Publishing.

McNamara, D.S., Graesser, A.C., McCarthy, P.M. and Cai, Z. (2014) *Automated Evaluation of Text and Discourse with Coh-Metrix*. Cambridge University Press.

Microsoft Corporation (2023) *Bing* (April 10 version) [AI-powered chat mode]. See www.bing.com (accessed September 2023).

Microsoft News (2023) Introducing Microsoft 365 Copilot – Your copilot for work. See https://news.microsoft.com/reinventing-productivity/ (accessed September 2023).

Mindzak, M. and Eaton, S.E. (2021) Artificial Intelligence is getting better at writing, and universities should worry about plagiarism. *The Conversation*, 4 November. See https://theconversation.com/artificial-intelligence-is-getting-better-at-writing-and-universities-should-worry-about-plagiarism-160481 (accessed September 2023).

Najjar, J. (2023) To AI or not to AI: That is the question in writing courses. Paper presented at the AMICAL 2023 Conference, 24–26 May, Ifrane, Morocco.

Najjar, J. and Akpan, E. (2023) Academic integrity: Issues and solutions. Paper presented at the AMICAL 2023 Conference, 24–26 May, (Ifrane, Morocco).

Nee, J., Smith, G.M., Sheares, A. and Rustagi, I. (2022) Linguistic justice as a framework for designing, developing, and managing natural language processing tools. *Big Data & Society* 9 (1). https://doi.org/10.1177/20539517221090930

Nerantzi, C. (2023) Creative ideas to use AI in education: A crowdsourced collection. See https://creativehecommunity.wordpress.com/2023/06/23/oa-book-101-creative-ideas-to-use-ai-in-education/ (accessed September 2023).

Nield, D. (2023) How to use generative AI tools while still protecting your privacy. *Wired UK*, 16 July See https://www.wired.co.uk/article/how-to-use-ai-tools-protect-privacy (accessed September 2023).

Olga, A., Saini, A., Zapata, G., Searsmith, D., Cope, B., Kalantzis, M., Castro, V., Kourkoulou, T., Jones, J., Abrantes da Silva, R., Whiting, J. and Kastani, N. P. (2023) Generative AI: Implications and applications for education. *CarXiv preprint arXiv:2305.07605*.

Oxborrow, I. (2022) Meta's new chatbot claims Donald Trump 'will always be president'. See https://www.thenationalnews.com/business/technology/2022/08/11/metas-new-chatbot-claims-donald-trump-will-always-be-president/ (accessed September 2023).

Pohl, J. (2023) What can psychology teach us about AI's bias and misinformation problem? *Berkeley News*, 22 June. See https://news.berkeley.edu/2023/06/22/what-can-psychology-teach-us-about-ais-bias-and-misinformation-problem (accessed September 2023).

Russell, S.J. and Norvig, P. (2016) *Artificial Intelligence: A Modern Approach* (3rd edn). Pearson.

Tang, Z., Yang, Z., Zhu, C., Zeng, M. and Bansal, M. (2023) Breaking cross-modal boundaries in multimodal AI: Introducing CoDi, composable diffusion for any-to-any generation. *Microsoft Research Blog*. See https://www.microsoft.com/en-us/research/blog/breaking-cross-modal-boundaries-in-multimodal-ai-introducing-codi-composable-diffusion-for-any-to-any-generation/ (accessed September 2023).

Thomas, A.M. and McCarthy, P.M. (2023) Multi-agent teaching. In J. Muller, J. Adamson, S. Herder and S. Brown (eds) *Re-envisioning Language EFL Education in Asia* (pp. 99–117). ITDI.

Villasenor, J. (2020) How to deal with AI-enabled disinformation. *Brookings*, 23 November. See Brookings. https://www.brookings.edu/articles/how-to-deal-with-ai-enabled-disinformation/ (accessed September 2023).

Vincent, J. (2023) OpenAI sued for defamation after ChatGPT fabricates legal accusations against radio host. *The Verge*, 9 June. See https://www.theverge.com/2023/6/9/23755057/openai-chatgpt-false-information-defamation-lawsuit (accessed September 2023).

Williams, R. (2023) AI-text detection tools are really easy to fool. *MIT Technology Review*, 7 July.

Yu, S., Zheng, Y., Jiang, L., Liu, C. and Xu, Y. (2021) 'I even feel annoyed and angry?': Teacher emotional experiences in giving feedback on student writing. *Assessing Writing* 48. https://doi.org/10.1016/j.asw.2021.100528

11 Learning English as a Second Language through Born-Digital Texts on Social Media in South Africa

Christopher Rwodzi and Lizette J. De Jager

11.1 Introduction and Background

This contribution provides an overview of how teachers and learners in South Africa can make use of the pedagogical opportunities of social media to support born-digital learners in achieving better educational outcomes in learning English as a second language. More specifically, it discusses how experiences of learning English as a second language on social media are used and integrated to effectively support African digital natives. ESL teachers' creativity and initiatives on pedagogic choices should consider selected subject-specific content knowledge, technological options and platforms within the socioeconomic ambit of South African society. Since English is widely used for communication in schools, for business purposes and social functions in South Africa, English in both education and business is at the top of the list of languages used in South Africa (Mutasa, 2006). Learners from townships and informal settlements are forced by the school curriculum and higher education requirements to use English for learning at school. Despite government policy demands, English is not their first language (Mbatha, 2016), which means that learners in township and informal settlement schools struggle to use English proficiently as a second language in academic domains. Learners from township and informal settlement secondary schools struggle to read and write in English with the competency expected to meet tertiary requirements. This is problematic since evidence from research clearly indicates that poor proficiency in English affects academic performance (Thanasoulas, 2001). The integration of digital technology in the teaching and learning of English is meant to improve learners' proficiency through the use of digital resources, which give them access to content and facilitate participation in global conversations.

Despite policy mandates on the inclusion of digital literacies in South Africa (Department of Basic Education, 2011), most townships and informal settlements are lagging behind in the implementation of digital tools and the provision of infrastructure needed, due to limited financial and material resources (Department of Basic Education, 2011: 33). The South African Department of Communications and Digital Technologies' Government Gazette (2020: 513), designed to fast-track the digitalisation process, clearly states that basic and intermediate digital skills can be acquired if all partners start with an awareness campaign and the training of teachers. Therefore, this chapter seeks to provide guidelines on policy framework and infrastructure development in the context of South Africa. Delivering learning in online contexts requires an adjustment in thinking, and the time students spend learning online needs to be structured differently from face-to-face sessions especially for born-digital learners. New pedagogical paradigms and practices are needed for online content knowledge delivery in a context of African ethical considerations.

Against this background, this contribution provides insights into English language teachers' initiatives and experiences on the use of digital platforms for teaching. Combining ESL learning and collaboration and socialisation on social media is a new phenomenon in Africa where language teaching methodology requires critical review. By social media socialisation, we mean that WhatsApp, Twitter, Instagram and Facebook text and audio chats involve conversation where teachers and learners inform each other, share and discuss social matters (Bock, 2017). The digitally-based chats combine academic issues and social matters discussed on digital platforms. The contribution therefore provides insights on initiatives and strategies of providing ESL learning online.

11.2 Current Trends in English Second Language Learning in South Africa

South African education is impacted by income disparities which affect provision and access to education through the use of digital spaces. In South Africa, former Model C schools (schools that were exclusively white but are now open to all learners since apartheid ended) were for the elite and ruling class during apartheid. In the apartheid system, schools were grouped and classified according to race. Schools of the elite and particularly white communities had access to resources, and upon independence and the implementation of democracy the schools continued to receive adequate resource materials for teaching and learning. Even today, learners from former Model C schools generally have more opportunities to access digital devices and WiFi for connecting to the internet with ease (Ebersöhn, 2017). In contrast to this point, learners from previously disadvantaged schools in townships and informal settlements still grapple with resources to access online educational services. For example, reports from teachers and learners in resource-constrained schools confirm that they share devices such as smartphones, laptops and computers for their online classes (Rwodzi & De Jager, 2021). To support these learners and enable access to shared devices and a stable internet connection, some parents in the informal economy make financial commitment and sacrifice their limited financial resources to buy digital devices to support their children in school. While this financial commitment and sacrifice from parents is greatly appreciated, the challenge is that the cost of WiFi and internet access means that learners should ideally spend a reasonable amount of time online doing their academic work. For example, the cost of mobile data packages is further increased by the poor network connection in the resource-constrained environments that the learners live in. Furthermore, electric cable theft and illegal power lines are prevalent in South African informal settlements, which often result in power cuts. Under such circumstances, learners are often not able to connect to the internet as required to accomplish academic tasks in ESL learning (Rwodzi & De Jager, 2021). On the basis of the conditions mentioned earlier, teachers using the internet and digital devices to teach English have to make informed choices on how to deliver content and which tasks they can give learners.

The outbreak of the global Covid-19 pandemic has triggered radical changes including lockdowns and a shift to online sites for the provision of educational services in South Africa and other parts of the world. National lockdowns and the restriction of human movement and interaction have had serious implications on curriculum implementation in South African schools since early March 2020. The devastating effects of the pandemic led to the closure of schools, and pushed English teachers to search for options to continue providing services to learners. In addition to the challenges brought on by the pandemic, three issues in South African education remain pertinent today, namely the need to improve English language proficiency, technology integration and the shortage of teaching and learning resources (Rwodzi et al., 2020). In view of the circumstances described above, and challenges brought on by the pandemic, learners and teachers had to find alternatives on modes of provision through online classes and discussions on Microsoft Teams, Zoom and other digital meeting platforms after schools closed. This also meant revisiting established ESL methodology and finding strategies suitable for the circumstances. To this end, we used the Technological Pedagogical Content Knowledge (TPACK) model (Mishra & Koehler, 2006) to explore experiences of teachers and learners in the use of social media for learning English as a second language. The model provides guidelines on how to integrate technology, content and methods in different teaching and learning environments.

11.3 Theoretical Framework

11.3.1 The Technological Pedagogical Content Knowledge (TPACK) model

Digital natives in the South African educational environment actively use social media for academic purposes, entertainment and social interactions. For educational activities, the TPACK model is a useful model to successfully integrate digital technology into teaching (Koehler *et al.*, 2017). TPACK (Koehler *et al.*, 2017) is a pedagogical theoretical framework seeking to support teachers, learners and educational practitioners in understanding the knowledge and skills required to provide support for learners. The framework has emerged as a strong guideline that helps teachers in the design of online lessons and the selection of appropriate tools for born-digital learners' learning programmes. The framework aims to specify the kind of knowledge that is required for teaching in digital contexts, and has garnered much attention across the field of education. In support of the application of the model, Dietrich (2018) and Santos and Castro (2021) indicate that TPACK is an important aspect in teacher training programmes, because it empowers educators with knowledge and skills necessary for most subjects in schools. For the African continent, Omoso and Odindo (2020) state that TPACK focuses on the intersection of technology, pedagogy and content for most technical and technology-based subjects. In Kenya, the model is used for pre-service teachers in order to empower them before they are deployed in schools (Omoso & Odindo, 2020). In this approach, school teachers can integrate knowledge, skills, technology and content. For South Africa, Gumbo (2020) strongly recommends that the model should be used by integrating it with indigenous knowledge systems in addition to the integration of teaching methods, technology and content, especially as TPACK presents a conceptual framework to support design thinking for developing digitally integrated lessons by language teachers in resource-constrained schools.

In view of the circumstances in South African schools at the time of writing, English teachers are expected to make pedagogical choices and integrate technology with content to support learners in virtual learning environments. In the South African context, one of the options widely used by ESL teachers for technology integration is Microsoft Teams, which they use to deliver lessons online. Learners attend virtual classes and can interact with teachers and other learners on academic matters. In resource-constrained schools in South Africa, technology motivates learners to complete tasks and access academic resources at relatively low cost as compared to the price of textbooks. Due to the lack of resources in informal settlements, learners collaborate and share devices with friends and family members to access information virtually, yet many challenges remain. However, the major advantage of using Microsoft Teams is that it combines audio, video, text and use of presentation software and other electronic images even on shared devices.

11.3.2 Social constructivism in digital spaces in the South African context

Social constructivism is a branch of constructivist philosophy and involves human interaction and socialisation, thereby creating opportunities for knowledge construction. Bell (2011: 35) posits that knowledge is a product of collaborative construction, a feature that is commensurate with digital literacy's connectivism, sharing, curating and networking (Reinders, 2018: 2–3). Knowledge construction takes place in a sociocultural context mediated by discourse and language (Wang, 2008: 413–416). Language learning happens through sharing, interaction, negotiation and transfer with the support of networked digital tools (Rose, 2009: 12). Language is fundamental in the digitally networked African academic space. The involvement of technology connects learners and teachers on social media platforms and therefore can spur pedagogical initiatives in line with English language teaching. The social and academic connection – as well as link between technology integration and social media – brings together teachers and learners in discussions, presentations and participation forums that generate knowledge and solve human problems thereby conforming to constructivism principles.

Covid-19 has increased technological developments in South Africa and, more generally, on the whole continent, which in turn necessitates that teachers and learners establish online relationships to be able to effectively deliver sessions. More specifically, teachers have moved towards use of online facilities to provide services to their learners. In South African resource-constrained secondary schools, social media platforms such as Facebook, YouTube and WhatsApp play a key role in connecting teachers and learners, although data costs and access to digital devices may limit learner participation. For example, social media platforms offer opportunities such as forming discussion groups, and the sharing of information among learners and teachers. Learners in the same subject form discussion groups and assessment chat sessions to complete academic tasks.

In terms of cohesion and coherence, for example, the participation in digital literacy activities of English language teachers and learners from disadvantaged communities improved their writing skills as a consequence of the methods and strategies used by the teachers (Rwodzi & De Jager, 2021). Findings from the research conducted by Rwodzi and De Jager (2021) indicate improved electronic writing skills by learners, as they were able to use online dictionaries and spelling and grammar checkers as part of Microsoft Office. In support of the constructivist trajectory, Abbas *et al.* (2013) state that a constructivist perspective provides insight on the combined use of digital technology and other remote learning capabilities in the process of providing educational service. While cognitivists and constructivists attune to mentally-based processes, Ebersöhn (2017) posits that human adjustments to new and adverse conditions require both emotional intelligence and mental cooperation, all destined to propagate resilience for performance accomplishment. In view of cognitivist ideas, the adjustments and initiatives taken by learners from resource-constrained schools, such as using devices in groups and borrowing devices from friends and family members, provide access to the digital technology which they use for learning English. The psychological process of adjusting to new digitally-based settings by incorporating behaviorist approaches as they manipulate devices with cognitive concepts is part of adaptive resilience because it involves modifications in teaching methods, approaches and strategies (Ebersöhn, 2017). In linking behaviorism and cognitivism to constructivism, learners and teachers' initiatives of looking for alternatives to shortages form part of collaboration and teamwork in problem solving. The initiatives are thus integral to the application of constructivist principles as learners watch videos, listen to online class presentations and discussions and share cellphones (Rwodzi *et al.*, 2020). ESL teachers from resource-constrained schools encourage learners to use the groups to help learners get access to academic content. Against this background, the following section reports on the findings of a research project which explored the experiences of and initiatives by ESL teachers in South Africa in an effort to improve their learners' language proficiency through the use of digital technology and in out-of-school digital literacy practices.

11.4 Methods and Modes of Inquiry

The study adopts a qualitative, interpretivist approach within a descriptive case study design. It is based on the view that teachers and learners in South Africa are struggling with online English reading and writing for academic purposes, as some teachers find it challenging to navigate computer software and electronic resources efficiently. In addition to the challenges which come with promoting digital literacy and proficiency in general, the lockdown period left most South African communities with the task of managing and administering online teaching and learning, especially in rural and township settings (Rwodzi & De Jager, 2021). Furthermore, some sections of society in South Africa have limited confidence in online modes of delivery and English language proficiency. In support of this view, the National Department of Basic Education in South Africa did not authorise national examinations for the senior high school certificate to be written online. In view of digital technology development and education in Africa and the world at large, teachers need to be digitally empowered in preparation for their role in the teaching and learning of born-digital learners (Maphalala & Nzama, 2014). Knowledge and proficiency in computer technology are a critical requirement for academic engagement.

For computer technology to support cognitive functions and encourage higher learning outcomes, teachers have a duty to conceptualise the way digital tools are used in the integration of theory and practice (Jonassen, 2006). In support of English language learning, cognitive functions will include the formation of linguistic concepts, linking views and opinions using digital technology as a resource. The conceptualised procedure should result in a shift away from a teacher-centred approach, to instruction towards an approach that attempts to engage learners in activities that support active knowledge construction. During conceptualisation, teachers create thought-provoking tasks which require learners to be creative as they attempt to solve problems in the learners' social and economic context. According to modern paradigms of language teaching, English teachers are not necessarily knowledge reservoirs, but facilitators who enable learners to discover and understand their environment as they solve problems. Furthermore, interaction among learners and teachers promotes community building (Reinders & White, 2016). In support of interactivity and community building, Savage and McGoun (2015) posit that digital classrooms, massive open online courses, cellphones, smartphones and video cameras as well as born-digital texts such as digital music, video games and other forms of digital entertainment, have created an environment for the born-digital generation to share and collaborate in academic spheres across national boundaries (Reinders, 2018).

Due to the Covid-19 movement restrictions, telephone and WhatsApp calls as well as text messages were used to interview participants in order to understand their role in learning English with social media (Dube, 2020). The participants comprised three EFL teachers from townships in Gauteng who have experience in teaching English as a second language. Additionally, six learners from the three township secondary schools that participated in the study were also interviewed. The participants were sampled from schools that took part in the data collection for the study (Rwodzi, 2018). We also interacted with participating teachers during e-learning cluster meetings, where we were appointed as teaching practice supervisors. The purpose of using two methods of data collection was to provide triangulation opportunities so that data are easily analysed in terms of emerging patterns in the experiences of teachers and learners when using digitally-based strategies for learning English as a second language. Sets of questions were used to explore both English teachers' and learners' experiences in learning English with digital devices. We also used document analysis by examining born-digital comments on social media produced by learners and teachers.

Patterns show that learners use social media platforms such as WhatsApp, Facebook, Instagram and Twitter for born-digital forms of communication such as sharing, transferring and sending information. As already mentioned, document analysis was also used to triangulate collection procedures. As Creswell (2013) states, documents provide valuable information in helping the researcher with the important aspects that are central to the phenomena in qualitative research. The documents, which included electronic documents, served as richer sources of information on how digital literacy is taught in English. Documents also provide tracks of human activity in the digital literacy landscape. The guiding idea in the use of documents is the view that parts of our daily lives leave traces in official and unofficial documents (Flick, 2014). Electronic documents and communication captions indicate that learners communicate with fellow learners, and their subject teachers constantly every day.

11.4.1 Data analysis

The aim of data analysis is to reduce, organise, interpret and substantiate data (Rwodzi et al., 2020). We used inductive thematic analysis, which involved procedures and processes leading to meaning-making by both researchers and participants (co-construction). Data analysis involved coding, sorting, coalescing and populating it according to themes and patterns at the end of field work. We grouped similar views together using the codes used to label the data, and then merged them to form a pattern. Digital texts, videos and pictures on WhatsApp groups and discussions relating to learning of English were collected for analysis. Guidelines developed by the researchers were used to provide focus and to eliminate bias in both data collection and analysis. We analysed texts from WhatsApp groups, Facebook, Twitter and Instagram which involved academic work, such as discussions of creative writing more broadly as well as poetic devices, summary writing, parts of speech, and so on. Texts in English included shared assignments and tasks but also born-digital texts such as pictures, diagrams and videos from YouTube and group discussions. The analysis of data involved checking the frequency of use of social media platforms and identifying discussions which involved academic work. In this case, we analysed images used by teachers and learners for learning purposes and how emojis and photos were used to improve proficiency in the use of English as a second language.

11.4.2 Findings of the study

Table 11.1 presents the summary of the findings outlined above and is discussed in more detail below and, more generally, in Section 11.5.

Findings for this study were a product of data analysed and produced patterns and themes as indicated on the summary of participants' views in Table 11.1. Findings from the collected data indicate that English teachers communicate with learners and subject experts in online teaching and learning on a regular basis. The presence of both teachers and learners on social media, and their participation in born-digital communication shows some level of collaboration. The collaborative strategies include

Table 11.1 Summary of findings

Broad view	Participants' views
Use of digital technology for teaching and learning	• It is a modern way of learning English as a second language in South African resource-constrained secondary schools. • There are limited digital resources in the informal settlements. • Most learners cannot afford data costs for learning all the subjects online. • Some students struggle with digital literacy and proficiency. • Electrical power supply is often disrupted leading to internet connectivity problems-cable theft and inadequate power supply
Social media platforms and English learning opportunities	• Common social media platforms used by both teachers and learners for ESL are WhatsApp, Facebook, Twitter and Instagram. • Teachers and learners share videos, text, scanned pages, emojis and other multimodal texts to learn English. • Discussion groups on social media are used by learners to complete assignments, online tasks and preparation for tests and examinations.
Digital devices and internet as information repositories	• Teachers and learners use digital devices to store information and as a tool to transfer and share knowledge. • Teachers also use devices for entertainment during their teaching and learning programme particularly when learners watch movies and drama performances such as *Macbeth* on YouTube. • Teachers and learners consult online dictionaries, and use spelling and grammar checkers when writing electronically. • Teachers create slides and learner activities, save videos and use them for future lessons.
Challenges faced by teachers and learners from resource-constrained secondary schools	• There is unreliable power supply due to load shedding and cost of electricity in the informal settlements. • There are network disruptions. • Efficient digital devices are expensive.

formation of social media groups named differently depending on the focus of the group (Czerviewicz *et al.*, 2019). Teachers initiate the formation of social media groups to create out-of-school contact with learners, although the schools and the Department of Basic Education do not provide financial support for teachers to buy data and digital devices for online English learning support. Learners form discussion groups with the guidance of teachers on social media, and they use the platforms to ask questions and initiate discussions regarding the content from the English syllabus. Learners share experiences and sources of information in their respective groups, while teachers provide guidance using online facilities even after school (Reinders, 2018). These conversations form part of digitally-based remote learning. The strategy allows virtual interaction between English teachers and learners, thereby extending the teaching and learning time even after school (Reinders & White, 2016). English teachers who participated in the study confirmed that most learners who struggled to complete homework have significantly improved, because they had a chance to ask for assistance from subject teachers and peers on social media.

In other cases, learners share tasks and documents, such as prompts and frames for essays and direct speech dialogues on social media. The sharing of information and documents in social media chats and other forms of communication such as email improved learners' electronic writing skills, and enhanced their awareness of the stages of writing. For example, learners share their essay plan, drafts and sketches on social media platforms and via email. Open and closed group discussions provide opportunities for learners to review and comment on specific aspects of learning English. The teachers who also participated in the conversations indicated that the sharing process provides learning curves for learners as they edit, correct and improve the structure of texts, correct grammatical and punctuation errors, and format the document. In other words, digitally-based writing skills developed through peer learning (Aljaad, 2016). Online dictionaries, textbooks and grammar books and articles provided additional guidance. During interviews both teachers and learners indicated that significant improvements in grammatical competence have been noted among those who participated in online learning. Specifically, a teacher from one secondary school indicated that learners are now able to use spelling and grammar checkers to correct their essays at Grade 9 level. As a result, improved proficiency in English language in both reading and writing creates access to academic knowledge repositories, because their ability has reached an advanced level (Rwodzi & De Jager, 2021). Initiatives taken by English teachers involve creativity, innovation and an ability to demonstrate job ability with the integration of digital technology, especially in adverse conditions (Reinders & White, 2016).

Discussions and observations yielded data on spelling competitions, word puzzles, essay writing skills and vocabulary development, which are activities meant to develop language skills in the born-digital learners at different levels. All participating teachers indicated that their role included creating assessment rubrics, assignment guidelines and portfolio folders online.

In support of their initiatives, participants used videos to create learning opportunities for learners by sharing the videos with friends and other learning partners in their out-of-school literacy practices (Reid, 2016). The key point at this stage is that modern learners, particularly born-digital candidates, experience learning in different modes and learning becomes exciting when it takes place in socialising contexts (Bock, 2017). The learning process involves the use of computers for typing to produce texts used for assessing creative writing and electronic tasks. In this strategy, learners learn to edit their work, use word-processing functions, custom animations, creation of images and other applications such as font size, bold and italics (Savage & McGoun, 2015). This teaching strategy also creates opportunities for learners to access online stories and pictures to support their creations, as well as access to easily accessible references from Google searches.

11.5 Discussion of Findings

Findings from the discussions and patterns emerging from the analysed documents indicate that initiatives centered around three main areas, namely the participating English teachers' creativity in the design of learner tasks (e.g. when developing activities, such as games and puzzles), as well as modification and curation of existing teaching strategies and skills to suit new learning settings. As mentioned earlier, teacher initiatives draw on the characteristics of the of teachers, namely human courage, language-learning readiness and being proactive in changing the learning landscape, for the benefit of their learners and highlighting the resilience of teachers in terms of technology integration for the improvement of teaching and learning of English in South African resource-constrained secondary schools. The creation of social media groups with a variety of topics and an acceptable array of skills helps to eradicate the challenges which come with the shortage, and allow learners to collaborate even after school hours. The acquired skills are the digital literacy skills that promote born-digital learners to participation on the educational platforms.

In addition to enhanced access to sources of information, English teachers and learners have an opportunity for born-digital literacy practices. Furthermore, increased online presence provides both entertainment and the opportunity to complete academic assessments. This means that learners can multitask and combine academic work and entertainment at the same time. In view of the major challenges, English language teachers and learners from resource-constrained schools state that data for connectivity cost them a lot of money because most learners from informal settlements are from lower income groups. Some teachers recommend that learners from informal settlements should get government subsidies on data, or local authorities should provide WiFi connection for educational purposes.

Technology centres and other educational training programmes offer opportunities to enhance teachers' awareness of the possibilities that technology offers, and to train teachers from technologically disadvantaged communities. The teacher training process involves creating, modifying and curating knowledge and skills which should equip learners with the skills to use social media and enable them to sit online exams. For teachers in the digital age, initiatives should include the cross-pollination of ideas, dynamism, creativity and interdisciplinary approaches to teaching digital literacy. The teacher-to-teacher initiative of peer collaboration seeks to integrate the teaching of English language concepts in all other subjects. Initiatives are time-specific tasks or projects that are necessary to achieve objectives. An initiative may support multiple objectives and determine readiness to embark on bold new ventures. In the context of this study, initiatives include investing time in learners' digital literacy and inculcation of a positive mindset towards that form of literacy. The creation of social media discussion groups and curation of content for sharing also form the additional role of English teachers in supporting learning on digital spaces. However, most teachers still only have pedagogic skills in teaching using pen and paper. For this reason, the need to re-skill and reorganise teaching into the electronic format is an imperative for teachers in the digital age. Critical issues raised by teachers during the interviews were the lack of pedagogic guidelines for using digital literacy in English and revisiting the policy on the use of digital devices for the teaching and learning of languages.

11.6 Conclusion

This chapter concludes by supporting that English teachers need progressive online training that provides further skills in the use of social media in teaching ESL. The experience of teachers in resource-constrained secondary schools in South Africa require development and training as well as digital resources to support online learning. The development could include retraining in some cases, and workshops at cluster level. The use of the TPACK model as a general framework should be encouraged in order to support the integration of technology in English language teaching. The combination of learning and socializing for teaching and learning of English is quite novel in townships but can significantly improve learners' language proficiency.

References

Abbas, P.G., Lei-Mei, L. and Haruil, N.I. (2013) Teachers' use of technology and constructivism. *I.J. Modern Education and Computer Science* 4 (1), 49–63.
Aljaad, N.H.M.A. (2016) WhatsApp for educational purposes for female students at a college of education – King Saud University. *Education* 137 (3), 344–367.
Bell, F. (2011) Connectivism: Its place in theory. *Informed Research and Innovation in Technology-enabled Learning* 12 (3), 1–8.
Bock, Z. (2017) Cyber socialising: Emerging genres and registers of intimacy among young South African students. *Language Matters* 44 (2), 68–91.
Creswell, J.W. (2013) *Research Design: Qualitative, Quantitative, and Mixed Methods Approaches* (4th edn). Sage.
Czerviewicz, L., Trotter, H. and Haupt, G. (2019) Online teaching in response to student protests and campus shutdowns: Academics' perspective. *International Journal of Educational Technology in Higher Education* 16 (3), 1–22.
Department of Basic Education (2011) *Curriculum and Assessment Policy Statement (CAPS). English Home Language.* Government Printer.
Department of Communications and Digital Technologies (2020) *Government Gazette.* Government Printer.
Dietrich, L. (2018) *Unpack TPACK in Your Classroom: Technology Integration Models and Barriers.* Press Books.
Dube, B. (2020) Rural online learning in the context of COVID-19 in South Africa: Evoking an inclusive education approach. *Multidisciplinary Journal of Educational Research* 10 (2), 135–157.

Ebersöhn, L. (2017) Enabling spaces in education research: An agenda for impactful, collective evidence to support all to be first among un-equals. *South African Journal of Education* 36 (4). https://doi.org/10.15700/saje.v36n4a1390 (accessed 23 November 2021).

Flick, U. (2014) *An Introduction to Qualitative Research* (5th edn). Sage.

Gumbo, M.T. (2020) Indigenizing technological pedagogical content knowledge in open distance learning. *Africa Education Review* 17 (4), 201–220.

Jonassen, D.H. (2006) *Modeling with Technology: Mindtools for Conceptual Change* (3rd edn). Pearson Merrill Prentice Hall.

Koehler, M., Mishra, P. and Cain, W. (2017) What is technological pedagogical content knowledge (TPACK)? *Journal of Education* 193 (3), 13–19.

Maphalala, M.C. and Nzama, M.V. (2014) The proliferation of cell phones in high schools. The implication for the teaching and learning process. *Mediterranean Journal of Social Sciences* 5 (3), 461–466.

Mbatha, N.G. (2016) An exploration of IsiZulu L1 students' attitudes towards Northern Sotho at a university of technology in Gauteng province. MTech dissertation, Tshwane University of Technology.

Mishra, P. and Koehler, M.J. (2006) Technological pedagogical content knowledge: A framework for integrating technology in teachers' knowledge. *Teachers College Record* 108 (6), 1017–1054.

Mutasa, D.E. (2006) *African Languages in the 21st Century. The Main Challenges*. Simba Guru.

Omoso, S. and Odindo, F. (2020) TPACK in teacher education: Using pre-service teachers' self-reported TPACK to improve pedagogic practice. *International Journal of Education and Research* 8 (5), 125–138.

Reid, J.M. (2016) New literacies for teachers: Researching the curriculum design, materials development, implementation and redesign of a compulsory, core course in literacy for first year BEd students. PhD thesis, University of the Witwatersrand.

Reinders, H. (2018) Technology and autonomy. In J.I. Liontas (ed.) *The TESOL Encyclopedia of English Language Teaching* (pp. 1–5). Wiley-Blackwell.

Reinders, H. and White, C. (2016) 20 years of autonomy and technology: How far have we come and where to next? *Language Learning & Technology* 20 (2), 143–154.

Rose, J. (2009) Independent review of the primary curriculum: Final report. See www.London.teachersnet.gov. (accessed May 2016).

Rwodzi, C. (2018) Exploring teacher initiatives on digital literacy in English. PhD thesis, University of Pretoria.

Rwodzi, C. and De Jager, L. (2021) Remote learning as an option by resilient English teachers in Gauteng resource-constrained township secondary schools. *Perspectives in Education* 39 (3), 62–78.

Rwodzi, C., De Jager, L. and Mpofu, N. (2020) The innovative use of social media for teaching English as a second language. *Transdisciplinary Research in Southern Africa* 16 (1), 1–7.

Santos, J.M. and Castro, R.D.R. (2001) Technological Pedagogical Content Knowledge (TPACK) in action: Application of learning in the classroom by pre-service teachers (PST). *Social Sciences & Humanities Open* 3 (1), 2590–2611.

Savage, J. and McGoun, C. (2015) *Teaching in a Networked Classroom*. Routledge.

Thanasoulas, D. (2001) Constructivist learning. See www.eltnewsletter.com/back/April2001/art54001.htm (accessed March 2021).

Wang, Q. (2008) A generic model for guiding the integration of ICT into teaching and learning. *Innovations in Education and Teaching International* 45 (4), 411–419.

12 'I'm going to teach differently': Changing Perceptions of Writing Instruction through Digital Text Creation

Maya Ashooh, Alecia Marie Magnifico and Bethany Silva

12.1 Introduction

Teachers have grappled with how to support students in developing digital literacy and composition skills, especially as playful, 'born-digital' compositions, such as tweets and memes, have become increasingly important genres of social and political communication. While many states have adopted digital- or media-based standards associated with composition (NH Dept. of Education, 2018a, 2018b), classroom writing in the United States still focuses strongly on alphanumeric, structured genres such as summaries, short-answer questions and formulaic essays (Gillespie *et al.*, 2014; Graham *et al.*, 2014; Ray *et al.*, 2016). When the term 'born-digital' focuses on texts that are 'created solely in digital formats' (Library of Congress, n.d.), this term becomes challenging for application to classroom writing, since teachers often ask students to begin composing on paper. Engberg (2007) articulates the problems of a definition that draws distinctions based on the drafting or creation of a composition. Further, paper multimodal texts like hand-drawn comics 'cannot be fully represented in print contexts alone' (Selfe & Hawisher, 2012; cf. Coppola, 2020) – another commonly-invoked aspect. Regardless of terminological differences, however, for students to successfully develop digital and media composition skills and literacies, it is clear that teachers must include such texts in the curriculum (McGrew *et al.*, 2018).

Mills (2016), Hicks (2015) and many others have argued that students benefit from the inclusion of digital and multimodal work in the classroom. When students compose born-digital texts that use a variety of media forms, they learn to think carefully about the meanings they wish to convey, and the options that exist for how to do this work. For example, when young writers translate textual ideas into a script, video, new story or visual composition, they adapt their meanings to the affordances or constraints of the new medium and work with a variety of media and tools to perform these translations and adaptations (Hicks, 2015; Rowsell, 2020; Stornaiuolo & Thomas, 2018). As Mills (2016: 68) puts it, 'translating semiotic content via a different expression plane necessitates the transformation of meanings'. Working in multiple modes sharpens young composers' sense of purpose and narrative meaning, as well as their awareness of the audiences who may interact with the product. Such composition builds awareness of texts as communicative and rhetorical, which readies students to see and interpret other creators' work (Fletcher, 2015, 2021). These critical media literacy skills are often absent from standards and thus not taught explicitly in schools, but they are crucial for 21st-century readers and writers (Janks *et al.*, 2014; Lyiscott *et al.*, 2021).

Media and literacy scholars may promote instruction in multimodal and media texts, as well as interest-driven digital literacy learning (Curwood *et al.*, 2013; Ito *et al.*, 2019), but school structures create tensions between this work and classroom implementation (Magnifico *et al.*, 2018). Educators who work with elementary-age children have noted that part of this tension comes from teachers, who typically position students as successful writers when they comply with task expectations and use proper grammar (Coppola, 2020).

English teachers who focus on writing have often discussed the importance of teachers writing alongside their students to model the often-cumbersome processes of drafting, false starts, revision and refinement (e.g. Chavez, 2021; Kittle, 2008; Murray, 2003). In order to develop a realistic sense of writerly identity, students need to see the extended writing processes of an expert writer – how an invitation to write, or even an idea, rarely leads immediately to a refined draft, or even to complete sentences. In our work, we explicitly extend this argument to multimodal and born-digital texts: to help teachers feel prepared to teach and assess such compositions, they first need to engage in the complexities of meaning-making that are inherent in multimodal, digital creation. They need to consider, draft and make born-digital texts.

We wonder if part of the reason that teachers have difficulty engaging in digital composition with their students is writing instruction's focus on skills and strategies such as KWL – what I know, what I want to know and what I learned about a topic (e.g. Beers, 2003; Beers & Probst, 2017; Graham *et al.*, 2016). While such skills and strategy-based pedagogies have been shown to be effective for improving students' work in writing to learn about content (e.g. responses to literature), and in explicit structured genres (e.g. exam-based essays), open-ended composition is often less straightforward, particularly in multimodal forms where meaning needs to be considered carefully, because it may be conveyed in a host of ways.

In recent years, some theorists have suggested that one potential way of sidestepping this tension and encouraging teachers' facility with born-digital texts is to explicitly include *play* with meanings and modes in the context of classroom composition. Wohlwend (2018, 2019) argues that play should be recognized as a literacy in its own right. Her work with young children argues that participating in creating and recreating narratives is not 'just' play, but vital early literacy work. Through the collaborative negotiation of pretend play, where meanings and stories are shared and shifted over time, often with the aid of a variety of physical objects and technologies, students create meanings by composing and revising playful narratives. Dyson's (2013, 2020) and Halverson's (2021) work on elementary classroom writing shows that in-class play with music and drama (e.g. 'Author's Theatre') can go hand in hand with storytelling and written compositions. Playful engagement with narrative can be helpful for secondary teaching, too; through fanfiction practices, students may engage with textual analysis and writing (Lammers & Magnifico, 2021), as well as examine and 're-story' diverse perspectives (Thomas & Stornaiuolo, 2016).

Whereas educational settings, particularly those for teenagers and adults, often see play, fun and student interest as secondary to the hard work that will prepare students for college and careers (Newkirk, 2021), Wohlwend's (2019) work sees and frames playful literacies as *fundamental* to students' development as writers, composers and meaning-makers. Black's (2008, 2009) early research on international young writers' fanfiction showed that playful texts inspired by anime characters helped writers to successfully practice and refine their English writing. Similar studies have examined spaces where media fandom participants (e.g. Agudelo Lopera, 2020; Curwood *et al.*, 2013; Martin, 2014; Sauro, 2017), students playing writing games in classrooms (Boscolo *et al.*, 2012; Liao *et al.*, 2018) and online gaming collectives (Horowitz, 2019; Mora *et al.*, 2020; Thorne *et al.*, 2009) learn languages by playing, chatting, composing and reviewing writing and multimodal texts together. Work from the perspective of Connected Learning (e.g. Ito *et al.*, 2018, 2019), more broadly, points out that these forms of interest-driven learning are pleasurable for teens and tweens because they extend across and beyond school subjects, drawing together students' virtual and face-to-face communities and their academic learning.

To successfully encourage playful writing and the composition of born-digital texts, educators need to take these forms of learning and teaching seriously, create such compositions themselves, and (perhaps most crucially) build ways for students to see these playful works as legitimate parts of in-class composition processes. Comber (2016) notes that educators' designs of spaces like their classrooms are vital but often overlooked. She draws on theoretical work from Massey (2005: 8), a critical geographer, to show that 'place ... does change us' in consequential ways. The places of classrooms are central elements of classroom curricula, marked by accepted composition processes like essays. Particularly by the time students reach secondary school, those processes are mediated by assessment that fosters a culture that discourages play. These composition processes and assessments shape students and teachers into people with particular identities and interests – 'good' or 'struggling' writers, for instance. When the classroom is a place where teachers play with texts, share messy drafts, doodle and allow students to participate in their revision, students begin to see such activities as normal parts of composition (Kittle, 2008). The nature of a classroom can powerfully influence the nature of student and teacher participation – and of what the participants see as writing, composition and literacy (Comber, 2016).

When considering students and their perceptions of school writing, it is necessary to think about what *they* think is valid and authentic learning. Behizadeh (2014) observed that students felt an assignment was more meaningful when they had a choice about its topic, because writing about their prior knowledge or interests increases its authenticity. However, authenticity does not solely stem from student choice: students also see writing work as more authentic when they value the content (e.g. their families), or believe it to be important beyond their communities. Approximately half of Behizadeh's participants reported that 'structured choice' was crucial to authenticity, rather than complete freedom. What is most important to keep in mind is that students who are engaged authentically in their work are likely to learn more effectively than those here who are not (Hillocks, 2011).

To create a space like this for playful textual and multimodal writing, and to learn more about how teachers and students might take up the creation of digital texts, our campus writing network hosted a National Day on Writing (NDOW) celebration. In doing so, we planned to promote playful, digital writing and hoped to help teachers envision including such texts in their curricula. Our National Day on Writing 'writing party' was an extracurricular, optional activity. Although we invited university faculty and local public school teachers to attend with their students, it was not centered in an academic class, and was not planned in accordance with specific writing outcomes or standards. Instead, we aimed to nurture an open, playful space to compose and discuss writing.

These questions guide our inquiry:

(1) How did participants respond to composing playful 'born-digital' writing? What were their motivations for participating?
(2) What kinds of compositions did participants contribute?
(3) What connections did participants draw between NDOW and writing instruction?

12.2 Methods

12.2.1 Context and data collection

The NDOW celebration was established by the National Council of Teachers of English in 2009 as an event 'to celebrate composition in all its forms by individuals from all walks of life' (Fink, 2020: para 2). In 2019, a group of leaders representing various campus writing groups from our school planned and hosted a NDOW celebration. University students, community members and other faculty and staff also helped get the word out about the writing celebration. We collect yearly data on this ongoing project to improve the program and to observe perspectives over time.

The writing celebration involves prompts that invite participants to engage with writing in many modalities, genres and styles. In 2019, prompts and exemplars were set up throughout a busy atrium, while a Twitter challenge ran online. The Twitter challenge was also projected onto a screen within the atrium. As participants composed, they posted their creations on the atrium's walls and also shared them via social media.

In 2020, the planning team moved the writing celebration online due to COVID19. We created a bitmoji classroom that contained multiple 'rooms', each hosted by a different writing group, as well as several Zoom rooms for synchronous writing. The NDOW Padlet provided a space to share writing asynchronously, giving participants opportunities to respond to prompts or design their own writing throughout the week. Prompts included multimodal and textual ideas, such as: 'Heart Map', 'Blackout Poetry', 'Favorite Quote' and questions like 'Where do you write from?'. Participants largely responded to prompts with added playful elements (pictures, designs).

The NDOW writing party was an open space for writers to contribute whatever they wanted to the Padlet, Twitter or Instagram thread without pressure to follow any structure or prompt. Because this celebration uses social media to share writing, many of these texts inherently include 'born-digital' elements. Some are tweets sharing or commenting on textual journal pages, while others are memes, short videos, or writings layered over pictures. Perhaps as a result of this encouragement to work across and through 'typical' writing, many of these texts are also playful.

12.2.2 Data sources and participants

- Survey data includes 24 respondents: two K12 students, 1 K12 teacher, seven university TAs and 14 university undergraduates (several who directly mentioned, or alluded to, plans to become teachers in their responses). Of these surveys, 19 were collected in 2019 and five were

collected in 2020. Key questions traced participants' purposes for attending, activities completed and beliefs about writing instruction.
- The Padlet gallery includes 54 posts and 69 responsive comments written by NDOW participants during the online 2020 NDOW celebration.

12.2.3 Data analysis

In this analysis, we examine participation data from 2019 and 2020, including the texts that writers shared, responsive comments and a participant exit survey. To analyze survey data, we tallied closed-ended questions and employed thematic analysis (Boyatzis, 1998; Saldaña, 2015) for multiple rounds of qualitative coding on open-ended questions.

Because the posts represent creative works, open to multiple valid interpretations, our analysis of the Padlet data drew on Call-Cummings *et al.*'s (2020) collaborative data analysis. Rather than seeking consensus, we sought to unearth the multiple meanings that could be gleaned from various posts. First, we organized all posts in a matrix, identifying forms, genres, written text, responses to prompt, modality and topics. We read through all posts, capturing first impressions individually. Over the course of five meetings, we shared our impressions, orally discussing each person's insights, themes observed and connections to other posts. We synthesized our individual impressions into 'collective impressions'. In that synthesis, two themes emerged: features of spaces that foster playful, digital writing and the ways participants intertwined multiple modes as they created textual meaning. We each then returned to the original Padlet posts and re-read them through the lens of our collective impressions, writing memos about our new understandings of spaces and intertwining of modes (Saldaña, 2015).

12.3 Findings

Formal school writing often does not attach much weight to writing that is playful or extracurricular, but through their surveys and participation in physical and virtual writing projects, participants suggested that the writing that they tried was meaningful to them. NDOW exposed them to creative writing ideas and approaches that introduced new perceptions of what classroom writing could be.

In these findings, we first examine focal texts, exploring how participants played with modes, created new meanings and built on each others' meanings in different interpretations of the various prompts. (In the examples that we share, we preserve the language of the original posts, including grammar and spelling.) Then, we discuss how our asynchronous Padlet created a born-digital writing space that offered structure to writers who wanted it, but also allowed openness and freedom to those who wanted to explore genres. Finally, we discuss the importance of playful writing to our participants – and, potentially, to their future classrooms.

12.3.1 Participants used a variety of modes to create meaning in their texts

In both 2019 and 2020, participants created multimodal texts, combining a variety of modes and genres to create the meanings that they wanted to share. Contributions used alphanumeric text (both handwritten and digital), images (handmade and digital in 2019, all digital in 2020), emojis and references to associated texts. In some cases, the text served as a complement to the writing, as was the case with this post (Figure 12.1) that Alecia (Author #2) shared on the NDOW Padlet, which combines an image of a tree with alphanumeric prose. Alecia used the title to refer to the prompt that inspired the writing, incorporating emojis of a plant and leaves. Within the post, she began by describing the image, referring to the 'jagged black scar' between two trunks. After describing the tree, she reflected on coppice-marks, scars from purposeful cuts on a tree, usually precursors to grafting. Alecia then reflected on how coppice-marks heal, relating them to the ways humans form scars as they heal. Throughout the writing, the only component where the text and image explicitly interact is in the description of the black scar at the center of the image.

Other writers created and posted multimodal compositions that only make sense through the intertwining of modalities combined with current cultural experiences. By itself, the text in Figure 12.2, 'One day, my whole life changed', is very general, and perhaps even clichéd. Readers might not connect with it because of this generality. But juxtaposed against an image of the world wearing a mask, the text takes on deeper cultural meaning. Time is an additional factor in a reader's interpretation: created in the middle of the Covid-19 pandemic, the composition can be read in a very specific way. Had the post been created one year earlier, a reader might have suspected that the sentence was the beginning of a dystopian novel or a memoir about an individual's illness. Additionally, the text's reference to the narrator's whole life changing through the use of 'my' creates a meaningful juxtaposition when placed in contrast with the image of the earth – is the point of the text that the narrator might be thinking individually, but the image emphasizes that the pandemic has impacted the whole world.

In addition to creating texts whose meaning depended on more than one mode, participants also created texts that referenced popular and classic stories as they made and shared meaning of their lives. One participant reflected on her identity formation through *Winnie the Pooh*, writing:

> ...[F]rom a young age, I loved Eeyore. He was so sad all the time and I was sad a lot, so I felt him a kindred spirit... As I got older and read the

'I'm going to teach differently' 193

> **Dr. Easley's #WriteOut**
> **"Stories happen in forests"**
>
> The birch's stems split, a jagged black scar between the trunks. Rough and exposed. I wonder if it's an old coppice-mark, a place where the original limb stretched high, now maybe adorns a room with clear-grained trim.
>
> Paper birches don't make paper anymore, but the bark still grows its own stories. The new pink inner skin creeps over a rough cut, scabs a scar, fuses membrane over membrane until the splinters wear and disappear. Broken white armor stretching over limbs.
>
> Coppice cuts take longer, and I wonder if they fully heal. Are they like the whorl on my scalp that marks my fall from a high deck, the knot of stomach-flesh that records Chris's appendectomy? We

Figure 12.1 Alecia's birch tree story and photo

Milne versions of all the Pooh stories, I found Eeyore less relatable and Piglet more representative of my life. Is this the progression of depression to anxiety? Maybe. (Padlet participant, 2020)

Another participant responded to a prompt to make a heart map and fill it with favorite songs. Underneath the heart, the author wrote, '"Send me on my way" takes me back to my very last volleyball game. My coach played this song for us to say goodbye and to find our way without volleyball'. As they referenced these texts within their own writing, participants also assumed readers who could relate to those texts and place them into new contexts that intertwined with their own deeper meanings. On one level, most readers might understand that Eeyore is sad and Piglet is nervous, but a reader who is able to connect memories of Eeyore's response to the destruction of his home or Piglet's overwhelming fear of wild animals might note the great depth of emotion in a 'progression of depression

[Figure: Image of a globe overlaid with a face mask, with the text "One day my whole life changed"]

Figure 12.2 Multimodal response to a 'one day' story prompt

to anxiety'. Similarly, from its title, a reader might infer that *Send Me On My Way* is a song about saying goodbye, but a reader familiar with the pulsing drumbeat and wailing lyrics of Rusted Root's song might feel a deeper connection to a former volleyball player's sense of loss.

When they came to NDOW, participants could create whatever they wanted to create. We had suggestions and prompts designed to encourage writers to play creatively with texts and media/modes, but there was no mandate to take any of them up, or to take them up in specific ways. Some participants used prompts or tried out the activities that we provided, and some did not. Particularly in 2020 when NDOW was fully digital, when participants made their contributions, they drew on a variety of modes and texts in their writing, often bringing their writing together with an image or another text to deepen their meaning or draw a connection to their own experiences. Through this play, writers were able to explore a variety of meanings, and to create new meanings with these juxtapositions.

12.3.2 What's posted becomes what's possible

With its focus on sharing and reflecting on composition across genres and modes, NDOW creates physical and digital space for textual play. However, our findings show that even when our participants had the freedom to contribute any piece of writing they wished, a majority chose to respond to a provided prompt, though they interpreted that prompt in many ways.

This phenomenon occurred explicitly and implicitly. Some posts explicitly suggested writing prompts or possibilities, creating a space for other writers to join in and try something similar. In 2019, participants filled one wall of our writing space with blackout poems, and another wall with illustrated treasure maps. Multiple examples of a prompt or a form seemed to encourage writers to try making their own version. We noticed this trend even more explicitly on the 2020 Padlet, a tool that allowed us

Landay Poems

A landay is a form of folk poetry from Afghanistan that consists of two lines, the first line having nine syllables and the second line having thirteen syllables.

See details and examples HERE and HERE.

Landays are traditionally composed in Pashto, one of the main languages in Afghanistan and Pakistan, but we invite you to create your own landay in the language(s) of your choice and post it here!

♡ 1   ⊙ 5

I sing even under my blue hood. My mother says I am a most determined songbird.

žlutá z podzimního lesa: s takovým zlatem vydržím další zimu.

Figure 12.3 Post and comments encouraging participants to write landay poems

to look at the order of submissions. For example, one Padlet post gave information about a traditionally Afghan poetry form, landay and invited people to contribute their own (Figure 12.3). While nobody made a new post on the Padlet that contained an individual landay poem, four comments on the original post took the form of landay responses to the prompt's original author.

In another instance, Bethany (Author #3), engaging in her facilitator role, took a photo of herself writing in a physical notebook and posted it on the Padlet with a note encouraging others to post their physical writing as well (Figure 12.4). This introduced a new medium to the Padlet: digitized physical writing. In response, other participants followed this lead and posted photos of themselves writing in their physical journals. Regardless of whether these texts originated as 'born-digital', they were

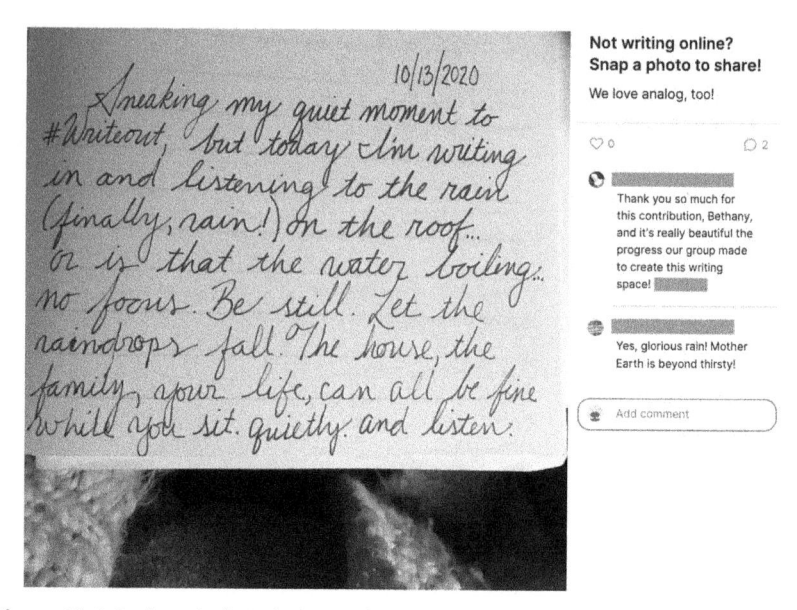

Figure 12.4 Bethany's digital photo of her physical journal

shared and distributed digitally and gained a responsive audience, members of which took this as a potential model for their own composition.

We also found implicit examples of the posts structuring further possibilities for writing. The majority of the Padlet posts responded to prompts from the NDOW bitmoji classroom slideshow. Furthermore, when Padlet posts prompted a new genre or style of writing, several other participants followed along, creating a series of similar posts or responses. For example, one participant added an Eleanor Roosevelt quotation to the Padlet in response to a prompt for 'favorite quotes' – and the next three posts that follow are all favorite quotes. Something similar happened after a writing club's participants tried posting a series of one-sentence responses to a 'One Day…' prompt that we had provided. Just a few hours later, individuals from outside the writing club began to attempt the same prompt and post their versions on the Padlet.

These chains of responses to our prompts varied greatly in content and form, but it seems as if writers typically chose paths that provided more structured approaches to writing even though the possibilities were vast. What was posted became an idea, perhaps even a template, for new possible writing. Even though writers were responding to each others' content in this way, we found that posts within the same prompt showed many differences in the content produced. For example, in the case of the favorite quote prompt, many participants only posted a quote and an attribution. Some chose to go further, though, adding explanations of what the quote meant to them or pictures of the originator. Participants did not seem to feel confined by the prompts – they chose how personal, reflective, or technical they wanted to get in their writing – but they consistently used the structure of prompts despite a wide-open space to create and share compositions.

This is not to say that participants never shared open-ended compositions. Fifteen of the 54 posts (28%), five of which were short poems written and layered over pictures by one member of our volunteer team, were not traceable to any prompts. This finding shows that participants did find and enact new creative affordances in the digital Padlet space. At the same time, 39 of the 54 of the posts (72%) responded to prompts, suggesting that providing options and mentor texts to seed participants' writing is a powerful practice that allows writers to imagine new composition possibilities. Following a prompt led to a wide array of written and multimodal content and offered the chance for participants to build from the posts that others made.

Altogether, these multimodal posts demonstrate a spectrum of what the students, pre-service teachers and teachers who participated *consider* writing. They also represent potential directions for future classroom writing, and a reminder that many successful compositions begin from a social response to a prompt or mentor text rather than from wide-open inspiration. Perhaps particularly in schools, playful creative writing does not happen automatically. Instead, intentionally constructing a space where writers can see prompts and responses helps to build confidence in new directions, ideas, or experiments that are authentic to the writers.

12.3.3 Participants thought differently about teaching and learning writing

Survey participants attended the NDOW writing party for a variety of reasons: in 2019, 12 of the 19 participants included 'I came here with my class' in their reasons for participation (the survey allowed multiple responses for this question), and 5 of the 19 included 'I love to write'. In 2020, 4 of the 5 participants included 'I love to write'. From this distribution, we infer that many people who already loved to write attended the writing party, but so did people who otherwise might not have tried an activity like this.

Participants reported that – across these reasons for participation – their experiences affected them. Across the two years, 20 of the 24 participants noted that NDOW writing shifted their perceptions of what it means to teach or learn writing. In the free response space for describing these shifts, they mentioned new ideas about incorporating 'art' or 'creative' writing, the success of multiple 'strategies' or 'prompts', and ideas about writing while teaching. One 2020 respondent who identified as university/college faculty described 'new ideas' about student and teacher writing: 'It gave me new ideas about prompts I could use in class and also helps me think about ways that I could engage myself in writing without the pressure of an assignment or a class'. A 2019 respondent who identified as an undergraduate student attending with their class noted new definitions of writing: 'It makes me realize writing can be fun and creative – it's not just about research papers and reports'. Doing various writing activities helped survey respondents imagine new possibilities that they might use in their own teaching.

Beyond finding playful and multimodal writing appealing or inspiring, teachers and learners described the potential for pleasure to develop greater interest in writing or motivation to write – both for themselves and for students. Twenty-one of the 24 survey respondents, including all participants who identified as teachers, saw potential benefits to adding new 'prompts', 'different ways' or genres of writing to their current or future teaching. For instance, one 2019 respondent who identified as a graduate student noted that '[i]t makes you think about your process differently. It emphasizes creativity and invention and following the path of an idea in interesting ways', while a 2020 participant reflected that the writing party was 'a reminder to experiment and have fun with language'.

The writing that participants posted to the atrium walls (in 2019) and to the Padlet (in 2020) also identified some of the writing party participants' experimentation – and thus the ways in which survey respondents expanded their ideas about possible approaches to writing. Teachers and students who participated tried new writing techniques and strategies. In the survey, they observed that creative, playful and multimodal writing asks them to shift their pedagogies and, as one pre-service teacher respondent noted, 'teach differently' (2019).

12.4 Discussion and Implications for Future Work

The National Day on Writing is a celebration of composition across forms and purposes. Because it is an event sponsored by the National Council of Teachers of English, its participants include a great number of English teachers and students. Ironically, however, the scope of classroom writing is often restricted. Coppola (2020) has observed that classroom teachers often value students' compliance with an assignment most highly, and repeated national surveys of writing tasks (Gillespie *et al.*, 2014; Graham *et al.*, 2014; Ray *et al.*, 2016) have demonstrated that shorter writing tasks like short-answer questions, outlines and summaries are the most common classroom writing assignments. Particularly at the secondary level, few teachers regularly include extended writing or imaginative, open-ended compositions like journals or stories. It seems, in schools, that a great number of students and teachers believe that the main purposes for writing are recording information and answering questions.

Our NDOW writing party was conceived in a more playful frame, in response to these typically tight strictures. We hoped to inspire teachers and students to try low-stakes, personal and multimodal composition, and we wondered whether or not these attempts would lead participants to think in new ways about the roles that writing plays in their own lives and classrooms.

Particularly in the born-digital artifacts that they produced in online spaces like the Padlet, most writing party participants combined their own composition with another text (e.g. the 'Send Me On My Way' heart map) or with an image (e.g. the 'One Day' one-sentence stories). Mills (2016) notes that such multimodal meanings are complex because the meaning-making does not rest solely in one kind of expression. For example, the meaning of 'one day, my whole life changed' shifts when a writer overlays this sentence on an image of the Earth wearing a surgical mask, and students in our increasingly digital world benefit from understanding the contributions of the different elements to the overall meaning – the composition's intertextuality. Wohlwend's (2019) and Dyson's (2013, 2020) work additionally reminds us that further representations of any text are possible, and, for many young writers, this (re)vision can be aided by continued imaginative play or use of digital tools (cf. Halverson, 2021). Brought together, such work indicates that playful and multimodal writing is more than a fun, playful diversion. It holds potential for valuable meaning-making, as well as broadening composition curricula.

At the same time, we observed that participants seemed to venture tentatively into playful writing. When they had the choice to write anything, the majority of writers tried out one of our prompts or activities rather than making a genre or text completely from their own invention. In 2020, the ordering of participants' writings on the Padlet demonstrated that only 28% of the posts introduced new genres or forms. Participants more commonly chose to respond to a prompt, suggesting that Behizadeh's (2014) insight that 'structured choice' can offer writers a comfortable level of autonomy and authenticity describes not just classroom writing experiences, but writing across settings.

Comber's (2016) work shows that the design of a classroom place, not just the designs of lessons, affects how students interact. Our writing parties are university-sponsored events that take place within academic spaces. Because research shows that school writing typically has a correct answer or formula, it also seems possible that participants followed prompts closely because they felt some pressure to submit compositions that were acceptable for a formal university space.

Additionally, the National Day on Writing is a short event, which suggests that careful design may be necessary for participants to be willing to truly take risks with their writing in this short window of experience. Many examples of such learning environments exist. For instance, Chavez (2021) describes spending most of each semester preparing her undergraduate creative writing students to explore new techniques and share them with others, and Halverson (2021) outlines extensive research on how 'gradual release of responsibility' (Fisher & Frey, 2013) can help a class quickly begin telling and improvising stories intended for dramatic performance. Similar research on pedagogies for playful digital writing does not yet exist on a large or generalizable scale, but if we truly want students to play with writing, it seems vital to work on creating spaces where experimental or boundary-pushing composition becomes safe to try. This need for further work on how teachers can encourage students to develop their language and writing skills by making playful and 'born-digital' texts is one important implication of this study.

Nevertheless, survey participants looked beyond the space of the writing party to their own current or future classrooms. Teachers' positive responses indicate the importance of experiences like the writing party for nurturing born-digital writing within classrooms. They described engaging in the messy act of composing similarly to Chavez (2021), Kittle (2008) and Murray (2003): when teachers are writers who compose their own physical, digital and/or multimodal writings, they better understand what processes and techniques are helpful for student writers. In other words, educators' participation in the writing party helped them envision ways to design digital writing spaces for their own students. Until educators themselves engage in digital writing, it is difficult for them to incorporate born-digital composing in their teaching.

Despite the limitations of time and space inherent in a one-day event, writing party participants who took our survey told us that their participation in playful, born-digital writing mattered to them. They engaged in real writing and described a sense of coming into contact with new ideas, and of trying writing that pushed their ideas about what 'counts' as legitimate composition. Several survey responses confirm the idea that students and teachers define writing as 'school writing' – formulaic and teacher-centered, like the 'reports and research papers' that one student participant mentioned. This finding suggests that students know and understand strategies for showing their school knowledge through test questions, but may be uncomfortable with creating new meanings or sharing writing that feels vulnerable because it is personal, or because it is an experiment in a new genre. Nonetheless, survey responses that suggest that teachers want to 'teach differently', show that participation in playful, open, digital writing spaces may play a vital role in showing teachers new visions for how authentic, multimodal and meaningful writing might happen.

References

Agudelo Lopera, Z.Y. (2020) Affinity spaces and multimodal texts for connecting english classroom and students' daily tasks. Unpublished MA Thesis, Universidad Pontificia Bolivariana.
Beers, G.K. (2003) *When Kids can't Read: What Teachers can Do.* Heinemann.
Beers, G.K. and Probst, R.E. (2017) *Disrupting Thinking: Why How We Read Matters.* Scholastic.

Behizadeh, N. (2014) Adolescent perspectives on authentic writing instruction. *Journal of Language and Literacy Education* 10 (1), 27–44.

Black, R.W. (2008) *Adolescents and Online Fan Fiction*. Peter Lang.

Black, R.W. (2009) Online fan fiction, global identities, and imagination. *Research in the Teaching of English* 43 (4), 397–425.

Boscolo, P., Gelati, C. and Galvan, N. (2012) Teaching elementary school students to play with meanings and genre. *Reading & Writing Quarterly* 28 (1), 29–50. https://doi.org/10.1080/10573569.2012.632730

Boyatzis, R.E. (1998) *Transforming Qualitative Information: Thematic Analysis and Code Development*. Sage.

Call-Cummings, M., Hauber-Özer, M., LePelch, V., DeSenti, K.L., Colandene, M., Sultana, K. and Scicli, E. (2020) 'Hopefully this motivates a bout of realization': Spoken word poetry as critical literacy. *Journal of Adolescent & Adult Literacy* 64 (2), 191–199.

Chavez, F.R. (2021) *The Anti-Racist Writing Workshop: How to Decolonize the Creative Classroom*. Haymarket Books.

Comber, B. (2016) *Literacy, Place, and Pedagogies of Possibility*. Routledge.

Coppola, S. (2020) *Writing Redefined: Broadening Our Ideas of What it Means to Compose*. Stenhouse Publishers.

Curwood, J.S., Magnifico, A.M. and Lammers, J.C. (2013) Writing in the wild: Writers' motivations in fan-based affinity spaces. *Journal of Adolescent & Adult Literacy* 56 (8), 677–685.

Dyson, A.H. (2013) *Rewriting the Basics: Literacy Learning in Children's Cultures*. Teachers College Press.

Dyson, A.H. (2020) 'We're Playing Sisters, on Paper!': Children composing on graphic playgrounds. *Literacy* 54 (2), 3–12.

Fink, L. (2020) The National Day on Writing 2020. *NCTE Blog*, 18 October. https://ncte.org/blog/2020/10/national-day-on-writing-2/

Fisher, D. and Frey, N. (2013) *Better Learning Through Structured Teaching: A Framework for the Gradual Release of Responsibility*. ASCD.

Fletcher, J. (2015) *Teaching Arguments: Rhetorical Comprehension, Critique, and Response*. Stenhouse Publishers.

Fletcher, J. (2021) *Writing Rhetorically: Fostering Responsive Thinkers and Communicators*. Stenhouse Publishers.

Gillespie, A., Graham, S., Kiuhara, S. and Hebert, M. (2014) High school teachers' use of writing to support students' learning: A national survey. *Reading and Writing* 27, 1043–1072. https://doi.org/10.1007/s11145-013-9494-8

Graham, S., Capizzi, A., Harris, K.R., Hebert, M. and Morphy, P. (2014) Teaching writing to middle school students: A national survey. *Reading and Writing*, 27 1015–1042. https://doi.org/10.1007/s11145-013-9495-7

Graham, S., Fitzgerald, J., Friedrich, L.D., Greene, K., Kim, J.S. and Booth Olson, C. (2016) Teaching secondary students to write effectively: What Works Clearinghouse educator's practice guide. IES National Center for Education Evaluation and Regional Assistance. Retrieved from: https://files.eric.ed.gov/fulltext/ED569984.pdf

Halverson, E.R. (2021) *How the Arts can Save Education: Transforming Teaching, Learning, and Instruction*. Teachers College Press.

Hicks, T. (ed.) (2015) *Assessing Students' Digital Writing: Protocols for Looking Closely*. Teachers' College Press/National Writing Project.

Hillocks, G. (2011) Commentary on 'Research in secondary English, 1912–2011: Historical continuities and discontinuities in the NCTE imprint'. *Research in the Teaching of English* 46 (2), 187–192.

Horowitz, K.S. (2019) Video games and English as a second language: The effect of massive multiplayer online video games on the willingness to communicate and communicative anxiety of college students in Puerto Rico. *American Journal of Play* 11 (3), 379–410.

Ito, M., Martin, C., Pfister, R.C., Rafalow, M.H., Salen, K. and Wortman, A. (2018) *Affinity Online: How Connection and Shared Interest Fuel Learning*. NYU Press.

Ito, M., Martin, C., Rafalow, M., Salen Tekinbas, K., Wortman, A. and Pfister, R.C. (2019) Online affinity networks as contexts for Connected Learning. In K.A. Renninger and S. Hidi (eds) *Cambridge Handbook of Learning and Motivation* (pp. 291–311). Cambridge University Press.

Janks, H., with Dixon, K., Ferreira, A., Granville, S. and Newfield, D. (2014) *Doing Critical Literacy: Texts and Activities for Students and Teachers*. Routledge.

Kittle, P. (2008) *Write Beside Them: Risk, Voice, and Clarity in High School Writing*. Heinemann.

Lammers, J.C. and Magnifico, A.M. (2021) Working with living texts: Building an argument for play in secondary ELA instruction. Paper presented at the American Educational Research Association Annual Meeting. (Virtual, April).

Liao, C.Y., Chang, W.C. and Chan, T. (2018) The effects of participation, performance, and interest in a game-based writing environment. *Journal of Computer Assisted Learning* 34, 211–222. https://doi.org/10.1111/jcal.12233

Lyiscott, J., Mirra, N. and Garcia, A. (2021) Critical media literacy and popular culture in ELA classrooms. James R. Squire Office on Policy Research, National Council of Teachers of English. Retrieved from: https://eric.ed.gov/?id=ED612183

Martin, C. (2014) *Learning the Ropes: Connected Learning in a WWE fan Community*. Connected Learning Working Papers. See https://clalliance.org/publications/learning-the-ropes/ (accessed September 2023).

Magnifico, A.M., Lammers, J.C. and Fields, D.A. (2018) Affinity spaces, literacies, and classrooms: Tensions and opportunities. *Literacy* 52 (3), 145–152.

Massey, D. (2005) *For Space*. Sage.

McGrew, S., Breakstone, J., Ortega, T., Smith, M. and Wineburg, S. (2018) Can students evaluate online sources? Learning from assessments of civic online reasoning. *Theory & Research in Social Education* 46 (2), 165–193. https://doi.org/10.1080/00933104.2017.1416320

Mills, K.A. (2016) *Literacy Theories for the Digital Age: Social, Critical, Multimodal, Spatial, Material and Sensory Lenses*. Multilingual Matters.

Mora, R.A., Gee, J.P., Hernandez, M., Castaño, S., Orrego, T.S. and Ramírez, D. (2020) Literacies of play: Blazing the trail, uncharted territories, and hurrying up – #TeamLaV's interview with James Paul Gee. In A. Garcia, S. Witte and J. Dail (eds) *Studying Gaming Literacies: Theories to Inform Classroom Practice* (pp. 53–62). Brill/Sense. https://doi.org/10.1163/9789004429840_006

Murray, D.M. (2003) *A Writer Teaches Writing* (rev. 2nd edn). Cengage.

New Hampshire Department of Education (2018a) *ICT Program Standards*. New Hampshire Department of Education. See http://www.nheon.org/ictliteracy/ictstandards.html (accessed June 2020).

New Hampshire Department of Education (2018b) *Computer Science Policy Statement*. New Hampshire Department of Education. See https://www.education.nh.gov/instruction/computer-science/policy-statement.htm (accessed June 2020).

Newkirk, T. (2021) *Writing Unbound: How Fiction Transforms Student Writers*. Heinemann.

Ray, A.B., Graham, S., Houston, J.D. and Harris, K.R. (2016) Teachers' use of writing to support students' learning in middle school: A national survey in the United States. *Reading & Writing* 29, 1039–1068.

Rowsell, J. (2020) 'How emotional do I make it?': Making a stance in multimodal compositions. *Journal of Adolescent & Adult Literacy* 63 (6), 627–637.

Saldaña, J. (2015) *The Coding Manual for Qualitative Researchers* (3rd edn). Sage.

Sauro, S. (2017) Online fan practices and CALL. *CALICO Journal* 34 (2), 131–146. https://www.jstor.org/stable/90014685.

Stornaiuolo, A. and Thomas, E.E. (2018) Restorying as political action: Authoring resistance through youth media arts. *Learning, Media and Technology* 43 (4), 345–358.

Thomas, E.E. and Stornaiuolo, A. (2016) Restorying the self: Bending toward textual justice. *Harvard Educational Review* 86 (3), 313–338.

Thorne, S.L., Black, R.W. and Sykes, J. (2009) Second language use, socialization, and learning in internet interest communities and online gaming. *Modern Language Journal* 93, 802–821. http://dx.doi.org/10.1111/j.1540-4781.2009.00974.x.

Wohlwend, K.E. (2018) Playing to our strengths: Finding innovation in children's and teachers' imaginative expertise. *Language Arts* 95 (3), 162–170.

Wohlwend, K.E. (2019) Play as the literacy of children: Imagining otherwise in contemporary childhoods. In D.E. Alvermann, N.J. Unrau, M. Sailors and R.B. Ruddell (eds) *Theoretical Models and Processes of Literacy* (7th edn, pp. 301–318). Routledge.

13 Fanfiction Experiences of Japanese Students: Connecting Wild Reading and L2 Learning

Tara McIlroy

13.1 Introduction

Reading experiences are becoming increasingly diverse in the digital age. As reading habits change, interactions with literature continue to develop. As a result of these changes, teachers and curriculum planners should consider how new types of texts, such as born-digital literature, could be used in second and foreign language (L2) learning contexts. The current chapter focuses on the potential for using fan-based practices and creations, particularly those with born-digital texts, as topics for exploration in language classrooms. While the texts which inspire fanfiction are not themselves born-digital, fanfiction itself exists wholly in its digital form and shares features, such as interactivity, with other born-digital texts. The ongoing trend toward integrating born-digital texts into language curricula is likely to gather pace due to contemporary approaches to learning, such as the digital literacies framework (Pegrum et al., 2018) and transformation model (Puentedura, 2013). Using the Exploratory Practice (EP) framework (Allwright & Hanks, 2009), the current discussion focuses on Japanese learners' choices of culturally familiar born-digital literature and discusses its potential for language learning. This provides an overview of the potential of integrating digital reading practices into L2 contexts. In doing so, the discussion addresses a gap in understanding how young adult language learners may be interacting with emerging forms of literature at the current time. This argument is related to earlier calls for greater integration of indigenous cultural references to language learning (Kramsch, 1993) and calls for helping learners to gain meaningful positive experiences from their interactions with literature (Paran, 2008). After a background introduction of fanfiction for L2 learning and an introduction to the methodology, learner reading preferences are presented, along with concrete examples of classroom practice. In the final sections of the chapter, the potential for born-digital texts for language learning is discussed along with theoretical and practical implications, with some suggestions for integrating contemporary reading practices and fanfiction into L2 classrooms.

13.2 Popular Culture in Contemporary Japanese Society

Popular culture has been deeply embedded in Japanese daily life at least since the Edo period (1603–1868) when Japan was effectively closed to the outside world. In the Edo period, printed literature of many varieties and genres were popular alongside traditional *kamishibai* (visual street theatre) and other cultural arts. Japanese literary culture changed rapidly in the Meiji Restoration (1868–1912), when Japan interacted with the West and adopted new styles of culture, including literature. Popular culture has been widely consumed and more recently produced and distributed digitally. As in many other countries, in Japan digital interactions with literature are part of everyday society. Visual storytelling in popular culture relies on less formal written forms of speech, while the writing system contains a combination of pictographs from Chinese, used concurrently with additional syllabaries (*hiragana, katakana* and *romaji*). Adopting new visual styles of literature is part of the Japanese literary tradition, with the latest innovation being the move towards digital literature. Rather than being a static environment for literature, interactions with digital literature are part of the evolving and changing visual culture and literary ecology.

Innovation continues in the Japanese cultural scene in the third decade of the 21st century. In the 1980s and 1990s, electronic literature and gaming were activities only available to those with home computers (a minority), unlike today's widespread use of mobile devices. *Convergence culture* (Jenkins, 2006), a term used to describe the meeting of old and new media, is now part of daily life in many countries, including Japan. Elements of convergence culture led to a prevalence of fan culture such as wearing the costumes of favourite characters (*cosplay*). Such creative practices may be viewed as an element of participatory culture (Jenkins, 2010), resulting in a meshing of real-world and online experiences. Participatory fan-based practices occur at the event Comic Market, known commonly as *Comiket*, held in Tokyo since 1975. *Comiket* is now advertised as the largest *doujin* (fan-made) event in Japan, with pre-pandemic attendance numbers of over 750,000 over four days (The Comic Market Committee, 2008/2014) and interest from international audiences (Kanazawa, 2016). At this event, there are displays of limited editions and other associated content called *doushinji* (self-published works). The event itself is a 'space' where participants can find fan-made comics, books, magazines, accessories, games, spin-off zines, parodies and costumes. The example of *Comiket* shows the ubiquitous nature of fan-based practices related to interactions with literature in Japan.

The activity of producing digital texts and disseminating them online has been a component of Japan's digital literary landscape for a number of years. In Japanese, the general term *netto shōsetsu*/ネット小説 can be translated as *internet novel* and the genre is similar to the Japanese *light novel* (young adult novel). In this genre of user-generated content, original writing by aspiring writers is uploaded and readers access the works online. One of the largest sites for the internet novel in Japan is *Shōsetsuka ni narō*/小説家になろう (Let's become a light novelist) available from https://syosetu.com/. Since 2004, *Shōsetsuka ni narō* has found both popular and commercial success with all works available freely. Today the site contains nearly 1 million novels and has over 2 million registered users (HinaProject, n.d.). Some of the digital fiction first published online using this site or similar websites become printed or adapted into film, manga or anime (the most successful works being commercially successful across different forms of media). Digital fiction and the social reading and interaction associated with it allows for new types of literary interactions in the digital landscape.

13.3 Born-Digital Literature

Born-digital texts are 'materials that have developed in the digital realm only and have no print or analogue counterpart' (Page & Thomas, 2011: 277). This born-digital literature cannot be printed and keep all its features such as hyperlinks. Non-linear digital texts, immersive interactive reading, multiple-path stories and gaming are examples of narratives that rely on their digital format. Instead of engaging with the binary nature of analogue vs. digital, the current chapter accepts the range of 'emerging forms of literature' (Thomas, 2020: 25) in the digital world, such as those involving social interactions on Twitter, Instagram and TikTok. Fanfiction itself, although not the original texts it was created using, can be considered born-digital literature, because of the interactive elements and connections between readers and authors. Informal or in-the-wild reading, which includes fan-based interactions, has received less attention than print-based literature. Hammond's (2016: 174) *Literature in the Digital Age* states that some kinds of new fiction 'finds new ways to bring readers more directly in contact with what it means to be alive in their place and time'. The current chapter focuses on aligning real contemporary reading experiences, which includes interactions with born-digital fiction, and L2 learning.

The idea that informal or wild reading (Miller & Kelley, 2014) can be used in classroom contexts simply refers to the idea that teachers should understand and recognise self-selected reading materials which students are already having in their own reading lives. Miller and Kelley (2014) surveyed over 800 adult readers and discussed the reading habits exhibited by lifelong readers. They called these prolific readers wild readers, and suggested that teachers should try to promote wild reading to learners in classroom settings. One aim of promoting wild reading is to connect learning in class with outside interests. Interactions with literature continue throughout life, and positive interactions with literature can lead to further interest and enthusiasm for reading (Paran, 2008). The elements positively correlated with lifelong reading were as follows: first, they dedicate time to read; second, they read self-selected material; third, they had opportunities for sharing books and reading with other readers; fourth, they had reading plans; and fifth, they understood how to show preferences for genres, authors and topics (Miller & Kelley, 2014: 23–4). From this perspective wild reading is desirable as it connects to engagement with reading and lifelong learning.

While other chapters in this collected volume may deal with traditionally non-literary genres, born-digital fiction should receive some attention because of its popularity and potential to interest L2 learners. Literature in language learning has been utilised in different ways throughout the last century and its popularity has changed over time (Kramsch & Kramsch, 2000). Recently, there have been calls for practice-based reports to describe uses of literature in specific contexts (Paran, 2008) and innovative ways of learning using literature in digital environments seem to be constantly evolving (Lütge *et al.*, 2019). This renewed interest in literature has seen the appearance of collections focusing on texts to motivate and engage L2 learners (Bland, 2018). This chapter recognises the value of printed texts, but also suggests that some content should come from outside the classroom, including students' choices of digital leisure reading. The main reason for this is that the constant evolution of digital reading affects how, what and why we read. These changes in reading habits and behaviours can be seen as learning potentials which are likely to occur when we connect in-class learning with activities from various informal situations (Benson & Reinders, 2011; Chik & Ho, 2017), including those including fan-based interactions and social reading experiences. For these reasons, the chapter argues for consideration of experiences learners have with born-digital literature, and how these experiences could be brought into the language classroom.

13.4 Previous Research Using Fanfiction: Key Findings

Fanfiction can be described as prose fiction of any length, style, genre and narrative technique that is produced by fans of a wide range of cultural products, including TV, movies, video games, manga and canonical literature (Page & Thomas, 2011: 205). A more recent definition states that it is 'stories that reimagine or reinterpret existing stories, characters and universes found in other texts and media' (Sauro, 2020: 139). The first definition seems to emphasise the form, i.e. 'prose fiction' while the second allows for the possibility of multimodal interpretations. Fanfiction has grown and changed from being a small subculture to 'the vast fan sites and communities' now available online (Thomas, 2020: 32). Reading and writing fanfiction is a leisure activity occurring in informal contexts. Fan-related practices are related to actions and activities conducted outside of simply reading or viewing a chosen film or book. Becoming a fan occurs 'by joining a "community" of other fans who share common interests' (Sauro, 2020: 140).

While arguably a sub-field, fanfiction is an element of popular participatory culture, potentially useful because of the dynamic relationships between readers and authors. Fanfiction has previously been explored in various fields, including cultural studies and media (Jenkins, 2006, 2010), tourism (Yamamura, 2020) and linguistics, from the perspective of developing identity (Black, 2006, 2009). Narrowing the view to L2 learning specifically, fanfiction research, usually 'research on fanfiction and its connection to reading skills, can be divided into two main areas: reading for the purpose of writing and reading for the purpose of giving feedback to support others' writing' (Sauro, 2020: 145). Of course, reading a collection of fanfiction in a printed anthology (Coppa, 2017) is not equivalent to reading the original works in the online spaces from which they emerged. Printed books have more durability, while the ephemeral nature of born-digital literature brings many benefits including the potential for mobile reading and sharing online. Therefore, the current discussion is not a case of either/or when discussing positive or negative points about digital and print-based literature.

Related to reading skills, identity and language learning together have previously been investigated. The results of these studies show how fan practices helped support reading skills for learners of English in an ESL setting (Black, 2006; Li, 2012). The situation for EFL learners may not be entirely comparable, but as Sauro (2020: 145) points out, 'the reading of fan fiction, but not school texts or textbooks, successfully served as input and scaffolding for their own future writing development'. Further investigation of reading preferences and reading practices may help shed light on the potential use of fanfiction in various contexts. Turning to writing, it is writing stories individually and collaboratively which can lead to gains for L2 users. Black (2009) looked particularly at the writers who offer themselves as readers, and the comments received from peers, and found many supportive comments and suggestions from others in fanfiction communities. While later fanfiction research has been conducted in classroom settings (Sauro & Sundmark, 2016, 2019), research in different international contexts may only just be beginning. One of these online reading communities is Fanfiction.net, a freely available, multilingual site available for browsing and reading in different languages.

13.5 Exploratory Practice and Wild Reading Choices

This chapter draws on the principles of Exploratory Practice (EP), an approach that focuses on both teachers and learners, referring to them as *key developing practitioners*. EP is closely related to other forms of practitioner research, such as action research (Burns, 2010), and has been used to investigate various topics, including peer reviews (Zheng, 2012). The notion of practice-as-research in EP takes a holistic stance, 'gearing research towards, and integrating it into, pedagogy, aiding learning and teaching rather than interrupting it' (Hanks, 2019: 170). Allwright and Hanks (2009) proposed an adapted version of Allwright's (2003) principles for inclusive practitioner research (Figure 13.1). What appealed about this approach for the current discussion was first that it recognises the learners' roles in creating meaningful classroom interactions using their own experiences. The approach combines 'creative pedagogy and research methods' (Hanks, 2019: 144) and emphasises the collective agency of learners and teachers as active participants in the learning process.

The following explains how puzzling led to pedagogical decisions in teaching with literature. In one university-level language and literature elective class, learners chose their favourite narratives for weekly presentations in English. The genre could be poems, songs, short stories, or other creative text in any language. Emiko (pseudonym) wrote about the songs in her favourite computer game (Figure 13.2), along with her interpretation of the lyrics and a discussion of her interpretations. In a presentation, Emiko discussed her interpretation of the meanings of the lyrics, using several pages of digitally painted manga-style images she created for the

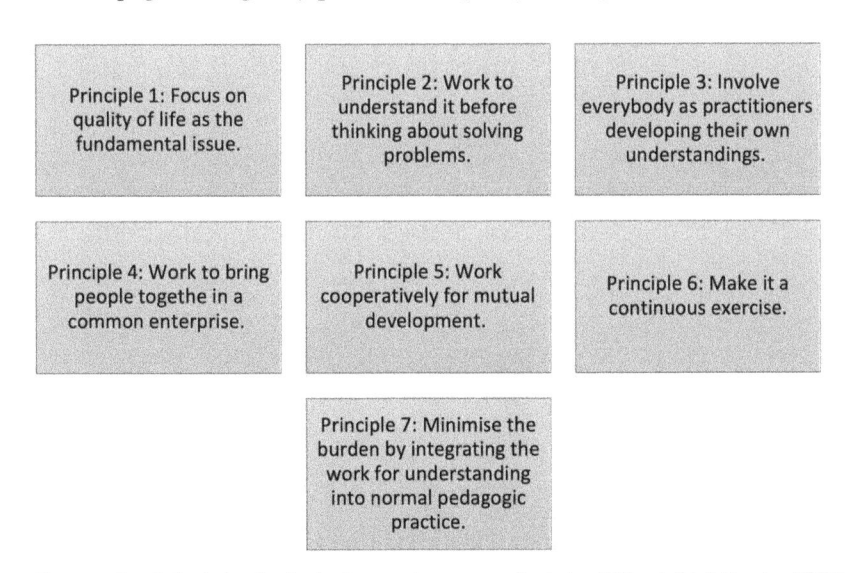

Principle 1: Focus on quality of life as the fundamental issue.	Principle 2: Work to understand it before thinking about solving problems.	Principle 3: Involve everybody as practitioners developing their own understandings.
Principle 4: Work to bring people togethe in a common enterprise.	Principle 5: Work cooperatively for mutual development.	Principle 6: Make it a continuous exercise.
	Principle 7: Minimise the burden by integrating the work for understanding into normal pedagogic practice.	

Figure 13.1 Principles for inclusive exploratory principles (Allwright & Hanks, 2009: 260)

210 Born-Digital Texts in the English Language Classroom

presentation. The song lyrics and her drawings contained complex feelings of nostalgia, regret and loss. Some of the pages were drawn in pencil, and some were colourful, particularly those depicting the most moving parts of the song. In addition, Emiko painted various scenes, from listening to the song's lyrics to describing what she imagined from this song more clearly. The example shows how reading interests outside the class can become materials for in-class learning.

The next step in EP is to consider what is already happening in the classroom by using Potentially Exploitable Pedagogic Activities (PEPAs). PEPAs are part of what the EP framework uses to refer to communicative activities which can be seen as puzzles and exploration (Allwright & Hanks, 2009: 157). Various kinds of communicative activities can be viewed as PEPAs, and what this means in practical terms is learning

Figure 13.2 Emiko's visual representation of computer game song lyrics (used with permission)

from pedagogic activities which are already being used. Essentially, PEPAs as investigative instruments benefit from being closely aligned with what teachers are already doing. Teacher-researchers use the PEPAs to create a kind of exploratory element that can illuminate issues and respond to puzzles. One example of this related to the gap between learners' in-class reading and their in-the-wild reading is to initially find out what kind of interactions learners are having with their choice of texts, genres and authors outside of class. A reading experiences survey becomes a PEPA when it explores out-of-class learning habits and gathers ideas to bring into the classroom. Instead of problem-solving, the EP approach looks at 'Why…?' questions as beginning points for investigation, using the notion of a puzzle (Hanks, 2017). Beginning with *puzzlement* means understanding an issue rather than simply seeing it as a problem to solve (2017: 156). In the context of the current discussion, the puzzle of why learners were more interested in their own reading choices than in-class reading serves as the beginning puzzle. Framed as an EP puzzle, this could become more of a series of questions, i.e. 'Why do my students read more varied genres outside the class?' or 'Why are some students lacking in interest or engagement with literature, even though this is a literature class?'. These questions naturally lead to considerations of aligning learners' interests with class content more successfully. In the next section, we consider some of the insights from learner comments from surveys and reflections about their in-the-wild reading choices and discuss implications for teaching and learning. Following that are two practical activities to engage learners in classroom activities related to their text choices.

13.6 Insights from Student Comments

At the beginning of the semester students completed a reading experience questionnaire and wrote about their personal reading histories. The exact format of questions differs depending on the purpose of the course, but the primary intention is to find out what learners are reading outside of class. The assignment includes more discipline-based questions when using literature with learners from a literature department. With classes containing students from any academic department, it is desirable to find common interests through literature. If teaching trainee language teachers, the focus is on educational experiences and personal reflection. Understanding reading practices can reveal schemas for reading (Jeffries & McIntyre, 2010) and provide valuable insights into the reading interests of L2 learners. The comments in this section come from answers to reading experience questionnaires and reflective papers and are used here as examples of PEPAs. Some of the comments were written originally in Japanese and have been translated.

13.6.1 Example 1

What kind of reading and writing do you like to do in your own time?

(1) When I was in junior high school, I watched the animation and I tried to write my own story. (Maiko)
(2) I write reviews of the books I read on my Twitter. It's a good way to keep track of what books I've read. (Haruki)
(3) I read crossover fanfiction which is mixing Japanese comics and *Harry Potter*. (Wakana)

With participatory popular culture so prevalent in broader society, it may seem natural that some learners explore fanfiction in their leisure time. Related to the first two aims of EP, concerning *quality of life* for everyone, and working primarily to understand *quality of life,* the key point is learning more about the backgrounds of the students and their interests. Sharing their experiences as readers and fans is one way to encourage connections and communication between these students from different academic backgrounds. Maiko wrote about her earlier experiences writing stories and, in her longer reflection, discussed how difficult it is to write this kind of story well. Haruki is using reviews to keep note of his own reading experiences. He listed some interactions with other readers on Twitter in the more extended reflection. Wakana is already interested in crossover fanfiction, with specific texts in mind.

13.6.2 Example 2

What do you think about fanfiction and how do you think it could be useful for language learning?

Fanfiction and social reading sound interesting, and I think it's a great way to expand your horizons by learning what other people think about a book. (Miho)

Miho's comment may be interpreted to show how students answer questions related to reading choices when considering their peers as potential readers of the comments. EP suggests using joint involvement in the work towards understanding collaboratively. This quote helps to show an interest in learning about other learners' views and seeing texts from multiple perspectives.

13.6.3 Example 3

Write about a favorite book you have read or re-read recently and explain why you recommend it.

(1) I love these books and I recently watched the video of my favourite actor who appeared in the movies of the books on TikTok. (Mayuko)

(2) I think that the reading of *The Promised Neverland* has had a great impact on me. I think this story shows both the tragedy and the beauty of the real world we live in, and it really gets to the heart of human nature. This story should be read by all people, regardless of age, because it shows the problems of modern society. (Hiroko)

Mayuko wrote her response about reading the *Harry Potter* books in English and Japanese. From Mayuko's comment, we can learn that some of her enjoyment of the books recently has meant augmenting the readings with social media in her free time. In the following comment, Hiroko explains her reasons for enjoying the dystopian series Yakusoku no Nebārando/約束のネバーランド (*The Promised Neverland*). This serialised story (Shirai, 2016–2020) became an international success and has been published in several international languages. While the series is not itself born-digital, the fan-based practices around writing using popular series as inspiration for new stories helps to feed the popularity more. The comment from Hiroko shows an interest in discussion of social issues, or problems in wider society, as a result of reading the series. These topics, and the connections between them, could be used in language learning contexts for discussion, analysis or critique. The final aim of EP is to consider ways that understanding can reduce burdens on teachers and learners and help them grow sustainably. The following section makes two practical suggestions for L2 learning with fanfiction.

13.7 Reading with Fanfiction: Crossovers

This section considers two ideas for using born-digital fanfiction in classroom practice. The idea first relates to reading, discussing or critiquing fanfiction, and the second is a writing and editing activity. These new creations based on familiar stories, are written online for online audiences. The fan-made texts are themselves born-digital, while the books they relate to may have been digital or print-based originally. On fanfiction.net, one of the popular sites for fanfiction, users can write and upload stories in chapters and as part of an original series. Readers can also interact with the stories and the authors by commenting and upvoting. The site was founded in 1998 with the tagline 'unleash your imagination' (https://www.fanfiction.net/). The guidelines state rules for authors and general advice about the community of amateurs who are creating content for the site. The site only accepts content acceptable for most ages (Guidelines, 2008). Crossovers have been included on fanfiction.net since 2009 and there are many different crossover fictions with Japanese literature, including popular manga and anime (Crossovers: Anime, n.d.). Crossovers may be seen in examples of remix literacy (Pegrum *et al.*, 2018) from the revised framework of digital literacies. The categories for crossover are anime/manga, books, cartoons, comics, games, plays, music and TV.

Popular manga series sell many thousands of copies in a year and the rankings show how popular series are (Oricon, 2020). Yakusoku no Nebārando/約束のネバーランド (*The Promised Neverland*) and *Shingeki no Kyojin*/進撃の巨人 *(Attack on Titan)* by Isayama (2009-present) are examples of series used in crossover digital fiction. *Harry Potter* is a popular novel for crossover fiction on the site, for example a Japanese wizard school teaching magic and techniques to defeat demons.

In the classroom, language learners new to fanfiction as well as those familiar with it can discuss open-ended questions such as the following:

(1) What kinds of anime and manga do you think are popular for crossover?
(2) How do you think a writer chooses elements of the story to include?
(3) What texts would you choose for crossover fanfiction?
(4) What do you think are some ethical issues around creating and sharing crossover fiction?

After discussing crossover fiction ideas, classroom activities could include reading some of them, then participating in discussions or collaborative writing activities. To save time and to focus on relevant topics and suitable content, the teacher can partially curate the choice of texts.

13.8 Writing with Fanfiction: Beta Readers

This second suggestion for using fanfiction for L2 learning is to look at the roles of beta readers in fanfiction and use them as examples in classroom discussions about social reading and reading communities. Beta readers are people who '[read] a work of fiction with a critical eye, with the aim of improving grammar, spelling, characterization and general style of a story prior to its release to the general public' (https://www.fanfiction.net/betareaders/). The beta readers in fanfiction.net can indicate their availability to work with different genres, including humour, romance, mystery, fantasy and adventure. As listed on their beta bio, the readers all have topics, genres, storylines, or languages as their special skills. A general introduction is available for each beta reader, including the following information:

- I like to think of myself as...
- I'm the kind of person who likes...
- I can...
- My strengths...
- My weaknesses...
- Preferred genre/project...
- I would rather not... (Beta Readers, n.d.)

The languages available for reading fanfiction include English but also Spanish, French, Indonesian, German, Japanese, Chinese and Portuguese.

Japanese students are often curious about how anime and manga reach global audiences and are generally interested in talking about the popularity of different books and series. Learners can make their own bios, offer comments or suggestions to individual beta readers, or discuss the possible ways in which online communities may be useful for developing L2 skills. Classroom activities using the 2018 Pegrum *et al.* framework of digital literacies could be used to create activities requiring critical literacy and ethical literacy, for example. Through discussion of fanfiction, including beta readers, learners can gain insights from fan-based literacy practices worldwide.

13.9 Implications for Further Research

Related to pedagogy specifically, we should consider elements such as the progression of learning materials, assessment and instructional procedures. One potential outcome of this investigation is to suggest research that aligns reading interests and curriculum content. Born-digital texts such as those emerging from online fanfiction practices are part of popular culture and informal learning. Informal learning often allows for connections between readers through shared interactions in spaces (including those online) where communities interact. Investigations of comics are not new, since we know that Norton and Vanderheyden (2004) found that they can motivate language learners. But engagement with reading communities such as those created in digital fanfiction spaces could build on everyday cultural experiences, aligning in-the-wild reading with classroom learning. The revised digital literacies framework categorises different levels of focus in learning with digital tools, from communication and information to the more complex collaboration and design/redesign (Pegrum *et al.*, 2018). According to this model, ethical literacy and critical literacy are part of the framework at the higher level of complexity.

The EP approach of using what is already being done in class to inform future curriculum planning can be made using feedback from PEPAs to guide course planning. The 'exploitable' part is most effectively viewed as an opportunity for creative interpretation. Examples include creating videos using an online tool Flip (https://info.flip.com/). Activities using Flip (previously named Flipgrid) can include asking students to create book introductions and reply to group videos. Such student-created videos are PEPAs because of their participatory nature. Interactions between students in video projects allow opportunities for collaboration and co-creation. Informal reading is what occurs in what has been referred to as the *digital wilds* (Sauro & Zourou, 2019: 2). These types of online reading occur spontaneously and include 'the dynamic, unpredictable, erratic character of technologies'. Wild reading is by its nature informal, but experiences of wild reading can be brought into the classroom via conversations about reading practices and the social practices. As with online gaming, fanfiction has in-built communities which could contribute to L2 learning opportunities for interaction and learner autonomy (see Chik, 2014). Learning more about how students are experiencing the digital wilds should be done while appreciating the constantly evolving range of experiences available to contemporary readers.

Using the *Common European Framework of Reference* known as the *CEFR* (Council of Europe, 2001) and the more recent *Companion Volume* or *CEFR-CV* (2018/2020) for planning helps position literature as a part of language learning. Literature variously appears in the recently revised *CEFR-CV* descriptors as first, reading as a leisure activity; second, responding to literature expressing a personal response to creative texts; and third, analysis and criticism of creative texts (Council of Europe, 2018, 2020). In the context of the current discussion, leisure activity could, of course, mean outside school learning done in informal contexts, interactions with digital fanfiction and reading or writing crossover fiction. Personal responses to literary texts related to fanfiction can be seen in interactions with the fanfiction itself, while the notion of personal response is related to critique. For the third of these descriptors, we can refer to examples of when fanfiction writers frequently interact with the audience by explaining their writing processes, asking for feedback, commenting on their differing views of earlier versions of the writing, and replying to reader comments. Also related to the *CEFR* is the key concept of plurilingualism as part of plurilingual and pluricultural competence. Plurilingualism encourages the bringing of the 'whole of one's linguistic equipment into play' (Council of Europe, 2018: 28), and the concept recognises and values the full linguistic repertoire of language use. Bringing in various literary experiences, texts and culture to language and literature classes can help to value the plurilingual aspects of developing linguistic use.

Comments from learners in the current investigation were centred around choices of fanfiction, interactions with digital platforms and digital reading, and general reading preferences. To investigate these elements further, teachers could work with the notion of literary competences as another area of potential exploitability related to fanfiction for language learning. While not yet widely used, the model includes empathic competence, cultural and discursive competence, aesthetic competence and interpretive competence (Alter & Rathheiser, 2019). Related directly to fanfiction in general and specifically to crossover fiction, the various competences in the model could become learning objectives for lesson plans and units of work.

One additional way for using fanfiction and literature for culturally relevant language learning could be by applying the higher levels of the SAMR model (Puentedura, 2013), used to evaluate curricular uses of technology. SAMR means *substitution, augmentation, modification, redefinition*, with the last two terms referring to transformation. Curriculum planners can use the model to gauge how far they have developed from an analogue approach to teaching and learning. The first two elements are when digital tools have been applied and are added to the learning environment to enhance it. Modification is when creativity occurs, and new ideas emerge in redefinition. Digital books such as ebooks are only the first step, and at the other end of the scale, creating new tasks and activities which were previously impossible begins to happen. Creative fan practices fit the SAMR model, including collaborative writing using digital tools and social interaction. Examples of redefinition/transformation are already emerging, as can be seen with the European *FanTales* (www.fantales.eu) project (discussed in Sauro *et al.*, 2020). Possible directions include choosing new paths to read and interact with, rewriting characters in crossover fiction and literary critique.

13.10 Conclusion

Teachers should look for ways to nurture connections between the culturally relevant literature most familiar to students and their L2 learning. Globally, culturally relevant literature can create literary experiences that are not yet fully utilised in L2 classes. One potential outcome of this discussion is to suggest ways to integrate reading interests and curriculum planning into L2 curricula more fully. Therefore, the discussion calls for a greater alignment of culturally situated reading practices with L2 learning. Integrating these new ways of experiencing literature is a possible way to appreciate the value of both print-based and born-digital content. Greater awareness of digital reading practices, and online interactions with fan-based communities, can help shed light on how born-digital and in-the-wild reading could be used for language learning. This chapter offered a perspective from the Japanese context on how digital in-the-wild reading experiences can be brought into focus for greater alignment with L2 learning. Using an EP approach the chapter aimed to discuss fanfiction as a part of the contemporary reading experience. Using EP as a framework for exploring student reading choices creates options for research and critical reflection. Given the diversity of digital reading experiences young adult learners are now experiencing in their daily lives, the opportunities to bring outside interests in the L2 classroom should be considered by curriculum planners. This chapter sought to argue for greater alignment between pedagogical approaches to L2 learning using literature through the integration of reading experience with language learning. The chapter finished with suggestions for including fan-based practices into L2 course design. By considering the diversity of interactions with digital literature such as fanfiction, learners and teacher-researchers can better understand learners' lives and thereby remove the gap between learners' reading lives and the language classroom.

Acknowledgements

All names are pseudonyms.

References

Allwright, D. (2003) Exploratory Practice: Rethinking practitioner research in language teaching. *Language Teaching Research* 7 (2), 113–141.

Allwright, D. and Hanks, J. (2009) *The Developing Language Learner: An Introduction to Exploratory Practice*. Palgrave Macmillan.

Alter, G. and Ratheiser, U. (2019) A new model of literary competences and the revised CEFR descriptors. *ELT Journal* 73 (4), 377–386.

Benson, P. and Reinders, H. (eds) (2011) *Beyond the Language Classroom*. Palgrave Macmillan.

Beta Readers (n.d.) Fanfiction.net. FictionPress. See www.fanfiction.net/betareaders/ (accessed December 2021).

Black, R.W. (2006) Language, culture, and identity in online fanfiction. *E-Learning* 3 (2), 170–184.

Black, R.W. (2009) Online fan fiction, global identities, and imagination. *Research in the Teaching of English* 43 (4), 397–425.

Bland, J. (ed.) (2018) *Using Literature in English Language Education. Challenging Reading for 8–18-Year-Olds*. Bloomsbury.

Burns, A. (2010) *Doing Action Research in English Language Teaching: A Guide for Practitioners*. Routledge.

Chik, A. (2014) Digital gaming and language learning: Autonomy and community. *Language, Learning and Technology* 18 (2), 85–100.

Chik, A. and Ho, J. (2017) Learn a language for free: Recreational learning among adults. *System* 69, 162–171.

Coppa, F. (2017) *The Fanfiction Reader: Folk Tales for the Digital Age*. University of Michigan Press.

Council of Europe (2001) *Common European Framework of Reference for Languages: Learning, Teaching, Assessment*. Cambridge University Press.

Council of Europe (2018) *Common European Framework of Reference for Languages: Learning, Teaching, Assessment. Companion Volume with New Descriptors*. Council of Europe.

Council of Europe (2020) *Common European Framework of Reference for Languages: Learning, Teaching, Assessment. Companion Volume*. Council of Europe.

Crossovers: Anime (n.d.) Fanfiction.net. FictionPress. See www.fanfiction.net/crossovers/anime/ (accessed June 2022).

Guidelines (2008) Fanfiction.net. FictionPress. See fanfiction.net/guidelines/ (accessed June 2022).

Hammond, A. (2016) *Literature in the Digital Age*. Cambridge University Press.

HinaProject (n.d.) *Shōsetsuka ni narō*/小説家になろう *(Let's become a light novelist)*. See https://syosetu.com/site/about/ (accessed December 2021).

Isayama, H. (2009) *Shingeki no Kyojin*/進撃の巨人 *(Attack on Titan)*. Kodansha.

Jeffries, L. and McIntyre D. (2010) *Stylistics*. Cambridge University Press.

Jenkins, H. (2006) *Convergence Culture: Where Old and New Media Collide*. New York University Press.

Jenkins, H. (2010) Fandom, participatory culture, and Web 2.0 – A Syllabus [blogpost]. See http://henryjenkins.org/blog/2010/01/fandom_participatory_culture_a.html (accessed December 2021).

Kanazawa, T. (2016) The *dojinshi* convention in Japan, Taiwan, Indonesia, and France. *Artes* 30, 153–160.

Kramsch, C. (1993) *Context and Culture in Language Teaching*. Oxford University Press.
Kramsch, C. and Kramsch, O. (2000) The avatars of literature in language study. *The Modern Language Journal* 84 (4), 553–573.
Li, G. (2012) Literacy engagement through online and offline communities outside school: English language learners' development as readers and writers. *Theory into Practice* 51 (4), 312–318.
Lütge, C., Merse, T., Owczarek, C. and Stannard, M. (2019) Crossovers: Digitization and literature in foreign language education. *Studies in Second Language Learning and Teaching* 9 (3), 519–540.
Miller, D. and Kelley, S. (2014) *Reading in the Wild: The Book Whisperer's Keys to Cultivating Lifelong Reading Habits*. Jossey-Bass.
Norton, B. and Vanderheyden, K. (2004) Comic book culture and second language learners. In B. Norton and K. Toohey (eds) *Critical Pedagogies and Language Learning* (pp. 201–221). Cambridge University Press.
Oricon (2020) Nenkan hon rankingu/Annual book ranking. See www.oricon.co.jp/special/55505/9/#link1 (accessed June 2022).
Page, R. and Thomas, B. (2011) *New Narratives: Stories and Storytelling in the Digital Age*. University of Nebraska Press.
Paran, A. (2008) The role of literature in instructed foreign language learning and teaching: An evidence-based survey. *Language Teaching* 41 (4), 465–496.
Pegrum, M., Dudeney, G. and Hockly, N. (2018) Digital literacies revisited. *The European Journal of Applied Linguistics and TEFL* 7 (2), 3–24.
Puentedura, R.R. (2013) SAMR: Moving from enhancement to transformation. See www.hippasus.com/rrpweblog/archives/000095.html (accessed December 2021).
Sauro, S. (2020) Fan fiction and informal language learning. In M. Dressler and R.W. Sadler (eds) *The Handbook of Informal Language Learning* (pp. 139–151). John Wiley & Sons, Ltd.
Sauro, S. and Sundmark, B. (2016) Report from middle earth: Fan fiction tasks in the EFL classroom. *ELT Journal* 70 (4), 414–423.
Sauro, S. and Sundmark, B. (2019) Critically examining the use of blog-based fan fiction in the advanced language classroom. *ReCALL* 31 (1), 40–45.
Sauro, S. and Zourou, K. (2019) What are the digital wilds? *Language Learning and Technology* 23 (1), 1–7.
Sauro, S., Buendgens-Kosten, J. and Cornillie, F. (2020) Storytelling for the foreign language classroom. *Foreign Language Annals* 53, 329–337.
Shirai, K. (2016–2020) *Yakusoku no Nebārando*/約束のネバーランド (*The Promised Neverland*). Shueisha.
The Comic Market Committee (2008/2014) *What is Comic Market?* Comiket. See www2.comiket.co.jp/info-a/WhatIsEng201401.pdf (accessed November 2021).
Thomas, B. (2020) *Literature and Social Media*. Routledge.
Yamamura, T. (2020) Contents tourism and creative fandom: The formation process of creative fandom and its transnational expansion in a mixed-media age. *Journal of Tourism and Cultural Change* 18 (1), 12–26.
Zheng, C. (2012) Understanding the learning process of peer feedback activity: An ethnographic study of Exploratory Practice. *Language Teaching Research* 16 (1), 109–126.

14 The Potential of Location-Based Technologies and Mobile-Assisted Language Learning for ELT

Carolin Zehne

14.1 Introduction

Mobile digital media have become intertwined with our everyday lives and continue to fundamentally change societal and cultural practices (Hepp, 2020; Stalder, 2016). Such changes also affect our spatial experiences (Buschauer & Willis, 2014), as mobile technologies enable us to carry the internet with us and thus make our use of it independent of a specific location. On the other hand, our location and the types of information we access become interconnected as 'location-based services and location-based social networks' (Souza e Silva, 2013: 117) are now 'an intrinsic component of mobile communication' (Souza e Silva, 2013: 117). The interconnectedness of our location, our mobile media use, as well as how we can access information is reflected in numerous ways: map services enable us to receive location-based directions or information, such as weather updates and reviews of particular places (see e.g. Zickuhr, 2013). We can further share our location in real time or tag our location in social media posts (see e.g. Wilken, 2014), experience cultural heritage sites via locative storytelling (see e.g. Millard *et al.*, 2020) or play (mobile) games such as *Pokémon Go* which make use of locality and mobility (Souza e Silva, 2017).

Smartphones, as typical mobile devices, and the internet play a vital role in students' free time in Germany (Medienpädagogischer Forschungsverbund Südwest, 2021) and beyond (see e.g. vom Orde & Durner, 2021). Despite the omnipresence of mobile and location-aware technologies, students are likely not to automatically acquire the necessary competences to handle digital information and digital tools. This seems to particularly apply to students from socially disadvantaged backgrounds (Bos *et al.*, 2014; Eickelmann *et al.*, 2019). Fostering digital competence has thus become an important aspect of helping students to become responsible citizens as a part of a move towards the types of literacies needed in our rapidly changing world today (see e.g. Cope & Kalantzis, 2009; New London Group, 1996). In this chapter, I follow the definition of Ferrari (2012), who specifies digital competence as:

> a set of knowledge, skills, attitudes […] that are required when using ICT and digital media to perform tasks; solve problems; communicate; manage information; collaborate; create and share content; and build knowledge effectively, efficiently, appropriately, critically, creatively, autonomously, flexibly, ethnically, reflectively for work, leisure, participation, learning, socializing, consuming, and empowerment (Ferrari, 2012: 3–4).

This definition is not only concerned with *using* 'digital artifacts' (Brinda *et al.*, 2019: 26) on a receptive and productive level or to connect with others, but it also includes the ability to analyze and critically reflect on digital artifacts and one's own media practices. The aspect of critical reflection is also connected to '[…] the way young people navigate in the digital world, how they use their applications, for what purposes they use them and how this affects cultural practices' (Steininger, 2020: 75). For educational contexts, this means that both digital media and digital media practices, not only need to be incorporated *in teaching* but also that digital competences should be fostered *through digitally-enhanced teaching and learning* (Kultusministerkonferenz, 2016, 2021; Maaz *et al.*, 2020). For teaching English as a foreign language, with its overarching aim of enabling students to take part in discourses in which English is used outside of the classroom (see e.g. Hallet, 2012), this thus also includes actively participating in and reflecting on *digital* discourses, environments and products in the school context. For many students however, taking part in (digital) English discourses outside the classroom clearly differs from their experience inside the classroom, e.g. in terms of using English to communicate (Zehne, 2022).

Taking this as a starting point, this chapter outlines a teaching project which capitalizes on students' smartphone use when creating their own city tours with annotated maps as born-digital texts within a mobile-assisted language learning (MALL) framework. Through devising their own tours by sharing their own experiences at particular places in their city, students are actively involved in creating born-digital texts with the tool *MyMaps*. They are further enabled to critically reflect on location-aware technologies and their use of such technologies in their everyday lives.

Students thus explore their role as cultural agents as well as the discursive practices they engage in (Freitag-Hild, 2018; Kramsch, 2013; Young, 2009) both in the analogue and digital spheres as they actively contribute their stories and experiences to selected places to create their own tours. The project follows general principles of modern English language teaching, such as learner-centeredness, task-based teaching and action-oriented forms of learning (Elsner, 2018) as a part of a wider sociocultural approach to learning (Kearney *et al.*, 2012).

I first summarize the theoretical background of MALL and its implementation in teaching with a focus on the framework by Kukulska-Hulme *et al.* (2015). I further connect the use of mobile media to locality and location-aware technologies. In a next step, the framework by Kukulska-Hulme *et al.* is utilized to outline a teaching project idea which lets students utilize mobile, locative media tools and expand their digital competence.

14.2 Blurring the Lines Between Inside and Outside of the Classroom Through Mobile-Assisted Language Learning (MALL)

MALL is specifically concerned with the use of mobile technology in language learning (Kukulska-Hulme, 2019; Miangah & Nezarat, 2012) and can be considered a subfield of mobile learning (Kukulska-Hulme, 2021), which in turn:

> [...] refers to teaching and learning with the use of mobile technologies such as mobile phones, media players, PDAs, smartphones, and tablet computers, which are potentially available anytime and anywhere. (Duman *et al.*, 2015: 198)

While many definitions of MALL exist, there are central characteristics which can be identified across publications. These are particularly related to 'the role of the learner, the mobility and the context' (Heinz, 2021: 64; see also Palalas & Hoven, 2016: 52–56). MALL can overcome barriers in relation to time and space, e.g. in terms of portability of devices or the potential to interact with others (Miangah & Nezarat, 2012), leading to '[...] learning across physical and virtual contexts' (Palalas, 2016: v). Thus, the lines between informal and formal learning become increasingly blurred – in- and out-of-classroom learning experiences can be linked. This may arguably result in learners becoming more autonomous and students taking responsibility for their own learning (Kukulska-Hulme *et al.*, 2017; Morgana, 2021).

MALL does not simply entail the use of mobile devices in the classroom, but also emphasizes learners' mobility and agency. Thus, mobility and flexibility as two of the main characteristics of MALL also entail increasing complexity of learning/teaching settings (Kammerl & Dertinger, 2020): as MALL has the potential to make learning more flexible and varied and thus to increase students' motivation as well as their independence, teachers need to provide appropriate structures to guide and support their learners in this process (Kammerl & Dertinger, 2020). This particularly applies to more complex uses of mobile technologies, for example when creating one's own texts or communicating with others (see also Pegrum, 2014, 2019). Within the different functions of MALL ranging from the mere delivery of content to productive uses such as communication and creation, the multimodality of mobile devices '[…] permits learners to exploit a range of modal affordances' (Kukulska-Hulme *et al.*, 2017: 221), such as taking pictures, creating audio recordings or videos.

In the literature, a move beyond the mere focus on content delivery through MALL has become more and more prevalent. There has been an ever-growing interest in exploring the opportunities MALL offers in the light of content creation on the part of students, as well as new ways of communicating through MALL (Morgana, 2021). In the following, the focus will be on a language-learning specific framework which aims at facilitating this type of more complex uses of MALL.

The framework proposed by Kukulska-Hulme *et al.* (2015) is intended to '[…] help teachers think about how any new language learning activity they might design for their mobile learners might be different from activities they may have planned or designed before' (Kukulska-Hulme *et al.*, 2015: 8). It outlines four aspects which should be considered when planning mobile learning activities in the light of language learning and teaching:

- Teacher wisdom, i.e. manifestations of the teacher's experience and role in enacting pedagogy, for example harnessing their learners' prior knowledge or their language proficiency.
- Device features which have the potential to enable multimodal collaboration and communication as well as language rehearsal.
- Learner mobilities which describe not only the places and times students can learn, but also the range of cultural settings and contexts, as well as the learners' goals which motivate them to learn beyond the classroom setting.
- Language dynamics which take into account the new ways of interpersonal communication and implement them in language teaching (Kukulska-Hulme *et al.*, 2015: 8).

Kukulska-Hulme *et al.* (2015) describe four connected concepts which frame the four aspects in the center of the model. The first, *Outcomes*, raises the question to what extent a particular activity leads to improved language proficiency and other outcomes which can also be specifically related to the use of MALL. These additional outcomes can include developing autonomy and digital competences. *Inquiry* focuses on the extent to which the activity relates to the constantly changing contexts of language use. Mobile devices can also be used to obtain insights into how language is used and how it changes in emerging social networks. *Rehearsal* is concerned with expanding chances for language practice through mobile media, while *Reflection* focuses on the ways in which mobile technology fosters reflection on learning processes (Kukulska-Hulme *et al.*, 2015: 9).

Particularly the four central aspects of the framework will guide the outline of the teaching idea and help to link students' use of locative media and MALL. The next section introduces the concepts of locative media in the light of use of mobile devices and their impact on locality.

14.3 Locative Media and Changing Conceptions of Place

The use of mobile devices for language learning, and the increasing flexibility and agency that comes with it, also means that learners perceive location and space differently.

Very broadly speaking, 'locative media involves [sic] the use of information, data, sounds, and images about a location' (Wilken & Goggin, 2014: 1–2). What had started as personal computing with the emergence of 'cyberspace' thought of as existing alongside physical space (Frith, 2015), has now turned into pervasive computing (Farman, 2015) with location, space and the internet becoming increasingly intertwined (Souza e Silva, 2013; Souza e Silva & Sheller, 2015). In this context, smartphones in particular have added to '[…] the way people interact with digital information' (Frith, 2015: II), as they enable us to access the internet anytime anywhere.

According to Tuters and Varnelis (2006), there are two types of locative media: *annotative* types allow users to actively and virtually tag the world they physically move in while *phenomenological* types trace the movement of users in the physical world. The concept of location thus acquires a dynamic meaning through location-aware mobile technologies: locations might take on multiple meanings as a result of the kind of information connected to them (Wilken & Goggin, 2014). Locative media contribute to a socially connected understanding of location in the sense of contributing to the social construction of place (Ryan, 2012). The *annotative* conceptualization of locative media provides the chance to add one's own experiences to a public place and thus allows people to contribute to the construction of locality (Manresa & Bacharach, 2016; Ryan, 2012) – to tell their individual stories and experiences tied to a particular place, e.g. by adding their own reviews or photos to online map services. Adding such individual stories to particular places is also utilized in mobile locative narratives as a part of letting people experience cultural heritage sites (Farman, 2014; Scarpati, 2019). By accessing information provided through annotative functions, we can gain an insider perspective with the help of locative media, even if we have not yet spent much time at a particular place (Buschauer & Willis, 2014).

The following practical project incorporates MALL and the construction of place as a part of using location-aware technologies to let students make use of the annotative function of locative media and to let them critically reflect on their own uses of such location-aware technologies. The use of mobile technologies can help to bridge the gap between in- and out-of-class learning and aid students to develop an understanding of the meanings attached to a place as a potentially shared endeavor, as outlined in the next section. At the same time, the project can also be used to foster the critical reflection of such technologies, particularly in connection with potential challenges, such as data protection and privacy concerns.

14.4 Practical Implications for the Classroom: Using Location-Aware Technologies to Tell Your Own Story – Reclaim Your City

In this project, students use location-aware mobile technologies to create their own guided tour through a selected part of their city in small groups. Their tour consists of places for which they all share a particular individual experience; these experiences in turn contribute to the meaning of the place. Students create an annotated map by adding their personal experience and stories to the places they have selected as an overall outcome of the project. They then publish their map and let other students (or an audience beyond the classroom) try out their guided tour.[1] In a final step, students critically reflect on their own practices of using location-aware technologies and potential dangers that come with them.

Google's MyMaps is one potential tool for creating such annotated maps. With this tool, customized maps can be designed by adding individualized tags to a Google base map. Tags can simply be placed on any location on the map and appear as editable icons. Custom tags can contain texts as well as pictures and videos. The tags themselves can also be customized, e.g. in terms of changing the type of icon used for the tag and its color. Individual tags can then also be connected on the map to create a tour to let Google Maps navigate participants from one tagged location to the next. Personalized maps can be shared with a wider audience via a link or making the map available on Google searches.

The project pursues several objectives. It is centered around the relationship between learners' use of mobile, location-aware technologies and their annotative potential which I have outlined in the preceding section. It aims at fostering a sense of agency on the part of the students by making use of mobile, location-aware technologies to let them tell *their own* stories related to particular places in their city, which they select themselves. The project further aims at fostering students' digital competences as they actively engage in creating their own city tour by making use of MyMaps and their smartphones. They furthermore use these two tools to use the target language to communicate with their peers, their teacher and a wider (online) community. While using location-aware tools for the project, students also critically reflect on aspects of location-aware technologies, such as sharing one's location and other personal information (see

226 Born-Digital Texts in the English Language Classroom

Teacher wisdom, language dynamics, device features, learner mobilities

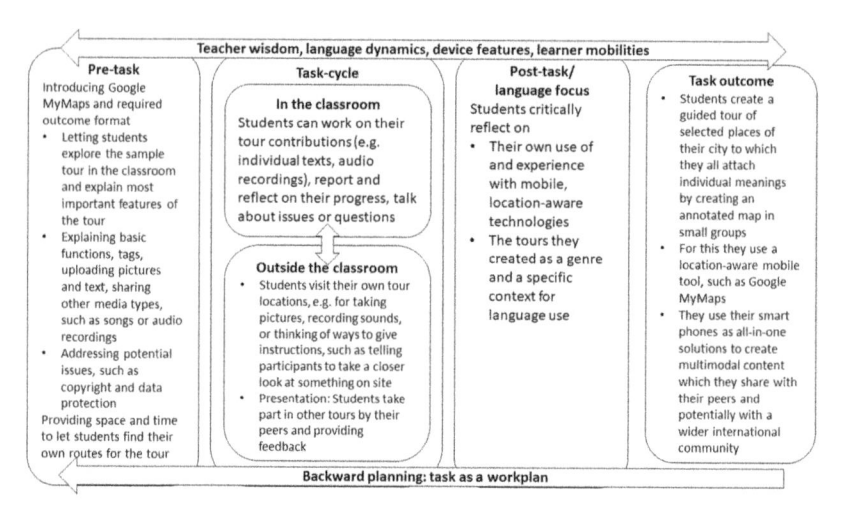

Pre-task	Task-cycle	Post-task/ language focus	Task outcome
Introducing Google MyMaps and required outcome format • Letting students explore the sample tour in the classroom and explain most important features of the tour • Explaining basic functions, tags, uploading pictures and text, sharing other media types, such as songs or audio recordings • Addressing potential issues, such as copyright and data protection Providing space and time to let students find their own routes for the tour	**In the classroom** Students can work on their tour contributions (e.g. individual texts, audio recordings), report and reflect on their progress, talk about issues or questions **Outside the classroom** • Students visit their own tour locations, e.g. for taking pictures, recording sounds, or thinking of ways to give instructions, such as telling participants to take a closer look at something on site • Presentation: Students take part in other tours by their peers and providing feedback	Students critically reflect on • Their own use of and experience with mobile, location-aware technologies • The tours they created as a genre and a specific context for language use	• Students create a guided tour of selected places of their city to which they all attach individual meanings by creating an annotated map in small groups • For this they use a location-aware mobile tool, such as Google MyMaps • They use their smart phones as all-in-one solutions to create multimodal content which they share with their peers and potentially with a wider international community

Backward planning: task as a workplan

Figure 14.1 Overview of task phases and the task outcomes

also Carretero *et al.*, 2017). Students are likely to have shared their locations outside of the classroom before, e.g. when using map services, sending their location to friends, or playing location aware (mobile) games. The teacher guides students' reflection of practices outside of the classroom as a part of the project inside the classroom, such as by providing the space for letting students report on their progress or for discussing sharing one's own location and personal information in connection with digital competence.

Figure 14.1 summarizes the basic project structure with essential task-based language teaching phases (see e.g. Ellis, 2009) and MALL elements as the central parts of the framework by Kukulska-Hulme *et al.* (2015).

Before students create their own guided tour in the task cycle, they need to be prepared to do so in the pre-task phase. As a part of their *teacher wisdom*, teachers need to introduce the format/genre of the task outcome and MyMaps with its features and functions as the tool students need to use. A sample tour created by the teacher can be used to illustrate the features of MyMaps and to make students aware of characteristic (linguistic) features of such a tour as a specific context of using the target language. A sample map with annotated places illustrates how the students' own tour on MyMaps could look like and which features might be important. The sample tour can be used to show how:

- a map should look in terms of fulfilling minimum requirements of the task;
- tags for individual places can look in terms of content and language;
- tags can be personalized by changing the icon and its color;
- pictures can be added to tags;
- other media such as sound recordings can be implemented;

- locations can be linked to create a tour with location-aware navigation instructions participants can use.

Teacher wisdom not only guides the selection of useful language and technical aspects to create the tour in the pre-task phase, but also throughout the task cycle. In the pre-task phase, students also freely exchange their experiences at certain places in their city to select spots for their tours.

While working on their tours in the task cycle, the classroom becomes a space for students to exchange their experiences and progress. In the light of *learner mobilities* (Kukulska-Hulme et al., 2015), students move between inside- and outside-the-classroom settings during this phase. Inside the classroom, students can reflect on their progress, plan their next steps with the help of the teacher, or address any problems they might face. Within their group, students negotiate which places they would like to include, which individual stories they would like to tell, and which types of media they could use in their tour (such as additional pictures, videos, or songs). Depending on the students' needs and abilities, the teacher can provide further scaffolding, such as technical and language-related support, e.g. tutorials for using MyMaps or useful words and phrases for coming up with content.

The *device features* of their smartphones (Kukulska-Hulme et al., 2015), such as video and voice recording as well as high-quality cameras, provide 'all-in-one solutions' for creating their tours. Students can take pictures and record videos or audio files on site, and either add them to their map on the go, or at home when they have WiFi available to avoid excluding students who might not have high mobile data volume at their disposal. As a part of *language dynamics* (Kukulska-Hulme et al., 2015), students can use their devices to not only engage in conversation and collaboration with their peers, but also to communicate with the teacher, e.g. during pre-determined office hours in case they have questions while working on the project or for receiving feedback.

In the presentation phase, students take part in other tours, share their outcome with other groups, as well as (potentially) the wider community of people who use MyMaps. This is then also connected to taking part in the discourse beyond the classroom and connecting to a wider international audience.

In the post-task phase, the classroom is utilized as a space to critically reflect on the construction of location, as well as the impact of location-aware mobile technologies on the students' lives. With their experience while working on the project and taking part in other tours as a starting point, students can critically reflect on their own practices of sharing their location and using location-based services. Students could check the settings of their phones to see which type of location information they share and to what extent they are aware of these settings. In a next step, students can discuss the potential, and dangers, of using location-aware technologies and sharing their location on a regular basis.

14.5 Suggestions for Future Research

Particularly in the field of MALL, numerous studies have been conducted to examine the use and effects of mobile technology. There are also a number of meta-analyses (see e.g. Burston, 2021, for an overview and detailed discussion). It appears that many studies measure the effect of MALL on the four basic skills of listening, speaking, reading and writing (Bozdoğan, 2015; Peng et al., 2021) as well as vocabulary learning (Peng et al., 2021), particularly in higher educational settings.

Ros i Solé et al. (2010) call for a move away from measuring effectiveness in language learning based on the four skills towards the everyday practices of language learners. Mobile learning involves more than merely letting students use certain applications for learning. Research and practice thus need to focus on the wide variety of ways in which mobile devices can be used (Stockwell, 2022). This also includes a more careful consideration of how learners already use their own mobile technologies outside of the classroom (Chwo et al., 2018). In the light of Stockwell's (2022) observation that there still is a relative lack of studies which use ethnographic approaches, research connected to the practical idea of this project could emphasize the students' experience while working on the task, e.g. when it comes to cultural learning, collaboration, or the use of their devices.

14.6 Conclusion

The ubiquity of mobile digital technologies requires competences in order to be able to successfully participate in society and become a responsible citizen. This also means that students need to be adequately prepared to take part in such changing discourses. Frameworks which model the required competences for educational contexts thus not only address the mere ability to operate digital tools, or to use them to look for information, but also include productive, active and reflective aspects.

Mobile technologies are omnipresent in students' lives outside the classroom and potentially open up new ways of (language) learning. Additionally, location-aware technologies fundamentally change the relationship between locations and the individual.

The teaching unit I presented in this contribution combines aspects of MALL with location-aware technologies to let students create their very own annotated tour of a part of their city with the help of MyMaps. Within a task-based framework, students can build on their digital competences by creating their own tour, and critically reflect on the use of location-aware technologies and potential dangers of doing so in their everyday lives.

Note

(1) A sample map which illustrates the basic functions of MyMaps and a potential outcome format for a city tour can be found here: https://tinyurl.com/4ubf2p4z

References

Bos, W., Eickelmann, B., Gerick, J., Goldhammer, F., Schaumburg, H., Schwippert, K., Senkbeil, M., Schulz-Zander, R. and Wendt, H. (eds) (2014) *ICILS 2013: Computer- und informationsbezogene Kompetenzen von Schülerinnen und Schülern in der 8. Jahrgangsstufe im internationalen Vergleich*. Waxmann.

Bozdoğan, D. (2015) MALL revisited: Current trends and pedagogical implications. *Procedia – Social and Behavioral Sciences* 195, 932–939.

Brinda, T., Brüggen, N., Diethelm, I., Knaus, T., Kommer, S., Kopf, C., Missomelius, P., Leschkem R., Tilemann, F. and Weich, A. (2019) Frankfurt-Dreieck zur Bildung in der digital vernetzten Welt: Ein interdisziplinäres Modell. See https://dl.gi.de/bitstream/handle/20.500.12116/28916/a1.pdf?sequence=1 (accessed December 2021).

Burston, J. (2021) Unreported MALL studies. What difference do they make to published experimental MALL research results? In V. Morgana and A. Kukulska-Hulme (eds) *Mobile Assisted Language Learning Across Educational Contexts* (pp. 10–35). Routledge.

Buschauer, R. and Willis, K.S. (2014) Introduction. In R. Buschauer and K.S. Willis (eds) *Locative Media: Medialität und Räumlichkeit – Multidisziplinäre Perspektiven zur Verortung der Medien* (pp. 1–25). Transcript Verlag.

Carretero, S., Vourikari, R. and Punie, Y. (2017) *DigComp 2.1 The Digital Competence Framework for Citizens: With Eight Proficiency Levels and Examples of Use*. European Commission.

Chwo, G.S.M., Marek, M.W. and Wu, W.-C.V. (2018) Meta-analysis of MALL research and design. *System*, 74, 62–72.

Cope, B. and Kalantzis, M. (2009) 'Multiliteracies': New Literacies, new learning. *Pedagogies: An International Journal* 4 (3), 164–195.

Duman, G., Orhon, G. and Gedik, N. (2015) Research trends in mobile assisted language learning from 2000 to 2012. *ReCALL* 27 (2), 197–216.

Eickelmann, B., Bos, W., Gerick, J., Goldhammer, F., Schaumburg, H., Schwippert, K., Senkbeil, M. and Vahrengold, J. (eds) (2019) *ICILS 2018: Deutschland Computer- und informationsbezogene Kompetenzen von Schülerinnen und Schülern im zweiten internationalen Vergleich und Kompetenzen im Bereich Computational Thinking*. Waxmann.

Ellis, R. (2009) *Task-Based Language Learning and Teaching*. Oxford University Press.

Elsner, D. (2018) Institutionalized foreign language learning – Teaching English at different levels. In C. Surkamp and B. Viebrock (eds) *Teaching English as a Foreign Language: An Introduction* (pp. 17–38). J.B. Metzler.

Farman, J. (2014) Site-specificity, pervasive computing, and the reading interface. In J. Farman (ed.) *The Mobile Story: Narrative Practices with Locative Technologies* (pp. 3–16). Routledge.

Farman, J. (2015) Stories, spaces, and bodies: The production of embodied space through mobile media storytelling. *Communication Research and Practice* 1 (2), 101–116.

Ferrari, A. (2012) *Digital Competence in Practice: An Analysis of Frameworks*. See https://op.europa.eu/de/publication-detail/-/publication/2547ebf4-bd21-46e8-88e9-f53c1b3b927f/language-en (accessed December 2021).

Freitag-Hild, B. (2018) Teaching culture – Intercultural competence, transcultural learning, global education. In C. Surkamp and B. Viebrock (eds) *Teaching English as a Foreign Language. An Introduction* (pp. 159–175). J.B. Metzler.

Frith, J. (2015) *Smartphones as Locative Media. DMS – Digital Media and Society*. Polity Press.
Hallet, W. (2012) Die komplexe Kompetenzaufgabe. Fremdsprachige Diskursfähigkeit als kulturelle Teilhabe und Unterrichtspraxis. In W. Hallet and U. Krämer (eds) *Kompetenzaufgaben im Englischunterricht: Grundlagen und Unterrichtsbeispiele* (pp. 8–19). Kallmeyer.
Heinz, S. (2021) Designing mobile language learning scenarios with digital tools. In C. Lütge and T. Merse (eds) *Digital Teaching and Learning: Perspectives for English Language Education* (pp. 61–84). Narr Francke Attempto.
Hepp, A. (2020) *Deep Mediatization*. Routledge.
Kammerl, R. and Dertinger, A. (2020) Guter Unterricht mit mobilen Medien. Eine Darstellung einschlägiger Konzepte und aktueller Forschungsbefunde. In D.M. Meister and I. Mindt (eds) *Mobile Medien im Schulkontext* (pp. 47–78). Springer Fachmedien Wiesbaden.
Kramsch, C. (2013) Culture in foreign language teaching. *Iranian Journal of Language Teaching Research* 1 (1), 57–78.
Kukulska-Hulme, A. (2012) Language learning defined by time and place: A framework for next generation designs. In J.E. Diaz-Vera (ed.) *Left to My Own Devices: Learner Autonomy and Mobile-Assisted Language Learning* (pp. 3–20). Emerald.
Kukulska-Hulme, A. (2019) Mobile-assisted language learning. In C.A. Chapelle (ed.) *The Concise Encyclopedia of Applied Linguistics*. Wiley-Blackwell.
Kukulska-Hulme, A. (2021) Reflections on research questions in mobile assisted language learning. *Journal of China Computer-Assisted Language Learning* 1 (1), 28–46.
Kukulska-Hulme, A., Norris, L. and Donohue, J. (2015) Mobile pedagogy for English language teaching: A guide for teachers. See http://oro.open.ac.uk/43605/1/__ userdata_documents3_lemn3_Desktop_E485%20Mobile%20pedagogy%20for%20ELT_FINAL_v2.pdf (accessed November 2021).
Kukulska-Hulme, A., Lee, H. and Norris, L. (2017) Mobile learning revolution: Implications for language pedagogy. In C.A. Chapelle and S. Sauro (eds) *The Handbook of Technology and Second Language Teaching and Learning* (pp. 217–233). Wiley.
Kultusministerkonferenz (2016) Strategie der Kultusministerkonferenz 'Bildung in der digitalen Welt'. See https://www.kmk.org/fileadmin/pdf/PresseUndAktuelles/2018/Digitalstrategie_2017_mit_Weiterbildung.pdf (accessed November 2021).
Kultusministerkonferenz (2021) Lehren und Lernen in der digitalen Welt. Ergänzung zur Strategie der Kultusministerkonferenz 'Bildung in der digitalen Welt'. See https://www.kmk.org/fileadmin/veroeffentlichungen_beschluesse/2021/2021_12_09-Lehren-und-Lernen-Digi.pdf (accessed December 2021).
Maaz, K., Artelt, C., Brugger, P., Buchholz, S., Kühne, S., Leerhoff, H., Rauschenbach, T., Rockmann, U., Roßbach, H.-G., Schrader, J. and Seeber, S. (2020) Bildung in Deutschland 2020: Ein indikatorengestützter Bericht mit einer Analyse zu Bildung in einer digitalisierten Welt. See https://www.bildungsbericht.de/de/bildungsberichte-seit-2006/bildungsbericht-2020/pdf-dateien-2020/bildungsbericht-2020-barrierefrei.pdf (accessed December 2021).
Manresa, G.A. and Bacharach, S. (2016) Digital street art. In S. Bacharach, J. Booth and S.B. Fjµrestad (eds) *Collaborative Art in the Twenty-first Century*. Routledge.
Medienpädagogischer Forschungsverbund Südwest (2021) JIM-Studie 2021. Jugend, Information, Medien. Basisuntersuchung zum Medienumgang 12- bis 19-Jähriger. See https://www.mpfs.de/fileadmin/files/Studien/JIM/2021/JIM-Studie_2021_barrierefrei.pdf (accessed January 2022).
Miangah, T.M. and Nezarat, A. (2012) Mobile-assisted language learning. *International Journal of Distributed and Parallel Systems* 3 (1), 309–319.

Millard, D.E., Packer, H. and Howard, Y. (2020) The balance of attention: The challenges of creating locative cultural storytelling experiences. *ACM Journal on Computing and Cultural Heritage* 13 (4), 35:1–35:24.

Morgana, V. (2021) Mobile assisted language learning across different educational settings: An introduction. In V. Morgana and A. Kukulska-Hulme (eds) *Mobile Assisted Language Learning Across Educational Contexts* (pp. 1–9). Routledge.

New London Group (1996) A pedagogy of multiliteracies: Designing social futures. *Harvard Educational Review* 66 (1), 60–92.

Palalas, A. (2016) Introduction to the handbook. In A. Palalas and M. Ally (eds) *The International Handbook of Mobile-Assisted Language Learning* (pp. I–XV). China Central Radio & TV University Press.

Palalas, A. and Hoven, D. (2016) Emerging pedagogies for MALL. In A. Palalas and M. Ally (eds) *The International Handbook of Mobile-Assisted Language Learning* (pp. 44–85). China Central Radio & TV University Press.

Pegrum, M. (2014) *Mobile Learning: Languages, Literacies and Cultures. New Language Learning and Teaching Environments.* Palgrave Macmillan.

Pegrum, M. (2019) *Mobile Lenses on Llearning: Languages and Literacies on the Move.* Springer.

Peng, H., Jager, S. and Lowie, W. (2021) Narrative review and meta-analysis of MALL research on L2 skills. *ReCALL* 33 (3), 278–295.

Ros i Solé, C., Calic, J. and Neijmann, D. (2010) A social and self-reflective approach to MALL. *ReCALL*, 22 (1), 39–52.

Ryan, M.-L. (2012) Space, place and story. In S. Füssel (ed.) *Medienkonvergenz – Transdisziplinär: Media convergence – across the disciplines* (pp. 109–128). de Gruyter.

Scarpati, J. (2019) Walking on code: Of mobile locative storytelling & augmented experience. *Urban Interfaces: Media, Art and Performance in Public Spaces* 22 (4). See https://www.leoalmanac.org/walking-on-code-of-mobile-locative-storytelling-augmented-experience-jessica-scarpati/ (accessed July 2022).

Souza e Silva, A. de. (2013) Location-aware mobile technologies: Historical, social and spatial approaches. *Mobile Media & Communication* 1 (1), 116–121.

Souza e Silva, A. de. (2017) Pokémon Go as an HRG: Mobility, sociability, and surveillance in hybrid spaces. *Mobile Media & Communication* 5 (1), 20–23.

Souza e Silva, A. de. and Sheller, M. (2015) Introduction: Moving toward adjacent possibles. In M. Sheller (ed.) *Mobility and Locative Media: Mobile Communication in Hybrid Spaces* (pp. 1–16). Routledge.

Stalder, F. (2016) *Kultur der Digitalität.* Suhrkamp.

Steininger, I. (2020) Towards a concept of Critical Digitalisation in the foreign language classroom. In D. Gerlach (ed.) *Kritische Fremdsprachendidaktik: Grundlagen, Ziele, Beispiele* (pp. 69–85). Narr Francke Attempto.

Stockwell, G. (2022) *Mobile Assisted Language Learning: Concepts, Contexts and Challenges.* Cambridge University Press.

Tuters, M. and Varnelis, K. (2006) Beyond locative media: Giving shape to the internet of things. *Leonardo* 39 (4), 357–363.

Vom Orde, H. and Durner, A. (2021). *International Data Youth and Media.* International Central Institute for Youth and Educational Television. See https://www.br-online.de/jugend/izi/english/International%20Data%20on%20Youth%20and%20Media.pdf (accessed July 2022).

Wilken, R. (2014) Places nearby: Facebook as a location-based social media platform. *New Media & Society,* 16 (7), 1087–1103.

Wilken, R. and Goggin, G. (2014) Locative media – Definitions, histories, theories. In R. Wilken and G. Goggin (eds) *Locative Media* (pp. 1–20). Routledge.

Young, R. (2009) *Discursive Practice in Language Learning and Teaching.* Wiley-Blackwell.

Zehne, C. (2022) Reconceiving the E in English Language Teaching in Germany – An investigation of teacher, student, and curricular concepts of English in the light of its global use. Unpublished doctoral dissertation, University of Bielefeld.

Zickuhr, K. (2013) Location-based services. *Pew Research Center*. See https://www.pewresearch.org/internet/wp-content/uploads/sites/9/media/Files/Reports/2013/PIP_Location-based-services-2013.pdf (accessed July 2022).

15 *Alice for the iPad*: Digital Storybook Apps in the EFL Classroom

Jeanine Steinbock

> 'And what is the use of a book', thought Alice, 'without pictures or conversation?'
> Carroll and Tenniel, 1865

15.1 Introduction

Digital media form a significant part of children's and adolescents' lives. Furthermore, studies such as the *KIM* and *JIM study* which examine the media consumption of children and teenagers, as well as their attitudes towards digital media have found that digital devices such as smartphones and tablets constantly rank among the top equipment next to internet access as their most prominent feature (mpfs, 2021: 5). In academic discourse, the question of whether digital media have an impact on teaching and learning is no longer debated; rather, groundbreaking concepts for the implementation of digital technology are being proposed and critically discussed (cf. Lütge & Merse, 2021; Strasser, 2018). Closely related to this, education policymakers are devising models for developing the digital literacies of both teachers and learners (cf. Redecker, 2017).

Digital technology makes new forms of multimodal texts possible, including digital adaptations of traditional texts and born-digital literature. For example, digital storybook apps such as *Alice for the iPad*, transform a printed text into a digital version, adding semiotic modes (cf. Hallet, 2015: 283–285), whereas born-digital texts unfold their potential through those digital affordances from inception. These digital texts offer new ways of meaning-making, which is why Becker-Mrotzek *et al.* (2019: 21) describe reading as 'a key skill in transition' from analogue to digital. Using storybook apps with learners brings new reading experiences to the classroom and can thus enhance learners' reading skills, literary literacy and digital competence (cf. Lütge *et al.*, 2019; mpfs, 2021). Taking this as a starting point, this chapter discusses the potential of digital literature in terms of multimodality and digital literacy, before presenting examples of storybook apps as adaptations of literary classics as well as born-digital texts.

15.2 Digital Literature in the EFL Classroom

Literature has a long tradition in the EFL classroom and is considered 'an integral part of language education' (Ludwig, 2021: 209). In the reading process, learners are attributed an action-oriented role, applying knowledge and experience to engage with a text (cf. Ludwig, 2021: 210). Literature allows for a holistic approach towards language learning by, for example, combining vocabulary and grammar acquisition as well as skills in analysis and interpretation (cf. Naji *et al.*, 2019: 3). Furthermore, '[w]ords in literary texts tend to carry cultural and emotional associations [...]' carrying the potential of responding to learners' thoughts, feelings and perceptions of the world (cf. Naji *et al.*, 2019: 36). With the evolution of digital – multimedia and multimodal – forms of literature, innovative approaches towards digital textuality gain prominence that in turn also redefine current perceptions of texts, tasks and activities (cf. Lütge *et al.*, 2021: 232).

With regard to traditional print literature, books and paper have been an inseparable combination for a long time, as Gralley (2006: 36) states in the context of picturebook analysis:

> After centuries of thinking of books and paper simultaneously, picture book artists who work digitally are beginning to uncouple books from print. More pointedly, we're becoming able to uncouple the idea of the book from 'paper thinking'.

This development also allows for the evolution of digital-born texts, making use of the multimodal characteristics of digital environments. Therefore, a closer look at the definition of *text* might be a good starting point. In a traditional sense, the Oxford English Dictionary (Stevenson, 2010: n.p.) defines text as:

> [t]he wording of anything written or printed; the structure formed by the words in their order; the very words, phrases, and sentences as written and further as ([a] unit of) connected discourse whose function is communicative and which forms the object of analysis and description.

Expanding this term in a linguistic sense, Hillesund (2006) states that the term 'text' can moreover refer to 'both written and spoken text'. Furthermore, texts are increasingly understood to also include visual and auditory modes such as videos and animations (Eisenmann & Summer, 2020: 57; Lütge *et al.*, 2021: 233). Developments in digital technology add digital and interactive components ranging 'from social media posts to video tutorials, digital newspapers and even virtual realities' (Lütge et al., 2021: 232). Due to this variety of elements that may contribute to a text, Dalton and Procter (2008: 300–301) posit that a digital text may be:

- a linear text in digital format;
- a text with integrated media;
- a text with response options;
- a single text;
- multiple texts [...];
- networked and either constrained or open (e.g. accessed via a server, which may or may not provide access to the internet);
- primarily visual, such as an animated graphic, video clip, photo slideshow, or image with little accompanying verbal information, and verbal information may be presented in auditory rather than written format.

Because of this range of elements, digital texts relate to the multimodal lives of learners, who can access texts, pictures, videos and animations anywhere and anytime (cf. Abraham & Farías, 2017: 60), and use them regularly to get information and to be entertained.

One such form of entertainment is digital literature which may incorporate multimodality, and this digital multimodality in turn influences text composition leading to 'new dynamics [in] creating innovative literary and aesthetic experiences for a "new" readership [...]' (Lütge et al., 2019: 521). Hence, Eisenmann and Summer (2020: 53) call for 'a broader definition of what constitutes literature'. Yet, finding a unanimous definition of digital literature remains a challenging task. For example, Lütge et al. (2021: 244) define digital literature as '[t]exts which are purposefully and aesthetically designed with a reliance on the interactive and multimedia affordances of digital tools and spaces'. Aspects of social constructivism, game-based activities, transmediality and hypertextuality are thus core characteristics of digital literature (Lütge et al., 2021: 245). With regard to how to deal with such texts in the classroom, there seems to be almost infinite potential to actively engage learners in reading digital literature as they co-create stories and produce new multimodal artefacts (cf. Kaminski, 2019: 176). In order to do so, both teachers and learners need a high degree of digital literacy, enabling them to select, read and understand digital texts. Therefore, Lütge et al. (2019: 522) emphasise the importance of combining literary learning with digital skills:

> [The] crossover of digitalization and literature in the context of EFL pedagogy must be accompanied by combining the didactic discourses of using literature and of using media in the classroom, which are currently considered in a fairly separate manner rather than being investigated for productive overlap.

If successful, this will allow both researchers and practitioners to develop new approaches to learning and teaching in the EFL classroom.

15.3 Multimodality and Digital Literacy

As Hallet (2015: 283) points out, there has been a significant development of multimodal literature over the last 20 years, both quantitatively and qualitatively. This multitude of digital texts and their multimodal nature requires learners to apply a plethora of meaning-making skills (Eisenmann & Summer, 2020: 57). The term 'multimodality' can be described as the 'interplay of a broad range of modes of communication, types of representation and signifying processes in cultural and social interaction' (Hallet, 2015: 284). In this, multimodality colocates with learners' everyday multimodal experiences. For example, learners' cultural and social interactions are in large parts defined by the 'affordances' (Kress 2010: 80, cited in Hallet, 2015: 287) of digital semiotic representation, meaning that, for example, emoticons can express emotions either in addition to, or instead of, written words. Hallet (2015: 283–284) concludes that:

> [In] combining various semiotic modes in addition to the verbal language, multimodal novels can be regarded as an imitation of the more complex, symbolically diverse ways in which meaning is generally made and communicated in cultural discourses and in the lifeworld.

Kalantzis *et al*. (2016: 2, cited in Lütge *et al*., 2019: 522) add a digital component to this when they say that '[...] we need to supplement traditional reading and writing skills with multimodal communications, particularly those typical of the new, digital media'.

First of all, the implementation of born-digital literature in the EFL classroom necessitates digital teaching and learning competences both on behalf of teachers and learners. With *DigCompEdu*, the Council of Europe has created a competence framework aligning teachers' and learners' quintessential skills for (digital) participation in modern-day society (Redecker, 2017). According to the framework, teachers need to be able to identify and select digital resources suitable for achieving curricular learning goals, as well as implementing methodological and pedagogical approaches (Redecker, 2017: 20). Moreover, teachers should actively foster their learners' engagement with digital media, thus enabling them to choose and use digital tools which help them to achieve their individual learning goals. With regard to literature this means that teachers should incorporate digital adaptations of print literature and born-digital literary texts which support learners in acquiring the digital reading skills which they need to understand and produce such texts. Even though there is some consensus on what modern-day digital literacy entails, some researchers perceive digital literacy as being subject to constant change due to a perpetually changing (digital) environment (cf. Naji *et al*., 2019: 14). Therefore, a constant debate on the interplay of digital skills and aspects of digital language learning is needed. In general, according to

Naji *et al.* (2019: 14), successful participation in modern-day digital society requires learners to obtain skills of 'creativity, imagination and criticality, problem-solving, collaboration [...], lifelong learning and flexibility'. In this, communicating and participating in written discourse serves as a basis for the acquisition of these skills. Through evolving forms, digital literature addresses these digital competences of creative expression, collaboration and being an active member of society in a sense of active authorship.

Digital storybook apps represent one way of engaging with literature. With some digital storybooks being browser versions, digital storybook apps differ in terms of accessibility and compatibility, for example some apps being specific to different operating systems. Within these apps, literary adaptations as well as born-digital literature are edited by picture book artists to be an aesthetically appealing and interactive language learning opportunity.

15.4 Digital Storybook Apps

Storybook apps, story apps or picturebook apps (Brunsmeier & Kolb, 2017; Ritter, 2013) consist of a (mostly) non-linear text in a digital format and can therefore be considered digital literature (Brunsmeier & Kolb, 2017: 2). They make use of technical features to combine texts with pictures, animations and sounds (cf. Brunsmeier & Kolb, 2017: 2). Ritter (2013) defines picturebook apps as: 'digitale Bild-Text-Erzählungen im Format der Anwendungssoftware für Mobilgeräte, wobei idealtypisch eine dominante und explizite Erzählung erkennbar ist'. [digital image-text narratives in the format of the application software for mobile devices, whereby ideally a dominant and explicit narrative is recognizable; translation by author] (Ritter, 2013: 4).

Methodological approaches for using storybook apps in the classroom focus on both their interactivity as well as their multimodal narrative functions. Lütge *et al.* (2019: 524) propose the FINaLe model for a 'systematic exploration and description' of digital literature consisting of four dimensions: functionality, interactivity, narrativity and the learner-reader-role; a model which can also be applied to storybook apps. In terms of functionality, the affordances of each individual storybook app are crucial for its value in English lessons, determining its position on a scale from a solely substitutional application to a redefinition of text's potential (Lütge *et al.*, 2019: 525–526). Furthermore, Lütge *et al.* (2019: 527–530) note that in terms of interactivity, there are different degrees of depth, ranging from peripheral interactivity to interactions affecting the narrative and plot line, to a full reshaping of a story by the reader. This creation of alternating storylines affects the narrativity itself, for it shifts the direction of the narration from 'multi-linear' to 'open' (Lütge *et al.*, 2019: 531), emphasising the range of choices that emerge for formerly passive readers. In game-based research this is often referred to as 'sandbox narration', with no fixed storylines and players building their own worlds and defining their own goals (Neitzel, 2012: 121). The fourth dimension specifies the depth to which the application allows readers to immerse themselves in the story ranging from being assigned the role of a peripheral reader to a character in the story, sometimes represented through an avatar (cf. Lütge *et al.*, 2019: 533–534). Combining all four dimensions of the FINaLe model leads to a multidimensional assessment of the digital storybook apps EFL teachers can use to find suitable stories.

However, in addition to the affordances of storybook apps, the composition of the text itself, including all modes and their 'narrative function[s]' (Müller-Brauers *et al.*, 2020a: 166), needs to be considered, as reading and understanding them requires a complex set of skills. For this purpose, Müller-Brauers *et al.* (2020a: 167) developed the ViSAR model (visual, speaker, animative, reader), which originated in the German language classroom for analysing digital storybook apps according to the levels of visual and animative features, as well as the role of the speaker and the reader. For the degree of visual features, the model draws on picturebook analysis, including narrative, verbal, pictorial, intermodal and paratextual dimensions (Staiger, 2014, cited in Müller-Brauers *et al.*, 2020a: 166). In this context, and as a crucial characteristic of picturebook evaluation, Staiger (2014: 15) proposes the description of text-image relations according to five criteria: symmetry, complementarity, enhancement, counterpoint and contradiction. In terms of animative features, Thiele (2000, cited in Müller-Brauers *et al.*, 2020a: 166) suggests that images are either 'parallel', 'contrapuntal' or designed as a 'plaited braid' in relation to the corresponding texts. Parallel text-image relations mean that the images function as a symmetrical mirror of the printed words, which is thought to be particularly beneficial for young learners, as the mode of operation of storybook apps for young learners should feature proximity and coherence of text and image (Brunsmeier & Kolb, 2017). To support young students' language learning through facilitating understanding and meaning-making, visual modes should occur in juxtaposition to their verbal reference, and 'text and images need to match' (Brunsmeier & Kolb, 2017). A contrapuntal array, on the other hand, displays an 'inconsistent relation between text and animated images/sounds', possibly even contradictory, through, for example, 'break[ing] the timeline', when an animation can be reactivated while the text tells it as a single event (Müller-Brauers, 2020b: n.p.). For a 'plaited braid' relation, images and texts are complementary, that is, both text and image provide different additional information for facilitating the meaning-making process.

In addition to these aspects of narrative modal functions, Müller-Brauers *et al.* (2020a: 166) note an illustrative or atmospheric function of images and illustrations in digital storybook apps, highlighting aspects of 'making space vivid [...] or evoking emotions', thus emphasising characteristics that make digital stories appealing to readers, and enabling an emotional and therefore personal connection to the story. As a third level, the model adds the role and characteristics of the narrator, highlighting the storytelling aspects, when storybook applications feature reading-out functions, which not all of them do (cf. Müller-Brauers *et al.*, 2020a: 172). These features add prosody and rhythm, and are therefore emulating early childhood reading experiences such as parents reading aloud to their children (cf. Müller-Brauers *et al.*, 2020a: 172).

Along with the evolution of these analytical models, an empirical foundation on digital storybook apps has emerged over time, where studies highlight the positive influences on language learning (cf. Brunsmeier & Kolb, 2017; Kaminski, 2019). For example, a research project on multimodal stories conducted among young learners showed that learners responded to 'all the different modes of the input', resulting, for instance, in the reproduction of 'multi-item chunk[s]' (Kaminski, 2019: 181). The visual input is crucial in the meaning-making process, resulting in learners' increasing tolerance of ambiguity towards word-for-word understanding (cf. Kaminski, 2019: 181). Research on storybook apps moreover indicates significant positive influences on learners' story comprehension and vocabulary development when working with storybook apps in the language classroom (cf. Smeets, 2012). Zipke (2017: 1695) conducted a study among pre-schoolers and was able to identify the read-out-loud function as beneficial for 'students' word recognition scores', as well as the positive influence of digital storybooks on learners' reading comprehension in an autonomous language learning setting. In the context of modern digital storytelling, Fibriasari *et al.* (2021) highlight the applicability of interactive storybooks for an action- and product-oriented approach in language learning scenarios facilitating learners' perceptions of ownership of a story, i.e. 'the right to tell it' (Shuman, 2015: 41). In their study setting, participants discussed features of digital storybooks and then transferred these theoretical concepts into the design of storybooks (Fibriasari *et al.*, 2021: 971). They conclude that even though participants were young and rather inexperienced, 'the end result succeeds admirably in meeting the user's requirements' (Fibriasari *et al.*, 2021: 975). Brunsmeier and Kolb (2017: 6) focused on 'features of the story apps the children benefit from during the reading processes' in the context of a study among primary EFL learners and identified five core characteristics: audio narration, animation and sound, vocabulary support and co-creation (Brunsmeier & Kolb, 2017: 8–12). Participants assessed aspects of self-regulated learning using audio options and repetitions, as well as the positive influence of parallel animations both on their vocabulary development and story comprehension as positive factors (cf. Brunsmeier & Kolb, 2017: 9–10). The study also suggests that learners intuitively comprehend aspects of co-creation, enabling them to personalise the story and develop their own plotline (cf. Brunsmeier & Kolb, 2017: 13).

The following elaborations will focus on the practical aspects of analysing digital storybook apps, both as adaptations of literary classics as well as born-digital interactive storybook apps.

15.4.1 *Alice for the iPad*: An analysis of 'Down the Rabbit-Hole'

Both the FINaLe and the ViSAR models will serve as a basis for an example analysis of the first chapter of the app *Alice for the iPad,* a storybook app containing the story of *Alice's Adventures in Wonderland* by Lewis Carroll (1865) for iOS. The two models will be used in a complementary manner as the FINaLe model allows for an analysis of interactive features of digital storybook apps whereas the ViSAR model affords a detailed look at the relation between images or animations and texts.

In the first chapter 'Down the Rabbit-Hole', Alice finds herself falling down a rabbit hole while following the White Rabbit and desperately trying to enter Wonderland by making herself grow and shrink. The app augments the literary experience by animating a piece of the literary canon and hence addressing multimodal meaning-making. *Alice for the iPad* provides a set storyline readers cannot influence, i.e. it offers peripheral interactivity, which Lütge et al. (2019: 527) argue to be 'particularly common with print books that have been adapted to adopt the aesthetics afforded by the digital medium'. Readers navigate through the storyline using bottom arrows allowing them to turn the page, but cannot alter their order. Thus, the narration itself also cannot be altered, as it is 'linear, predetermined and closed' (Lütge *et al.*, 2019: 531). This affects the role of the reader, as it remains 'external and exploratory' (Lütge *et al.*, 2019: 533) and thus the reader is not a part of the story itself but merely a spectator.

The visual and animative functions of the first chapter are manifold. However, there is no reading-out-loud function included. Generally, the animation only comprises animated objects moving across the pages, following the tablet's motion, seemingly defying gravity. Additionally, the storybook app provides images, some of which are taken from the printed text whereas others have been added to the digital version. In the introduction of the first chapter, for example, an image of a sleeping Alice is added to the story app. As the text does not explicitly mention Alice falling asleep, this image can be viewed as an 'enhancement' (Staiger, 2014: 20) and foreshadowing as, following the printed text, readers would not find out until the end that Alice was in fact dreaming (Carroll & Tenniel, 1865: 105). On the next page, when Alice thinks of daisy chains, readers can animate a watch by flipping the tablet, causing the watch to swing from a letter. However, as there is no mention of a watch until the next page, this animation can be argued to be contrapuntual as it lacks proximity and coherence (cf. Brunsmeier & Kolb, 2017; Müller-Brauers, 2020a: 166). When Alice falls down the hole, a jar of orange marmalade can be animated moving across the page when the tablet is tilted or turned upside down. This animation adds a visual component to the scene. It can, however, also be viewed as contrapuntal as the text clarifies how Alice emphasises the importance of putting the jar back into a shelf while the animation does not allow for the jar to be put on a shelf (Carroll & Tenniel, 1865: 7). After several pages, the reader gets a glimpse of Wonderland through a small door into garden-like scenery. This was, however, described on the page before, so while this animation displays parallelity, it lacks proximity. It could be viewed as an enhancement instead, as it combines an image from the printed text with an animated section, as Alice, like in the printed text, moves a curtain to look at a closed door.

A similar animation can be found on the next page when Alice finds the bottle saying 'DRINK ME', with an animated labelled bottle being shown. The chapter's final animation shows Alice 'shutting up like a telescope' (Carroll & Tenniel, 1865: 9) as an animated image of the printed text. However, in the printed version, this image does not appear until chapter two. Although there is coherence, proximity and parallelity, this animation could also function as a contrapuntal animation, as readers are able to reactivate this animation an unlimited number of times, although in the text it happens just once (cf. Müller-Brauers *et al*., 2020b: n.p.).

Lütge *et al*. (2019: 527–528) discuss the question whether the interactivity of these forms of only peripherally interactive storybooks are intended to scaffold the meaning-making process of the reader and/or highlight the aesthetics of the text as a part of literature. In support of the

Figure 15.1 Shrinking Alice from Alice for the iPad; Screenshot courtesy of Oceanhouse Media Inc.

former, it could be argued that the narrative functions of the animations make the complex storyline easier to understand. On the other hand, since the storyline is predefined and the interactive elements are only peripheral, it could also be argued that they are predominantly enhancing the aesthetics of the narrative rather than supporting the learning process (cf. Lütge et al., 2019: 530).

Not all digital storybooks based on literary classics, however, limit the interactivity to peripheral elements. Other examples abandon the linear storyline and grant the reader the utmost freedom in developing the story while preserving the original plot. In contrast to *Alice for the iPad*, the interactive storybook *80 Days* (Inkle Ltd., 2015), for example, can be considered a move towards digital-born interactive storybooks as it allows readers to take 'ownership' (Dyer, 2014: n.p.) of the story ideally resulting in a text that has a personal meaning rather than solely being an artefact of literary history. The storybook *80 Days* is based on the classic novel *Le Tour du monde en quatre-vingts jours* by Jules Verne (1873) and incorporates excerpts while at the same time enabling readers to go on the journey themselves, planning and organising destinations within the time limit of 80 days. As such, *80 Days* immerses the reader in the storyline through a high degree of interactivity and sandbox narration.[1]

In addition to animations of literary classics, digitisation allows for born-digital texts that embrace the possibilities of digital technologies to realise their full potential. In the following, two examples of born-digital storybook apps for advanced and for young learners will be discussed.

15.4.2 Born-digital interactive storybooks for young and advanced learners

The different storybook apps available on the market range from pure paper book substitutions (e.g. *Oakrot – It's Literally a Book*, Morel, 2021) to open-world narrations, offering a maximum degree of reader autonomy with regard to what to read. In the following section, the storybook apps *The Last Survey* and *Paperbark* are presented as examples of storybook apps for advanced and young learners, respectively, particularly focusing on their potential for multimodal language learning.

15.4.2.1 Example 1: The last survey

The Last Survey (O'Brien, 2020) is a born-digital storybook for advanced learners about sustainability and the future of the planet. In the story, a geologist, hired by a mining company, discovers the disparity of the supply and demand for nickel, silver, cobalt and platinum used in computer production and a coming shortage of these commodities. This app includes 'interactivity creating variations in a predefined story' (Lütge et al., 2019: 529) because the reader takes up the role of the geologist delivering the alarming discovery and has to make decisions about the actions and statements of the main character. The basic storyline is predetermined, so the interactivity involves conversational choices that affect the behaviour of the mining company and therefore offers a multi-linear narrativity. In terms of the learner-reader role, readers experience an internal and exploratory setting, as they can choose between 'different narrative paths' (Lütge *et al.*, 2019: 533–534), which, however, have no influence on the overall storyline in the sense of the text being co-constructed (Lütge *et al.*, 2019: 533–534). Readers navigate through the story using bottom arrows with each page containing a paragraph of text at the bottom and animations taking up the top two thirds of the page. A distinctive element of the animations is that the images are merging into each other, looping until each page is turned again. In terms of their narrative function, the animations display both parallel and plaited braid features. Some of the animations mirror the text, e.g. the word 'caterpillar truck' corresponds to an emerging vehicle of this type. Other animations enhance the written word, for example, the colocation 'overactive socialising' is linked to an animation of two clinking wine glasses. All animations feature a consistent display of coherence and proximity, which makes this app appealing for learners despite the advanced vocabulary (e.g. economic terminology). With its gloomy design in black and white, the app not only supports readers' understanding by scaffolding important vocabulary but also addresses the aesthetic sense of literature, which in turn can be part of follow-up tasks and activities.

15.4.2.2 Example 2: Paperbark

An example for young learners is *Paperbark* (Paper House, 2018), the story of a wombat and its journey through the Australian bush in search for food. Readers steer the wombat along the way, collecting all sorts of insects and plants and facing dangers, such as wildfires. The story predominantly unfolds through readers sliding their fingers over the screen and uncovering previously hidden sceneries, including plants and insects to be eaten by the wombat. In between these game-based activities, the story unfolds in a predefined storyline, with text elements shown at fixed points throughout the main quest. The interactivity therefore constitutes a peripheral interactivity, where readers' gaming strategies may vary but cannot influence the progress of the storyline. Although it can only be viewed from a bird's-eye perspective, readers experience an internal and exploratory role in the narration. Throughout this storybook, text and animations show coherence and proximity by being either parallel or enhancing, which is appropriate for young learners (cf. Brunsmeier & Kolb, 2017: 9–10). The written text is composed of short sentences with repeated vocabulary and syntax. The fact that it can be read through in a relatively short amount of time (approximately 60 minutes) adds to the suitability for young learners in a classroom setting.

15.5 Implications for Further Research

As the studies discussed in Section 15.4 show, research on storybooks predominantly focuses on early language learning (cf. Bus *et al.*, 2020; Neumann, 2020; Son *et al.*, 2020). Yet, there is still scope for further research leading to an even deeper understanding of the impact of individual characteristics of storybook apps on reading comprehension in the context of early literacies in language learning. As Müller-Brauers *et al.* (2020b: n.p.), point out:

> [T]here is still a lack of research on how the specific conditions in digital reading impact children's understanding of stories and how shared reading interaction and adults' responsive strategies during digital reading are affected by the digital device.

In addition, Brunsmeier and Kolb (2017: 16) suggest taking a 'closer look' at the reading process itself and how distinctive characteristics of storybook apps help foster reading and meaning-making skills in a longitudinal study design. Where research on early childhood focuses on a deeper understanding, research in advanced learners' perceptions and effects on learning with storybook apps lacks correspondingly in-depth empirical foundation. Especially in the context of reader-response-criticism, storybook apps targeting an advanced audience are designed to address topics of personal and global impact. In this context, aspects of reading strategies, literary aesthetics and a critical perception of born-digital interactive literature are of special interest.

15.6 Conclusion

Storybook apps offer a unique language learning experience by combining text, image, animation and sound. They not only adapt literary classics and famous children's novels but also include born-digital storybooks which are both graphically sophisticated and intuitively operable. This form of multimodal interactive literature has found its way into EFL classrooms for young, intermediate and advanced learners, especially as research continues to show the positive effects of reading digital storybooks in the context of modern English teaching, promoting connected authorship, autonomy and action-orientation. The text-image stimuli in digital stories encourage learners to engage with the subject matter while, at the same time, training their multimodal meaning-making skills. Future research on storybook apps could aim at compiling a literary canon of born-digital storybook apps and identifying their value for EFL purposes. This, in turn, would lead to initial insights into the genre, and furthermore, foster debate among teachers, researchers and learners.

Note

(1) For a detailed analysis, see Lütge et al. (2019).

References

Abraham, P. and Farías, M. (2017) Reading with eyes wide open: Reflections on the impact of multimodal texts on second language reading. *Ikala* 22 (1), 57–70.

Becker-Mrotzek, M., Lindauer, T., Pfost, M., Weis, M., Strohmaier, A. and Reiss, K. (2019) Lesekompetenz heute – Eine Schlüsselqualifikation im Wandel. In K. Reiss, M. Weis, E. Klieme and O. Köller (eds) *PISA 2018. Grundbildung im internationalen Vergleich* (pp. 21–46). Waxmann.

Brunsmeier, S. and Kolb, A. (2017) Picturebooks go digital – The potential of story apps for the primary EFL classroom. *Children's Literature in English Language Education Journal* 5 (1), 1–20.

Bus, A.G., Hoel, T., Aliagas, C., Jernes, M., Korat, O., Mifsud, C.L. and van Coillie, J. (2020) Availability and quality of storybook apps across five less widely used languages. In O. Erstad, R. Flewitt, B. Kümmerling-Meibauer and I.S.P. Pereira (eds) *The Routledge Handbook of Digital Literacies in Early Childhood* (pp. 308–321). Routledge.

Carroll, L. and Tenniel J. (1865) *Alice's Adventures in Wonderland. Wisehouse Classics – Original 1865 Edition with the Complete Illustrations by Sir John Tenniel*. Penguin.

Dalton, B. and Proctor, C. (2008) The changing landscape of text and comprehension in the age of new literacies. In J. Coiro, M. Knobel, C. Lankshear and D.J. Leu (eds) *Handbook of Research on New Literacies* (pp. 297–324). Lawrence Erlbaum Associates.

Dyer, M. (2014) 80 days review. See https://www.ign.com/articles/2014/12/04/80-days-review (accessed October 2021).

Eisenmann, M. and Summer, T. (2020) Multimodal literature in ELT: Theory and practice. *CLELEjournal* 8 (1), 52–73.

Fibriasari, H., Baharuddin, Gultom, S., Restuati, M., Ritonga, W., Dalle, J., Putra, A., Biyatmoko, D., Mutalib, A., Azizah, C. and Andayani, W. (2021) Developing digital storybook to improve children's language learning. *Advances in Social Science, Education and Humanities Research* 591, 967–977.

Gralley, J. (2006) Liftoff: When books leave the page. *Horn Book Magazine* 1, 35–39.

Hallet, W. (2015) Teaching multimodal novels. In W. Delanoy, M. Eisenmann and F. Matz (eds) *Learning with Literature in the EFL Classroom* (pp. 283–298). Peter Lang.

Hillesund, T. (2006) Digital text cycles: From medieval manuscripts to modern markup. *Journal of Digital Information* 6 (1). See https://journals.tdl.org/jodi/index.php/jodi/article/view/62/65> (accessed December 2021).

Inkle Ltd. (ed.) (2015) *80 Days*. Digital Storybook App.

Kaminski, A. (2019) Young learners' engagement with multimodal texts. *ELT Journal* 73 (2), 175–185.

Ludwig, C. (2021) Teaching literature with digital media. In C. Lütge and T. Merse (eds) *Digital Teaching and Learning: Perspectives for English Language Education* (pp. 207–230). Narr.

Lütge, C. and Merse, T. (eds) (2021) *Digital Teaching and Learning. Perspectives for English Language Education.* Narr.

Lütge, C., Merse, T., Owczarek, C. and Stannard, M. (2019) Crossovers: Digitalization and literature in foreign language education. In A. Lämmerer and S. Mercer (eds) *Studies in Second Language Learning and Teaching. Border Crossing in Language Education* (pp. 519–540). Adam Mickiewicz University.

Lütge, C., Merse, T. and Stannard, M. (2021) Digital textualities: Innovative practices with social media, digital literatures and virtual realities. In C. Lütge and T. Merse (eds) *Digital Teaching and Learning: Perspectives for English Language Education* (pp. 231–256). Narr.

Medienpädagogischer Forschungsverbund Südwest (mpfs) (eds) (2021) *JIM-Studie 2020. Jugend, Information, Medien.* Landesanstalt für Kommunikation.

Morel, L. (2021) *Oakrot – It's Literally a Book.* Digital Storybook App.

Müller-Brauers, C., Boelmann, J.M., Miosga, C. and Potthast, I. (2020a) Digital children's literature in the interplay between visuality and animation. A model for analysing picture book apps and their potential for children's story comprehension. In K.J. Rohlfing and C. Müller-Brauers (eds) *International Perspectives on Digital Media and Early Literacy* (pp. 161–179). Routledge.

Müller-Brauers, C., Miosga, C., Fischer, S., Maus, A. and Potthast, I. (2020b) Narrative potential of picture-book apps: A media- and interaction-oriented study. See https://www.frontiersin.org/articles/10.3389/fpsyg.2020.593482/full (accessed October 2021).

Naji, J., Subramaniam, G. and White, G. (2019) *New Approaches to Literature for Language Learning.* Palgrave Macmillan.

Neitzel, B. (2012) Erzählen und Spielen. Zur Bedeutung des Erzählbegriffs in den *Game Studies*. In M. Aumüller (ed.) *Narrativität als Begriff. Analysen und Anwendungsbeispiele zwischen philologischer und anthropologischer Orientierung* (pp. 109–128). De Gruyter.

Neumann, M. (2020) Teacher scaffolding of preschoolers' shared reading with a storybook app and a printed book. *Journal of Research in Childhood Education* 34 (3), 367–384.

O'Brien, N. (2020) *The Last Survey.* Digital Storybook App.

Oceanhouse Media Inc. (eds) (2006) *Alice for the iPad.* Digital Storybook App.

Paper House (eds) (2018) *Paperbark.* Digital Storybook App.

Redecker, C. (2017) *European Framework for the Digital Competence of Educators: DigCompEdu.* Publications Office of the European Union.

Ritter, M. (2013) Innovative Grenzgänge oder oberflächliche Effekthascherei? Tendenzen der Transformation literarischer Welten in Kinderbuch-Apps. *Zeitschrift ästhetische Bildung* 5 (1), 1–27.

Shuman, A. (2015) Story ownership and entitlement. In A. De Fina and A. Georgakopoulou (eds) *The Handbook of Narrative Analysis* (pp. 38–56). John Wiley & Sons.

Smeets, D.J.H. (2012) *Storybook Apps as a Tool for Early Literacy Development.* Narcis.

Son, S.-H.C., Butcher, K.R. and Liang, L.A. (2020) The influence of interactive features in storybook apps on children's reading comprehension and story enjoyment. *The Elementary School Journal* 120 (3), 422–454.

Staiger, M. (2014) Erzählen mit Bild-Schrifttext-Kombinationen Ein fünfdimensionales Modell der Bilderbuchanalyse. In J. Knopf and U. Abraham (eds) *BilderBücher. Theorie* (pp. 12–23). Schneider Verlag.

Stevenson, A. (ed.) (2010) Text. *Oxford Dictionary of English.* OUP.

Strasser, T. (2018) *Mind the App 2.0. Inspiring Internet Tools and Activities to Engage Your Students.* Helbling.

Verne, J. (1873) *Le tour du monde en quatre-vingts jours.* Gallimard.

Zipke, M. (2017) Preschoolers explore interactive storybook apps: The effect on word recognition and story comprehension. *Education and Information Technologies* 22 (4), 1695–1712.

16 #Literature Goes Digital: Digital Transformations in the ELT Literature Classroom

Christian Ludwig, Michaela Sambanis and Georg Hartisch

> Lovers of print are simply confusing the plate for the food.
> Douglas Adams (as qtd. in Gliksman, 2015: 89)

16.1 Introduction

The goal of English as a foreign language teaching (ELT) is to create meaningful learning experiences which help students to acquire the knowledge and skills they need to live and prosper in the 21st-century digital world. This entails equipping students with strategies to navigate the modern multimodal and hypertextual media landscape where information is no longer just passively consumed but actively produced, altered, remixed and disseminated instantly. With regard to reading, digital platforms are rapidly transforming when, where, what and how we read (Johnson, 2021). Print literature, it seems, is destined to disappear into oblivion in an age in which the physical boundaries of the print-bound text may seem unimaginable to a new generation of reader-writers. Print literature and digital technology, however, may not be as incompatible as one may assume, digital media provide new ways for students to engage and experiment with print-based literature.

Yet, to simply look at the potential of digital media for working with print literature in the classroom at the dawn of 2022 would be far too narrow, as literature itself is evolving. It no longer simply dabbles in trying to emulate the typical look of born-digital texts on paper (Androutsopoulos, 2011; Groenke & Maples, 2010: 38; Kersten, this volume) but is increasingly born-digital itself. In the words of Hayles, literature in the 21st century is 'computational', it is 'digital born, created on a computer and meant to be read on it' (Hayles, 2007: 99). Particularly with the rapid evolution of social media platforms, which are no longer limited to the desktop but can be accessed through apps from basically anywhere and at any time, new formats of literature seem to evolve which are characterised by the increasing intertwining of literary, cultural and social media practices (Thomas, 2020).

In this chapter, we explore the potential of digital technology (Ludwig, 2022; Sambanis, 2020) with regards to literature education in English language teaching. However, we do not suggest a mere swap of paper for the screen but instead advocate for a more reflective use of both traditional and digital literature, not ignoring the fact that more (interdisciplinary) empirical evidence regarding, for example, the use of screen-based, instead of paper-based, texts as well as down-to-earth classroom practice is needed. According to the Stavanger Declaration Concerning the Future of Reading, evidence shows an inferiority effect of screen compared to paper 'regardless of age group and of prior experience with digital environments' (COST, 2018: n.p.). However, the same research initiative reaches the conclusion that '[d]igital texts offer excellent opportunities to tailor text presentation' which, in turn, can be beneficial for comprehension and motivation (COST, 2018: n.p.).

Taking this as a starting point, this contribution attempts to place (born-print) literature and digital media in dialogue with each other, arguing that their intricate and complex relationship is worth exploring with regard to multimodal and digital literacy instruction in the contemporary classroom. The first part of this paper discusses how digital technology can support students' critical and interactive engagement with print-based literature, especially as digital platforms offer new and innovative spaces for critical dialogue and creative expression (Ludwig, 2021: 209–232). To illustrate this, selected results of a mixed-method study conducted at a secondary school in Berlin in 2020 are presented, illustrating in an exemplary fashion how digital reading logs can enhance students' literary competences as they engage with literature on a deeper level, discuss their ideas with their peers, and critically reflect on their reading. The following part then moves on to explore the potential of born-digital literature for ELT. It focuses on how these new forms of literature can help deconstruct the discursive borders between literary and digital education (Lütge *et al.*, 2019: 519–540). The contribution concludes by exploring how Instapoetry and poetry performances on TikTok, as examples of born-digital literary texts, can be integrated into the English as a foreign language classroom and how they can help to give rise to a new generation of critical, self-conscious and digitally-literate wreaders (writer-readers) (Landow, 1992) in an increasingly less analogue world.

16.2 Literature in the (Digital) ELT Classroom: The State of Play

As Lockhurst (2016: n.p.) once poignantly put it, 'every technological breakthrough tends to be accompanied by anxious announcements of its catastrophic effect on literature'. The claim that literature is dying in the digital age (Hammond, 2016) seems to be supported by teachers who complain about and lament on the fact that students overwhelmingly no longer read (printed books). As Mrs Schmidt, (pseudonym), the teacher who participated in the project discussed in more detail in Section 16.3, states:

> In general, our students read very little. […] This means that I have some students who have never read a book before, and even more students who have never read a book in English before they had to read one in their English lessons [the German word *Schüler* in the original explicitly refers to male students]. They are not used to it. Well, let us put it this way: they are not used to it but maybe they can do it. But initially there is some sort of defensive attitude. Books are out. (Translation C.L.)

However, today's generation of adolescents, one may argue, does not necessarily read less but simply differently to their past peers. They read in non-traditional, digital formats brought about by an increasingly predominant digital culture. They listen to audiobooks, play video games, or consume what their news feeds offer them (*cf.* Schildhauer & Kemper, this volume); formats which challenge our traditional understandings of concepts such as literature, reader, writer, author and fan (cf. e.g. Sauro, 2017: 131–146). Thus, 'the subject of ELT is increasingly challenged to reconfigure and rethink its fields of engagement in light of digital changes and transformations currently underway' (Lütge & Merse, 2021: 13).

However, it may be premature to throw print books away as digital tools may offer a number of benefits for students when it comes to reading print-based literature (cf. e.g. Hetland, 2016). They may, for example, promote more autonomous reading, provide platforms for collaborative forms of engagement and participation, and encourage students to share their ideas and perspectives as well as express themselves creatively (Thomas, 2020: 7). Despite the assumed potential of digital tools to enhance students' literary experience, there seems to be 'the need to investigate further the advantages and disadvantages of paper-based reading and reading on digital devices' (Delgado *et al.*, 2018: 23–38) but even more so how literature is actually read and taught in schools in the digital age (Gabrielsen *et al.*, 2019: 2).

16.3 Background of the Study

Literary texts play an important role in the foreign language classroom as they provide numerous benefits, including ample exposure to the foreign language and different cultural contexts. In addition, they can also provide authentic and enjoyable reading experiences for the students who may be encouraged to critically reflect on real life events and their own experiences. Yet, literature seems to have become highly contested, especially since the advent of competence orientation and the rise of an increasing test culture. As Paran (2010: 146) rightly observes: 'If the teaching of literature is not linked quite clearly to assessment, it might simply disappear'. This is also reflected in the lack of descriptors for working with literature in both the 2001 *Common European Framework Reference for Languages (CEFR)* and the 2018 *CEFR Companion Volume*, despite the new scales which have been added for working with different types of texts.

In order to respond to a purely 'mechanistic', language-oriented approach to teaching literature (Bland, 2018: xi) and to justify the reading of literary texts in the competence-based classroom, literary competence models have been developed. These models not only 'distinguish subcategories that pay tribute to the potential of literary texts' (Alter & Ratheiser, 2019: 2) but also try to make students' experiences with literature measurable and testable. Based on prior understandings of literary competence, Brumfit and Carter, as early as 1986, defined literary competence as 'an interesting combination of linguistic, socio-cultural, historical, and semiotic awareness' (1986: 18). Since then, several models of literary competence have been suggested, including, by Spiro (1991), Burwitz-Melzer (2007), Hallet (2009), Rössler (2010), Steininger (2014), Diehr and Surkamp (2015), and Alter and Ratheiser (2019). These models conceptualise literary competence in different ways, for example through can-do descriptors (Blume, 2007) or emphasising the fact that reading literary texts is a highly individual process (*cf.* Decke-Cornill & Küster, 2010: 256; Diehr & Surkamp, 2015: 21–40). The model by Surkamp (2012), as shown in Figure 16.1, divides foreign language literary competence into seven distinct components (Surkamp, 2012: 83–84), with all of the components, or sub-competences, covering a broad range of skills and competences. Affective, e.g. refers to the reader's subjective responses to a literary text, their emotional engagement and their ability for empathy, while emotional covers aspects such as finding pleasure in reading and avoiding critical thinking or logic (suspension of disbelief). Productive refers to students' creative responses to a text (narrative competence) as they, for example, adapt a text into a different medium.

The study discussed in the following focused on two selected components of learners' literary competence, namely their linguistic-discursive competence (*sprachlich-diskursive Kompetenz*) and reflexive competence (*reflexive Kompetenz*). While the former describes the students' ability to draw on their linguistic knowledge and discourse competence to gain access to the text and, at the same time, use the text to further develop their language competences as they engage in communication about the text, the latter refers to the students' ability to reflect the major themes, norms, values and characters' actions represented in a text, relate them to things they have seen or done themselves (*Lebenswelt*) and reflect on their own reception process, alone and in collaboration with others.

Figure 16.1 Dimensions of literary competence (based on Surkamp, 2012, cf. Section 3.4 for a more detailed discussion)

There are numerous reader-response methods and pedagogical tools which promote the (student) reader's experience of, and interaction with, literature including, for example, writing as a character or writing oneself into the story, or responding to a text in a reading circle (Woodruff & Griffin, 2017: 108–116).

Reading diaries, which come in many different shapes and forms and which are the focus of the study discussed here, can have a number of benefits in the literature classroom as they 'encourage students to take greater risks, especially in speculating about a text and asking questions' (Dorn & Soffas, 2005: 47). Thus, they may also be considered particularly suitable to develop students' literary competence as they encourage students to engage with a text on a deeper and more personal level. Depending on the age of the students and their prior experiences with reading literary texts, reading diaries may be more or less guided. It may include different aspects such as language (e.g. new words and expressions), character descriptions, important quotes, questions about the text as well as other aspects, allowing students to keep important details about the story which can also be used for further in-class discussions. Closely related to this, reading journals may be used as a means of communication between the students and the teacher as well as between students. Last but not least, reading diaries can serve as an instrument to 'record introspective reflection in first person about someone's learning or teaching' (Lopera Medina, 2013: 115), including language learning strategies.

Against this backdrop, the partial results of a study presented in the following aim to provide empirical data on and a critical discussion of the use of digital technology in the EFL literature classroom. The results illustrate the potential of digital technology in foreign language teaching, especially for enhancing students' literary competence.

16.3.1 The study

The LitCom 2.0 study was conducted at an *Integrierte Sekundarschule* in Berlin in late 2020, a still relatively new type of school in the educational landscape of Berlin, characterised by highly heterogeneous and diverse groups of students with a great need for differentiation. The objective of the study was threefold, namely to gain a better understanding of how:

- the teacher and students perceive the use of digital tools in the English (literature) classroom in the light of their digital media consumption outside the classroom;
- digital media can inform the foreign language (literature) classroom;
- digital tools can potentially enhance students' literary competences, particularly focusing on their linguistic-discursive and reflexive competences.

More specifically, it addressed the following research questions:

RQ1: How do the teacher and the students experience the use of digital media in the EFL (literature) classroom?
RQ2: What are the perceived benefits and drawbacks of using digital reading journals in combination with print-based literature?
RQ3: How can digital reading diaries help to enhance students' literary competence, more specifically their linguistic, discursive and reflexive competence?

16.3.2 Design and instruments

In order to answer these research questions, a mixed-method research design was used, including the following sources of data:

- a pre- and post-questionnaire (open-ended and closed questions as well as multiple choice and Likert scale items) for the students;
- a pre- and post-questionnaire (open-ended and closed questions, multiple choice and Likert scale items) for the teacher;
- a pre- and post-interview (semi-structured) with the teacher;
- a qualitative analysis of the students' contributions to the digital reading diary.

The pre-test questionnaire investigated the students' social media use, their reading behavior, their experience with and attitude towards literature in the English classroom as well as their experiences with using digital media in EFL learning. Furthermore, it also included questions about the students' expectations concerning the use of a digital platform to share their thoughts, ideas, questions about a literary text and reflect their reading comprehension. The pre-test questionnaire for the teacher consisted of a similar set of questions, for example asking for her experience with using digital technology in her lessons and her expectations towards the results of the project. The post-test questionnaires mainly focused on the students' and the teacher's experiences with the digital reading journal. The qualitative analysis of the students' contributions to the digital reading diary was used as an in-depth investigation of how students negotiate meaning and share their thoughts and reflections digitally, and to find out if and how the engagement with the text enhanced their literary competence. For this purpose, all contributions to the reading journal were coded to identify common aspects and themes. In order to increase the reliability of qualitative findings, all entries were coded by multiple coders.

16.3.3 Procedure

A digital reading diary, which was created on LearningApps.org, a free-of-charge Web 2.0 platform which offers its users interactive and multimodal components to create learning content and activities, was used in a year 11 EFL class, consisting of 17 students of 15 to 17 years old, as part of a series of seven double lessons (90 minutes each).

The unit was built around George Orwell's allegorical novella *Animal Farm* (1945), a political satire which illustrates how the utopian dream of a more equal society is corrupted. Each week, the students were required to read one or two chapters of the novella at home and add their thoughts, ideas and questions to the interactive reading journal. In order to promote the students' use of the diary and active engagement, they were given a set of guiding questions and tasks each week (see Table 16.1 as an example).

As can be seen in Table 16.1, the tasks encouraged students to share their thoughts about the text (Task 1) and engage more deeply with the content of the novella (Task 2). Furthermore, the tasks encouraged them to discuss their ideas regarding selected aspects of the text (Task 3) and to share their questions with each other (Task 4). Last but not least, the students were also asked to reflect their individual reading experiences (Task 5).

Table 16.1 Guiding questions and tasks for week 4 of the project

	Tasks
1	What are your first thoughts after reading this chapter?
2	What shows that there are already problems in the leadership of the new government?
3	Discuss with one another. Do you think that the animals are fair to each other? Why or why not?
4	Here you can discuss contents, assumptions, or open questions you have and support each other.
5	Share your thoughts on your reading process for chapter 4 (problems, experiences).

> (3) The book contains many extremely effective scenes. Some are humorous or witty, others are bitterly ironic or pessimistic. Which scene did you find most memorable and effective? Why?
>
> T.
> 19.12.2020   14:12

> (4) Here you can discuss contents, assumptions, or open questions you have and support each other.
>
> E.
> 18.12.2020   22:23

> (5) How did you find your reading process for these chapters? (problems, experiences) Share your thoughts with each other.
>
> T.
> 19.12.2020   14:13

> 15.12.2020   22:39
> I like how the humans lost against the animals in the fight, because it's very unrealistic and funny.
>   N.

> 16.12.2020   10:45
> I think it was when boxer regrets that he "killed" an human because that shows how different he was and that he have a moral he was my fav character
>   S.

> 17.12.2020   11:01
> I agree with b. When napoleons dogs chased snowball off the farm it was the point where the reader knows that napoleon is a terrible leader
>   G.
> 18.12.2020   09:34

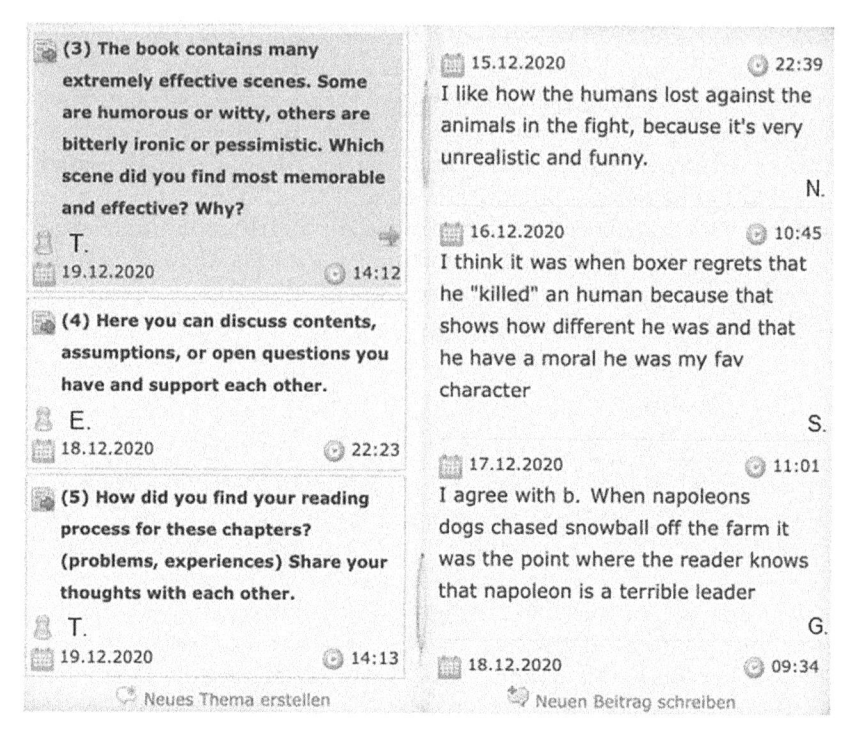

Figure 16.2 Example of a reading diary page

The tasks and questions were designed to promote students' reflexive as well as their linguistic-discursive competences, especially by encouraging the learners to exchange their questions, ideas and thoughts, and comment on each others' contributions respectfully (see Figure 16.2 for an example). Each project week would start with an in-class discussion of the students' reading log entries.

16.3.4 Selected results and discussion

Mrs Schmidt's overall impression that '[b]ooks are out [of fashion]' among adolescents was largely confirmed by the students' responses in the questionnaire survey. Fifty percent never read books in their free time, whereas the other 50% only spent up to one hour per week reading books. While the reasons for the unpopularity of books may vary, students mostly refrain from reading print books in English because they experience problems in understanding long sentences, colloquial language and what they deem to be 'old English'. Furthermore, students also expressed numerous challenges related to talking about literature in the English classroom. Due to gaps in their productive vocabulary, they find it hard to engage in discussions and are intimidated by speaking English in front of the whole

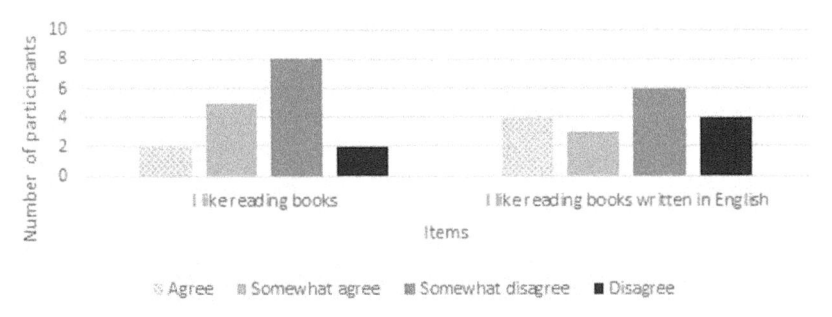

Figure 16.3 Students' attitudes towards reading books in general and in English

group. Some also claim that they cannot take part in in-class discussions, especially when spontaneous utterances are required.

With regard to RQ1, all students, as well as the teacher, stated in the pre-questionnaire that they use social media in their private lives, with most students using social media for between two and three hours, and five participants even spending between four and five hours on social media platforms such as Instagram (16 participants), YouTube (15 participants), WhatsApp (15 participants), Snapchat (15 participants) and TikTok (11 participants). Only one of the students had used LearningApps.org outside the classroom before. Interestingly, most participants indicated that they use social media for communicating with others and less for other pastime activities such as watching videos.

Despite the omnipresence and ubiquity of digital and social media in students' lives, digital tools and platforms are only scarcely used in the educational context of the class and seem mostly to be restricted to 'the classics', such as watching videos on YouTube or playing vocabulary games on Kahoot. Less than half of the participants had used social media in their English lessons (41%) and none of them had used digital tools in combination with literature. Similarly, Mrs Schmidt stated that she mostly uses YouTube videos to facilitate listening comprehension tasks, but not in combination with literary texts. However, all but one of the participants who had already worked with social media in their English classes found using them enjoyable. In contrast to the teacher, 10 students had already worked with LearningApps.org in school. Yet, they had mostly used it for submitting assignments and practicing their linguistic skills. Overall, the participants stated in the pre-questionnaire that they appreciate the use of digital media in general and social media in particular in their English lessons.

With regard to RQ2, the study results overall show that digital tools can potentially enhance students' traditional reading experiences as they help them to explore and critically engage with print-based literary texts, express their reactions to the text, and participate in (classroom) discussions with their peers. Although the number of students who answered the guiding questions varied slightly, on average 15 students participated in the discussions with eleven students participating every week, four students not completing the tasks between one and three times, and one student completing fewer than half of the assignments. On average, 56 contributions were posted each week. The use of a digital reading log was largely perceived as beneficial. In the pre-questionnaire, 16 out of 17 responded that the digital reading log would help them to better reflect on both their own reading process and on the content of the novella. After the sequence of lessons, 16 participants confirmed that the diary had helped them to reflect on their reading. Closely related to this, the students' answers revealed a number of perceived benefits of using a joint reading log, some of them are listed in the following. The digital reading log:

- encouraged me to engage with the novel on a deeper level;
- allowed me to reflect on my reading immediately or shortly after reading the chapter;
- made it possible for me to check how others were doing;
- helped me to see the story through the eyes of my peers;
- supported me in understanding the novel better;
- motivated me to reflect on my reading process in general.

Those students who considered the tasks less helpful mostly did so because they usually completed the assignments late in the evening, as anticipated by Mrs Schmidt.

As far as RQ3 is concerned, the results indicate that, as perceived by the study participants, the digital reading diary can promote students' linguistic-discursive and reflexive competences as well as most of the other sub-competences depicted in Figure 16.1. This underlines Surkamp's (2012: 82) assertion that all sub-competences work together. Here, the following student post may serve as an illustrative example as S12 subjectively responded to the text and was emotionally engaged (affective dimension), intentionally avoided logic in responding to the text (motivational dimension), and used language from the text to make their statement (linguistic-discursive dimension):

> I'm SHOCKED!!! Napoleon is crazy and super brutal! Napoleon no longer adheres to the motto 'Four Legs good, two legs bad'. He just kills everyone who doesn't follow him. (S 12)

In the pre-project interview, Mrs Schmidt explicitly stated that she anticipated the digital platform to have a positive motivational effect. She also assumed that the weekly tasks and questions would encourage students to complete their reading assignments. However, she did not expect the students to take the tasks seriously:

> On the other hand, I think that the exchange among the students can be very interesting. However, I believe that there will only be limited discussions as they are going to quickly complete the tasks the night before the lesson [and] that the opportunities for discussion will not be used as much as it would be possible.

Yet, in the post-project interview, Mrs Schmidt was positively surprised by the students' use of the platform. She stated: 'By dealing with the content before discussing it in the lesson, the students could more quickly engage in more profound discussions about the text in the classroom'. This perception is confirmed by the questionnaire results: some of the respondents stated that the questions helped them to engage more deeply with the novella, which, in turn, enabled them to contribute more actively to discussions during the lessons.

According to Surkamp (2012), linguistic-discursive competence comprises the students' ability to use their existing linguistic and discursive knowledge, make use of the language that the text offers to expand their own linguistic resources and discuss what they have read and convey their ideas and thoughts as they collaboratively create meaning (*gemeinsame Bedeutungsaushandlung*). All three components can be found in the analysis of the students' posts. They frequently employ expressions from the novel as the following examples illustrates:

> I think that the new principle that Snowball creates by reducing the 7 commandments to one contains the heart of Animalism. […]. (Week 3; S 16).

Furthermore, they actively asked for their fellow students' opinions to confirm their interpretations as the following diary excerpt shows:

> S 11 for sure! I don't like Napoleon at all! He's horrible! Does anyone agree with me?' (Week 5; S 12). (4)

Closely related to this, they negotiated meaning as the following examples from project week 2 and 7 illustrate:

> S 16: 'Who do you think took the milk away?!'
> […]
> S 14: 'Me too. The cat is suspicious.' (Week 2)
> S 3: 'At the end very unrealistic.'
> S 17: 'I think it doesn't have to be realistic. It's a fable and has the purpose of retelling the Russian revolution.' (Week 7)

Mrs Schmidt initially considered the journal's potential to promote students' communicative skills to be low as she expected her learners to revert to German on the platform. Yet, she changed her opinion in the post-interview, stating that by reading their peers' contributions the participants were provided with authentic language input from the text, which, despite possible language errors, could be more helpful and motivating than her, the teacher, providing it. However, while online chats can serve as authentic stimuli for in-class discussions, some of the participants explicitly stated in the post-questionnaire that online discussions cannot replace face-to-face discussions in the classroom:

> Taking up selected posts in class is, on the one hand, a token of appreciation, which cannot be expressed on the platform and, on the other hand, ideas can be developed further in face-to-face discussions. (S14)

The study also provides data regarding the development of the students' reflexive competences, as they frequently reflect on the actions of the characters and ethical and moral values inherent in the text, relate the content of the novella to their own lives, and reflect on their own reading processes. The following comment shows how one of the participants reflects the harsh living conditions of the animals:

> The first chapter of the book left me surprised and shocked. Of course, we all already know that animals live in very bad conditions, but it's actually sad getting it all from the perspective of the animals that are getting harmed. (Week 1; S 9)

With regard to the second dimension of the sub-competence, the following quote illustrates how one student relates one of the events in the novella to their own lived reality:

> [...] I've faced the exact same thing in reality and saw how powerful men try to push someone's name in dirt, because they couldn't be responsible for what they did. It is 'bitterly ironic' how easy they can convince other people. (Week 7; S 16)

As far as reflecting on their own reading is concerned, many of the students' comments relate to Surkamp's sub-competence cognitive I: reading comprehension (*kognitiv I: Leseverstehen*). Here, questions such as 'How fast did I read? How much did I understand? Which difficulties did I encounter?' were foregrounded as the following entry illustrates: 'I realised that I became a little bit faster in reading the chapter, although there were so many new words.' (S 17). Some of the comments also explicitly address the students' personal reception processes as well as how the platform helped them to critically look back at their own reading as one of the students poignantly puts it:

> I could probably get the message of the book without the reading diary but it was good that it has brought me to the point that I paid attention to every single part. (S 9)

Despite these positive results, some caveats should not be ignored. First, the vast majority of contributions on the social platform are rather short, with some contributions simply being copied or reposted more than once, often by the original author. Closely related to this, some of the students who rated the platform as beneficial in the pre-questionnaire, for example, found that the vocabulary used by their peers was too simple and thus did not help them to expand their own vocabulary and that some of the posts were too short. Even more importantly it was remarked that errors in the digital reading diary were not corrected by the teacher, which meant that they could not learn from each other's mistakes or improve their written English skills. Additionally, the use of the diary entries as discussion prompts was considered invasive by one student who thought of the platform as the students' private, personal space although it had never been framed as being this kind of space. These comments underline the importance of clear rules for using the diary, including, for example, a minimum number of words, but also to emphasize the fact that in-class discussions should not be limited to the content of a piece of literature but also its language. Last but not least, the layout of the platform was important to the students; a more user-friendly layout would have been conducive to more communication on the platform.

To conclude, the results of this admittedly small-scale study show that digital tools and platforms can potentially enrich the foreign language literature classroom, although digital media per se do not make learning better (cf. e.g. Schmidt & Strasser, 2016), especially as their didactic potential is not an inherent component of digital media (Koschel & Weyland, 2019: 43). Thus, the results are in line with existing research which emphasises the fact that it is important to consider how to bring digital and face-to-face learning together. Furthermore, modern foreign language teaching should also take into account both tools that students use outside the classroom as well as their 'in-the-wild readings', paying tribute to the fact that new forms of literature are evolving.

16.4 Born-Digital Literature in English Language Teaching

Undoubtedly, a paradigm shift away from the print to the digital format is taking place or as Hayles (2012: 56) already argued 10 years ago: 'people read less print, and they read print less well'. This assumption not only influences which (literary) texts we read with students, but also how we read and how we talk about them. However, despite the rapid developments in technology in recent years (Bündgens-Kosten & Schildhauer, 2021; Lütge & Merse, 2021) and the fact that we live in an era of digital ubiquity, both literary studies and English language teaching seem to remain slow in addressing the interactions between digital and print literacies (Hayles, 2012: 59) and filling the gaps in our existing knowledge. This is particularly concerning considering the fact that new literary text formats are evolving outside the classroom, many of which seem to be closer to traditionally non-literary formats such as video games than actual print literature (cf. Ensslin, 2014; Thomas, 2020). Without entering into the discussion on the literariness of video games and the gamelike qualities of digital fiction, it appears clear that students need to be prepared to think critically about these formats and how to read, analyse, and respond to them also with regard to developing their literary competence (cf. Section 16.2).

Most, if not all, of these texts can be subsumed under the umbrella of born-digital literature. Compared to print-based literature, born-digital, often synonymously referred to as electronic literature or e-literature, is a recent form of literature whose rather short history is inextricably linked with the advent of the computer (Hayles, 2008: 3; cf. also Rettberg, 2018: 203). Heckman and O'Sullivan (2018: n.p.) define electronic literature as 'work that could only exist in the space for which it was developed/written/coded – the digital space' while Wardrip-Fruin (2010: 29) understands digital literature as literature that requires 'digital computation'. For the purpose of this contribution, born-digital literature is defined as all literary texts which have originated in digital format, i.e. they have exclusively been created on, and for, digital devices, and have not originally existed in analogue format (for a more detailed and critical discussion of born-digital literature see, for example, Gibson, 2021; Hayles, 2004; Thomas, 2020).

Born-digital literature requires us to conceive literature in different and new ways as it challenges the traditional idea of the book as 'a stable, fixed object with [a] clear [beginning], [middle] and [end], or recognizable characters, plots and settings' (Thomas, 2020: 25). Furthermore, electronic literature – not necessarily in contrast to print text – comes in a lot of shapes and sizes (Rowberry, 2018: 319–332). There is a cornucopia of genres of electronic literature, such as interactive fiction, hypertext fiction, locative narratives, network fiction and generative texts (see Rettberg, 2018, for a more detailed discussion of some of the distinct genres of electronic literature) and more (sub-)genres will certainly be added as digital technologies evolve. These genres distinguish themselves from each other, for example, through the ways in which the user may enter, follow, or change the story. Despite their differences, there are some characteristics which most born-digital literary texts seem to share. First, electronic literature 'remains closely associated with nonlinear texts that foreground the activity and agency of the reader' (Thomas, 2020: 30). Second, it is multimodal as it often combines different semiotic systems such as written language, (moving) visuals, and audio, a shift which, Thomas (2020: 31) points out,

> is not solely determined by technological change, but is equally the result of the profound cultural shifts […] as literature adapts to rather than competes against other media and cultural forms.

Third, born-digital literature may never reach a state of fixity or completion as 'wreaders' add to a story, change, or share it; born-digital texts provide places where readers and authors congregate. Last but not least, born-digital literature is interactive. As Hammond (2016: 154) emphasises:

> Interactivity is the most recognizably innovative, potentially revolutionary, and intellectually intriguing of the born-digital affordances. Indeed, it is arguably the only born-digital affordance to offer something genuinely unprecedented to the literary experience. [...] There is no pre-digital version of a written text that asks you to act out the role of its protagonist, to determine the unfolding of the narrative, and to directly affect its outcome.

Social media provides new platforms for electronic literature to evolve, especially with the opportunities for collaboration, participation, and 'kinds of participatory performance' (Rettberg, 2018: 175 as cited in Thomas, 2020: 29) these platforms offer. With regard to the classroom, they require students as wreaders to access, engage with, and interpret literary texts in new ways. In other words, students have to acquire new forms of literacy as discussed in the following section.

16.4.1 #poetryisnotdead: *Instapoetry and TikTok poetry*

Digital media have brought about fundamental changes for writers as they increasingly use social media platforms for marketing and publicity but also to produce literary texts and interact with their fans and followers (Laing, 2017: 254–267). As Thomas (2020: 1) points out, social media platforms provide spaces for the 'production and dissemination of innovative creative works, as well as radically transforming modes of engagement with those works'. This seems to be more true for poetry than any other literary form. Poems first published on the internet, as well as using aspects associated with the internet (e.g. programming language in code poetry; Shakargy, 2020: 325–341) exist in superabundance. While some of them are original pieces of work, often deliberately using non-standard spelling or no punctuation, others are words put together from Google searches or composed from Spam mail content (Spam poetry) with the intent of 'abandoning anything that resembles traditional poetry' (Gittins, 2017: n.p.). Despite the harsh criticism it sometimes receives, for example that Instapoetry is nothing more than 'appropriation of self-help culture' (Pâquet, 2019: 296–314), some would go as far as to say that social media poetry has saved poetry from extinction. One thing seems to be sure though: the internet and social media in particular have changed the way poetry is viewed, as anyone can be a poet.

As discussed in the following, Instapoetry, as one example of born-digital literature (poetry), not only allows students to encounter literary texts on platforms they use on a daily basis but to actively act as wreaders as they intervene with the story through liking, sharing, or posting it as well as adding information of their own, often in form of music, images, or videos (cf. Barry, 2018: 68 as cited in Thomas, 2020: 30–21). While there seems to be no universal definition of Instapoetry, it is generally understood as modern-day poetry which is short, free-in-verse, straightforward, easily accessible and written with the intent of being shared, often accompanied by a photograph or drawing. Some of the most famous Instapoets, many of which publish across multiple networks, such as Atticus, Amanda Lovelace and Rui Kaur, have millions of followers and their poems have also been published in print with great success (cf. e.g. Thomas, 2020: 88).

Instapoems receive as much praise as harsh criticism (Penke, 2019: 451–479). While they are widely celebrated for being authentic, intense, and personal, they are also criticised for being simplistic, self-contained, and without context. As Berens (2019: n.p.) contends, Instapoetry is 'simplistic, little more taxing than reading a meme. It is almost always inspirational or emotional', alluding to the engaging nature of poetry shared on social media.

An even more recent emergent trend is poetry on TikTok, where poets share their experiences through oral performance poems. TikTok is currently the fastest growing social media app where users can create and post short videos. Especially among young people, TikTok has become one of the primary platforms to express themselves for example through singing, dancing, or lip-synching. According to the 2020 *JIM* study, a regular large-scale data collection which explores the media behaviour of 12 to 19 year-olds, TikTok has become the favorite social media platform of one in 10 teenagers, an increase of 9% compared to 2019 (Medienpädagogischer Forschungsverbund Südwest, 2020: 36).

TikTok is used by professional artists to showcase their work, but also by individual users to be creative as they read and perform classic and contemporary poems, often combined with music or text-on-screen elements. Furthermore, TikTok artists leave poetry recommendations for their followers, allowing them to choose poems depending on their moods. Poems on TikTok are easy to find under common hashtags such as #poetry or #poetrylover.

With regard to the foreign language classroom, Instapoetry and poetry videos on TikTok offer possibilities for students to engage in contemporary and authentic born-digital literature; a form of literature which 'transcends time and space boundaries in a globalized, digital world to remix language modes as part of the meaning-making process' (Kovalik & Curwood, 2019: 186). Thus, these modern forms of poetry can help improve students' multimodal literacies as well as their communicative skills (Passler, 2020) as they read, analyse and respond to Instapoems. Furthermore, the fact that Instagram and TikTok poems often tackle universal human themes, complex or even taboo issues, common social media problems such as cyberbullying or public shaming is a convincing reason to discuss them with students especially in order to enhance their critical literacies (cf. Becker, 2020; Gerlach, 2020; Ludwig & Summer, 2022).

16.4.2 Using *Instapoetry*: A practical classroom example

The potential of digital tools to make students' poetic encounters more manageable and enhance their personal engagement with born-print poems in the classroom has been explored in various publications on the topic (Ludwig, 2021: 209–232; Ludwig & Grubecki, 2022; Skorge, 2021: 57–68) Yet, as discussed in the preceding section, poetry is also thriving in the digital realm and (born-digital) poetry resembles the ways in which the younger generation communicates or, as the poet laureate, Carol Ann Duffy, put it in a *Guardian* interview (2011: n.p.):

> The poem is a form of texting [...] it's the original text. It's a perfecting of a feeling in language – it's a way of saying more with less, just as texting is. We've got to realise that the Facebook generation is the future – and, oddly enough, poetry is the perfect form for them. It's a kind of time capsule – it allows feelings and ideas to travel big distances in a very condensed form.

Thus, the potential of born-digital poetry for the classroom should not be eschewed but embraced by educators and teachers. The Digital Competence Framework 2.0 defines five key components. Reading and creating Instapoetry may be related to all five sub-competences as students should be able to manage, share and develop digital content appropriately, be aware of behavioural norms, manage their digital identities, and 'seek opportunities for self-empowerment and for participatory citizenship through appropriate digital technologies' (Vuorikari *et al.*, 2016: 8).

Instagram and TikTok may be short lived phenomena in the fast-paced social media world. Therefore, a lesson sequence on born-digital poetry should not simply focus on the discussed examples but also address both born-digital poetry and literature in general, allowing students to transfer what they have learned to other platforms and emerging formats and genres of born-digital literature. Here, questions such as the following appear to be vital, not least as they take into account the claim by the Stavanger Declaration Concerning the Future of Reading (COST, 2018) that 'students should be taught strategies they can use to master deep reading and higher-level reading processes on digital devices':

- *How do I read it?*
- *How do I engage with it?*
- *How do I write?*

The ensuing series of lessons follows the three guiding questions above and illustrates how Instagram and TikTok poetry can be approached both from a theoretical as well as practical angle as students analyse poetry and also create their own poems. The sequence encourages teachers to practice differentiation as students can decide whether they want to create a short, written poem, record their self-written poem for TikTok, or perform an existing (classic or modern) poem.

Step 1: How do I read it?

Real poems written in the style of an Instapoem, such as the following may provide a useful stepping stone towards studying Instapoetry, as the following two examples illustrate. In both poems the author takes a critical stance on everyday racism which is neither always overt nor explicit, also by using different (visual) techniques to enhance the meaning of his words.

Students could be asked to read the two poems and collect ideas of what they think could be common elements of Instapoems such as that they are short (free verse, epigrams, or blackout poetry), use consistent topics and themes, employ emotional language, are usually illustrated, and explore the *conditio humana*. Yet, as Strickland (2009: n.p.) suggests, 'reading e-literature requires taking an aesthetic attitude toward the textscape as an object that stimulates the sense'. Thus, aspects such as color, spacing, capitalisation, or font seem to be equally important as figurative devices to imagery.

Step 2: How do I engage with it?

Now that students are familiar with some of the main characteristics of Instapoetry, they could be asked to collect ideas on how to intervene with existing poems, including following the poet, liking or sharing it, or leaving a comment.

Step 3: How do I write?

During the last stage, students are asked to write their own Instapoem, paying attention to the characteristics of Instapoems collected at the beginning of the lesson. They should pay attention to the following guiding questions:

- *Which topic do I want to write about?*
- *Which canvas do I want to use?*
- *Which photos do I want to use?*
- *What do I want to use the caption for (e.g. explaining the poem)?*
- *Which hashtags would I like to use?*
- *Which imagery do I want to use?*

Regardless of whether students share their Instapoems or not, critical aspects of posting poems on Instagram should not be ignored but

Danilo Killisch

black and white
in art: harmonious
in life: ...

Is it called racism
 because somebody
  always wants to
   be faster
    than somebody else...?

d. k. 2021

Liked by C. L. and 1,212 others
Danilo Killisch "black and white in art harmonious in life..."

View all 42 comments

Figure 16.4 Example of two Instapoems in one post

explicitly addressed in the classroom. We want students to navigate the digital space safely, and also understand the power structures that shape media representations, including born-digital literary texts. These critical issues include, among others, cybersecurity, cyberbullying and harassment as well as the terabytes of data that are harvested from Instapoets and their followers (cf. e.g. Vuorikari et al., 2016).

16.5 Conclusion

Digital technology may be viewed as stealing the limelight from print-based literature in the classroom. Yet, digital tools can help students engage with literature in new and different ways. Moreover, as the margins between print-based and born-digital literature are vanishing, born-digital texts provide opportunities for students to indulge in the multi-modal experience of both reading and using new forms of literature.

References

Alter, G. and Ratheiser, U. (2019) A new model of literary competences and the revised *CEFR* descriptors. *ELT Journal*. See https://doi.org/10.1093/elt/ccz024 (accessed December 2019).

Androutsopoulos, J. (2011) Language change and digital media: A review of conceptions and evidence. In N. Coupland and T. Kristiansen (eds) *Standard Languages and Language Standards in a Changing Europe* (pp. 145–159). Novus Press.

Barry, R. (2018) A Media of One's Own: The Future of Criticism, in Retrospect. In H. Barekat, R. Barry, and D. Winters (eds) *The Digital Critic: Literary Culture Online* (pp. 68–78). OR Books.

Becker, D. (2020) Global, Digital and (Slightly) Scary: New Forms of English Literature in The EFL Classroom. Workshop at Teachers' Day 2020 (Saarbrücken, 1 October)

Berens, K.I. (2019) E-Lit's #1 Hit: Is Instagram Poetry E-literature? See https://electronicbookreview.com/essay/e-lits-1-hit-is-instagram-poetry-e-literature/ (accessed December 2021).

Bland, J. (2018) Introduction: The challenge of literature. In J. Bland (ed.) *Using Literature in English Language Education Challenging Reading for 8–18 Year Olds* (pp. 1–22). Bloomsbury.

Blume, O.M. (2007) Die Lücke schließen. Versuch eines Kompetenzmodells zur Textarbeit. *Der Fremdsprachliche Unterricht Französisch* 41 (28), 36–41.

Brumfit, C. and Carter, R. (1986) *Literature and Language Teaching*. Oxford University Press.

Bündgens-Kosten, J. and Schildhauer, P. (eds) (2021) *Englischunterricht in einer digitalisierten Gesellschaft*. Beltz Juventa.

Burwitz-Melzer, E. (2007) Ein Lesekompetenzmodell für den fremdsprachlichen Literaturunterricht. In L. Bredella and W. Hallet (eds) *Literaturunterricht, Kompetenzen und Bildung* (pp. 27–157). WVT.

COST = The European Cooperation in Science and Technology; E-READ = Evolution of Reading in the age of digitisation (2018) The Stavanger Declaration Concerning the Future of Reading. See ereadcost.eu/wp-content/uploads/2019/01/StavangerDeclaration.pdf (accessed November 2021).

Council of Europe (2001) *Common European Framework of References for Languages: Learning, Teaching, Assessment*. Cambridge University Press.

Council of Europe (2018) *Common European Framework of References for Languages: Learning, Teaching, Assessment. Companion Volume with New Descriptors*. Council of Europe.

Decke-Cornill, H. and Küster, L. (2010) *Fremdsprachendidaktik*. Narr Francke Attempto.

Delgado, P., Vargas, C., Ackerman, R. and Salmerón, L. (2018) Don't throw away your printed books: A meta-analysis on the effects of reading media on reading comprehension. *Educational Research Review* 25, 23–38.

Diehr, B. and Surkamp, C. (2015) Die Entwicklung literaturbezogener Kompetenzen in der Sekundarstufe I: Modellierung, Abschlussprofil und Evaluation. In W. Hallet, C. Surkamp, and U. Krämer (eds) *Literaturkompetenzen Englisch. Modellierung – Curriculum – Unterrichtsbeispiele* (pp. 21–40). Friedrich.

Dorn, L.J. and Soffas, C. (2005) *Teaching for Deep Comprehension*. Stenhouse Publishers.

Duffy, C.A. (2011) Poems are a form of texting. *The Guardian*, 5 September. See www.theguardian.com/education/2011/sep/05/carol-ann-duffy-poetry-texting-competition (accessed December 2021).

Ensslin, A. (2014) *Literary Gaming*. MIT Press.

Gabrielsen, I.L., Blikstad-Balas, M. and Tengberg, M. (2019) The role of literature in the classroom: How and for what purposes do teachers in lower secondary school use literary texts? *L1- Educational Studies in Language and Literature* 19 (1), 1–32.

Gerlach, D. (ed.) (2020) *Kritische Fremdsprachendidaktik: Grundlagen, Ziele, Beispiele*. Narr Francke Attempto.

Gibson, R.H. (2021) *Paper Electronic Literature: An Archaeology of Born-Digital Materials*. University of Massachusetts.

Gittins, P. (2017) Internet Poetry. *The London Magazine*. See www.thelondonmagazine.org/essay-internet-poetry-paul-gittins/ (accessed December 2021).

Gliksman, S. (2015) *Creating Media for Learning: Student-Centered Projects Across the Curriculum*. Corwin.

Groenke, S., Maples, J. (2010) Young Adult Literature Goes Digital: Will Teen Reading Ever Be the Same? *The ALAN Review* 37 (3), 38–44.

Hallet, W. (2009) Romanlektüre und Kompetenzentwicklung: Vom narrativen Diskurs zur Diskursfähigkeit. In W. Hallet and A. Nünning (eds) *Romandidaktik: Theoretische Grundlagen, Methoden, Lektüreanregungen* (pp. 73–88). WVT.

Hammond, A. (2016) *Literature in the Digital Age*. Cambridge University Press.

Hayles, N.K. (2004) 'Print is Flat, Code is Deep: The Importance of Media-Specific Analysis.' *Poetics Today* 25 (1), 67–90.

Hayles, N.K. (2007) Hyper and Deep Attention: The Generational Divide in Cognitive Modes. *Profession*, 187–199.

Hayles, N.K. (2008) *Electronic Literature: New Horizons for the Literary*. University of Notre Dame.

Hayles, N.K. (2012) *How We Think: Digital Media and Contemporary Technogenesis*. University of Chicago Press.

Heckman, D. and O'Sullivan, J. (2018) Electronic Literature: Contexts and Poetics. Literary Studies in the Digital Age. An Evolving Anthology. See https://dlsanthology.mla.hcommons.org/electronic-literature-contexts-and-poetics/ (accessed December 2021).

Hetland, T. (2016) *Teaching Literature with Digital Technology: Assignments*. Bedford Books.

Johnson, M.J. (2021) *Books and Social Media: How the Digital Age is Shaping the Printed Word*. Routledge.

Koschel, W. and Weyland, U. (2019) Das Potenzial digitaler Medien im Unterricht. *Pflegezeitschrift* 72, 42–44.

Kovalik, K. and Curwood, J.S. (2019) #poetryisnotdead: Understanding Instagram poetry within a transliteracies framework. *Literacy* 53 (4), 185–195.

Laing, A. (2017) Authors Using Social Media: Layers of Identity and the Online Author Community. *Publishing Research Quarterly* 33 (2), 254–267.

Landow, G.P. (1992) *Hypertext: The Convergence of Contemporary Critical Theory and Technology*. Johns Hopkins University Press.

Lockhurst, R. (2016) Modern literature and technology. See www.bl.uk/20th-century-literature/articles/modern-literature-and-technology (accessed December 2021).

Lopera Medina, S. (2013) Diary Insights of an EFL Reading Teacher. *Profile* 15 (2), 115–126.

Ludwig, C. (2021) Teaching Literature with Digital Media. In C. Lütge and T. Merse (eds) *Digital Teaching and Learning: Perspectives for English Language Education* (pp. 209–232). Narr Francke Attempto.

Ludwig, C. (2022) *Digital Englisch unterrichten: Grundlagen, Impulse und Perspektiven*. Friedrich Verlag.

Ludwig, C. and Grubecki, D. (2022) 'Every word is a poem': Mehrsprachige Gedichte im Englischunterricht'. In C. Ludwig and M. Sambanis (eds) *English and beyond: Impulse zur Förderung von Mehrsprachigkeit im Englischunterricht* (59–63). Brigg Verlag.

Ludwig, C. and Summer, T. (2022) *Taboos and Challenging Topics in Foreign Language Education: An Introduction*. Routledge.

Lütge, C. and Merse, T. (2021) Revisiting Digital Education: Dialogues and Dynamics in Foreign Language Teaching and Learning. In C. Lütge and T. Merse (eds) *Digital Teaching and Learning: Perspectives for English Language Education* (pp. 9–20). Narr Francke Attempto.

Lütge, C., Merse, T., Owczarek, C. and Stannard, M. (2019) Crossovers: Digitalization and Literature in Foreign Language Education. *Studies in Second Language Learning and Teaching* 3/2019, 519–540.

Mpfs – Medienpädagogischer Forschungsverbund Südwest (ed.) (2020) JIM-Studie 2020 – Jugend, Information, Medien. Basisuntersuchung zum Medienumgang 12- bis 19-Jähriger. See www.mpfs.de/fileadmin/files/Studien/JIM/2020/JIM-Studie-2020_Web_final.pdf (accessed December 2021).

Orwell, G. (2008[1945]) *Animal Farm*. Penguin.

Paran, A. (2010) Between Scylla and Charybdis: The Dilemma of Testing Language and Literature. In A. Paran and L. Sercu (eds) *New Perspectives on Language and Education: Testing the Untestable in Language Education* (pp. 143–164). Multilingual Matters.

Passler, A. (2020) #instapoetry in the EFL Classroom. The What, the Why and the How. Unpublished MA thesis, Universität Innsbruck.

Pâquet, L. (2019) Selfie-Help: The Multimodal Appeal of Instagram Poetry. *The Journal of Popular Culture* 52 (2), 296–314.

Penke, N. (2019) '#instapoetry. Populäre Lyrik auf Instagram und ihre Affordanzen. *Zeitschrift für Literaturwissenschaft und Linguistik* 49, 451–475.

Rettberg, S.R. (2018) *Electronic Literature*. Polity Press.

Rössler, A. (2010) Literarische Kompetenzen. In F.J. Meißner and B. Tesch (eds) *Spanisch kompetenzorientiert unterrichten* (pp. 31–136). Klett.

Rowberry S. (2018) Continuous, not discrete: The mutual influence of digital and physical literature. *Convergence* 26 (2), 319–332.

Sambanis, M. (2020) Potenziale und Grenzen von digitalen Medien: Befunde aus der Neurowissenschaft, Psychologie, Pädagogik und der Fremdsprachendidaktik. In M. Eisenmann and J. Steinbock (eds) *Sprachen, Kulturen, Identitäten: Umbrüche durch Digitalisierung? – Dokumentation zum 28. Kongress für Fremdsprachendidaktik der Deutschen Gesellschaft für Fremdsprachenforschung (DGFF)* (pp. 203–214). Schneider.

Sauro, S. (2017) Online Fan Practices and CALL. *CALICO Journal* 34 (2), 131–146.

Schmidt, T. and Strasser, T. (2016) Digital classroom. *Der fremdsprachliche Unterricht Englisch* 50, 144, 2–7.

Shakargy, N. (2020) Internetica: Poetry in the digital age. *International Journal of Cultural Studies* 24 (2), 325–341.

Skorge, P. (2021) Poetry writing in the secondary EFL classroom – digitally triggered and transfigured. In J. Bündgens-Kosten and P. Schildhauer (eds) *Englischunterricht in einer digitalisierten Gesellschaft* (pp. 57–68). Beltz Juventa.

Spiro, J. (1991) Assessing Literature: Four Papers. In C. Brumfit (ed.) *Assessment in Literature* (pp. 16–83). Macmillan.

Steininger, I. (2014) *Modellierung literarischer Kompetenz. Eine qualitative Studie im Fremdsprachenunterricht der Sekundarstufe I*. Narr.
Strickland, S. (2009) Born Digital. The Poetry Foundation. See www.poetryfoundation.org/articles/69224/born-digital (accessed December 2021).
Surkamp, C. (2012) Literarische Texte im kompetenzorientierten Fremdsprachenunterricht. In W. Hallet and U. Krämer (eds) *Kompetenzaufgaben im Englischunterricht: Grundlagen und Unterrichtsbeispiele* (pp. 7–90). Klett.
Thomas, B. (2020) *Literature and Social Media*. Routledge.
Vuorikari, R., Punie, Y., Carretero Gomez, S. and Van Den Brande, L. (2016) *DigComp 2.0: The Digital Competence Framework for Citizens. Update Phase 1: The Conceptual Reference Model*. Publication Office of the European Union.
Wardrip-Fruin, N. (2010) Five Elements of Digital Literature. In R. Simanowski, J. Schäfer and P. Gendolla (eds) *Reading Moving Letters: Digital Literature in Research and Teaching A Handbook* (pp. 26–57). Transcript.
Woodruff, A.H. and Griffin, R.A. (2017) Reader response in secondary settings: Increasing comprehension through meaningful interactions with literary texts. *Texas Journal of Literacy Education* 5 (2), 108–116.

Index

\# symbol 76
\#notmypresident (#nmp) 75, 76, 78, 81–84

21st Century Skills 125
80 days 242

Abbas, P.J. 177
Abbasova, M. 137
abbreviations 31, 32, 49, 78
Abihsira, V. 34
academic integrity 154–162
Ackermann, J. 122, 123
actor-network theory 93
'added value' 55
addressee orientation 128
affective contouring 75
affiliations 8
affordances
　AI-generated texts 140
　as concept 32, 33–34
　definition 76
　devices 58, 175, 223, 227
　digital literacies 125, 236
　digital storybook apps 237
　digital text creation 187
　digitally-mediated tasks 57, 58
　discursive affordances 79–81, 83, 87
　hashtags 71–88
　linguistic affordances 36, 37, 77–79, 84
　live text 107
　mobile-assisted language learning (MALL) framework 223
agency
　artificial intelligence (AI) 141
　to burst bubbles 90
　collective agency 209
　computational agents 94
　of learners 60, 79
　locative media 225
　mobile-assisted language learning (MALL) framework 222
Ahmed, K. 163, 165
AI Video Generator 166
Aitwani, S. 6
algorithms
　algorithmicity 8, 90, 94, 102–103
　blackbox algorithms 94
　debiasing techniques 161
　filter bubbles on Instagram 89–105
　student understanding of 97–102
　teacher education 141
Alice for the iPad 240–242
Aljaad, N.H.M.A. 182
Allwright, D. 204, 209, 210
Alter, G. 216, 250
alternate reality gaming 58
alternate worlds 126
American International Consortium of Academic Libraries (AMICAL) 155
Amiri, F. 141
Androutsopoulos, J. 30, 32, 38, 247
Animal Farm (Orwell, 1945) 253
Animal Safari 60–66
animations 49, 50, 59, 131, 182, 234, 235, 237–239, 240–241, 243
anime 47, 213, 214
annotative locative media 224
anonymity 9
antisocial behaviours 52
APA 157–158
Appel, G. 158
appellative functions 76, 78
applied linguistics 107
artificial intelligence (AI)
　AI-generated texts 137–152
　Artificial Intelligence-Mediated Communication (AI-MC) 137–138
　and the digital writing process 153–172

arts 5
assessment 250
asynchronous writing 190, 191
audience design 35
audience participation 111
audio
   device affordances for audio recordings 58, 227
   digital literature 260
   games as audiovisual texts 124
   integral versus marginal part of texts 46–47
   reading-out functions on books 239, 240
   voice recordings 227
Australia 51
authentic problems in tasks 59, 113, 127–128, 156
authentication 160–161
authenticity in texts 19, 58, 189, 199, 257
author-reader, blurred line between 13 see also 'wreaders'
authorship
   Artificial Intelligence-Mediated Communication (AI-MC) 138, 157–158
   born-digital texts 12, 13
   collaborative authorship 12
autonomous learning 2, 58, 64, 199, 216, 222, 239, 242 see also choice, student
Auto-Peer 168, 169

Baker, S. 64
Bal, M. 72
Ballweg, S. 62
Bankhead III, M. 156
Bär, M. 124
Bard 159, 161, 163, 164–165, 166
Barton, D. 15, 34, 35, 39, 44
Bateman, J. 109, 113
Battelle for Kids 125
Beagrie, N. 43
Beam, M.A. 90
Beaugrande, R. 10, 11
Beavis, C. 13
Becker, D. 129, 130, 132
Becker-Mrotzek, M. 233
Beer, D. 107, 187
behaviorist approaches 178

Behizadeh, N. 189, 199
Bell, A. 35
Bell, F. 177
Berens, K.I. 262
beta readers 214–215
bias 51–52, 93, 97, 160
Bieswanger, M. 32
big data 8, 92
Bildungsstandards für die Allgemeine Hochschulreife 127, 128
Bing 158, 161, 163, 164, 166, 167
bitmoji 190, 196
BitsBoard vocab cards 65
Black, R.W. 55, 188, 208
Black Lives Matter 96
blackbox algorithms 94
Bland, J. 207, 250
Blank, G. 92, 93
blogs 34, 58, 106, 107, 117n(3)
Blommaert, J. 111
Blume, C. 64, 132
books, as haptic object 12
born-digital, definition of 10, 42–43, 138–139
Boud, D. 168
boundaries of literacy, establishing 45
brainstorming 163–165
Brennan, S.E. 31
Brinda, T. 221
Brinker, K. 73
Brooks, M. 20
Brumfit, C. 250
Brundidge, J. 92
Bruns, A. 90, 91, 92
Brunsmeier, S. 237, 239, 240, 243, 244
Bucher, T. 33, 34
Bündgens-Kosten, J. 129, 259
Burns, A. 78
Burriss, S.K. 93, 94
Burrows, R. 107
Burwell, C. 124, 129
Busch, F. 36, 37, 38

Çakir, D.C. 124
calendar aphorisms 74
Call-Cummings, M. 191
Cameron, D. 45
canon, traditional 48
capitalization 110
Carrillo, C. 143
Carrington, V. 1, 93

Carter, R. 250
Caruso, C. 58, 59, 60, 61
Castro, R.D.R. 176
CEFR (Common European Framework of Reference) 86, 113, 127, 128, 216, 250
Charta of Digital Education (2020) 141, 142
chatbots 138
ChatGPT 154, 157–158, 159–160, 161, 162, 163, 169
Chavez, F.R. 199, 200
choice, student 189, 194, 197, 206–207
Chovanec, J. 106, 107, 111
Chubb, J. 157
Chung, M. 98
chunks 59, 66, 239
circulations 8
citations 140, 157–158, 159
citizenship 8, 48, 93, 221, 263
classroom design 188–189, 199
clicks 9
climate change discourse 102
close reading 80, 85
co-construction
    of context 35
    discursive affordances 80
    human/non-human agents 94
    of knowledge 177
    of meaning 36, 180, 257
    multimodal texts 188
    negotiation of meaning 59, 63, 257
CoDi 166
coding 139, 144, 169
coercive power 51
cognitivism 177–178, 179
coherence 11, 73, 177, 241, 243
Coiro, J. 113
cold start problems 94–95
Cole, M. 44
collaborative authorship 12
collaborative data analysis 191
collaborative learning 51, 65, 180–182, 257
collaborative problem-solving 8
college-level writing 153–172
collocations 77
Comber, B. 188, 189, 199
comedy journalism 112
comics 47, 205
Comiket 205–206

commentary-style writing 110
comments 8, 13, 213
communality 6–7
communicating of the self as a narrative 123
communication studies 107
communicative affordances 78–80, 84
communicative competences 58, 59, 61, 78–80, 86, 127–128
communicative contouring 75, 77, 79
communicative frames 75
communicative functions 11, 73, 75, 77
Communities of Practice 7, 19
community membership 8
Community of Inquiry 143
community-building 179
Companion Volume CEFR 86, 216, 250
composition 186
comprehension monitoring 64
computational agents 94
computer-mediated communication 31, 32
Connected Learning 188
Conners, J.L. 98
connotative interpretations 47
Consensus 166
constructivism 56, 177–178 *see also* social constructivism
contect-specific learning materials 18
context collapse 35
context design 35–36
contextualization cues 37
convergence culture 205
cooperative learning 144
Cope, B. 80, 114, 221
Coppa, F. 208
Coppola, S. 186, 198
copyright 43, 140, 158
corpus analysis 78, 110
cosmopolitan practice 6
cosplay 205
COST (Stavanger Declaration Concerning the Future of Reading) 248, 263
Coughlan, S. 9
Council of Europe 79, 86, 93, 128, 216, 236
Covid-19 51, 96, 175, 177, 179, 190, 192
creation tasks 186–203, 223
creative use of language 58
creativity and AI 157, 163

creators of born-digital texts 50
credibility of information 9, 160–161
Creswell, J.W. 179–180
critical analysis assignments 157, 162–163
critical digital literacy framework 89–105
Critical Discourse Analysis 95
critical ethnography 50
critical geography 189
critical literacy 93, 94, 187, 215
critical reflection 62, 114, 221, 223–224, 227
critical self-reflection 62
critical thinking 125, 250, 255
cross-boundary collaboration 179
cross-disciplinary research 147–148
  see also interdisciplinarity
crossovers 213–214
Crystal, D. 30, 32
cultural agency, students' 57, 221–222
cultural bias 51–52
cultural capital 48, 50
cultural diversity 50–52, 80, 155, 217
cultural heritage 48
cultural processes 5
Curwood, J.S. 262
cyberbullying 265
Czerviewicz, L. 181

DALL-E 159, 167
Dalton, B. 235
dark side of information society 9
data analysis 180
data coding 180
data protection 158
data security 132, 265
Davidson, C. 1, 15, 50
Davison, W. 97
De Jager, L. 175, 177, 178, 182
debiasing techniques 161
debunking 161
decentralized cultural production 8
deficit views of digitally-mediated communication 31, 38
Del Vicario, M. 9, 89, 91
Delagrange, S.H. 46, 52
Delgado, P. 249
democratic citizenship 8, 93
Dertinger, A. 222–223
Descript 166
descriptive case study methods 178

Developmental Language Disorder (DLD) 56, 62–66
devices 58, 175, 223, 227
dictionaries 59, 65, 177
Diehr, B. 79
Dietrich, L. 176
differentiation 56, 62
digital biosphere 3
digital competence 16, 138, 141, 147, 148, 221, 237
Digital Competence Framework 17, 18, 38
Digital Competence Framework for Educators (DigCompEdu) 141, 144, 236
digital condition 5
digital culture, living in 2–9, 89
digital exclusion/inequality 50, 174
digital humanities 19
digital journalism 106
digital literacies 125, 141, 174, 183–184, 204, 215, 233, 235, 236–237, 248
digital literature 235, 247–269
digital natives 138, 176, 178
digital preservation 43
digital reading logs 248, 253–259
digital reading skills 49–50
digital storybook apps 233–246
digital text creation 186–203
digital tools for scaffolding 59
digital wilds 215
digital-for-print 43, 45
digitalization 1, 174
digitally-enhanced teaching 221
digitally-mediated interaction (DMI) 30–41
digitally-mediated tasks 55–70
digitized physical writing 195–196
discourse analysis 95
discourse communities 166
discourse competences 80–81, 85, 86
discursive affordances 79–81, 83, 87
discussion groups (online) 177, 181
disinformation 160
dispreferred responses 37
document analysis 179
Donick, M. 126
Dorn, L.J. 251
Dressler, W.U. 10, 11
Dubois, E. 92, 93
Duffy, C.A. 263

Dyer, M. 242
Dyson, A.H. 188, 199

Eaton, S.E. 154
Ebersöhn, L. 177, 178
echo chambers 90–91, 92
Eick, D. 13
Eisenmann, M. 235, 236
eLearning 143
elementary classrooms 187, 188
Elicit.org 165
e-literature 260, 264
elliptic constructions 73, 78, 84
Ellis, R. 59
email 140, 143
emojis 31, 36, 192
emoticons 31, 32, 36
emotional intelligence 178
emotional meaning 47, 123, 126, 238–239, 250
empathy 71, 250
emulated speech 110
English as a lingua franca 57, 127
English literature 48
entertainment 112, 183, 235
e-publishing 46
Erway, R. 10
ethical guidelines 161
ethical literacy 215
ethical questions 126, 147, 156
ethnographic research 228
ethnography of communication 35
European literature 48
evaluation 148, 216
everyday practice, measuring learning effectiveness by 228
exclusion of certain texts from the classroom 48
'exclusively digital' texts 43
Exley, B. 46
exophoric reference 110
experimental research 92, 95, 99–100, 103
ExplainPaper 166
Exploratory Practice (EP) framework 204, 209–211, 213, 217

Facebook 9, 177, 179–180
fact-checking 161
fake news 98, 99
false information 159, 160

fanfiction 58, 188, 204–219
FanTales 217
Faustina Joan, S.P. 139
favoriting 33, 34
fear of change 42
feedback 168–169, 182
feeds (social media) 89, 95
Ferrara, E. 147
Ferrari, A. 16, 221
Fibriasari, H. 239
fiction 204–219
Field, H. 159
figurative meanings 76
filter bubbles on Instagram 89–105
FINaLe model 237–238, 240
'finding your tribe' 9
Fink, L. 190
Fischer, S. 123
Fletcher, J. 187
Flick, U. 180
Flip 215
Flores, M.A. 143
Floridi, L. 3, 4
folksonomies 17
formulaic expressions 74, 110
forums 32
Framework of Digital Literacies 17
Frisch, S. 79
Frissen, V. 4
Frontiers 157
full stops 36–37
functional communicative competence 128

Gabrielsen, I.L. 249
gaming
    alternate reality gaming 58
    digital literature 235
    digital storybook apps 238
    gamification of learning tasks 148
    gamification of society 4
    gaming clans 58
    Japanese popular culture 205
    Let's Plays (LPs) 122–136
    literariness 260
    location-based technologies 220
    as pedagogical tool 124–126
    software code as digital text 139
    writing games 188
García, O. 60
Gardner, H. 158

Garrison, R. 143
Gass, S.M. 62
Gee, J.P. 44
gender differences 125
generative AI 154–162, 163
Generative Pretrained Transformer 3 (GPT3) 138, 140
genre
  blogs 34
  digital literature 260
  digitally-mediated interaction (DMI) as new 31
  internet novels 206
  modified genre structures 49
  writing instruction 187
Georgakopoulou, A. 14
Gerlach, D. 56, 94
Germany 220, 238, 249, 252
gesture 47
Gibson, J.J. 33, 76
Giesau, M. 133
Gillespie, N. 147
Giovanelli, M. 48
Girmen, P. 14
Gittins, P. 261
Given, L.M. 159, 160, 161
Glaser, U. 138
Global State of Digital report (2022) 33, 38
globalization 79, 80
Gmail 140, 143
Goggin, G. 224
Goh, C.C.M. 78
González-Lloret, M. 58
Google 7, 8
Google Bard 159, 161, 163, 164–165, 166
Google MyMaps 221, 225–227
Google Translate 155
Göpferich, S. 73
Gralley, J. 234
grammar *see* syntax
grammar checkers 157, 177, 182
graphic novels 47
Grau, M. 58
Griffin, R.A. 251
Grimm, N. 56, 57, 65
Grosche, M. 56
Grubecki, D. 263
Grünberger, N. 123
Guardian, The 108, 115–117
guided tours 225–228

Gumbo, M.T. 176
Gutierrez, A. 43

Haenlien, M. 137
Hafner, C.A. 31–32, 94, 125
Hallet, W. 57, 80, 81, 85, 86, 99, 127, 233, 236
hallucinations 159
Halverson, E.R. 188, 199
Hamilton, K. 161
Hammond, A. 206, 249, 261
Han, B. 2–3, 4, 9
Hancock, J.T. 137, 138, 140, 145, 148
Hanks, J. 204, 209, 210, 211
Harris, R. 50
hashtags 71–88, 262
Haugen, F. 9
Hausendorf, H. 73–74, 75
Hauser, S. 106, 110
Hautzinger, N. 12
Hawisher, G. 42, 43, 46, 47, 186
Hayles, N.K. 247–248, 259, 260
Heap, J.L. 155
heart/like buttons 34
Heckman, D. 260
Heick, T. 169
Heidkamp, B. 12
Heinz, S. 222
Helmond, A. 33, 34
Hendricks, J. 159
Hennekes, M.A. 129
Hepp, A. 1, 220
Herring, S.C. 31, 32
heterogeneity in the classroom 56–57, 60–66
Hicks, T. 186, 187
hierarchies of analogue/born-digital texts 48–50
Hill, S.J. 92
Hillesund, T. 234
Hirvela, A. 144
Hitchcock, E. 15
Hofmann, J. 58
Hohenstein, J. 140, 141
Holmes, W. 19
homo ludens 4
Honan, E. 20
Houghton, K.J. 31, 37
Hübner, A. 132
Huizinga, J. 4
humor 112

Humphrys, J. 31
Hutson, M. 140
Hutz, M. 77
hybridity
    hybrid analogue-digital tasks 59
    hybrid learning tasks 46
    Let's Plays (LPs) 124
    live text 106–121
    remixed digital texts 5, 124, 213
hyperlinks 49, 74
hypermodality 49
hypernyms 77
hypertextuality 235, 247

identity
    as a reader 208
    revelation of 9
    as a writer 187, 189
ideological questions
    filter bubbles on Instagram 96
    hierarchies of analogue/born-digital texts 48
    text selection in the classroom 49
    which texts 'count' 45
ignorability assumption 92
images
    AI-generated texts 167
    creators of born-digital texts 50
    digital literature 260
    digital storybook apps 237, 238
    digital tools for scaffolding 59
    image-based analogue texts 47
    integral versus marginal part of texts 46–67
    layout/presentation 47, 108
    live text 111
    parallel text-image relations 238
    placement of images 47
immersive exposition to linguistic input 127
immersive imaginative texts 124, 126
Imo, W. 36
imperatives 75, 78, 85
inclusion, definition of 55–56
inclusive EFL classrooms 55–70
inclusive teaching approaches 56, 59
incomplete texts 78
indigenous cultural references 204
indigenous knowledge systems 176
Indigenous students 51
individualized learning needs 56, 57, 59
inductive thematic analysis 180

inequalities 156, 174
InferKit 138, 140, 142
inforgs 3
informal learning 215
informal reading 206
informal writing practices 110, 112, 113
information diversity 92–93
information overload 3
information skills 114
infosphere 3
in-service teacher education 20, 144
insider/collective knowledge 111
Instagram 34, 50, 89–105, 155, 179–180, 190, 263
instant messaging 49 *see also* WhatsApp
Instapoetry 248, 261–265
instructivism 56
intellectual property 158 *see also* copyright
intelligent tutoring systems 19
interactional (socio)linguistics 36
interactive texts
    algorithmicity 90
    digital literature 261
    digital storybook apps 237, 240, 243
    fanfiction 216
    hashtags 75
    Let's Plays (LPs) 123
    live text 106–107, 111
interactive whiteboards 65
intercultural competences 58, 62, 114, 138
interdisciplinarity 125, 147–148, 183, 248
interest networks 89, 111
interjections 110
International Center for Academic Integrity 154
internet access 174, 183, 220, 233
interpersonal skills 80, 141, 145
interpretivist approaches 178
intertextuality 199
invitation to action 76, 78, 111

Jackson, D. 106
Japanese students 204–219
Jenkins, H. 8, 9, 58, 205, 208
Johnson, M.J. 247
Jonassen, D.H. 179
Jones, R.D. 127
Jones, R.H. 31–32, 94, 125

journalism 106–121
journals 157, 166
Jung, M. 140, 141

Kahoot 255
Kalantzis, M. 80, 114, 221, 236
Kaminski, A. 239
Kammerl, R. 222–223
Kaplan, A. 137
Kelley, K.J. 154
Kelley, S. 206
Kemper, K. 102
Kenya 176
Kergel, D. 12
Kerres, M. 57
Kersten, S. 78
Kesson, H. 14
Kieffer, M.J. 50
Kim, N. 98
Kittle, P. 200
Klee, M. 161
Klumpp, T. 63, 64
Knobel, M. 2, 16
knowledge
  co-construction 177
  indigenous knowledge systems 176
  insider/collective knowledge 111
  knowledge distribution 58
  legitimate forms of knowledge 48
  sociocultural context of knowledge construction 177
  Technological Pedagogical Content Knowledge (TPACK) model 175, 176–178, 184
Koehler, M. 175, 176
Kolb, A. 237, 239, 243, 244
Költzsch, D. 148
Kordt, B. 76
Koschel, W. 259
Kovalik, K. 262
Kramsch, C. 204, 207, 221
Kreps, S. 140
Kress, G. 44, 45, 47, 52, 236
Krommer, A. 55
Kuhlen, R. 13
Kuhn, B. 123
Kukulska-Hulme, A. 222, 223, 226, 227

La Rocca, G. 71, 75, 76
Laing, A. 261
language, expanding conceptions of 44–46
language awareness 38
language dynamics 227
Lankshear, C. 2, 16
Last Survey (O'Brien, 2020) 242–243
Lauer, M. 158
Lave, J. 7, 19
layout/presentation 47, 108
Leander, K.M. 93, 94
learner mobilities 227
learner-centered approaches 18, 57, 66–67, 125, 179, 222
learner-learner interaction 60 *see also* peer learning
learning design development 142–143
learning materials design 147–148
learning objectives 127
LearningApps.org 253, 255
Lee, C. 15, 34, 35, 39
Lee, T. 98
legitimate forms of knowledge 48
Lemke, J.L. 49
Let's Plays (LPs) 122–136
lexical neighborhoods 77–78
lifeworld discourses 39, 81, 85, 86, 126
light communities 111
likes 7, 33, 34
Linell, P. 36
linguistic affordances 77–79, 84
linguistic biases 51–52
linguistic competences 17, 19
linguistic justice 156–157, 168
linguistic repertoires 61, 216
linguistics 30–41
listening strategies 64
LitCom 2.0 study 252
literacy, expanding conceptions of 44–46
literary competences 216, 250, 251, 256, 257, 260
literature, born-digital 206–207, 234–235
literature classrooms 247–269
Liu, Z. 50
live text 106–121
living in a digital culture 2–9
local norms 37, 38, 39
location-based technologies 220–232
locative media 224–225
locative storytelling 220
Lockhurst, R. 248–249
logocentricity 46, 47
longitudinal studies 147, 244
Lopera Medina, S. 251
Lotze, N. 78

Lowood, H. 139
ludification 4
Ludwig, C. 234, 248, 263
Luke, A. 48, 93
Lütge, C. 16, 113, 114, 207, 233, 234, 235, 236, 237, 238, 240, 241–243, 248, 249, 259

Macedo, D. 62
Macken-Horarik, M. 48
Mackey, A. 62
Mahapatra, A. 90, 93, 95
Mahesh, G. 43
Mammadova, N. 137
manga 213, 214
manipulation of information 9
maps 44, 220, 225
marginalized students 50–51, 157, 174–175
marketing 71, 80
Marks, D.-K. 64
Martens, G. 73
Marx, K. 127
Mason, J. 48
Masrour, F. 91, 92
Massey, D. 189
Matz, F. 80, 132
May, S. 61
Mayr, A. 95
McAdoo, T. 158
McCarthy, P.M. 153, 163, 165, 167, 169
McGoun, C. 179, 182
McGrew, S. 186
McLuhan, M. 4, 10
meaning, focus on 59
meaning-making
  choosing resources for 52
  co-construction of 36, 180, 257
  in communities 8
  digital literature 262
  digital storybook apps 233
  diversification of 129
  functions of a text 73
  interactional (socio)linguistics 36
  multimodality 12, 199, 239
  negotiation of meaning 59, 63, 257
  New Literacy Studies 46
media convergence 113
media studies 107, 122, 124, 187, 208
mediated quasi-interaction 111
Mehlhose, F.M. 92
memes 6, 7

mentorship 8
Merse, T. 113, 114, 249, 259
meshing 50
message-final full stops 36–37
metacognition 64
metadata 17, 139
metalinguistic awareness 38
metaphorical meanings 76
Michael, H. 107, 110
Michler, C. 123
micro-blogging 107
Microsoft 365 Copilot 161
Microsoft Bookmarks 169
Microsoft Teams 175, 176
micro-storylines 82
Miller, D. 206
Mills, K.A. 44, 45, 46, 47, 48, 49, 50, 51, 114, 186, 187, 199
Mindzak, M. 154
Mishra, P. 175
misinformation 9, 159, 160
Mittal, R. 43
mixed-method studies 248, 252
mobile data 175
mobile phones 52, 108, 175 *see also* smartphones
mobile-assisted language learning (MALL) framework 220–232
Molloy, E. 168
monetization of clicks 9
monolingual bias 61–62
moral panics 15
motivational effects of digital media 57, 79, 125, 189, 207, 215, 222, 256
Motsch, H.-J. 64
Müller-Brauers, C. 238, 239, 240, 241, 244
multi-authored works 113, 114
multiculturalism 48, 49, 80
multi-layered texts 113, 114
multilinearity 237
multilingual learners 60–62, 64–66, 80, 131
multiliteracies 13–14, 44, 45, 48, 50, 127, 128–129
Multimodal Critical Discourse Analysis 95–96
multimodality
  affordances 33
  AI writing tasks 162

born-digital texts 13–14
classroom texts 16
co-construction 188
digital literature 247, 248
digital storybook apps 233–246
digital text creation 186–187
drafting multimodal assignments 166–167
fanfiction 208
hypermodality 49
images 47
key skills of 2
live text 107, 108, 111–112, 114
meaning-making 12, 199, 239
Microsoft Teams 176
misinformation 160
mobile-assisted language learning (MALL) framework 223
multimodal literacy 114
National Day on Writing (NDOW) 192–198
textuality, criteria of 12
theory 44, 45, 46, 48
writing assignments 156
multitasking 50, 71, 183
Murray, D.M. 200
MyMaps 221, 225

Nagel, F. 141
Naji, J. 234, 236, 237
Najjar, J. 155, 156, 162, 163, 164, 165, 166
Nantke, J. 12
narratives
digital storybook apps 233–246
hashtags 75, 81–82
playful literacies 188, 200
National Archives 138–139
National Day on Writing (NDOW) 189, 190–198
Natural Language Processing (NLP) 139–140, 154, 156
Nee, J. 156
negotiation, producer-recipient 11–12
negotiation of meaning 59, 63, 257
Neitzel, B. 238
Nerantzi, C. 163, 167
Netspeak/Internet English 30, 32
network structures 91
networked communities 92
neural networks 138

New Literacy Studies 44, 45–46, 48
New London Group 44, 45, 127, 129, 221
news websites 108
Newton, C. 34
Nield, D. 159
non-book texts, expanding notions of 'literacy' to include 44–46
non-human agents 94 *see also* artificial intelligence (AI)
nonlinear data/texts 109, 112, 237, 260
non-neutral products, texts as 93
non-standard spellings 32
Norton, B. 215
Nöth, W. 5
#notmypresident (#nmp) 75, 76, 78, 81–84
novice/expert reversal 60, 62
Nunan, D. 59

Oakhill, J. 85
OBS Studio 132
obsolescence of research on born-digital texts 32–33
Odindo, F. 176
Omoso, S. 176
onlife 3
online education 51, 175, 177, 178, 180–182
open news discourse 106
open tasks 56
open teaching methods 19
OpenAI 159
oral skills 167, 262
Oregon Trail 123
Ortega, L. 58, 61
O'Sullivan, J. 260
Othold, T. 124
Otrel-Cass, K. 9
Owczarek, C. 14
ownership 157

Padlets 116, 190, 191, 194–195, 196–198, 199
Page, R. 207
Palfrey, J. 138
Panagiotopoulou, A. 62
pandemic *see* Covid-19
Paperbark (Paper House, 2018) 243–244
Pappert, S. 36
Pâquet, L. 261

paralinguistic cues 31
parallel text-image relations 238
Paran, A. 207, 250
paraphrasing AI tools 155
paratextual material 111, 124
Pariser, E. 90, 91, 92, 97
participant networks 89
participatory culture 8, 9, 58, 205, 208, 212, 263
passive voice 96
peer learning 60, 182, 257
peer review 167–168
Pegrum, M. 17, 204, 213, 215, 223
Penke, N. 262
Pereira, A.J. 14
permanence lack of in born-digital texts 13
personalized learning
　algorithmicity 90, 91
　digital storybook apps 239
　as key concept 2
　as key element in foreign language classrooms 18–19
　technology-enhanced 18–19
Petko, D. 19
phenomenological locative media 224
phono sapiens 3
photorealistic images 111
pictographic writing systems 205
picture books 47, 234
plagiarism 154, 155, 161
playful literacies 4, 188–189, 191–198, 199 see also gaming
plurilingualism 65, 216
Podcastle 166
podcasts 58, 166
poetry 261–263
Pohl, J. 160
polarization 90, 91
polyphony 75
polysemy 75
polyvocal discourse 113
popular culture 205–206
postmodernism 5, 6
post-reading tasks 85–86, 116
post-truth 9
Potentially Exploitable Pedagogic Activities (PEPAs) 210–211, 215
power 50, 94, 156
power cuts 175
PowerPoint Karaoke 167

Prain, V. 45
pre-reading tasks 85, 115, 117
pre-schoolers 239
presentation tools 167
pre-task exercises 132
privacy 158
processing load 84
Proctor, C. 235
producers of texts, students as 6, 8, 58, 141
productive tasks 86, 115, 117, 129–133, 144–145, 223 see also creation tasks
professional development 20, 147
prompt engineering 164
prompts for writing 194, 196, 197–198
pronunciation, replication in written communication 110
prosumers 58, 107, 112, 113
prototype theory 11
proxemics 47, 240–241, 243
pseudo-digitalization 16
Puentedura, R.R. 204, 216
punctuation
　AI tools 157
　informal writing practices 36
　as interactional cues 37
　live text 110
　message-final full stops 36–37
　non-standard punctuation 32, 36–37
Punie, Y. 141, 142, 144
punishment, writing as 51
puzzlement, as starting point 211

Quillbot 155
Quora 32

Raessens, J. 4
ranking systems 95
Rathheiser, U. 216, 250
ratings 13
reading
　digital reading skills 49–50
　reading communities 214, 215
　reading comprehension 84–86, 113, 114, 258
　reading skills 84, 87, 208, 233, 239
　reshaping the nature of 49
　wild reading 206–207, 209–211, 215, 259
reading histories 211–213
reading logs 248, 251

read-out-loud functions 239, 240
reappropriation of content 5
reception theory 123
recommendation algorithms 93
recreation/remixing/mashing up 5, 124, 213
Reddit 32
Redecker, C. 141, 142, 144, 233, 236
referentiality 89
reflective practice 99, 101, 113, 126, 223–224, 250, 253, 258
Reinders, H. 177, 179, 181, 182
Reinhardt, J 117n(3)
remixed digital texts 5, 124, 213
remote education 51, 175, 177, 178, 180–182
reporting verbs 110
research, using AI for 165–166
ResearchRabbit.ai 166
re-storying 188
retweets 33, 76, 82
Ritter, M. 237
Rohde, A. 56
role plays 65
role reversal techniques 167–168
Ros i Solé, C. 228
Rose, J. 177
Rowberry, S. 260
Rwodzi, C. 175, 177, 178, 179, 180, 182
Ryan, H. 10

SafeAssign 154
Sambanis, M. 248
Sampson, W. 10
SAMR model (substitution, augmentation, modification, redefinition) 216–217
Samuel, S. 137
sandbox narration 238
Sandig, B. 11, 12
Sandvig, C. 93
Santos, J.M. 176
Sauro, S. 208, 215, 217
Savage, J. 179, 182
scaffolding/support
 digital storybook apps 241
 digital tools for scaffolding 59
 digitally-mediated tasks 59, 64–66
 inclusive teaching approaches 56
 Let's Plays (LPs) 131
 live text tasks 117

Schick, K. 56, 63, 64
Schildhauer, P. 102, 129, 259
Schmid, R. 19
Schmidt, A. 127
Schmidt, T. 56, 127
Schönauer-Schneider, W. 63, 64
Schulz, L. 55
Schuman, A. 239
Scott, K. 6
Scratch 144
Scribner, S. 44
Scrivener, J. 78
search engines 7, 158, 166
self-directed learning 51
Selfe, C. 42, 43, 46, 47, 186
self-programmed algorithms 92
self-published works 205–206
self-referentiality 5
self-regulation skills 50, 57
semantics 75, 77
semiotic systems 13–14, 45, 47, 108, 187, 233, 236, 260
sentences, and the criteria of textuality 73
Sergeant, P. 35–36, 38
Shakargy, N. 261
Shōsetsuka ni narō 206
Siehr, K.-H. 112
Silverstone, R. 4
similarity principle 91, 93
single-word texts 73, 74, 77
situated digital media practices 49
situated language ecology of individual users 35
situational appropriateness 128
Skorge, P. 263
slide decks 167
slogans 74
small stories paradigm 14
small texts 73–75, 77, 78, 79, 83, 84, 85, 86
smart learning management systems 19
smart replies 140, 143
smartphones *see also* mobile phones
 living in a digital culture 3–4
 locative media 224, 225
 mobile-assisted language learning (MALL) framework 220, 222
Smith, W. 52
Snapchat 50
social bookmarking 17

social capital 35, 71
social constructivism 56, 177–178, 224, 235
social convergence 35
social homogeneity 9
social media
  apps 248
  augmentation of reading 213
  born-digital texts in South Africa 173–185
  comments 8, 13, 213
  creators of born-digital texts 50
  digital literature 261
  filter bubbles on Instagram 89–105
  hashtags 76, 79
  likes 7, 33, 34
  location-based technologies 220
  National Day on Writing (NDOW) 190
  poetry 261
  ubiquity of 255
social reading 212, 214
socializing contexts 182
social-semiotic resources 47
sociocultural approaches to learning 222
sociocultural competence 107
sociocultural context of knowledge construction 177
socioeconomic differences 50, 220
Soffas, C. 251
software code 139, 144
solidarity 71
song lyrics 209–210
South Africa 173–185
Souza e Silva, A. de. 220, 224
space and locative media 224–225
spatiotemporal interactive media 108–109
special educational needs 56, 57, 62–64
speech acts 78, 80
spelling
  instant messaging 49
  non-standard spellings 32
  spellcheckers 157, 177, 182
spoken conventions emulated in written texts 110
sports live text 108, 110
Sprachbad 127
stacking 50
Stadler-Heer, S. 148
Staiger, M. 238, 240

Stalder, F. 4–5, 6, 7, 8, 9, 89, 220
stance 110
Statista 7, 89, 102, 106
Stavanger Declaration Concerning the Future of Reading (COST) 248, 263
Steininger, I. 221
Stevens, M.D. 52
Stockwell, G. 228
storybook apps 233–246
streaming 122, 125
Street, B. 44
Strickland, S. 264
Strive/Thrive/Arrive 143
student choice 189, 194, 197, 206–207
style guides 157
stylistics 106, 110–111, 113
subtitles 131
Summer, T. 235, 236
Sunstein, C. 91
Surkamp, C. 250, 251, 256, 257, 258
survey research methods 92
Sykes, J.M. 71, 79, 80, 86
syntax
  hashtags 75, 78, 85
  live text 110
  small texts 74
Synthesia 166

Tagg, C. 13, 35–36, 38
tagging literacy 17, 225
Talarico, M. 58, 59
Talk to Transformer website 138
Task-Based Language Teaching (TBLT) 55–70
Tate, T. 50, 51
teacher education
  AI-generated texts 144, 147
  Artificial Intelligence-Mediated Communication (AI-MC) 161
  born-digital texts 19–21
  digital competence 141
  digital literacies 183–184
teacher-researchers 211
teachers
  digital competence 141, 144, 236
  as expert 60, 62, 66
  as facilitator 57, 60, 179
  key developing practitioners 209
  mobile-assisted language learning (MALL) framework 223

modeling writing 187, 189, 200
open teaching methods 19
play as literacy 198
professional development 20, 147
role in intercultural awareness 62
role in online learning 182
in-service teacher education 20, 144
Task-Based Language Teaching (TBLT) 57
teacher networks 20, 223
teacher wisdom 226
usage of AI 142–143
technological determinism 31
Technological Pedagogical Content Knowledge (TPACK) model 175, 176–178, 184
temporal data 109
test culture 250
text, definition of 10–11, 72–73, 234
text linguistics 10
text messaging 31, 36
text ownership 140
text selection in the classroom 48–49
textbooks 48, 127, 176
text-in-motion 106, 113
text-in-process 106
text-to-speech 59
textual shapes 74
textuality, criteria of 10, 11, 73
thematic analysis 180, 191
think-pair-share 131
third-person effects 97–99
Thomas, A.M. 169
Thomas, B. 206, 207, 208, 248, 249, 260, 261, 262
Thompson, C. 145
Thornbury, S. 77
Thorsen, E. 106
Thurman, N. 106, 107
TikTok 7, 50, 102, 248, 262–264
Tilgner, A. 123
time stamps 108
Towndrow, P.A. 14
transformation model 204, 216–217
translanguaging 60
translation 35, 155, 187
transmediality 235
traveling concepts 72
trust in texts 147, 160 *see also* credibility of information
Tufekci, Z. 93

Turckle, S. 9
Turner, K.H. 20
Turnitin 154
Tuters, M. 224
Twitch 125
Twitter
    #notmypresident 81–84
    affordances 33
    fanfiction 212
    hashtags 76, 79–80
    live text 107, 108
    National Day on Writing (NDOW) 190
    online learning in South Africa 179–180
    reading comprehension 84–86
    retweets 33, 76, 82

Unsworth, L. 114
US presidency 81–84, 90, 94–97, 108, 115–117
usernames 9

Valli, S. 139
van Leeuwen, T. 47, 52
Vandergrift, L. 64
Vanderheyden, K. 215
Vanilla Ice 123
varieties of English 156
Varis, P. 111
Varnelis, K. 224
verbalizations 127
verification of information 160–161
video conferencing 132, 175
video essay tasks 162–163
videogames *see* gaming
videos
    creators of born-digital texts 50
    device affordances for video recordings 58
    filter bubbles on Instagram 96
    hybrid learning tasks 46
    integral versus marginal part of texts 46–47
    Let's Plays (LPs) 122–136
    live text 108
    Potentially Exploitable Pedagogic Activities (PEPAs) 215
Villasenor, J. 160, 161
viral challenges 7
ViSAR model 238, 240

visual design 47
visual grammars 47
visual storytelling 205
vocabulary learning
   digital storybook apps 239
   digitally-mediated tasks 64–66
   literary competences 258
   live text 110, 116, 117
Vock, M. 56
voice recordings 227
vowel lengthening 110
Vuorikari, R. 16, 18, 38, 51, 263, 265

Walters, A. 106, 107
Wang, Q. 177
Wardrip-Fruin, N. 260
Warschauer, M. 50, 51
Wathall, J.C. 143, 144
Wei, L. 60
Wenger, E. 7, 19
Werner, V. 106, 107, 108, 109, 110
Western bias in text selection 48
Weyland, U. 259
WhatsApp 36, 37, 177, 179
while-reading tasks 85, 116
White, C. 179, 182
whiteboards 65
Wikipedia 58
Wikström, P. 33

wild reading 206–207, 209–211, 215, 259
Wilken, R. 224
Williams, R. 155
Williamson, B. 93
Windmüller-Jesse, V. 58, 59
Wohlwend, K.E. 188, 199
Woodruff, A.H. 251
word clouds 65
Word Macros 169
'wreaders' 261, 262
Writers' Conferences 133
writing
   AI and digital writing 153–172
   changing perceptions of writing instruction 186–203
   fanfiction 208
   Instapoetry 264

X *see* Twitter
Xbox Game Bar 132
XKCD 42

YouTube 122, 124, 125, 139, 177, 180, 255

Zangwill, I. 42
Zipke, M. 239
Zoom 132, 175, 190
Zourou, K. 215

Milton Keynes UK
Ingram Content Group UK Ltd.
UKHW020041020524
442042UK00006B/125